VIDEO
WORLD-WIDE

an international study

D0939156

VIDEO
WORLD-WIDE

an international study

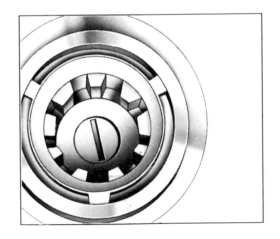

Edited by
MANUEL ALVARADO

UNESCO

BROADCASTING RESEARCH UNIT

John Libbey
LONDON · PARIS

British Library Cataloguing in Publication Data
Alvarado, Manuel
  Video world-wide : an international study
  Manuel Alvarado
  1. Video systems. Social aspects
  I. Title
  302.2'34

  ISBN 0-86196-143-9 (John Libbey)
  92-3-102521-X (UNESCO)

Published by
United Nations Educational, Scientific and Cultural Organization
7 place de Fontenoy, 75700 Paris, France (1) 45 68 10 00
John Libbey & Company Ltd
80/84 Bondway, London SW8 1SF, England (01) 582 5266
John Libbey Eurotext Ltd
6 rue Blanche, 92120 Montrouge, France (1) 47 35 85 52

Printed in Great Britain by Whitstable Litho Ltd, Whitstable, Kent

VIDEO WORLD-WIDE
An International Study

*In collaboration with Karoly Kozma, Imre Marczi, Peter Muller, Sandor Revesz, Andras Szekfu, Emoke Valko and Josef Zelnik.

PREFACE

For a number of years, Unesco has carried out studies on the international flow of information, and published them in the series 'Reports and Papers on Mass Communication'. Two of these studies, which appeared in 1974 and 1985, looked at the international flow of television programmes.

The recent emergence of video as one of the most rapidly developing communication media, with a variety and diversity of possible applications, has of course affected the distribution of television programmes and this was one of the reasons for the inclusion of 'a study on the international flow of video hardware and software' in Unesco's Approved Programme and Budget for 1984-85.

This study, which covers 39 countries, was undertaken in collaboration with the London-based Broadcasting Research Unit and Manuel Alvarado, Research Fellow in the New Technologies with the BRU, acted as its international co-ordinator as well as overall editor.

Manuel Alvarado, author of several books on television drama and a former editor of *Screen Education*, also co-ordinated the studies in Western Europe. In other regions he was assisted by a number of regional co-ordinators: Jerzy M. Pomorski (Eastern Europe), Paul E. Cahill (United States and Canada), Rafael Roncagliolo (Latin America and the Caribbean), Binod Agrawal (South and South East Asia), Douglas Boyd and Nawaf Adwan (Arab States), Momar Kebe N'Diaye (Western Africa), and Pauline Dodgson (Southern and Eastern Africa).

The opinions expressed in the report are those of the authors and do not necessarily reflect the views of Unesco.

FOREWORD

This study of the global distribution of video hardware and software presents a unique body of data, which should be of enormous use to those with a professional, commercial and academic interest in the future of video. Quite simply, never before has so much information about video been brought together in a single volume. These pages provide a chronicle of the extraordinary explosion of video around the globe, the creation in the blinking of an eye of a whole new medium of communication, which is fundamentally individualistic, anarchic even, almost beyond institutional organization, save by entrepreneurs who feed the demand. As such, it is a medium profoundly worrying to many governments as it dances with ease around their efforts to control the directions of their cultures. It has become a medium for sexual liberation, or abuse, according to one's disposition. It has become a political medium, nurturing and sustaining political opposition whose only previous means of communication lay with print. But most of all it bespeaks the ever greater importance of television as entertainment. These pages also document the grip which Japan has over hardware and Hollywood over software, with here and there, in India for example, something very different evolving as indigenous culture is carried by cassette.

The study may be compared to one of these fascinating pictures of the earth taken by satellite and much favoured by illustrated magazines. In the one, as in the other, there is a great deal of fine and interesting detail, providing a considerable amount of information to examine. The picture may provide a feeling for the topography of a structure and even, sometimes, the basis for strategic decisions. In this study, however, as in the satellite pictures, what is missing is the street life.

What these pages do not tell us because they were not meant to, is just what it all means. When the project was first discussed, the possibility was considered of examining not just the distribution but also the consumption — social experience perhaps expresses it better — of video. Budgetary constraints made this impossible. The social role of video, however, clearly remains as one of the most beguiling problems we face in establishing a proper understanding of the place that audio-visual culture plays in the life of nations and peoples.

It is, I think, no exaggeration to suggest that we have barely begun to scratch the surface of understanding the place of televisual images in social life. This is equally true whether we are speaking of understanding the role of television within the domestic life of first and third world countries, or of understanding television as an imported culture from the former to the latter. We have not so far sufficiently distinguished between the development of television — which is used here generically to include television programmes, video, cable and satellite — as a knot of strategic decisions which must and are being made, and television as a force for, allegedly, the shaping of culture and consciousness.

While it is both important and useful as a first step to delineate patterns of flow within and between video societies, and to dissect the facts which reveal the interplay of influences on that flow on a global scale, it is also essential to go further. We need, in short, to be able to focus on the street life. Of course that is easier said than done and anyone seeking to shift from the descriptive to the sociologically analytical quickly runs into enormous problems of conception and methodology, as well as the problems of funding. Yet we cannot move from the fact of television in people's lives to assumptions about the role of television in those lives, unless we construct, however difficult that may be, the intellectual tools which will allow us to make that all important leap.

One of the most fundamental errors made about television as a source of cultural and social influence in, for example, the debate about cultural imperialism, is to equate the fact of its *presence* within a culture with the fact of its *influence* within that culture. To lend weight unproblematically to television, whether delivered by video cassette or by transmitter, is not only to open the way to misunderstanding television, but equally to a misunderstanding of cultures and their internal dynamics.

The logic of this position implies that there should be no more research undertaken which examines only the physical flow of television and that all future work should include an examination of the sociological meaning of such flows of cultural products. In other words, future research must engage with the audiences for those products. This has to be emphasized both because this type of research tends to be neglected, and because *all* research of the 'how much TV products flow and in which direction' kind has within it ill-explored assumptions about the meaning of such flows. These assumptions, by their very nature, neglect even the most elementary understanding of how many people actually watch a TV programme or video cassette and what their basic responses might be, let alone the more complex questions of attitudinal and behavioural influences, and the alleged shaping of cultures and consciousness through audio-visual products.

We are still, however, left with the problem of how, empirically, to get at the nature of the social influence of television. The more analysis pursues the ostensibly objective truth of abstract statements based on survey returns, or the import/export figures for video hardware and software, the more one loses touch with what one might call the human truth. Often the sociological imagination, in the field of communications research, seems loftily removed from the real world, bled dry of any human content. It seems to want to avoid what E. P.

Thompson has called 'the collisions of evidence and the awkward confrontations of experience'. All of us who are involved in debates about information and cultural flows, and more particularly in the one about cultural imperialism, should see Thompson's comment as a gentle rebuke.

In *The Great War and Modern Memory*, Paul Fussell considers the ways in which the 1914-18 War influenced the internal structure of western thought and thus provided an emotional and intellectual watershed in modern history, leading to a shift in the very sensibility of modern man. Fussell dissects language at that particular moment, especially that of poetry, fiction and autobiography and shows how 'meaning' or consciousness were transformed from within the awfulness and the enormity of war. His work is not quoted as some kind of absolute model for research on television and its products, and certainly not as coded support for semiological analysis, but rather as an example of the need to get close, very close to the human experience of television. Ultimately, understanding of the place of television in history will evolve not from counting the number of hours of this or that kind of television, nor by pinpointing who precisely owns which programmes. It will be found through the close examination of the socio-cultural fine grain of the human mood, explored through any and every available method, but essentially through an intimate understanding of audiences as people and not as abstract undifferentiated aggregates to which some of us, in a rather superior way, believe things to happen. It is a form of examination which almost all research on international communication has avoided, with a resulting intellectual impoverishment which has been the hallmark of too much debate in recent years.

The implication here is clear: new strategies need to be developed for understanding the patterns and meanings that emerge when an audience in one culture watches television programmes from another. The problem is how to capture a cultural experience, employing widely recognized methods and conceptual frameworks, without reproducing evidence that is so abstract as to be devoid of any real engagement with given experience. In short, to have the sharpness of the acute critical eye, while holding to the recognized verities of social science.

In all research on television, there is an overwhelming need to employ both quantitative *and* qualitative methods. It would be relatively simple to construct a questionnaire addressing issues of television use and consumption. The problem is that there is no obvious connection between the type of information such a questionnaire would provide, and the more general and problematic questions that are now frequently posed concerning the socio-economic and cultural impact of communications on societies and cultures, and which have provided so much of the momentum for this study.

There are methodological options that would link the simple

demographic information with the more complex problems concerning the social and cultural implications of the flow of television. In these terms, any study of the consumption of television becomes the central point for a broader discussion of the relationship between leisure and culture, work and family, ethnicity and national sovereignty.

In terms of techniques, what is required is a marriage of quantitative and qualitative methods. On the quantitative side is the traditional sample-survey of audience uses, with which we are all familiar. By this method, it is possible to examine differences in demographic characteristics, patterns of leisure, family interaction and so on, between those who are, for example, heavy and light television viewers. In-depth, small-group questionnaires could be used to focus on the more complex problems of the relationship between viewing certain types of product and the functioning of national and cultural identities.

Another possibility for building on this technique would be to tie diaries, or a panel study, to the families of the discussion groups. Still another option would be one developed by the Liebes and Katz *Dallas* study, in which small groups in Israel and the United States filled in quite simple questionnaires about the amount of time they spent watching *Dallas*, who they watched with and so on. The researchers then watched an episode of *Dallas* with them and conducted an interview afterwards. The interviews were open-ended but the interviewers had a check list of issues they had to raise. It would be possible to extend this to other areas of imported television. Groups of, say, ten people would discuss their viewing, considering the individual gratifications as well as the broader issues such as linguistic and national identity.

One might also develop more ethnographically based, participant, quasi-anthropological studies to understand the meaning of television within a given culture. If nothing else of benefit emerged, this would have the positive effect of re-engaging communications research with some of the classic texts of sociology. Such methods could and should be balanced with the other methods of interview, group discussion and survey.

Such research would of course need to be undertaken by locally based researchers, rather than imported or travelling experts. It is also evident that such a strategy would require some radical rethinking on the part of major funding agencies which, for whatever reasons of finance and ideology, tend to be locked into providing the resources for grand if rather superficial pieces of research of the 'counting' kind rather than the much more difficult, long-term but ultimately more profound research proposed here.

Communications researchers then need to produce more empirically, sociologically and anthropologically based analyses and to spend less time on the preparation of grand theory and on the exercise of social science as ideology. Researchers should at least lower their sights and actually go out and meet the objects of their passion and concern. To do so will be certainly quite painful, since it is clear that the simple truths which have prevailed within the debate about television as a global process will be shredded by the complex realities of man in society. Manuel Alvarado and the authors of this study have performed the important function of clearing the pasture. Now it is time to plant the crop. Perhaps the most appropriate way to start will be by discussing at length the relevance and utility of different methods, and to collate the experience of such field research as has been undertaken in, for example, Latin America and increasingly, within Europe. If we do not develop such debate and continue to examine international television simply as a series of product exchanges with an unproblematic social meaning, then we may well continue to excite those for whom social science is the cerebral dimension to political conflict, but we will also further deepen the hole which we have already been furiously digging for a decade or more.

Michael Tracey
Broadcasting Research Unit
June 1988

INTRODUCTION

The history of video tape goes back quite a long time. Ampex were the first company to demonstrate and market video equipment in 1956, but it was then intended purely for broadcast television where, in fact, it went on to transform television production practices. The Senior Managing Director of Sony, on the other hand indicated that as far back as 1948 when Sony first began to develop audio tape recorders the company was studying the possibility of recording images on magnetic tape, a project they undertook in earnest in 1953. The important difference between Ampex and Sony was that the latter, from the outset, was convinced of the possibilities of a domestic format.

The first domestic systems did not however, appear until 1969 when both Sony (1/2") and Akai (1/4") began to market separate first generation systems of black and white reel-to-reel recorders. Five years later Philips introduced the first colour cassette recorder, but it was not until 1978 that the first reliable colour cassette systems came on to the market – Sony's Beta and JVC's VHS systems, which have since come to dominate the international markets.

Let us now look at the situation to-day, for in a very short period of time, video has revealed its potential as a world-wide medium. It is one of the driving forces of the fast-growth consumer electronic, entertainment and marketing industries and its rapid development and expansion have occurred against a background of deep global recession and fierce competition between video manufacturers producing incompatible systems and formats.

There are four 'video rich' areas of the world: Japan and South East Asia; the Arab countries; Western Europe; and North America. The video markets in these regions vary enormously in growth rates, in the way video technology is being used and in ultimate levels of penetration, but the markets in these areas have expanded far beyond those of Eastern Europe, Africa and Latin America.

This report provides information about the expansion and development of video and offers insights into a number of factors that affect social and cultural change in different countries and their relative importance. It offers information about producers, assemblers, exporters and importers of VCRs and tapes; the size and extent of the current world markets; an assessment of the nature of the videogram market; the current situation regarding piracy and illegal recording; relevant government regulations and censorship; and

1

some information on the use people are predominantly making of video. There is also, on occasion, information about the interrelation between video and national television systems and its effects on film distribution patterns.

The research project involved 29 researchers working in 39 countries and some explanation should be given as to why the countries which feature here were chosen.

The reasons guiding their selection were, in many cases, rather complex with what often began as fine principles eventually giving way to decisions made on largely pragmatic bases. Initially, the intention was to select four countries from most regions on the basis of the two with the highest and lowest video penetration and the two with the highest and lowest Gross National Product per capita. Thus in the case of Western Europe, the United Kingdom and Italy were chosen for having the highest and lowest video penetration respectively, and Sweden and Spain for having close to the highest and lowest GNP.[1]

It is important to stress here however, that direct comparisons were not made between countries in any one group or between regions. Rather, what is offered are discrete accounts of video developments in each country which it is hoped will provide a baseline for future work.

For the regions other than Western Europe the decisions were rarely so clear cut. In the case of a region with relatively low penetration (or where no figures were available) it became more a matter of covering those countries where research was already being conducted or where it was possible to make contact with people or organisations interested in undertaking such work.

Since an extremely wide range of countries is covered, it is important to stress that the nature of the information collected varies enormously. It was possible, for example, to obtain a considerable amount of information about the tiny market that exists in Belize, or in an officially well documented state such as the United Kingdom, but it was extremely difficult to obtain very detailed information for the African states in general.

Mexico, as one of the world's major producers of cinema films and a substantial producer of television, was considered essential in the Latin American section, but the tragedy of the massive earthquake in the middle of 1985 made research impossible.

The African Continent is possibly the least 'videoed' and also the most expensive in which to conduct research. It was for this reason that it was decided to commission two co-ordinating researchers who found nevertheless that their coverage of Africa could, on the finances available, only be conducted by working from their home bases of Senegal and Zimbabwe.

It is also important to note that much of the information comes from institutional sources – albeit of a very wide range – around the world. In many cases, such figures as we have arrived at are substantially different from previously published tables. However, whilst we have striven for the greatest possible accuracy, it must be noted that our sources were rarely in a position to offer reliable information on the illegal or parallel markets that exist for video. Furthermore, we are aware that our enquiries into video piracy and smuggling were unlikely to reveal an accurate picture of the international flow of video through illegal channels since the financial stakes in this market are very high.

In this brief introduction to the report the first question that must be addressed is that of the relative size of the various markets.

After a remarkably slow start the United States is now the world's largest market with 40 million videos having been sold. This is double the figure for Western Europe.

The highest growth areas in percentage terms are, predictably, those areas with the lowest penetration of video, but the figures are still strikingly high. In Latin America, current growth rates overall are running at 49 per cent although certain countries such as Uruguay have 100 per cent growth rates; in North Africa they are 61 per cent but in China the figure is 117 per cent.

Clearly therefore, video seems to figure very highly in terms of people's technological desires and the Japanese electronics company JVC which recently tried to quantify the significance of video in world terms released some 'partial' figures (September 1986) which argued that video is about to become the world's leading communication tool. At present, radio leads with an estimated 1,600 million units world-wide followed by TV and telephones with an approximate 600 million units each. However, by the end of 1986 it was estimated that video will have achieved 120 million units – a figure which has been reached within the last decade, half of those sales having taken place in the last two years. Furthermore, 50 of those 60 million sales were VHS machines.

Software sales are similarly high. There are currently 70 million pre-recorded tapes being sold annually and the figure for blank tapes is 500 million a year.

Another important question is the effect of video on the already established mass audio-visual media particularly on the cinema.

Until the 1960s television and cinema seemed to develop quite separately and research would now seem to indicate that in the developed countries at least, TV cannot be solely or even largely blamed, for the drop (and eventual demise) of interest in the cinema[2]. What in fact has happened since the early 1970s is that the introduction of new technologies has substantially re-arranged the structures of communications systems and the mass media. This process has not yet reached a first stage of equilibrium and the splintering effect that video, cable and satellite would seem to have had on the more traditional audio-visual media has yet to be charted, let alone understood.

It has been suggested however, that this splintering effect, instead of creating the conflicts and contradictions between the media that one would expect from the play of such powerful and competitive market forces, is leading rather to new convergences and inter-relations. This is not, perhaps, surprising, given that the major players on the world's stage are relatively few in number. On the one hand, the major Japanese multi-nationals such as Sony and JVC are consolidating their world supremacy in the field of electronics production and on the other the media magnates and entrepreneurs are increasingly consolidating their distributive empires.

It would therefore be more useful to investigate the levels of convergence if the real implications of video are to be understood. Video offers a degree of individual and personal control over a new technology which other delivery systems do not. Instead of simply having to choose between what has already been produced and/or transmitted by the major broadcasting organisations, individuals can, with video, make selections similar to those made when choosing a book to read.

Furthermore, there is the additional, and increasing, use of low cost video cameras and editing suites by both individuals and small groups of people to record events and make programmes about issues which the mass media ignore. In many cases, this is quite understandable where, for instance, a recording is being made of a family occasion such as a wedding or holiday. However, there are also many instances in which such equipment is used to make statements which present alternatives or are even in direct opposition to the institutional voices of the majority culture.

There are a number of elements to take into account when attempting to measure the effects of video:

1. It is a fallacy to suggest that video destroys the cinema. British research indicates that the prime video users are also significant film-goers and vice-versa. The conclusion that is being drawn in the United Kingdom is that those people who make regular conscious decisions to watch a particular film or TV programme display a commitment to audio-visual culture generally that is unlikely to wane or fluctuate very much. It will be very interesting to see if the same holds true in other countries[2].

2. Furthermore, it is possible to put forward a positive argument about the relationship between video and cinema. The most recent research in the United States would seem to indicate that since the advent of video, cinema attendances are rising for the first time in decades.

3. In the United Kingdom, the advent of the £6.99 film for purchase on video has been crucial. It has ensured a new lease of life for many hundreds of film titles. This would also seem to be in line with American market research conducted by Paramount in conjunction with the UCLA. They found that at $50 there was a 2 per cent interest in buying a copy of the film *Superman*, whereas at $20 there was a 42 per cent interest. Obviously, the problem for the film distributors is to decide at what price they maximise their profits. This research also indicates that between 70 per cent and 80 per cent of all video films purchased have already been seen by the purchaser.

4. The sales of 'adult' or pornographic tapes is falling dramatically due to the increasing 'family' orientation of the market. Again whilst this is not necessarily the case in every country, it is a clearly discernible trend.

5. The area of cinema that has been hit the hardest are the 16 mm educational and film society distributors. This sector of the market has literally

disappeared in the United Kingdom: a phenomenon that is already being repeated around the world.

It might yet be the case that video could prove to be the saviour of a medium which at present seems threatened with destruction.

It is clear therefore that the nature of the relationship between cinema and video is not as straightforward as might first be imagined. But what use do people make of their videos?

The research defined four key variables in the diffusion of video: a) price; b) government restrictions/taxes; c) income distribution; and d) the content of broadcast television.[3] To give one of the most extreme examples of the difference of the diffusion of video between two regions, Kuwait, with a very high average *per capita* income per annum, has a very high penetration with many homes having two machines. The total number of VCRs in the African countries south of the Sahara on the other hand was estimated in 1983 to be 778,000 and the price of a machine was 29 times the minimum annual salary.

The research also defined the three main uses of video as being (in descending order of importance): a) time-shifting (recording transmitted TV programmes for later viewing); b) viewing non-broadcast professional material (primarily, but not solely, movies); and c) viewing non-broadcast non-professional material ie 'home movies'.

There are many aspects of each of these uses which are interesting and one will be selected for each usage here. In the case of time-shift viewing American research has found that only 58 per cent of off-air recordings made are viewed in the same week. The more startling finding is that if the recording is not viewed in the same week then the figures suggest that it is never viewed.

In the case of non-broadcast professional material it is clearly films that dominate the field but certain 'hobbies' type videos and pop videos have enjoyed large international circulation. It is however important to note that if one looks at the migrant communities then the situation is very different. For Asians working in the Gulf States, for groups of Yugoslavs in different countries, or for Indians living in minority communities in a country like the United Kingdom, video is a way of helping them to maintain close links with their home culture.

To some extent this is also the case with the third main use of video – for example the recording of weddings and other special events is a way of keeping in touch with home. However, in a more direct political sense video is also clearly playing a part as an alternative means of mass communication. The use of video by aboriginal people in Australia to record meetings and to present their land rights case in places hundreds of miles from where they live, is extremely important.

Furthermore, similar practices are important as part of the majority/minority cultural divide that exists in many countries. The alternative views about, for example, the Miners' Strike in the United Kingdom, or the social and community tapes made in São Paulo, reflect the increasing use of video to present messages which are different from those produced by the majority 'mass' media of the dominant culture.

The introduction of any new form of media is likely to lead to attempts at censorship. In February 1984 the Legal Affairs Committee of the European Parliament expressed concern about both the pornographic and violent aspects of certain video tapes in circulation. In such cases, it is the effect such material can have on children that is of prime concern. Research was conducted in Sweden (in 1981 and published in 1983) and in the United Kingdom in 1983 about the influence of video on young people. In this latter case it led to the passing of the Video Recordings Act in July 1984 which required that all videos should be classified by the re-named British Board of Film Classification.

This Act requires that every film released on video, no matter in which year it was processed, has to be re-classified. The general result is a massive project that will take many years to complete. Moreover, this legislation designed to 'protect' children has, in fact, other implications and consequences. A tape which is to be distributed must have a certificate from the Board (a private commercial body). The certificate fee which is paid by the producer is high and community video groups, for example, find it very difficult, if not totally prohibitive, to pay the classification fees.

This one example provides an indication of the importance a government may attach to what is essentially a piece of domestic consumer electronic equipment, and it is still not yet clear to what extent the legislation may provide a model for other countries. This report offers an indication of the way in which many governments are thinking about the issue of censorship.

This report on the current situation of video is extremely long, because the field of enquiry is so large, and so ill-documented, that it was felt necessary to provide as much detailed information as possible. Ironically, at the same time what follows is both limited and partial. Many countries are not covered and for those that are it was often difficult to obtain reliable and up to date data. In addition, at this early stage in a technology's life, the world situation is fluctuating and changing at a dramatic speed. Nevertheless, this report provides an invaluable base line of information – one from which it is hoped that many more reports will proceed.

Notes

1. There were always additional factors which determined our final choices. For example, in the case of Italy we were additionally interested in the relationship between video and the de-regulation of television in 1976; in the case of Spain we were also interested in investigating the possibility of there being a specific and particular flow between Spain and the Spanish speaking countries of the Americas.

2. It is also worth noting here that despite the fact that many commenta-

tors have argued in the past that the United Kingdom has always lacked a majority film culture, the country did have for quite a long period after the Second World War, the highest cinema attendance figures in the world. This would seem to suggest that there is a strong cultural tradition of film, and by extension video, viewing.

3. The quality or volume of broadcast television in a country can lead to contradictory responses regarding the question of the value of possessing a video recorder. Many people would argue that video is successful because the indigenous television is poor or limited in range. On the other hand, it is argued that one of the main reasons for high video penetration in the United Kingdom is that the TV system is good – people enjoy the programmes so much they either don't want to miss them or they want to keep them for later re-viewing.

Chapter 1

UNITED KINGDOM

The United Kingdom has a population of approximately 55 million people. There are currently four broadcast television channels, two of which are run by a public corporation – the British Broadcasting Corporation – and two by commercial companies regulated by a government body – the Independent Broadcasting Authority.

The BBC is the largest broadcasting organisation in the world and initiated the world's first regular daily television transmissions in 1936. However, with the onset of the Second World War and the subsequent rebuilding programme this necessitated, television did not become a mass medium until the mid 1950s. Today the four channels reach 99 per cent of the country's population and, judging by audience figures, is hugely popular with the BBC's top serial *EastEnders* regularly achieving a weekly audience of 25 million viewers.

The annual turnover of both the BBC and the 18 commercial companies that make up the ITV and Channel 4 Networks is more than £1,000 million and the international sales of these organisations is second only to the American companies in terms of revenue. It is within this context that the size and speed of the development of video in the United Kingdom are studied.

THE VIDEO PHENOMENON

The first question to be addressed is *how* video is used. Discussion of this is followed by presentation of the data on the current video situation.

There are a number of interrelated, but nevertheless distinct, ways in which video is used in the United Kingdom. Firstly, and most important, video is used for 'time shift viewing'. It is still generally felt – perhaps with some justification – that the country has one of the best television systems in the world and people do not wish to miss favourite programmes: the VCR frees people from the 'tyranny of schedulers' and allows each owner, to become in effect, a mini-scheduler.

The second most popular way of using video is in the hiring of feature films which are between 6 months and 3 years old since the television channels are not allowed to transmit such films. There are at present approximately 15,000 retail outlets in the United Kingdom which offer video hire from £1.00 upwards (although videos may be hired for the evening for as little as 35p). These outlets range from a shelf in the local grocery shop and mobile vans travelling around local council estates to specialist shops in the middle of all sizeable conurbations and cities. To give an idea of the figures involved, a successful film will achieve an average sale of 15,000 units with a highly successful film achieving a sale figure of 30,000 units. By comparison an 'art house' film might achieve sales of a few hundred with only a really successful film achieving up to 5,000 units. Werner Herzog's *Fitzcarraldo*, for example, despite a large amount of publicity only achieved sales of around 1,500 but this was possibly because the film was transmitted at about the same time on television.

Video has also had a major effect on the 'non-theatrical' sector of the film distribution system, such as educational users, film societies and so on. Some years ago, all the major film companies distributed on 16mm (and more recently video) and they combined to create 3 major distributors: – 1) Columbia/EMI/Warner (including 20th Century Fox); 2) Rank (including MGM, United Artists, Paramount, Universal); 3) Harris (including Walt Disney, RKO, Allied Artists). In late 1984, however, these three combined under Harris leaving only a few small independent companies still distributing their own titles. It was video that led to this development. Because copyrighted feature films could be rented from a local shop and then publicly screened, the companies were effectively forced to join together in order to fight these practices – which they have done increasingly succesfully via FACT (the Federation against Copyright Theft) and the BVA (the British Videogram Association). However, this development would also seem to indicate the soon to be expected demise of the Film Society Movement whose membership has dropped by over 50 per cent. On the other hand, the business of the small independent distributors would seem to be quite healthy for the reasons indicated below.

Another interesting development is the way in which a community such as the British Asian Community is a particularly heavy user of video for the showing of Indian films which would not otherwise be available in this country. A recent study of the use of video in the London Borough of Wandsworth for example, revealed that amongst the numerous retail outlets for Asian films in the area, one had a list of 30,000 titles and a membership of 5,000 people.

Other, more detailed, studies are currently being conducted within similar communities in Leicester and Bradford. The findings of this research have yet to be published but it is worth mentioning one or two of their early findings. For example, 74 per cent of the Gujerati community in Bradford have access to video but only 59 per cent of their use of the equipment is to record programmes off-air. Thus a significant proportion of their use of the equipment is to view films imported from India – a situation which is not the case with other ethnic minority groups such as families with a West Indian background. Furthermore, videos of Pakistani TV news and satirical shows are available for the Pakistani communities. It is within the context of these findings, which touch upon the experience of living within two cultures, that Charles Husband (the project Director) talks of video offering a new source for cultural mobilisation and maintenance and as constituting at the same time a vehicle for political mobilisation.

This example may also explain the fears of many people about Government policies which may attempt to control and regulate video – through use of the copyright law and with the introduction of the new censorship act both of which effectively limit a whole range of 'alternative' and 'oppositional' uses of video.

The third main area of video use – one which exercises the minds of government officials and industrialists alike – is for the viewing of pornography, 'video nasties' and pirated, new release movies. As a result of a 'moral panic' about such material there has been much Parliamentary debate, the introduction of the Video Recordings Act (requiring the registration and classification of *all* video tapes by the re-named British Board of Film Classification), and a Consultative Document on video copyright law. The implications of these developments for the concepts of free speech and expression are fundamental but the full force of the legislation has yet to be felt. What is clear is that it would not be difficult to introduce political control under the guise of moral and sexual censorship for the small, independent and potentially politically oppositional video producers who would be most affected by a law which requires a relatively large payment for the official categorisation of all their productions.

The Video Recording Act (often referred to as the 'Bright Act' after Graham Bright, the original mover of the Bill in Parliament) has essentially been brought about as a result of approximately 40 titles (the 'Video Nasties') out of over 7,000 currently available on tape. It became law on 1 September 1985 and eventually all pre-recorded video cassettes and discs will have to be certified but, because of the enormous backlog of material (every tape has to be certified even if they have been in general circulation for many years and *all* movies have to be re-certified) there are 5 phases of classification lasting until 1 September 1988. There will be no prosecutions under the new Act until then but when fully implemented fines for infringement will be up to £20,000 for distributors and/or retailers ('library operators').

There will be exemptions under the Act as follows:

'Material designed to be informative, educational or instructive, or concerned with sport, religion or music, is exempt unless it deals 'to any significant extent' with human sexual activity, violence towards humans or animals or human genital organs, urinary or excretary functions. Neither are videos in the above categories designed 'to any significant extent' to stimulate human sexual activity or violence towards humans or animals exempt. It is up to the supplier to decide initially whether a tape is exempt. It is to be hoped that distributors will clearly label such product as such to avoid future confusion. Exempt supplies under the act include: (a) If the supply is neither for reward or in the course of business. A gift is an exempt supply, but a free gift as part of a business promotion, or one that takes place on business premises is not; (b) Where an original supplier supplies a videogram to another supplier as long as it is not intended to reach the public; (c) Exports; (d) Supplying video made to record events like weddings for those who took part in them and don't depict or are designed to stimulate sex or violence; (e) Supplies to *bona fide* cinemas and broadcasters used to the censoring authority are exempt, along with medical training films.

(*Video Business* 16 September 1985 p 12)

The fourth, increasingly important, area of video use is to make 'home movies'. When the new generation of video recorders was introduced colour cameras could be bought and plugged directly into a video recorder. However, the amateur movie maker was still constrained by the size and weight of the recorder and the length of the mains lead. Recorders became increasingly portable until the stage was reached in 1984 where both the Beta and VHS systems introduced 'camcorders' or cameras with inbuilt video recorders, and Sony have now introduced a new 8mm format.

What has been described so far are the main ways in which video usage has developed in the United Kingdom, but there are of course other forms of audio-visual material that have become available for the first time. The widespread popularity of video would seem to have led to the creation of markets of new kinds of video tape material which are being exploited and developed by producers and distributors. For instance a) general interest and 'hobby' tapes; b) pop music videos; c) re-cycled popular TV programmes; d) famous sporting events and festivities; e) publicity tapes for leisure activities such as holidays.

General interest tapes would include videos about gardening, cooking, 'keep fit' (with Jane Fonda's tape being particularly successful), motor repairs etc. For this category and that of general publicity tapes there are no accurate figures for the level of hire or sale. However, there are some interesting figures for the other categories. Pop music, for example, would seem to maintain the highest level of sales, although it is only the occasional tape by the most successful artists that sell in really big numbers. The average figure tends to be around 10,000 with Duran Duran having reached sales figures of 24,000, Culture Club 40,000 and Michael Jackson's *Thriller* 150,000 copies.

The television companies have now begun to exploit what they hope will be a very lucrative market in the future. Thames Television International has set up a new marketing wing – Thames Video – to distribute some of its more popular programmes and BBC Enterprises has been very successful with the sale of *Fawlty Towers* which topped the video charts for some weeks and sold over 20,000 copies. The Royal Wedding sold over 15,000 copies and sport (primarily Snooker and Wimbledon) averages sales of between 3 and 6,000.

This proliferation of commercially produced and distributed films, television and video programmes on cassette has led to another interesting, and politically significant development in that video would now seem to be challenging broadcast television as an alternative network system. The week of 25 February 1985 offers an interesting example. In that week a Channel 4 television programme – *20/20 Vision* which was about MI5 – was banned by the IBA, and there was an institutional struggle between the BBC and Thames TV over *Dallas* which led to the withdrawal of transmissions of future episodes of that series by the BBC. Video tapes of the Channel 4 programme and of the next three episodes of *Dallas* were available within three days in video shops.

In some ways an even more interesting development has been the growth of the independent video sector – both in production and distribution terms. For example *The Miners' Campaign Tapes*, filmed by video workshops across the country and edited centrally, were designed to offer the miners' account of their strike which had not been represented on broadcast television. About 8,000 copies of these tapes were sold. Since such tapes would have been viewed by fairly large groups at meetings for example, they must have reached an audience perhaps 50 times that size. Furthermore, there are now many independent video groups in the country producing tapes about a large range of the political and social affairs of local communities. London alone has more than 50 such groups and an increasing number of public libraries are beginning to provide loan systems in competition with the High Street trader. As already mentioned however, it is such video groups who have the most to fear from new video legislation. The cost of having their work vetted and classified (and they will be required by law to do so) may be prohibitive and thereby lead to the disappearance of such groups.

There are also an increasing number of both management and trade union schemes for using video in the education/re-training of workers – the significance of which is not lost to either side. For example, in August 1985 Austin Rover Cars (part of the British Leyland group) launched a £60,000 video scheme to inform their workers of company policy and to improve industrial relations. TV monitors have been placed at key points in the work place to keep workers informed about the company's prospects, plans and successes. The company is also considering expanding the information service by allowing workers to ask specific question and screening the answers.

The trade union movement has expressed grave misgivings about this new move by managements. They see the 'combination of novelty, time off work, and sometimes a very effective programme' as leading to 'measurable attitude changes in the views of workers treated in this way'. (Joel Cayford 'Beating the Bosses' Message' in *New Socialist* November, 1985). In order to counter these developments, most of the large trade unions have experimented with their own use of video and have, as in the case of The National and Local Government Organisation (NALGO) produced tapes such as *Working Terms* which '... deals with the introduction of new technology in a local authority office. In it the management view is shown alongside workers' views and the interviews reveal the bargaining positions and the consequent working condition improvements' (ibid).

VIDEO DATA

HARDWARE

1984 marks the turning point in many aspects of the video market in the United Kingdom. Since the level of video penetration is one of the highest in the world it is not surprising to find that the country has substantial domestic production, very high import figures and significant export figures. For example in 1984 over 268,000 domestically produced machines were sold and over 1,500,000 were imported. Of this combined figure of over 1,750,000 nearly 300,000 were exported.

It is however, interesting to note that these figures mark the levelling out of the domestic video market as the figures for 1983 were substantially higher. In 1983, a million more machines were imported and whilst domestic manufacture increased by approximately 200,000 machines this rise was matched by export sales (Table 1).

Between 1982 and 1984 the net imports of domestic VCRs were 5,941,366 machines. British production in 1983 and 1984 was about 300,000 machines (this is based on the assumption of approximately 40,000 machines being for non-domestic use). In that same period, according to industry estimates, sales were 5,480,000.

There have been three formats in the British VCR market. However, the V2000 produced only by Philips didn't survive 1985, whilst Sony's Betamax system lasted only two years longer. The domination of VHS has had nothing to do with technical superiority, merely with economies of scale: by combining in Europe with Thorn-EMI and Thomson, JVC secured a large share of the VCR market, thus squeezing out other manufacturers who failed to fall into line. Both Sanyo and Toshiba, originally manufacturers of Betamax VCRs, have gradually moved to VHS. Philips and Grundig have set up plants to produce VHS VCRs and the smaller manufacturers such as Bang and Olufsen have followed suit. Meanwhile, the success or otherwise of the new Super 8 format has yet to be measured (Table 2).

In order to overcome trade restrictions, Japanese manufacturers have taken to building and assembling VCRs in the United Kingdom to supply not only the British market but also that of the other EEC countries. This state of affairs is now changing, with Thomson becoming the major supplier. British 'manufacture' was in fact almost entirely constituted by the assembly of imported kits, of which net imports were 434,961 units.

The British market was the first and quickest to develop. It is also the first to reach saturation (penetration is far higher in the Gulf States but the market is still increasing), a state of affairs precipitated in part, according to the industry, by the effects of recession. The figures are given in Table 3 and they may perhaps indicate the sort of growth and flattening off that markets may well follow in other countries.

Since estimates of market penetration are complex and varied, three sets of figures are given in Table 4. The Financial Times Business Information (FTBI) figure for new installations in 1984 is the correct one. BREMA, the British Radio and Electric Manufacturers' Association, is likely to have underestimated VCR penetration, in order to exaggerate the potential market. Given that net imports of VCRs designed for domestic use in 1983 were 2,352,591, MINITEL's figures of VCR sales in that year, if correct, would indicate overstocking to the extent of 374,591 units. BREMA's figure of 2,180,000 units sold in 1983 is probably the most accurate, although perhaps as many as 9 per cent (200,000 units) were bought second-hand.

The FTBI estimates of the total VCR base seem to be exaggerated. Based on an aggregate rate of replacement of 10 per cent per year from 1980 onwards, the total VCR base at the end of 1984 would be about 6,500,000 or 29 per cent of households. However, given that 10 per cent of rented machines (5 per cent of new installation in 1983 and 4.7 per cent in 1984) have been returned, this figure should be reduced to 6,325,000 units (28.6 per cent of households).

The retail market for video machines is dominated by Thorn EMI/JVC who account for 50 per cent of all sales. Their market competitors are Panasonic, Hitachi and Sony who each account for 10 per cent of sales.

In 1983 Thorn EMI joined forces with JVC and the Thomson controlled Telefunken companies to form J3T. Throughout Europe it enjoys an unassailable market position. National Panasonic, having failed to set up a Europe-based manufacture/assembly plant, is threatened by those companies that have done so, especially Hitachi, Sharp, Matsushita and Sanyo Marubeni which have all recently established factories in the United Kingdom.

Demographics of VCR Acquisition

In March 1985, a national opinion poll was carried out. Of the 2,045 respondents. 164 had acquired a VCR in the previous twelve months. This would suggest that VCR purchases and rentals in the United Kingdom were 1,760,000 in that period. In a poll undertaken a year previously, the proportion of respondents who had acquired a VCR was 10 per cent. By the analagous calculation this would indicate that VCR purchase and rentals in 1983 were 2,200,000. This represents a discrepancy of 25 per cent in relation to the 1,400,000 estimated in this report as the actual number of acquisitions, and can only be partially explained by referring to the rate of return of rented VCRs after the first year.

1985 NATIONAL OPINION POLL SURVEY OF VIDEO OWNERSHIP

Sample Size: 2,045   % of adults acquiring: 8%

		% of sample profile	% of acquirers
SEX	Male	47	56
	Female	53	44
AGE	15–24	20	22
	25–34	18	31
	35–44	15	24
	45–64	28	20
	65+	19	3
SOCIO-ECONOMIC GROUP			
	AB	17	17
	CI	22	30
	C2	31	35
	DE	30	18
REGION	London	19	23
	S & SE	9	10
	SW	4	4
	Wales & W	7	4
	E	7	6
	NW	13	13
	Midlands	17	18
	Yorkshire	10	7
	NE	6	6
	Scotland/Border	9	8
	Scottish Highlands	1	2

The interpretation of these figures by the pollsters indicated that the high proportion of male buyers (it was 53 per cent in 1983) was attributable to both the increased cost of purchasing a VCR and a decrease in rental take-up. They also found that the AB social group had reached saturation, while the DEs were affected by economic depression. It might also be noted that in the HTV (which covers South Wales) and Yorkshire regions, both centres of the miners' strike, acquisition ran considerably below the national rate. In this period 17 per cent of respondents acquired a new television.

The Market Assessment Product Group Research Report (the MAPGR Report), in common with the many other market research reports consulted, took a rosy view of the future of the VCR market, even while characterising the drop in 1984 as 'catastrophic'. These projections, that envisaged the market steadying off at 1,450,000 to 1,550,000 units sold or rented a year, were based on an economic recovery and on the introduction of cheaper playback machines. There was also the suggestion that Video Disc players might be re-introduced once the small technological problems were resolved.

Discounting each of these possibilities, it seems more likely that VCRs will be sacrificed quickly by households trying to spread diminishing income further, and that the decline in the VCR market will continue in its present, precipitous downward curve.

What is surprising is the inability of British manufacturers to undertake licensed manufacture of Japanese models, let alone to develop machines better suited to conditions in the country. Because of this, the VCR market has produced an extraordinary negative trade balance, slightly disguised by the export of a small number of non-domestic VCRs that accounted for the major part of the trade revenues for VCRs.

Since the 1950s the TV rental market has always been a large one in the United Kingdom and it is not therefore surprising that by 1983 VCR rentals had reached the level of 50 per cent of the installed base. By 1985, the rental sector had sunk to 40.5 per cent of the VCR market, representing 2,560,000 machines. Up to 10 per cent of rented VCRs are being returned at the end of an initial twelve month rental period.

Shares of the rental market are similar to those for rented television, although Visionhire, which was slow to switch from Betamax to VHS, is weaker. Again, Thorn EMI are in the dominant position and in 1985 accounted for 50 per cent by renting out 907,000 machines. Their nearest competitor was Granada which is also the ITV contractor for North West England and which accounted for 20 per cent of the market.

BLANK SOFTWARE

The market for blank video tapes also reached a plateau in 1983 with imports dropping slightly in 1984 from 30.4 million to 27.9 million. However exports rose by 2.2 million to 13.9 million over the same period. Both these figures indicate the striking increase in the domestic production of video tapes. The two production companies with factories in the United Kingdom – 3M and Maxell – increased their sales by nearly 8 million units over this period which represented a 135 per cent increase (Table 5).

Demographics of Blank Video Cassette Purchase

In 1985, a survey of End User profiles for 1984 purchasers was carried out. Of the 2,045 person sample, 22 per cent had bought a blank tape in 1984.

This represents 11.66 million end users. By far and away the largest user group are the C2 socio-economic group, who while representing only 31 per cent of the sample, accounted for 37 per cent of the users. Similarly, in regional terms, Londoners, who represented 19 per cent of the sample, accounted for 24 per cent of the users.

The 1985 data has several interesting implications. First, a comparison of the profile of VCR users versus blank tape purchasers reveals the following:-

S/E group	% of pop	% Sample owning VCRs	% Sample buying blank tapes	% Sample buying renting v. grams
AB	17	17	21	17
C1	22	30	24	23
C2	31	35	37	37
DE	30	18	17	23

One can infer from this comparison that C2s are dissatisfied with what network television has to offer, compared with ABs, a dissatisfaction that extends to scheduling times, since C2s also resort to time-shifting more than other groups.

Scotch (3M), one of only two videotape manufacturers in the United Kingdom, employed 6,400 people at the end of 1983. Given that their turnover is £291 million, and video accounted for no more than £48 million, about 1,000 of Scotch's employees could be expected to be involved with videotape. At the other end of the spectrum, TDK, equally active in audio and video tape markets, employed only 37 people.

VIDEOGRAMS

There was a very large increase in the number of videograms imported over the years 1983 and 1984 (1,271,657 in 1984 as opposed to 730,208 the previous year) *but* hardly any change in the value of this business due to a substantial drop in prices. With many pre-recorded video tapes currently retailing at only £6.00 there is clearly a greatly increased demand for old American films. Sales of domestically produced material increased by approximately 14 per cent over this period but it was the level of exports which increased dramatically with the number of units nearly doubling (Table 6). Again, if ones looks at the overall figures for the period 1978–84 it is clear that the volume of trade peaked in 1983 (Table 7).

The price for videograms varies widely from £6 to £54. Titles that have recently received national theatrical releases are sold for between £35 and £54, although CIC, the distributor with the largest market share (see below) have taken to releasing even the most successful titles, notably *Raiders of the Lost Ark*, at £10.95. They have vastly increased the volume of sales in this way.

Music videos are sold for between £20 (for pop videos) to £40 (for opera and ballet). Increasingly the videogram catalogue comprises older films, video feature releases (with no theatrical run), TV compilations and specialised titles (eg *Jane Fonda's Exercise Tape*).

It was announced in the *Sunday Times* 6 October 1985 that the videogram market which had been stagnant for 2 years was to be given a new lease of life in a cut-price cassette campaign by 2 of the largest British High Street chain stores. Marks and Spencers used 10 stores to test market 6 'coffee table' cassettes all custom made for the store by BBC Video Productions and sold at £9.99 (roughly half the average price for a tape). The six titles were David Attenborough's *Animals of the British Countryside*; Ken Hom's *Chinese Cookery*; Cliff Morgan's *Great British Sporting Moments*; Willie Rushton reading *Winnie-the-Pooh*; highlights from recent Royal tours and a cartoon compilation.

Woolworth's, on the other hand, are using all 860 of their stores to present 'The Video Collection' which is intially 50 cartoon and classic feature films selling at £6.99. On the whole the titles are bought from BBC Enterprises at a reduced price but even so, with the current cost of a blank tape plus packaging plus labelling coming to £4.50, to which has to be added the cost of duplication, distribution, publicity, copyright payments, tax and VAT, the profit margin is very small indeed. Woolworth's must therefore aim to sell at least 20–30,000 copies of each tape.

In a 1985 a new label, 'Channel 5', began distributing a large range of old movies for £5.99. It would seem that the title of the series confirms the argument put forward earlier about video beginning to constitute the 5th channel in the British TV system.

Possibly the most significant single area of videogram sales is that of pop music videos. Certainly the production of these tapes has had a stimulating effect on the British independent film industry. In 1984, for example, about 800 pop videos were made in the United Kingdom at a cost of approximately £12 million making the country the second largest in this field in the world (the United States produced nearly 2,000 in the same year – France and the Federal Republic of Germany each produced 100). Sales are substantial and, as with records, a weekly 'hit' sales chart is compiled. These tapes are available at most record stores and all branches of the countries largest book and newspaper chain store, W H Smith.

The rental market is still expanding: 328 million transactions took place in 1984. This means that between 1979 and 1984 the cash value of rentals increased from 3 million to 425 million.

There are approximately 15,000 outlets for videograms in the United Kingdom with specialist shops dominating the market (Table 9).

Use of Videograms

The industry believes that 60 per cent of VCR owners and renters rent an average of 1.5 tapes per week. This would give a figure for rental transactions of 296,010,000, a reduction of around 15 per cent (depending on the extent of undisclosed pirate transactions) on 1984 levels.

In a 1985 opinion poll, of the 2,045 people interviewed, 12 per cent had bought or rented a videogram in the preceding 12 months. This would give the figure of 6,400,000 for the number of videogram users (a figure that compares favourably with the 6,325,000 VCRs given above).

Table II illustrates the extent to which the videogram market is volatile. Factors such as a film being available only to rent, or a single very successful title skewing all the proportions (eg Michael Jackson's *Thriller* video in 1984), make the breakdown above quite arbitrary. At the same time, a pattern emerges according to which people rent rather than buy war films, horror films and thrillers. This suggests that tapes are bought on the grounds that they will be viewed repeatedly.

VIDEO PIRACY

In 1982, according to the Economist Intelligence Unit, the loss to the videogram market caused by the activities of the pirate sector amounted to £100 million, compared with an official market worth £155 million (retail plus rental). Up until August 1983, the proportion of piracy to official sales would have been at or above 1982 levels, that is to say it would have represented about £142 million. Piracy then began to decline (see below) to the point that, in 1984, the industry guessed the amount to be about £96 million (Table 10).

There are four forms of video piracy:

a) pure pirate – a copy of a motion picture that has not been released in domestic video cassette format;

b) counterfeit – a copy of a legitimate videotape dressed up in illicit packaging (sleeve, labels, etc) in order to pass it off as a genuine cassette;

c) imported pirate – a copy made from a film print or cable TV transmission outside the United Kingdom that is then imported, either as a 1/2" tape or as a U-matic master, from which 1/2" copies can be made;

d) back-to-back copy – a 1/2" copy of a 1/2" orginal, made by a private individual or a dealer from either a legitimate or pirate cassette.

As a result of the work of the video industry's own policing body, the Federation Against Copyright Theft (FACT), pure pirate and counterfeit copies are no longer being made, though there are still a certain number in circulation and presumably new 1/2" copies are continuing to be made from pirate U-matic masters.

From 1981 until the summer of 1983, every single film released by the industry in the United Kingdom was pirated. Prints were stolen from the projection booths of cinemas in which the films were shown, dubbed on a telecine machine onto U-matic copies from which the 1/2" copies in turn were made. The film prints were then returned to the cinema. The practice was to make five U-matic masters of a film, one for each of the British distribution centres: London, Birmingham, Manchester, Glasgow and Belfast. The 1/2" copies were sold and rented by pirate and legitimate video stores.

This practice came to an end when FACT prevailed on the film industry to code each release print of a film. Pirate video copies could then be traced back to the print from which they were made, and the individuals who had allowed the prints in their charge to be pirated, prosecuted. Security for prints in cinemas has also been improved. Counterfeiting was ended by FACT tracking down the suppliers of the packaging and closing them down, as well as by video distributors adopting forge-proof cassettes, marked under the glass or made of specially printed plastic. The public has apparently been relentless in supplying FACT and the police with information on pirate copies being circulated.

It is virtually impossible to stop imported pirate copies coming into the country. Nor is it possible, however, for them to take the place of the pure pirate copies, since they are often subtitled, or, if taken from American cable transmissions, they will be marked with the HBO logo, etc, and they tend not to be available in the sorts of numbers that previously characterised pure pirate copies. According to FACT, back-to-back copying is the largest area of piracy today, though it is impossible to quantify.

The recent finding against Amstrad, in a suit brought by the British Phonographic Industries about Amstrad's retail marketing of a fast-copying audio cassette deck, reflects the concern by the copyright owners to restrict the availability of such technology. At the same time Sharp's double-headed VHS deck, made principally, it would seem, for the Gulf States, is being imported from India or Pakistan (not by Sharp) to be sold in the United Kingdom. The machine, the 5W20, is capable of handling SECAM and PAL(B), but can be converted easily to PAL(M). It retails at £800.

In 1982, video piracy accounted for 50 per cent of the videogram retail and rental market. Today it is estimated to represent about 20 per cent of the market.

FACT suggests that one of the greatest disincentives to piracy would be for the commercial video release to coincide with the cinema release; once a title becomes officially available on video, piracy of that title decreases. They advocate the sale of videograms in cinemas and claim that this would not adversely affect cinema box office figures.

TABLE 1

VIDEO CASSETTE RECORDERS - INTERNATIONAL TRADE 1985 UNITED KINGDOM (EXPORT-IMPORT)

Year	Cat	Units	Value(£)	Unit value (£)
Imports				
1983	Home	2,428,615	542,492,103	223
	Kits	0	0	0
	Professional	26,500	42,469,633	1,603
	All VCR	2,455,115	584,961,736	238
1984	Home	1,603,010	264,162,857	249
	Kits	443,422	61,647,832	139
	All Home	1,506,432	325,810,689	216
	Professional	34,965	49,186,886	1,407
	All VCR	1,541,397	374,997,575	243
Exports				
1983	Home	76,024	22,264,057	293
	Kits	0	0	0
	Professional	10,989	31,118,360	2,832
	All VCR	87,013	53,382,417	613
1984	Home	258,433	68,786,166	266
	Kits	8,461	2,219,102	262
	All Dom	266,894	71,005,268	266
	Professional	14,576	45,105,669	3,095
	All VCR	281,470	116,110,937	413

SALES BY UK MANUFACTURERS

	Units (based on unit price of £400)	Value(£)
1983	70,275	28,110,000
1984	268,115	107,246,000

NET UK VCR TRADE (IMPORTS + UK MANUFACTURE - EXPORTS)

1983	2,422,866	559,689,319
1984	1,507,653	366,132,638

TABLE 2

UK VCR MARKET BY FORMAT AND % OF SALES AND RENTALS BY VOLUME OF UNITS, 1981–1984

Year	VHS	Betamax	V2000
1981	60	30	10
1982	65	28	7
1983	70	25	5
1984	83	13	3

Sony estimated that, by the end of 1984, Betamax accounted for 30% of the installed base. This figure computes well.

TABLE 3

VALUE OF THE UK VCR MARKET

Year	Volume (000s units) with % increase (% decrease) on previous year		Value (£000,000s) with % increase (% decrease) on previous year		Average unit price (£)
1978	80		31		388
1979	155	+94	60	+94	387
1980	410	+158	155	+165	378
1981	1,035	+152	375	+142	362
1982	1,900	+84	650	+73	342
1983	2,180	+15	720	+11	330
1984	1,400	−56	560	−29	400

These figures include both sales and rentals. On the basis of these figures, total VCR sales and rentals up until the end of 1984 were 7,160,000 units. This fact makes a mockery of some of the estimates of market penetration that, to be accurate, would entail that every single VCR ever bought or rented is still in operation.

TABLE 4

1983	New installations	Total VCR base
FTBI (1985)	2,125,000	5,750,000 (26.1% of homes)
BREMA (1985)	2,180,000	4,100,000 (18.6% of homes)
MINTEL (1984)	1,978,000	4,840,000 (22.0% of homes)

1984	New installations	Total VCR Base
FTBI (1985)	1,400,000	7,150,000 (32.5% of homes)
BREMA (1985)	1,550,000	6,600,000 (30.0% of homes)

TABLE 5
BLANK VIDEOTAPE INTERNATIONAL TRADE 1978-1984

Year	Volume Million	%Change In Volume	Value (£ Million)	Unit value (£)	% Change in
Imports					
1980	8.8		34.7	3.94	
1981	13.7	+47[a]	79.5	5.80	+56
1982	30.3	−5	166.6	5.50	+121
1983	30.4	−38	121.9	4.00	no change
1984	27.9	−8	103.4	3.70	−9
Exports					
1980	4.0[b]		15.5	3.86	
1981	4.5[b]	+50[a]	26.0	5.78	+13
1982	11.4	−22	54.2	4.75	+153
1983	11.7	+4	57.7	4.93	+3
1984	13.9	−17	58.5	4.21	+19
Net Imports					[c]
1980	4.80		19.2	4.00	
1981	9.2		53.5	5.82	+92
1982	18.9		112.4	5.95	+105
1983	18.7		64.0	3.42	−1
1984	14.0		44.8	3.20	−25
Estimated Sales by UK Manufacturers (domestic sales only)[d]					
1980	0.7		2.7	3.86	
1981	1.0		5.8	5.78	+43
1982	n.a		n.a	4.75	n.a
1983	5.7		29.6	4.93	n.a
1984	13.4		58.8	4.21	+135
UK Sales of Blank Video Cassettes, 1978-1984					
1978	0.7		7.0	10.00	
1979	1.7		18.0	10.59	+142
1980	5.5		47.0	8.55	+224
1981	8.2		74.8	9.12	+49
1982	17.6		120.0	6.82	+115
1983	24.4		155.0	6.35	+39
1984	27.4		156.0	5.69	+12

Notes
a) The extreme price fluctuation is influenced by the proportion of the volume taken up by 3/4" U-matic tape.
b) These figures are estimates only.
c) These figures indicate the UK balance of trade. They also indicate that U-matic tapes constitute a higher proportion of exports than they do of imports, hence the variation in unit value.
d) 3M, one of the two UK videotape manufacturers (the other is Maxell) is unaccountably unwilling to reveal even broad figures for their sales. This tends to make all the above figures approximations, and very difficult to check. Maxell, on the other hand, were very helpful.

24

TABLE 6

VIDEOGRAMS - INTERNATIONAL TRADE

Imports (Source: HMCE 3512/132200/page 6219/281184 S3FA 01)

Year	Units	Value (£)	Unit value (£)
1983	730,208	9,468,348	12.97
1984	1,271,657	9,983,126	7.85

The main sources of imports are the United States, EEC countries and Scandanavia.

Exports (Source: HMCS 3512/132200/page 6219/281184 S3FA 01)

1983	1,499,932	15,476,678	10.32
1984	2,830,113	20,817,344	7.36

*Sales by UK Manufacturers** (Source: BVA; MCE 3512/132200/page 6219/281184 S3FA 0)

1983	3,623,158	74,854,447	20.66*
1984	4,109,066	60,773,086	14.79*

*   Estimates, based on the relationship between the export unit value and the UK sales unit value in 1985, indexed to the export unit value in the two previous years.
Note. The BVA, whose figures for sales and exports in 1983 and 1984 correspond exactly with those given above, but which omit figures for units sold and exported, give the following data for the 1st & 2nd quarters of 1985: –

Units	Value (£)	Unit value (£)
1,550,527	33,389,386	21.60

This huge variation in unit value may or may not be due to the fact that the Customs and Excise figures include so-called 'distressed' merchandise, that is used, defective or deleted material with consequently smaller market value. This, at least, is the explanation of the BVA.
   The Customs and Excise figures given here include a tiny proportion of so-called 'other duplications'. This has been ignored in compiling these figures.

Net UK market for Videograms (Imports + UK Domestic Sales – Exports)

1983	2,853,434	68,846,117	24.13
1984	2,550,610	49,938,868	19.58

TABLE 7

UK VIDEOGRAM SALES AND RENTALS – MARKET VOLUME 1979-84

Year	Units	% Change Vol. of units	Value (£)	Unit value (£)
1979	100,000		3,500,000	35.00
1980	500,000	+400	17,500,000	35.00
1981	1,000,000	+100	35,000,000	35.00
1982	1,800,000	+ 80	55,000,000	30.56
1983	4,300,000	+139	129,000,000	30.00
1984	2,200,000		55,000,000	25.00
2ndQ. '85	680,715	-57	14,806,494	21.75

Note

It is evident that these figures are a little crude, also that there is a huge disparity between the 1983 Net UK Sales figure given above and the volume of sales in 1983 indicated here. To what extent video piracy has contributed to this discrepency is impossible to judge, as is the extent to which under-reporting by Customs and Excise (unlikely) and over-reporting by the Trade (more likely) are factors.

The Department of Trade's figures for UK Sales are considerably less than those indicated here, since they ignore manufacturers' output where the units manufactured are for export.

TABLE 8

OFFICIAL RENTALS

Year	Volume of transactions	Value (£)	Unit value	% Change of transactions
1979	1,200,000	3,000,000	2.50	
1980	3,800,000	7,000,000	1.84	+216
1981	10,600,000	19,000,000	1.79	+179
1982	66,000,000	100,000,000	1.52	+523
1983	207,000,000	310,000,000	1.50	+214
1984	328,000,000	425,000,000	1.30	+ 58

TABLE 9

DISTRIBUTION CHANNELS FOR VIDEOGRAMS

There are now about 15,000 videogram outlets

Outlet	Purchases (% of units sales)		Rentals (% of transactions)	
	1983	1984	1983	1984
Videotape specialists	35	55	42	72
Video hardware specs	16	4	7	1
Audio records and tape specialists	6	4	6	3
Audio and other electrical hardware specs	5	4	4	4
Mail Order	9	6	n/a	n/a
TV rental specialists	0	2	9	4
CTN	n/a	1	n/a	3
Garage	n/a	1	n/a	2
Others/user does not remember*	29	23	32	11

* This category may well relate to use of pirated videograms.

TABLE 10

Year	Official market (£)	Pirate market (£)	Total (£000,000)	%Change
1982	155,000,000	100,000,000	255	
1983	439,000,000	232,000,000	671	+163
1984	480,000,000	96,000,000	576	−16

TABLE 11

USE OF VIDEOGRAMS BY CONTENT CATEGORY PERCENTAGE OF MARKET VOLUME

Year	Purchases		Rentals (Last tape rented)	
	1983	1984	1983	1984
Comedy	31	13	13	19
Comic/Thriller	9	5	16	18
Musicals/Music	5	20	2	3
Science Fiction	4	11	4	8
General Features	4	12	8	9
Adult	2	14	5	8
Horror	2	6	15	17
Sport	1	3	2	1
Children's	–	1	5	7
Western/War	5	neg	21	12

27

TABLE 12

Videogram Distribution Market Shares – 1984

	%
CIC (Paramount)	21
Warner	15
RCA/Columbia	10
Thorn EMI	10
Rank	10
Others	34

Based on share of rentals for the period December 1983 to November 1984, the league of distributors went in this order: 1) CIC, 2) Warner, 3) Thorn EMI, 4) CBS/Box, 5) Columbia, 6) Rank, 7) Guild, 8) Walt Disney, 9) Enterprise Video, 10) MGM/UA, 11) Embassy. These eleven companies control 85% of the market.

Chapter 2

SPAIN

HARDWARE

Up to 9 per cent of households in Spain have a VCR. Table 1 illustrates market penetration. Other sources, notably Antich (1984), show that in 1984 the total supplies of VCRs reached a figure of 1,405,000, which represents 13.8 per cent of households.

From Table 1, it can be deduced that the market for VCRs in Spain, although some way off saturation point, will only experience relatively slow growth. This slow increase can be accommodated by the national industry if the industry is safeguarded by the imposition of effective protective tariffs. At present, total sales equal total imports.

Portable video camera equipment, aimed at replacing Super 8 cine cameras, has, as yet, made very little impact on the Spanish market.

PRODUCTION

Two subsidiaries of Japanese companies – Sony Espana, SA, (Sony Corporation) and Industrial Electronica Aznarez, Sa, (Sanyo Electric Trade Corporation) – began manufacturing home video cassette recorders (VCRs) in Spain in 1985. For their part, two Spanish subsidiaries of European companies – Philips and Grundig – have applied for licences for VCR production.

Sony Espana, SA, with a turnover of $98 million in 1983, plans to reach output levels of 125,000 units by 1987. Industrial Electronica Aznarez, SA, with a turnover of $111 million in 1983, has plans for similar output (*Formento de la Produccion*, [Development of Production] 1984).

DISTRIBUTION

Five companies – Sony España, National Panasonic España, Industrial Electronica Aznarez, Philips Iberica and CEDOSA – control 64 per cent of the VCR retail market in Spain. The rest of the market is divided up into segments of less than 5 per cent.

Table 2 presents details of the transactions of these companies and, if compared with Table 1, allows us to observe the concentration in production and distribution, as well as the importance of VCRs, in the overall growth of companies in the electronics sector.

Source of imports

Until 1985, when VCRs began to be manufactured in Spain, Japanese imports greatly exceeded those from any other country (see Tables 2 and 3).

CONSUMPTION

The majority of VCRs are for home use (up to 90 per cent). However the number of videos for institutional use, ie those used in schools, bars, on coaches, in video clubs, for company presentations of annual reports etc; and by public institutions, is quite high and accounts for 9.5 per cent of VCRs supplied (Torres, 1984: 32).

This number is not matched by optimal utilisation. In Spain, VCRs have often been acquired, along with all the necessary equipment, by schools, companies and institutions that have then been unable to use them properly for their communication needs. Statistical evidence is not available for these uses. We can only cite the case of one experience of video in a Catalan school, where the utilisation has not exceeded 25 per cent of original estimates.

BLANK SOFTWARE

PRODUCTION

There are no companies in Spain that manufacture either blank tapes or video discs.

DISTRIBUTION

According to figures obtained from the *Anuario El Pais 1985* [*El Pais* Yearbook] and *La Vanquardia* (April 30, 1984), the total number of tapes sold in 1984 was 4,100,000 units.

A study of the figures for the company 3M de Espana, SA, shows that in 1984 total video cassette sales reached 7,500,000 units, of which 3,400,000 were pre-recorded and 4,100,000 were blank tapes.

The recommended retail price for a blank tape was $12.40 in 1984. The forecast of revenues for that year therefore was $93.3 million.

According to figures obtained from the A. C. Nielsen Company, SA, sales of tapes by format were: VHS 51 per cent; Beta 42 per cent; V-2000 7 per cent.

Distribution companies

Only one company – Sony Espana, SA – has achieved a market share greater than 20 per cent. Another four large companies have achieved shares greater than 6 per cent. Comparing the figures with those for the distribution of hardware, it can be seen here the number of companies involved in the market is slightly larger. The top five companies share 54 per cent of the market in tapes, while with hardware the figure is 64 per cent (see Table 4).

Sales outlets

The principal sales outlets for blank tapes are, on the one hand, shops that specialize in the sale of photographic supplies and domestic appliances (televisions and VCRs), and, on the other, large department stores.

In 1984, according to Torres (1984: 43), there were 13,385 sales outlets for blank tapes in Spain, classified as follows:

Domestic appliance shops	8,800
Photographic shops	2,100
Other small shops	1,250
Markets	600
Video clubs	390
Department stores	245

The number of businesses, however, cannot be related to the quantity of sales. The big stores – especially 'El Corte Ingles' and 'Galerias Preciadas' – are the outlets that sell the greatest number of tapes.

CONSUMPTION

In 1984, the total number of tapes made available on the Spanish market was close to twenty million. The growth rate must be considered 'extraordinary', given that, in 1980, the number of units sold was only 350,000 (see Table 5).

According to other sources – *Feria de Barcelona* (1984: 44) – the total number of units sold between 1981 and 1984 was 17,636,000, while the Scotch Centre for Video Information puts the total number supplied, for 1984, at 10,700,000 units.

Trends in domestic consumption

In 1984, the distribution of tapes in the Spanish market was as follows: 60.6 per cent for the domestic sector (private homes); 37.8 per cent for the indsutrial sector (distributors and video clubs); and 1.6 per cent for the professional sector (the recording of weddings and christenings, video production, etc.). This confirms the fact that clearly the greatest social use of video, in Spain, as in other European countries, is for the passive consumption of feature films on domestic VCRs, while active and participatory uses remain marginal and of little quantative importance (see Table 6).

VIDEOGRAMS

PRODUCTION

Major TV Programme Producers

In Spain there are two national television channels: TVE 1 and TVE 2, both belonging to the state institution, Spanish Radio and Television (RTVE). Since 1982, two independent channels have been in operation: TV 3 in Catalonia, and Euskal Telebista in the Basque Country. More recently, in June 1985, independent television began transmissions in Galicia.

At present, and before the anticipated arrival of more independent television channels, television production is almost exclusively in the hands of RTVE and production breaks down as indicated in Table 7.

Although not specified in Table 7, domestic production of taped studio production by RTVE for broadcast between January and September 1984 consisted of 642 hours on TVE 1, and 526 hours on TVE 2, and 563 hours and 221 hours, respectively of taped on location productions. Of the other programmes broadcast, 100 hours and 53 hours respectively were taped programmes produced by other Spanish production companies. This accounts for 40.04 per cent of the total broadcasting of TVE 1 and 37.07 per cent of the total broadcasting of TVE 2. The remainder is spread among domestically produced live programming (whether studio or location), filmed production (including Spanish language material), and foreign produced programming from Eurovision, satellite, etc.

The profits of RTVE's 'home production' have increased, not only those from sales abroad but also, and most importantly, those from the home market through sales of books, videos, films for theatrical distribution, etc.

DISTRIBUTION

Various types of companies are involved in video distribution and each of them deals with a different phase, or form of distribution:

Production Companies: in Spain these are exclusively producers of theatrical feature films on 35mm. *Sole Agents*: companies which acquire the exclusive distribution rights for films. *Distributors*: companies which produce or package software, either in their own or an outside laboratory. *Laboratories*: their principal activity consists in making duplicates of other companies tapes. *Sales Agents*: companies which sell films to distributors. *Wholesale Agents*: handle films on video; they may also run video clubs. *Video Clubs*: rent films to individual customers.

Videos handled by the video clubs are, for the most part, films already showing in cinemas and produced by cinematographic producers – Spanish or foreign – who have sold the distribution rights for this new home market. However, the cinematographic distributors (whose clients are cinemas) must not be confused with video distributors, even though both offer the same product. They have different technical back-up needs, and supply different recreational environments. It is also important to note that many companies active in the video sector call themselves 'producers', even though in fact they limit themselves to the distribution of feature films.

The total number of companies involved in the production and sales of video in Spain was estimated at more than five thousand in 1984. They are shown in Table 8 and the distributors – the most powerful companies in the video market – are given in Table 9.

Many companies in this sector operate through different, but integrated, subsidiaries. It is estimated that the total number of companies does not exceed 140, although there are an additional 50 pirate distributors, who are not registered, and who are therefore omitted from Table 10.

The main Spanish distributors managed to secure their position in the market before the arrival in Spain of the transnationals. The following list includes a sample of such companies:

Videoespana: with five hundred titles in its catalogue and with a production capacity of more than three thousand recorded tapes.
Video Disco: the Spanish dealer for the world's leading company, Media Home Entertainment, with sales of about $50 million.
CYDIS Video: at the moment this company has an exclusive sales network

with about fifty agents. It has announced its expansion into the Latin American market.

Universal Video: went from a turnover of $890,000 in 1982 to $2,500,000 in 1984.

The headquarters of these national distributors are concentrated in the two biggest Spanish cities, 56 per cent of the total business is based in Barcelona, 36 per cent in Madrid.

Factors Favouring the Entry of Transnationals

The demand for video has undergone spectacular growth in the last four years. During this time many new national companies have been set up; some have achieved significant and fast growth. Nevertheless, control of production is in the hands of a few of the transnational companies. As in the rest of Europe, this has already begun to affect the national sector as the transnationals set up their own distribution networks.

The dominance of Barcelona is beginning to decline, as the transnational film distributors, though few in number, increase their turnover and volume. They are tending to set up offices in Madrid, where they already have their own distribution offices.

CONSUMPTION

It is calculated that, at present, there are between six and seven thousand titles available on video in the Spanish market. Twenty-five per cent of these titles are Spanish productions, as shown in Table 11. For the most part, this breakdown of video titles conforms to the traditional trends in the commercial cinema. Although small, there is a proportion of educational material.

Video Clubs and Video Shops

The point of direct contact with the video consumers is the video club, a centre for the sale and rental of videos.

This sector has been marked by the extraordinary growth in the number of video clubs between 1979 and 1983 (see Table 8) and their subsequent decline in number due to the increasing competition of rental chains and large enterprises.

The basic economic conditions in the video club sector can be summed up in the following way.

Investment Costs

Several entrepreneurs have stated that the investment necessary to open a video club is between fifty and sixty thousand dollars.

Marketing and Purchasing of Tapes

The entrepreneurs in this sector are concerned, firstly, with economies of scale and their effect in lowering the price of the copies. The video club buys a recorded tape from the distributor for about $50. After two years, when the film has exhausted its market, they will be able to sell the tape to a smaller video club for less than half its original cost, that is to say $20.

It must be remembered that the video club buys the rights from the video distributor who, in turn, has obtained these from the film's producers.

The actual rental price is beteen $0.60 and $3.75 per transaction, with an average price of $1.87. The entrepreneurs in this sector estimate, for their part, that the rental price of a tape, if it is to generate profit, should average about $3.

Geographic Concentration

The actual penetration of video hardware varies from region to region. Such variations correspond, to a greater or lesser extent, with other inequalities – economic, social, demographic and cultural. An example may be seen in the geographical distribution of video clubs: while there are two self-contained markets – Madrid and Catalonia – that stand out from the rest of the country, and which are, moreover, the two regions with the highest levels of penetration, there are others, like Galicia, which are underprovided.

Business Concentration

The conditions of supply described above correspond to the patterns of demand. Like the product itself, they are subject to changes in fashion and other such variables. Because of this, the volume – of both titles and copies – becomes a basic condition for the business survival of the video club. This is what determines the progressive disappearance of small video clubs and the growth of the large companies capable of maintaining the necessary stocks. For example, the current top video club in Spain, Videcor, SA, is a subsidiary of the biggest department store chain in Spain, 'El Corte Ingles', with outlets in all the principal Spanish cities.

As a result of this evolution there has been a drop in the total number of video clubs in Spain. There were six thousand in 1982 and 4,700 in 1985. At the same time, the total number of registered copies in circulation has risen from 150,000 in 1980, to 6,145,000 in 1985.

The concentration of business is a clear trend in the field of the production, sales and marketing of hardware and software, as well as in video clubs. In 1984, a total of three hundred companies controlled over 30.36 per cent of video club membership, 30.35 per cent of the total turnover of the subsector and 41.97 per cent of the total supply of films on video.

Cinema and Video

The turnover of the video clubs, in 1984, exceeded $166 million and therefore, for the first time in Spain, the revenues from video overtook those from cinemas.

Professionals, researchers and business – people in this sector do not interpret these figures in terms of competing industries, but rather as showing the necessity to co-ordinate the two.

Meanwhile, the aggregate revenues of video clubs and cinemas have remained more or less stable since 1980 (see Table 12). An overall increase will occur in programme distribution via broadcast and narrowcast television. The future of the video club business will certainly be much less clear once the supply of software through television is extended by the appearance of private channels, and the various expansions forecast for Direct Broadcast Satellite (DBS) and for cable television.

Alongside the rate of profit and the evolution of the video sector, it is important to emphasize the change that the communication system itself will undergo with the gradual disappearance of cinemas. It is estimated that, within some twenty years, cinemas will be used only for major spectacular productions or for specialised consumption by social groups, such as the young, whose demand for entertainment outside the home does not appear to be falling.

The trend towards the 'mega-spectacle' that aims to compete with the small television image, started in the 1950s with the technique of large panoramic screens: Cinemascope, Cinerama, etc. The increase in the size of domestic television screens (video projection systems, high definition image, etc) does not solve all the problems, among which is that posed by the interior design of most houses that does not always allow for such large screens. In the cinematographic business the technical challenge of projection onto a giant hemisphere is already being explored (for example, the *Geode* in Paris).

The consequences that these changes may have on the international circulation of audiovisual products, lead the professionals in the sector to conclude that the future growth of video clubs, making film titles available at the same price as film theatres, implies a greater scope for exporting Spanish productions, although this expectation is yet to be confirmed.

USES OF VIDEO

The video sector in Spain, is going through a period of expansion. This expansion is however unevenly spread among different social forms and uses. In general terms, it may be said that alternative uses, such as art, educational or community video remain marginal.

VIDEO IN EDUCATION

The main use of video in education is in the teaching of foreign languages, especially English.

Particular mention should be made of the project being carried out in the historically autonomous communities in Spain. In the Basque Country there are experiments with video to teach the Basque language in 'ikastlas' (schools). The Government of Catalonia has carried out various experiments using video in its programme for standardising the Catalan language, but it has also proposed a special plan to equip schools with videos, in order to introduce them into the teaching of various subjects in secondary schools. To this end it has set up the first educational video libraries.

Despite the many difficulties that are encountered in the development of these programmes, the educational use of video in Spain is on the increase, as much for specialized productions as for the recording of conventional television programmes, especially in the case of those that deal with the humanities, literature, history, etc.

VIDEO ART

The first examples of video art in the pursuit of new trends originating in the United States, were produced in Barcelona during the first half of the 1970s. among the most famous video artists is the Catalan, Antonio Muntadas (Bonet, 1985). Works of video art have met with great difficulties, not only in production, but also in distribution (Dols Rusinol, 1985). The only videos seen on television are pop videos produced by the transnational record companies.

Spanish artists, with a few exceptions, have been unable to count on the usual art exhibition circuits of museums, art galleries, foundations, etc. Their works have become known only through a few festivals and small screenings (Perez Ornia, 1984a). The principal institutional platforms that promote video art are the video section of the San Sebastian Film Festival and the Video Festival of Madrid, inaugurated in 1984.

COMMUNITY VIDEO

The first examples of community video in Spain came about as a continuation of the anti-Franco cinema. With the arrival of democracy in 1976, several projects were set up that carried on the attempt to encourage social participation through the use of video. These projects were based on the flexibility of video and its ability to involve users on various levels, as much in production as in representation.

With the passage of time, it is becoming clear that these projects cannot survive if the Government does not adopt the medium as part of its own communication strategy.

VIDEO AND THE GOVERNMENT

The majority of video productions made for or by national, regional and local government have mostly been public relations exercises rather than communication projects to encourage social participation. Because of this there is no difference, either in kind or form of production, between them and industrial and promotional videos.

The current situation in Government use of video is illustrated by the fact that, as yet, no start has been made to introduce experimental programmes for rural broadcasting, despite this being such a fitting use for the medium.

PIRATE VIDEO MARKET

In 1984, according to various sources in the video sector, the pirate market represented between 80 and 90 per cent of total turnover. This amount seems somewhat exaggerated, but it is certain that the pirate market phenomenon is of such a size as to merit special attention.

As far as is known, video piracy has its roots in the ease with which video tapes can be duplicated, the necessity for video clubs to offer competitive prices – films are sometimes rented for as little as $0.30 – and, until recently, the complete lack of any adequate legislation.

In the first half of 1984, the police seized some 750 masters and around 80,000 video tapes, representing 800 different titles. It is believed that a video club makes three illegal copies for every tape legally acquired.

A pirate copy, in most cases, passes along the following route: the pirate video is either made in the cinema that is showing a successful film or in a film laboratory, sometimes with the help of the person who actually transports the reels and who then returns them to the distributor. The illegal copy is generally made from a 35mm print. This service can cost between $300 and $1,200. From this copy the pirate makes a number of masters that are distributed to business accomplices, for a price of between $1,850 and $5,600. About a thousand copies are made from each master. These are then sold to video clubs for about $370 each, and to individuals for about $600. The piracy chain ends when the video clubs, in turn, copy the copies, taking the final figure from a thousand initial copies to some six thousand per title (Antich, 1984).

An economic study carried out by a group of North American experts on the illegal video sector in Spain, yields the figure of $185 million, obtained through pirate tapes in 1984. The most important centres for the manufacture of pirate tapes, were found to be, in descending order, Barcelona, Valencia and Madrid.

From a figure of 5,400,000 pirate tapes in the market, the net profit generated could reach $110 million. In this estimate special attention must be paid to the material, copied both from legal and illegal tapes, that accounts for 4,250,000 copies annually (*Video Actualidad* [Video Today] 1985).

In order to protect themselves from illegal activity and to bring cases discovered to court, the associations of publishers and legal video distributors set up the anti-Pirate Federation (FAP) in June 1984.

FAP, which is modelled on FACT (Federation against Copyright Theft) set up in the United Kingdom in 1982, has put aside, in its first year, about $185,000 to be used in the prosecution of fraud. In fact, lately, a large part of the Spanish police's success in discovering clandestine laboratories has been due to information provided by FAP.

However, despite this small success, the illegal sector works with such large profit margins and is so efficiently organised that it is hardly affected by the police raids. This is partly because illegality does not necessarily mean working 'underground': much of the work is carried out in laboratories that can be easily assembled and dismantled (Misse, 1984).

Another question that is of concern to the business sector is what is called private communal video – not to be confused with community video mentioned above. According to an FAP report, the broadcast of films on communal video in Spain is costing about $9 million a year in copyright theft.

At the last count, there were about 500 communal video set-ups in Spain, with an average of 150 customers each, which means 75,000 households are receiving at least three films a day via their television set, for about $9 a month. From these figures FAP calculates that the communal video organisations are broadcasting 45,000 films a month and taking about $700,000 from them, which accounts for the $9 million annually stated above.

Communal video began in 1981 when a Barcelona firm, Televecino Club [Tele-neighbour Club], installed equipment to provide transmissions to the residents of an area of the city, by means of a VCR connected to a collective aerial through which, by using a decoder, broadcasts could be received by residents who subscribed to the service.

Communal video companies generally proceed as follows: a) a contract is made with a group of residents, whereby, for a previously determined sum (about $37), the company agrees to install a transmitter and do the necessary wiring, to transmit the video films that they programme and that can be seen on each of the group's television sets; b) once the equipment has been installed, films are transmitted (for a monthly fee of $9) by using video tapes rented for home use from any video club.

Current legislation does not cover the existence of communal video, which is considered private viewing. But the business sectors, whose interests are directly affected by this competition – and this is mostly those self same video clubs – believe that it is illegal competition and demand protection, from the Government, through prosecution under the existing legislation covering copyright theft (*Video Actualidad*, 1985).

More recently, however, the Generalitat de Catalunia [the autonomous Government of Catalonia], enacted a law on October 4 1985 that bans communal video, because the companies do not have the legal concession granted under section 4 of the 1980 Radio and Television Act. This law has yet to come into force, but it could affect some 60,000 housholds, mostly in the metropolitan area of Barcelona (Fondevila, 1985).

VIDEO LAW

The legislation in Spain that deals with audio-visual material, that is laws concerning its distribution and public showing, have gone through two different stages in the last few years. The first stage, corresponding to the former regime, was characterized by strict Government regulation of content, through censorship. This covered both the initial project and the audio-visual material that came from it. The second stage corresponding to the present democratic regime, is characterised by the Government's interest in eradicating video piracy, so as to protect not only the rights of the creators and producers, but also those of the consumers.

Here we will briefly refer only to the current situation, where we have two main laws, the 'General Police Regulation of Public Performances and Recreational Activities', which covers public showings of audio-visual material in bars, cafeterias, pubs, discotheques and other such establishments, and the Royal Decree 2332/1983 which sets specific standards for the public sale, distribution and exhibition of audio-visual material.

As well as safeguarding the rights of creators and customers, the Government has considered it reasonable to apply the same legal rules to cinematographic and audio-visual works, because of the similarity between them in terms of public showings, circulation and content. These rules consist, basically, in restricting access of minors to some material, using a simple code.

However this reveals the following problem: the Royal Decree, cited above, is not clear; it considers audio-visual material as 'merely a reproduction of cinematographic works that conforms, without exception, to the regulatory norms that apply to cinematographic theatres'. It appears, from this, that it is the the medium that determines the difference in juridical treatment, while the content is treated in the same way (Hernandez Marques and Munoz Contreras, 1984).

The certificate given by the Ministry of Culture, must accompany every video, whether it is destined for public sale, distribution or showing. When more than fifty copies are being produced, it is enough that the cassette cover of each copy should be printed with the wording of the certificate itself. When the content of the audio-visual material is a straightforward reproduction of a cinematographic work already classified by the Ministry of Culture – as is most often the case – this will be given the same grade as that of the film at the time of its release. In these cases, it will be specified that the audio-visual material may not be shown except in film theatres (Beaumont, 1983).

The distribution and cinematographic import sectors and those that have direct commercial dealings with legal video in Spain, welcomed the Royal Decree when it came into effect. However, the demands made on the Government by the business sectors did not end there. In November 1983, they persuaded the Government to set up an enquiry into the spread of video piracy. Two months later, in January 1984, the Ministry of Culture published a bill to extend the scope of the Royal Decree 2332/1983, in which each step of the procedure to be followed by the owner in order to be within the law concerning the exploitation rights of an audio-visual work was described.

The present law in Spain concerning copyright, dates from 1879. The Ministry of Culture has worked out a bill that, after consultations with those sectors directly involved, will go to Parliament for discussion and ratification. This future law looks at the existing new technologies, including video, and at other audio-visual material (Mallofre, 1985), and one of its fundamental aims is to bring Spanish regulations into line with those of the rest of the EEC. It deals with international piracy and the co-ordination of international protection of the rights of the author.

The autonomous Spanish communities also intend to establish regulations regarding video and the control of piracy, but, so far, only the Generalitat de Catalunia [Government of Catalonia] has passed a specific law, which is soon to set up periodic inspections and create a register of audio-visual companies in Catalonia (Department of Culture, 1985).

TABLE 1

GROWTH OF VCRs IN SPAIN

	1981	1982	1983	1984
No. nationwide (units)	115,000	335,000	620,000	1,020,000
Annual sales (units)	90,000	220,000	285,000	400,000
Volume of sales ($ millions)	97.5	218.3	216	317
Market share by system (%)				
VHS	44.2	48.5	49.5	48.7
Beta	53.9	44.3	41.5	44.0
V2000	1.9	7.2	9.0	7.3

Sources: *Anuario El Pais* (1984 and 1985), with figures from the Scotch Centre for Information on Video, for 1981–1982 and from A. C. Nielsen for 1984.

TABLE 3

MARKET SHARE OF VCR IMPORTS BY COUNTRY OF ORIGIN

Origin	Videos (in units)	Value (in $ millions)	%
Japan	247,950	271.7	87
EEC	19,950	21.8	7
United States	2,850	3.1	1
Rest of the world	14,250	15.6	5
Total	285,000	312.2	100

Source: Our own compilation with figures *from Feria de Barcelona* (1984: 38) and *Anuario El Pais 1984* (1984: 196).

TABLE 2

DISTRIBUTION OF VIDEO HARDWARE IN SPAIN

Video hardware distributors	Head-quarters	Share of Spanish market %	Units sold	Video turnover $ millions	Total turnover $ millions	% Of total turnover represented by video	No of employees	Ultimate owner international headquarters
Sony España SA	Madrid	21.20	80,420	66.4	98.3	67.55	278	Sony Corporation Japan
National Panasonic España SA	Barcelona	16.00	45,600	49.9	93.5	53.37	434	Matsushita Electric Corp Japan
Industrial Electronica Renaree SA	Barcelona	15.00	42,750	46.8	111.4	42.01	977	Sanyo Electric Trade Corp Japan
Philips Iberica SA	Madrid	5.90	16,815	18.4	321.3	5.72	1,177	Philips Holland
CEDOSA	Madrid	5.80	16,530	18.1	105.2	17.20	700	Thomson Brand France
Unilec SA	Barcelona	4.00	11,400	12.5	21.6	57.87	41	Akai Japan
Soba Espana SA	Barcelona	3.90	11,115	12.2	-	-	-	Soba West Germany
Electranica Bertran (ELBE)	Barcelona	3.60	10,260	11.2	75.9	14.76	271	Sharp Corp Japan
Mobel SA	Barcelona	2.40	6,840	7.5	3.5	-	40	Mitsubishi Japan
DIELSORSA	Barcelona	2.10	5,985	6.5	-	-	-	Toshiba Corp Japan
EURA SA (JVC)	Barcelona	1.60	4,560	5.0	-	-	-	Victor Company of Japan
Inter Grundig SA	Barcelona	1.40	3,990	4.4	89.2	4.93	930	Grundig West Germany
Hitachi Sales Iberica SA	Barcelona	1.00	2,850	3.1	-	-	-	Hitachi Japan
CECSA (Emerson)	Barcelona	0.40	1,140	1.2	-	-	-	-
Otras empresos	-	15.70	44,745	49.0	-	-	-	-
Total España	-	100.00	285,000	312.0	3,476	8.98	-	

Source: Data gathered by the *Feria de Barcelona* (1984: 36), *Amuario el País* (1984: 196) *Fomento de la Produccion* (1984)

TABLE 4

DISTRIBUTION OF BLANK TAPES IN SPAIN

Name of distributor	Head-quarters	Share of Spanish market for blank tapes	No of units sold	Turnover of tapes $ millions	Total turnover $ millions	% Of total turnover represented by turnover of tapes	No of employees	International headquarters
Sony España SA	Madrid	22.30	735,900	6.7	98.3	6.81	278	Sony Corp Japan
Cimax SA (Maxwell)	Barcelona	9.80	323,400	2.9	-	-	-	Maxell Japan
3M Espana SA (Scotch)	Madrid	9.40	310,200	2.8	61.4	4.56	793	3M USA
Mayro Magnetics SA (TDK)	Madrid	6.80	224,400	2.0	-	-	-	TDK Japan
Agfa-Gevaert SA	Barcelona	6.50	214,500	1.9	98.7	1.92	415	Agfa Gevaert West Germany
BASF Española SA	Barcelona	4.60	151,800	1.4	183.4	0.76	978	BASF West Germany
Philips Iberica SA	Madrid	3.90	128,700	1.2	321.3	0.37	1,177	Philips Holland
Ind. Electronica Aznarez	Barcelona	3.00	99,000	0.9	111.4	0.81	977	Sanyo Japan
DIELORSA	Barcelona	2.70	89,100	0.8	-	-	-	Toshiba Corp Japan
Fuji Film España SA	Barcelona	2.60	85,500	0.8	10.4	-	80	Fuji Japan
National Panasonic España	Barcelona	2.50	82,500	0.7	93.5	0.75	434	Matsushita Electric Japan
Eure SA (JVC)	Barcelona	2.00	66,000	0.6	-	-	-	Victor Company Japan
Inter Grundig	Barcelona	1.60	52,800	0.5	89.2	0.56	930	Grundig West Germany
Otras empresas	-	22.30	735,900	6.7	-	-	-	-
Total España		100.00	3,300,000	29.9	-	-	-	-

Source: Data gathered by the *Feria de Barcelona* (1984: 36), *Anuario el Pais* (1984: 196) *Fomento de la Produccion* (1984)

TABLE 5

CONSUMPTION OF VIDEO TAPES

Total tapes	Until 1980	1981	1982	1983	1984	Total no.	Growth rate %
Units sold *	350	1,050	3,350	6,150	8,150	19,050	2,228
Mean annual price**	39	26	19	13	10	–	-74
Total sales***	13.6	27.3	63.6	79.9	81.5	–	499

* – in thousands
** – in dollars
*** – in $ millions
Source: Our own compilation with figures from Torres (1984) and Argandona and Garcia Duran (1985: 136).

TABLE 6

DISTRIBUTION OF TAPES IN 1984

User group	Total no of tapes	% of total
Domestic users	11,546,500	60.60
Homes with fixed VCRs	11,234,500	59.00
Homes with portable VCRs	312,000	1.60
Industrial users	7,200,000	37.80
Pre-recorded tapes for video clubs	6,145,000	32.00
Pre-recorded tapes for private users	750,000	4.00
Pre-recorded tapes for distributors	305,000	1.60
Professional users	303,500	1.60
Photographers, weddings, christenings	150,000	0.80
Producers	53,500	0.30
Others	100,000	0.50
Grand total	19,050,000	100.00

Source: Authors Data, with data from Torres (1984: 46 & 47)

TABLE 7

COMMERCIALISATION OF AUDIOVISUAL PRODUCTION

	1975	1979	1983	1984(to Sept)	Growth rate %
Total sales	581	1,327	2,698	1,230	364
Sales to Latin America				277	
Commercialisation in Spain	279	663	1,514	2,815	442
Total	860	1,990	4,213	4,045	389

Source: Our own compilation with figures from RTVE (1984: 69 and 437). [Figures in $ millions]

TABLE 8

TYPES OF VIDEO COMPANY, IN 1984

Companies	Total number
Production Companies	20
Sole agents	5
Distributors	190
Laboratories	20
Sales agents	200
Wholesale	150
Video clubs	4,700
Total	5,285

Source: Torres (1984: 56), with estimated figures.

TABLE 9

VIDEOGRAPHICS DISTRIBUTORS IN 1984

	Distributors		Titles	
	Total	%	Total	%
Transnationals	9	4.74	630	10.48
Large national	30	15.79	2,400	39.92
Medium national	90	47.37	2,250	37.42
Small national	61	32.10	732	12.80
Total for Spain	190	100	6,012	100

Source: Torres (1984: 54 and 57), with estimated figures.

TABLE 10

PRINCIPAL DISTRIBUTORS ACTIVE IN SPAIN

Transnationals	*Spanish*
Metro Goldwyn Mayer United Artists	Centre Internacional del video
RCA Columbia Pictures	CYDIS Video
Warner Brothers (Paramount, Universal)	International Video Sistemas
Thorn EMI	Odin Video
Twentieth Century Fox	Tele-Jector Espana
Walt Disney	Universal Video
Cinema International Corp.	Vadimon
CBS Fox	Video Club de Espana
	Video Disco
	Videospana
	C. B. Films

Source: Rodriguez-Berzosa (1985), Torres (1984).

TABLE 11

COUNTRY OF ORIGIN OF VIDEO AND FILMS DISTRIBUTED IN SPAIN

Producing country	Video	Films
	Total	%
United States	1,804	30
Spain	1,503	25
Italy	962	16
United Kingdom	601	10
France	421	7
Federal Republic of Germany	180	3
Scandinavian countries	180	3
Latin American countries	60	1
Other countries	301	5
Total	6,012	100

Source: Torres (1984: 58).

TABLE 12

REVENUES FROM BOX OFFICE AND FROM VIDEO CLUBS

	1980	1981	1982	1983	1984	Growth rate %
No. of cinemas	4,096	3,970	3,939	3,820	3,510	−14.31
Cinema revenues	314.6	282.9	248.0	199.6	165.0	− 47.55
No. of Video clubs	300	900	1,900	3,900	4,700	1,466
Video club revenues	11.4	31.3	83.8	136.9	166.7	1,362
Total revenue for cinemas and video	326	314.2	331.8	336.5	331.7	1.75

(*) - Revenue figures in $ millions.
Source: Our own compilation with figures from the Ministry of Culture (1985) and from Torres (1984: 63 and 95).

Chapter 3

ITALY

Since the end of 1984, after two years of economic recession, the Italian consumer electronics market has shown signs of recovery. This is despite the government tax of 16 per cent imposed in January 1983 on almost all electronic equipment whether produced internally or imported. The reduction in the rate of inflation and interest rates has contributed to an increase in sales, even if socio-economic differences and the increase in the level of unemployment widens the gap between classes, thereby excluding large sections of the population from a certain type of luxury consumption.

In particular, there was a significant increase in the sale of video hardware in 1984, for which a continuous development is foreseen. The colour TV market is on the increase (1,750,000 sets sold), and remained stable in 1985. Lombardy is the region which has recorded the greatest number of sets sold. Overall, it is calculated that 60 per cent of Italian families possess a colour TV.

It should be noted that overall the Italian market is notably less developed in comparison with the other European countries, especially in the video sector where penetration is still low. However, the prospects are favourable for a further expansion in all sectors, especially in the video sector, where the accumulated delay has encouraged a very high development in percentage terms (+30 per cent in 1984), while other countries are heading towards market saturation.

VIDEO MARKET

The video market in Europe has slowed down in those countries in which this sector developed first whereas countries which entered the market later are still able to sustain growth.

In Italy, the video phenomenon has not yet reached dimensions of great significance and remains marginal on the world market. Notwithstanding the large increase in percentage terms in recent years, the Italian market is not highly diffused in absolute terms. Although one of the seven most industrialised countries in the world, Italy shows percentages similar to a developing country and, in any case, lower than those of other nations whose GNP is similar.

At the end of 1984, the penetration of video recorders among Italian families was approximately 2 per cent and there are a number of reasons for the very low figure.

First, the price of VCRs is among the highest in Europe. An enquiry conducted in 1983 by the European Bureau of the Union of Consumers, indexing the average British price of a VCR to be 100, gave a relative price of 123 in the Federal Repulic of Germany, 131 in France, and 155 in Italy. Only Spain, Greece and Denmark show higher figures. This is because of government taxes and distribution costs, but also because of the commercial strategies of the importers. In comparison with the Federal Republic of Germany, distribution costs are 7–8 per cent higher, consumer tax is 16 per cent higher, and VAT (IVA) is 6 per cent higher.

The VCR is normally used in conjunction with a colour TV set, and the relatively sparse distribution of the latter (market saturation around 60 per cent) constitutes another restraining factor. Moreover, many of these colour TVs have been acquired recently, and a further heavy expense based on TV cannot be expected within a short period of time.

Another cause lies in the lack of advertising. Last year 80 per cent of the advertising budget was sustained by Philips and Sony. Furthermore many of the companies operating in Italy are branches of foreign companies (above all Japanese) and have at their disposal an advertising investment strictly proportional to the volume of sales.

Moreover, the poor quality of the advertising information has not contributed to the creation among clients of that indispensable culture of the image. Advertising objectives have been limited to 'selling' the superior quality of products, with no attention paid to public education about the advantages and uses of the product. From this derives a certain resistance based on a lack of familiarity with the technology and with the workings of video-recorders, not only among the public, but also among the retailers.

One of the elements which influences the diffusion of video is the large number of television programmes available. On this point opinions differ. According to some operators, the presence of private television and the enormous range of programmes offered chokes the market. Others argue that the presence of an abundant and qualified television system, such as the Italian one, should favour the use of VCRs for time-shifting. However, the amount and variety of programmes offered by the Italian networks together with the limited spread of VCRs, has not encouraged the extensive development of the sectors of pre-recorded software. Moreover, commercially succesful titles are not easily available and there is little to encourage the mass development of hardware.

There has recently been an effort on the part of distributors to offer the public the widest possible choice of titles including those on the market for the first time and it is this which has stimulated the growth rate of the Italian market.

Nevertheless, the present taxation policies consider VCRs to be luxury products and therefore subject to high taxation.

The expansion of sales outlets for video materials has been rapid and they are now available in almost all consumer electronics and photographic shops.

In the opinion of commercial operators a 'true' video market is one where distribution has reached at least one and a half million VCR units. It is forecast that this target, in the absence of extraordinary new developments, will be reached at the end of the 1990s. By that time video in Italy will have become a mass medium. For the moment, it is still an elite phenomenon.

HARDWARE AND BLANK SOFTWARE

The Italian video hardware sector is dominated by foreign – and in particular Japanese – industry. National production is limited to a few companies, of which the most important is Zanussi.

Distribution is carried out by Italian import companies which ensure national distribution on the basis of contracts with the producers. The most powerful companies have branches in Italy. The high cost of manpower limits the possibilities of assembling VCRs in Italy.

The number of VCRs in Italy is amongst the lowest in Europe, but there is an increasing rate of annual development, indicative of an already irreversible process of penetration, even if very slow when compared with other nations.

In spite of the fact that Italy has the greatest variety of television programmes in Europe, sales of video hardware in Italy increased 40 per cent in 1984 and 50 per cent in 1985. The region which records the most substantial sales of VCRs is Tuscany. Portable VCRs represent 20 per cent of the market, as against an European average of 8 per cent. In terms of volume, sales of portable sets in Italy are comparable with those in the rest of Europe, although there has not been a corresponding sale of fixed units. The progressive expansion of the market will no doubt modify the percentage of portable sets in the overall market.

The sales of blank videocassettes continue to grow slowly but surely: 1,500,000 units in 1984 which should reach 1,800,000 in 1985. It is thought that the eventual introduction of a tax for the safeguarding of copyright, which is being discussed at the EEC Commission, would have negative repercussions on sales.

As far as the proportion of the various formats in the market is concerned, the prevalence of VHS is confirmed, with a slight increase in the proportion of the Video 2000 format. This is the result of a policy of price reductions in order to exhaust stocks with a view to withdrawing it from the market. With regard to the Betamax format it should be noted that Sony controls the market.

Opinions of those working in this sector attribute a larger percentage of the market to the VHS format than the percentage shown by available statistics. Such opinions suggest 80–90 per cent of the market and this at the expense of the Video 2000 to which not more than 5–10 per cent is attributed, in spite of the fact that its superior quality is recognised.

It should be made clear that interviews show that one of the major causes of market inhibition is the lack of a standardised system and the rapid evolution of hardware. The public hesitates to buy a unit which could be replaced on the market by something considerably better within a few months. This situation may change with the introduction of the 8mm format, even if the diffusion of VHS would appear to make universal acceptance of a different system difficult.

VIDEOGRAMS

The home-video market in Italy has slowed down. One development strategy could be reductions in the price of units, a practice which has led to a wide diffusion of VCR units in the United States. This depends however on both governmental policies and commercial policies of the importers. Not only is the VCR heavily taxed as a luxury item, but the number of imported units is limited, because of limits on the import of Japanese electronic products.

As far as taxation is concerned, within the framework of the Italian economy and of the effective purchasing power of the citizens, it cannot be denied that the VCR constitutes a luxury item. There is therefore no reason to expect a reduction in the price of hardware in the short run, which might substantially modify the movement of the market.

The general situation is stagnant because the limited number of video recorders installed does not encourage a massive distribution of the video cassette titles most in demand (and therefore more costly from the point of view of reproduction rights), while the scarcity of available titles does not stimulate the acquisition of hardware.

In this context, the locomotive is the software sector. Distribution here has been almost excessive given the present market situation, but the aim is to accelerate the development of home-video.

In 1984, approximately 30 new video titles came out each month. The average sale of each title was about 500 copies and up to 3,000–4,000 copies in the case of best sellers. For 1985 some estimates predict the sale of 400,000 pre-recorded cassettes, and a further 150,000 made illegally.

The penetration of the Italian home-video market by multinational cinema and disc companies has played a fundamental part in the expansion of the available software. The emergence of new labels which offer specialised catalogues has also contributed to a wide and diversified offering. All these companies seek to corner a slice of the market which is growing continuously even if no large profits can be expected immediately .

There is considerable demand from the overseas market and particularly from the several million emigrants whose requests are mainly for films of typical Italian comedy. In countries where the home-video sector is more developed the reproduction rights to films by the great Italian cinema directors such as Fellini, De Sica, Rossellini, Antonioni etc, are much in demand.

A further incentive to the development of the software market comes from the now established practice of renting. The rental of a videocassette for three days costs about 10,000 lira (US$5). Renting of VCRs on the other hand, is less widespread, although it is possible to exploit the normal channels, which function according to a principle similar to leasing. In this case the monthly cost is around 10 per cent of the value.

In specialised centres rental arrangement show a ratio of 15:1 to sales (source Arci-Media). On the other hand, because of the large circulation of software, there is an ever greater diffusion of illegal reproductions, and for this reason many companies no longer rent videocassettes.

Films make up the greater part of available video libraries and their success is due in large part to the reduction in the time between the cinema issue and the videocassette edition. The association of producers and the association of cinema managers (Anica and Agis) have protested that the time lag is too short and have requested a period of at least one year between the two issues. It is necessary to consider however that the simultaneous issue of a film on these two fronts makes for the most efficient advertising campaign and also leaves less room for piracy.

Collections of videocassettes featuring the same protagonist or theme have met with considerable success. In the case of video music the decision of gramophone record manufacturers to distribute videocassettes of their own artists has been a determining factor in their diffusion, especially considering that almost all the high quality products come from abroad.

Cartoons also achieved excellent results after Walt Disney Home Video and Warner decided to sell and not simply to rent titles from their own catalogue. Moreover, this type of cassette, unlike most films, may be viewed many times especially by children.

Educational programmes still remain marginalised, in spite of the excellent programmes available from the Schools Education Department of RAI and from other scientific and education catalogues. The reason for this is to be found above all in the reluctance of the Italian school system to adopt audio-visual teaching and until recently in a lack of educational software. Although the problem of the modernisation of the school system is a national one, the individual efforts made by numerous school principals should be mentioned.

The lack of training for teachers in the use of the new technology is particularly serious. The instinctive familiarity of the young with computers in particular, and with electronics in general, is in stark contrast to this. The knowledge and use of the new technologies thus remains for the time being excluded from the education system which, will have to be opened up to these new developments if it is not to become divorced from reality.

The development of educational software owes much to the success of the televsion programme *Quark* which has aroused a great interest in scientific matters, and revealed a new and stimulating ways of imparting knowledge.

Interviews confirmed the fact that pornographic videocassettes account for the greater part (40–50 per cent) of pre-recorded software. In absolute terms, the circulation of this type of product probably corresponds to the European average, while the acquisition of videocassettes of other types does not enjoy a great success among the public. It would appear that the many and varied offerings of Italian television do not encourage demand for software.

The ratio between VCRs installed and pre-recorded cassettes sold annually, should provide some idea of the dimensions of the software market. However, this ratio is about 350,000:400,000 and implies an average annual sale of 1.14 videocassette for each VCR, which is certainly a disconcerting figure for the industry bearing in mind the number of rentals. It would therefore appear that these data are scarcely reliable, or alternatively that there are a very large number of pirate copies on the market.

The tables were drawn up on the basis of 1984 catalogues. For some categories we have calculated percentages, with and without pornographic products: in the one case to have a picture of the market and in the other to leave these particular products out of consideration.

THE ILLEGAL MARKET

An overall evaluation of the circulation of pre-recorded software cannot ignore the importance of illegal copies. This problem concerns not only the field of video-recordings, but also audio cassettes and computer software. More generally it afflicts every type of commerce based on the storing of information by magnetic means.

Given the presence of small scale piracy, organised crime and copies as favours or for personal use, it becomes very difficult to establish the incidence of pirate copies in the videocassette market. The few facts which are certain concern police operations connected with the confiscation of materials and installations. For the rest, it is necessary to rely on estimates and on the opinions of shop owners and distributers.

The average price of videocassettes is high – about 70,000 lire (US$35) for the types most in demand. According to all operators interviewed this figure is too high for the average user. Many people prefer therefore to acquire pirate copies, certainly of inferior quality, but at a lower price.

In theory, the renting of cassettes should be a valid deterrent to the illegal market, given the offer of films at very low prices. In practice, the large amount of software circulating for rentals has allowed the great majority of users to obtain original copies, to reproduce them and to exchange or resell them at a low price.

According to some distributors there may even be retailers who produce illegal copies to increase their earnings.

It is a widely held opinion that the greater part of the Italian parallel market operates through these private channels rather than on the basis of large scale counterfeiting, for the present limits of the market do not make this sector attractive to organised crime. It should nevertheless be noted that the situation differs from region to region. In some regional centres connections between the activity of the underworld and aspects of this market can be perceived. Moreover it is necessary to consider that, though the Italian market may be small the situation is very different in other countries and smuggling should not be discounted. Indeed the joint initiatives by the EEC Governments to combat audio-visual piracy by the resolution published in the official EEC Gazette of 3 August 1984, reveal the seriousness of the situation.

As far as the Italian situation is concerned, *Video* estimates sales of 150,000 pirate cassettes in 1985 as compared with 400,000 legal ones. This figure meets with the unanimous scepticism of the interviewees, who declare that the volume of trade in pirate cassettes is at least equal to, if not higher than that of legal copies. They consider that their estimates are correct taking into account rentals, while for sales they estimate the ratio between the two markets to be 5:1 in favour of illegal copies.

We emphasise once again that these proportions are not 'official' they are the opinions of retailers and distributors. However, it is important to keep these impressions in mind, and to remember that circulation of copies deriving from small-scale piracy renders every type of statistic problematic and approximate. In fact, the 'official' data are very far from offering reliable information on the dimensions of the phenomenon. The annual report of the president of the SIAE on the occasion of the presentation of the final budget for 1984, states that there were 812 police operations against violations of the laws of copyright. These led to the seizure of 15 reproduction installations equipped with the most modern facilities, 587,159 counterfeit music cassettes and 5,360 illegal videocassettes (as compared with 658 in 1983).

Though the growth of the illegal video cassette market is evident from the above, it is also clear that the figures reported do not offer an adequate description of the parallel market, because police operations concern offences perpetrated on a large scale, and the greater part of the circulation of illegal copies occurs through domestic channels.

The duplication of pre-recorded cassettes is among the most widespread forms of piracy. The practice of 'bootlegging' is not very widespread, given the great availability of TV channels, but it occurs on occasions of exceptional events such as the Live Aid mega-concert, the marriage of Prince Charles and Lady Diana etc.

Cinema piracy suffered a severe blow when almost all the large distribution companies published, in videocassette format, entire catalogues, making new films available at the time of their release on the big screen. Moreover, the policy of immediate rental of video cassettes of newly released films has eliminated a large part of the area in which the illegal 'video cassette cinema' market operated.

In general, there exist at least two channels, which are always connected, for the circulation of pirate videocassettes. On the one hand there is organised counterfeiting of a criminal nature; on the other hand there is domestic duplication, with which it is sometimes intended to make a little money, but which mainly expresses the tendency towards supplying software at low costs.

The key element regarding this dual development of illegal software is the difference in quality between the professional and domestic copying systems. In fact, the poor quality of duplicated videocassettes is notable, especially if reproduced at home with non-professional equipment. Therefore one can, with all probability, predict a parallel development of the two markets, each offering a certain product, price and service.

The results of the interviews undertaken reveal a recent increase in the demand for quality videocassettes, and this would indicate a certain disaffection on the part of the public with poor quality products. On the other hand, to those who have economic problems many retailers propose the convenient solution of renting.

It would however be incorrect to expect a drastic reduction of the illegal market through this strategy because the lowest cost will continue to constitute an important preferential factor to the advantage of the pirate market. The two markets for the circulation of software seems likely to remain in place for some time.

CONCLUSION

Our focus up till now has been on the contexts within which the video phenomenon has developed in the domestic situation in Italy. The figures clearly indicate the still embryonic state of video although the rate of growth is high. On the other hand it may be supposed that, within a few years, Italy will be more in alignment with the other EEC countries in which the first signs of market saturation have appeared in the last few years. It is important to note here the striking increase in the last few months of the availability of pre-recorded software, which presumably indicates a precise marketing strategy.

Considering the fact that domestic video-recording is fundamentally linked to television, we have sought to describe the present situation of television which represents one of the most important and disconcerting phenomena of the last decade. Since the end of 1984 private television in the absence of adequate legislative regulation, has been in reality a monopoly. The Berlusconi Group owns the main networks and has made advantageous business agreements with the other minor networks. At this point legislation is too late and one can only acknowledge the situation which has been created.

It is within this context that the 'power' of the 'telecommander' sees its role significantly reduced and videorecording appears as a means of liberation, at least partially, from the ties of the television schedules.

However at the present stage it seems that VCRs are seen essentially as a product which confers on its owner, a particular status of comfort and modernity. The possibilities of video independence offered by video recording are thus a potential rather than a reality.

It should not be forgotten however that the price of a VCR in Italy is still among the highest in Europe and constitutes for the average buyer a committed acquisition.

The widespread diffusion of portable VCRs and the conspicuous sale of telecameras would however indicate a strong tendency to creative or individual use of video as an instrument for capturing images. It remains to be verified if, with the evolution of the market, such a tendency will be confirmed.

In this context it seems reasonable to foresee a market development of very large dimensions, which will presumably lead to a stratification in the use of video-recording. It is hoped therefore that the VCR can also become an instrument for the satisfaction of many needs, not only those of entertainment and recreation, but also those of television self-management, as well as for creative uses and communication.

TABLE 1

VIDEO FORMATS: ITALIAN SHARE OF MARKET

	1983 %	1984 %
VHS	63	60
Betamax	23	20
Video 2000	14	20

Source: Ace International

TABLE 2

VIDEOCASSETTES AVAILABLE ON ITALIAN MARKET – 1984

	Number	*%*
Film	816	44.06
Music	200	10.79
Educational	140	7.55
Documentary	134	7.23
Sport	82	4.43
Pornography	481	25.96
Total	1,853	100.00

TABLE 3

FILMS AVAILABLE ON VIDEOCASSETTE

Genre	Number	%Excl porno	% Incl porno
Comedy	170	20.83	13.11
Drama	157	19.24	12.10
Adventure	83	10.17	6.40
Comic	74	9.07	5.71
Western	50	6.13	3.86
Cartoon	44	5.39	3.39
Detective	42	5.15	3.24
Horror	25	3.06	1.93
Historical	25	2.06	1.93
Spy	24	2.94	1.85
Romantic	23	2.82	1.77
Science fiction	22	2.07	1.70
War	19	2.33	1.46
Thriller	16	1.96	1.23
Erotic	16	1.96	1.23
Musical	15	1.84	1.16
Fantastic	11	1.35	0.85
Pornographic	481	–	37.08
Total excl porno	816	100.00	–
Total incl porno	1,297	–	100.00

TABLE 4

VIDEO CASSETTE CATEGORISATION

	Number	% Excl prono	% Incl prono
Film/entertainment	816	59.5	70.0
Music	200	14.6	10.8
Science	127	9.2	6.9
General interest/education	115	8.3	6.2
Sport	82	6.0	4.4
Instruction/how-to	19	1.4	1.0
Fine arts	12	0.9	0.6
Children	1	0.1	0.1
Total excl porno	1,372	100.00	–
Total incl porno	1,853	–	100.00

TABLE 5

WHAT IS THE USE OF A VIDEORECORDER?
— Inquiry among Italian daily paper readers

	%
Recording for future viewing	81.1
Recording by video camera	25.3
Hobby	12.3
Viewing pre-recorded cassettes	11.1
Working	9.1
Teaching	9.1
Time-shifting	8.7
Studying	6.7
Video libraries	5.5
Others	4.4

Source: Video TV

Chapter 4

SWEDEN

HARDWARE AND BLANK SOFTWARE

PRODUCTION

There are no companies manufacturing VCRs or tapes of any kind in Sweden. All video cassette players and unrecorded tapes sold in Sweden are imported.

DISTRIBUTION

There are approximately 30 companies importing VCRs into Sweden, of which 23 are members of the industry association SRL. It is data provided by them that is used below on sales of VCRs and tapes. There are roughly the same number of importers of tapes, however, these are not necessarily the same companies.

In 1984, 135,000 VCRs were sold in Sweden, 96 per cent of which were VHS and 4 per cent Beta. Philips have practically disappeared from the sales statistics, although a few percent of total stock are still of this standard. In 1985 it is predicted that 160,000 VCRs will be sold (96 per cent VHS).

The value of the VCRs sold in 1984 was SEK 708 million before VAT, or 870 million including VAT. The same year 5,000 video cameras were sold at a value of 30 million before VAT and 37 million including VAT.

The range of sales prices of new video players is wide, from SEK 4,000 to 7,500. What consumers actually pay depends very much on the timing and conditions. A well informed consumer can get a very favourable price, by waiting for the right moment. The appropriate value might then be the statistical average between sales revenues and number of VCRs sold. The sales tax on VCRs is SEK 600.

In 1984, two million blank cassettes were sold at a value of SEK 120 million before VAT and 150 million including VAT. There is a considerable amount of smuggling, black marketing and false definitions of cassettes sold in Sweden because of the high tax on audio and video tapes. Sales of tapes in 1984 ought to have yielded SEK 90 million to the Treasury, but the tax revenues received amounted to only a third of that.

For 1985 it is estimated by the industry that 2–2.5 million cassettes will be sold, of which 0.6 million will be smuggled and 0.5 million will come from stocks dating from before 1983 (the year when the tax was introduced). The number of cassettes sold and reported for taxation, is estimated to be around 1 million in 1985. The balance, up to half a million cassettes, could thus be sales not reported to the Treasury.

The tax on blank video cassettes has been recently lowered to SEK 15 per cassette, in an effort to limit smuggling and fraud.

CONSUMPTION

In Sweden there are approximately 1,500 dealers in TV, radio and video who sell VCRs and tapes. Some of these shops also rent VCRs, as a response to increased competition from rental companies (such as Granada and Thorn) but also as a response to a tightening consumer credit market. Approximately 20 per cent of all VCRs are rented and 80 per cent are sold to consumers. To this number has to be added about 20,000 so-called Movie Boxes, video players with no recording capacity, rented together with pre-recorded cassettes at many software dealers, to extend the software market to consumers without VCRs.

It is impossible to give official rent charges for hardware and software, because they vary considerably, depending on the conditions. But around SEK 200–250 per month seems to be a normal charge level for a standard VCR, higher for more sophisticated equipment, shorter periods, etc. Temporary offers can go as low as below 100 per month. The total rental business can be estimated to amount to about SEK 250 million including VAT in 1985.

VIDEOGRAMS

PRODUCTION

The film industry in Sweden release their products on cassettes on the rental market. To this group has to be added the national public service television companies and a few special production houses. The importing companies provide only the technical preparation of foreign films for release and are not included here.

AB Svensk Filmindustri (SF) is the biggest film production company in

Sweden, as well as the biggest cinema chain. It has merged with several video companies and is now one of the leaders in video distribution. Its turnover of video proper is not known. Total turnover of SF in 1984 was SEK 277 million, with a negative net result of 14 million. SF is also involved in negotiations for a Swedish pay-TV channel. Finally, SF is exploring cable TV services. SF's mother company, the publishing house Bonnier, is involved through a Danish subsidiary, Borsen, in an experimental broadcast TV station in Copenhagen (Weekend TV).

ESSELTE Video AB is the other video market leader in Sweden. It is a subsidiary of ESSELTE, which has interests in office supplies, the graphics industry and book publishing. ESSELTE is financially very strong and the video division can benefit from that and the fact that the company is operating multinationally. The video division had a total turnover in 1984 of SEK 230 million, net profit of 21 million, from operations in Scandinavia and Benelux. ESSELTE Video is now starting to build its own chain of cinemas and to invest in film productions. It owns shares in Film Net, the Dutch pay-TV channel, and the company has plans to introduce Film Net in Scandinavia.

Together, SF and ESSELTE may well have 70 per cent of the video market in Sweden. *Sandrew Film & Teater AB* and *Sonet Film AB* also have roots in film production. Most other producers of films are very small. *Sveriges Television AB (SVT)* and *Utbildningsradion AB (UR)* are subsidiaries within the Sveriges Radio AB group. They produce TV programmes and educational material for circulation on the home market as well as on the institutional market. SVT operates through other distributors on the home market. UR is the educational radio and TV company which produces material for the school system and for adult education.

Since 1963, the Swedish film industry has had an agreement with the *Swedish Film Institute (SFI)* to contribute to the financing of domestic film productions. Ten percent of the gross revenue from ticket sales in major cinemas are contributed to the SFI production funds. In 1983, when the agreement was extended for another period of ten years, the video industry was included in the support system. The video rental business now provides approximately SEK 20 million a year to the SFI funds. For each cassette copy put out for circulation, SEK 40 has to be paid to the SFI funds for films longer than 73 minutes (the fee for shorter films is SEK 25).

During the last two years, new incentives have been found to stimulate investments in Swedish films. Investors are now found outside the traditional film industry and outside the video industry. The cinema showing is still the heart of a film's commercial success, but video circulation offers important extra revenues. This is the reason why film and video are now more or less integrated. Film companies buy video distributions, and video companies are engaged in film production.

DISTRIBUTION

The market for video software distribution has been turbulent but there are now signs of a growing maturity. The market is more and more dominated by a few big companies. Distributors of any importance are members of The International Federation of Producers of Phonograms and Videograms (IFPI). The market is very competitive and thus unwilling to give a comprehensive record of turnover or market shares for each individual company. In some instances, too, the turnover figures may include business in other countries by the same company.

Data from consumer surveys and estimates from observers in the business, indicate a total turnover in the video software business of approximately SEK 450 million in 1984 before VAT (a figure likely to grow to 550 million in 1985). Including VAT (23 per cent), the cost to consumers in 1984 equalled SEK 550 million.

The number of cassette rentals during 1984 is estimated to be about 16 million, at an average cost of SEK 34 (based on interviews). The range of rental charges vary from SEK 10 per day to SEK 75 per weekend for premium films. A common level is SEK 40 per day, but every third consumer reports some kind of discount agreement with the dealers.

The biggest distribution companies are Swedish: ESSELTE, with subsidiaries in Denmark, Norway, Finland, Holland, Belgium and the United Kingdom; Bonnier, with Svensk Filmindustri (SF), Transfer, Europafilm; Viking video; Media Network (co-owned by Swedish VTC and Dutch VCL); Walthers; Sandrews; Sonet; Juno Media.

The following are owned, wholly or partially, by foreign companies: Thorn/EMI; Warner Home Video; Select (owned by Danish publishing house Gutenberghus); RCA/Columbia (with Video Trade); Hem films and MDC (owned by the Norwegian film and video company VIP Scandinavia); Vestron Video International.

Video rights are bought for more than one country at a time. A prevailing pattern is to procure more than the video rights in the deals. It seems to be a pattern to group together the Scandinavian and the Benelux countries in these packages and to get the video, cable, satellite rights with TV production as well. It is not possible to ascertain the extent to which this is the norm today.

The channels through which the consumers have access to rental cassettes are many and are fairly evenly spread throughout the country. According to the IFPI records, there are more than 3,330 rental dealers, to which has to be added 400 Pressbyrå news stands (similar to WH Smith in the United Kingdom). The 3,300 dealers can be divided into four groups: service stations, radio and TV shops, special video rental dealers, and local grocery shops.

Of the revenues, specialised video rental dealers account for approximately 40 per cent and a growing share. Local grocery shops have about 15 per cent and a growing share. TV and radio shops, showing less and less interest in the rental business, still account for about 15 per cent. Service stations and the Pressbyra chain account for approximately 10–15 per cent each.

The total number of cassettes circulating on the rental market has been estimated at around 0.8 million. Since about 0.4–0.5 million new copies are released each year, the conclusion must be that the average life of a copy is roughly two years. A negligible number of pre-recorded cassettes are sold in Sweden.

Due to the large number of rental dealers, the relatively small number of copies in circulation, and the relatively small number of VCRs in Sweden (October 1985, approximately 750,000), it is clear that average rental revenues per dealer are low. Competition among rental outlets has led to narrow profit margins, something the industry is now trying to alleviate through information and co-operation.

CONTENT

There are no up-to-date accounts of the content of available titles on the Swedish market. In 1982, the Swedish Broadcasting Corporation conducted a study which revealed that there were then 3,500 titles available for consumers to hire. The distribution of categories was the following:

Thrillers, adventures, entertainment	47%
Pornography	36%
Children/Family oriented	10%
Music	1%
Non-fiction	6%

According to estimates made by IFPI, the total number of titles available today through its members is 4,000, and from non-members of IFPI another 1,000. To this figure should be added an unkown number of pornographic titles (in 1982 estimated at more than 1,000). It may thus be assumed that in 1985 there were roughly 6,000 titles available on the Swedish market. A qualified guess about the composition of the content available in 1985 would be: of the 5,000 non-pornographic titles available, roughly 19 per cent are children/family, sports and music; 5 per cent non-fiction and 75 per cent thrillers, adventures and entertainment. Roughly 10 per cent of the titles are domestic productions and 90 per cent foreign.

Software for the institutional market has never been researched. There is an established system serving this market with films and other audio-visual media, and video is simply another means of distributing such material.

The broadcasting company UR is providing the educational system in Sweden with almost all the videos used. Educational programmes are broadcast and recorded off air by more than a hundred local AV Centres or by the schools directly. In 1983, some 100,000 video copies of educational TV programmes were thus used by the schools, according to a study by UR. Most schools have access to video players.

A special video network has been created for the merchant navy, embassies and groups of Swedes abroad, such a those serving in a UN military capacity. Every month packages of programmes from national TV are sent out on video for circulation.

Another special network has been created for deaf people. Public resources support professional productions of video programmes, specially designed for deaf viewers, who can order these by mail. The system can be seen as a parallel to the books and newspapers on sound cassettes for the blind.

Video is also used for in-house training by many enterprises and organisations. However no systematic information as to the volume and extent of this market is available.

LEGAL PERSPECTIVES

The parallel market situation is very orderly in Sweden compared with that in many other countries. Video cassettes are, however, very attractive to consumers and the number of thefts in rental shops is fairly high. An estimate 6,000 rental cassettes are stolen each year.

CENSORSHIP

There is no compulsory censorship of videograms for private use, but in August 1982 a criminal law was passed prohibiting the distribution of cassettes with extremely violent content. The public prosecutor is responsible for bringing such cases to court. A new law came into effect from January 1986 introducing censorship of cassettes intended for public screening.

VIDEO USE

Table 1 gives the rate of penetration of video in Swedish homes. The penetration is uneven, especially by age group. While more than 30 per cent of people under 24 years of age have access to a video player in their homes, only 3 per cent of people older than 65 have players at home. The metropolitan areas have a higher rate of video ownership than smaller towns and farming areas. Stockholm has 34 per cent, Gothenburg and Malmö around 24 per cent, smaller towns around 15 per cent and the countryside approximately 10 per cent.

In comparison with the diffusion of television and of colour television sets, the penetration of video has been rather slow. Television reached almost 60 per cent after five years. Five years after its introduction, colour TV had found its way into every third household, while video after five years was found in only 13 per cent of households.

The average number of blank cassettes per recorder is now around 10–12. Over the years, some 9 million cassettes have been sold, of which 8 million have been bought by individual consumers.

There is now a long series of figures measuring the total extent of video consumption in Sweden. Every year in October, the Audience and Programme Research Department of Sveriges Radio reports how many Swedes watch video on an average day (as well as a range of other mass media activities – the 'Media Narometer'). Table 2 gives the annual figures.

As in the case of television, use of video varies both seasonally and over the course of the week. The variations in the 'watch TV' column is almost entirely explained by the time of the year at which the survey is made.

When broadcast television offers an attractive programme, people prefer to watch the transmission directly if possible. When there is 'nothing on', literally or figuratively speaking, video households will fill in with home recordings of earlier programmes or rental films.

The reason the daily use of video does not increase at the same rate as ownership of video is the fact that only about 25–30 per cent of video owners use their players every day. This figure is stable, as is the proportion of non-owners who watch video. The daily average video viewing among them is around 2 per cent. These two figures give the daily total video audience in Sweden.

A question of the greatest importance to television is what share of video use goes to recorded TV programmes. It has been found in Sweden that the new owners of video are very active in renting cassettes, but interest wears off rather quickly. Already after some months it levels off. On the average, owners of video players rent 2–3 cassettes per month.

A balance seems now to have been achieved between recorded programmes and rental programmes. Table 3 summarizes the situation.

Swedish and foreign studies of home video all confirm the medium's role as an *entertainer*. This applies to those who have their own video as well as to those who watch video in others' homes. This is true of young people especially, but the same applies to older groups, as well.

The longer a household has had a video recorder, the less the inclination to rent films, and the greater the share of recorded television programmes in the video diet. More highly educated video owners use their recorder to 'timeshift', more ie to free themselves from programme schedules, than do other groups.

Video serves as a *complement to television* and reflects television output in mirror fashion. The less interesting the regular TV programming, the more video is used as a means of 'plucking the raisins out of the pudding', so to speak.

So far video has not had any noticeable impact on the average level of consumption of television. It has most probably led to less TV viewing among young people, but heavy consumers of television have, thanks to video, been able to increase their consumption of TV fare overall.

Clearly video is in more direct competition with cinemas. During the last few years annual sales of cinema tickets have decreased, down 30 per cent since 1979. Today, more than 3 times more people watch films on video than in cinemas. In 1984, the economic turnover in video rental was higher than that of ticket sales in cinemas for the first time.

The majority of Swedish viewers use video for entertainment. Efforts have been made to make titles of special interest available in libraries and book shops, but none of these channels has been very successful. Another effort to use an alternative non-commercial channel of distribution involves the Swedish Postal Service. The Swedish Television Company has an agreement with the postal service, by which a selection of some 100 television programmes are made available via mail order. The system is a practical means of serving a limited and geographically dispersed market, but it requires rather considerable marketing efforts.

There are some specialised channels: magazines and journals, hobby clubs and interest organisations offer their customers and members a selection of targeted titles, but this market is small in Sweden. Building up a mass distribution apparatus for other than broad-appeal, commercially successful feature films and entertainment programmes will take time and cost money. On the other hand, such a development has time on its side. The number of video owners whose interests and tastes are broader than those of the 'teen market' is growing. Public interest in the overall selection of videograms that are actually available will only increase with time. The major drawback in the case of Sweden is the limited size of the total market and the costs of producing or translating foreign special interest programmes.

TABLE 1

ACCESS TO VIDEO RECORDERS IN SWEDEN

Year (December)	VCRs	% homes (000s)	% population (7-79 yrs)
1978	40	1	no data
1979	70	2	no data
1980	120	3	4
1981	285	8	9
1982	435	13	15
1983	530	16	18
1984	665	19	21
1985	825	23	25
1986	990	27	29

TABLE 2

SHARE OF POPULATION WHO WATCH VIDEO

Year	Watch video	Watch tv	% Population with video
1980 Oct	1	79	4
1981 Oct	5	76	9
1982 Oct	4	79	15
1983 Jan	6	79	18
1984 Jan	6	79	19
1985 Aug/Sep	7	72	24

TABLE 3

DISTRIBUTION OF VIDEO USE BETWEEN RENTAL CAS-SETTES AND RECORDED TV PROGRAMMES

	Winter 81/82	Feb 84	Feb 85	Oct 85
Rental	51	43	42	48
Rec. TV-prog.	51	59	53	51
Other	–	–	5	1

(Multiple responses possible)

Chapter 5

JAPAN

Japan is a democratic state with a constitutional monarchy. The official language is Japanese. That all citizens speak and understand Japanese without difficulty may be largely attributed to the historically rapid growth of radio which helped to unify the language. Traditionally, Japan has been relatively isolated because of its geographical location and the foreign and economic policies which obtained from 1639–1858.

After the Second World War – which marked the end of a period of institutionalised militarism – commercial broadcasting was introduced to encourage freedom of speech and to stimulate the process of an increasing exchange of information. Television expanded extremely rapidly – based upon an equally rapid economic growth – and this enabled the Japanese people to experience a far wider range of experiences of the outside world via this new media.

There are two types of broadcasting organisations in Japan – two public broadcasting corporations and 102 commercial broadcasting companies. One of the public corporations – NHK (Nippon Hoso Kyokai) – is financed via an annual licence fee, and the other – the University of the Air – is owned by a government funded corporation.

NHK has two nationwide networks covering the whole of Japan and about 90 per cent of all programmes are produced in Tokyo. Total production amounts to approximately 252 hours per week.

The commercial companies are financed through sponsored advertising and there are 1 minor and 4 major networks. Total tele-casting in Tokyo alone amounts to more than 560 hours per week. Network arrangements are made between the stations but strictly speaking there are no 'networks' in that Broadcasting Law prohibits the ownership of multiple stations by any individual company.

VIDEO HARDWARE AND BLANK SOFTWARE

PRODUCTION

Japanese companies are not prepared to disclose either their annual rate of turnover, the volume of video recorders exported or company estimates for projected growth rates, but overall collective figures can be provided. Thus for example, in 1984, 27,124,000 units were produced of which 26,085,000 were sold – 22,071,000 of them on the international markets. This means that almost 85 per cent of all production was exported. Table 1 shows the growth rate.

VHS had 80.4 per cent of the market and Betamax 19.6 per cent, whilst figures were still not available in 1985 for the new 8mm format.

Retail prices in Japan ranged from $324 to $719 with wholesale prices representing 75 per cent of the retail price. Meanwhile the average income of a worker (aged 42.8 years) with 3.8 family members was $1,696 per month (including bonuses and after taxes).

With regard to blank video tape production 931,745,000 tapes were produced in 1984 which marked an increase of over 215 million units over the previous year. However, sales dropped from $6,200,000 to $3,800,000 in value. Tables 2 and 3 provide basic production information for both video recorders and blank tapes.

DISTRIBUTION

Both the international and domestic distribution of equipment is carried out by the production companies themselves and there are no significant wholesalers independent of a production company. Domestically, most manufacturers have wholesale outlets in various districts and these dealers organise the numerous retail outlets.

There are seventy thousand electrical appliance shops in Japan. In every town, no matter how small, there are always rice dealers, drugstores, fishmongers, greengrocers, and the electrical appliance shop. The Matsushita Electric Industry is very strong in this area, with about thirty thousand shops in which more than 80 per cent of the retail commodities are Matsushita products. Sony has fifteen hundred shops of this kind, and other manufacturers have their own 'series' shops.

Video recorder rentals represent a very small proportion of the Japanese market and account for only 1.8 per cent of total income for members of the Japanese Video Association in 1984.

Predictably, the markets for Japanese video recorders are dominated by North America and Europe which accounted for 60.6 per cent and 22.6 per cent respectively of all units sold (see Table 4).

CONSUMPTION

The rental trade for video hardware is almost negligible and the largest market for videotape recorders is the domestic market – institutional use represents a very small area of the business. For example, primary schools which are regarded as a fairly large institutional market, possess 40,000 video recorders, but this figure is less than 0.3 per cent of the total number in private homes.

There are also 843 audio-visual Education Libraries which provide a wide range of educational back up services. Eighty per cent of these are equipped with VCRs but they still seem to function far more on the basis of 16mm film. For example, in 1983 they rented out an average of 925 film titles a year against only 140 video titles.

VIDEOGRAMS

PRODUCTION

There are 52 video tape production houses which belong to the JVA (the Japanese Video Association) and the five largest account for 66 per cent of the business. In addition there are three significant non-JVA members – Warner Pioneer, CIC-Victor Video and RCA-Columbia. These three companies were originally dealers in American films but since 1984 they have emerged as strong video software producers. Their main titles are, of course, Hollywood movies and they also rent out tapes and function as copyright agents.

COPYING AND FACILITY HOUSES

There are dozens of facility houses but three dominate the field – Sony, Toyo Recording Company and Toyo Genzosho – which are known as the 'Big Three'. Each company has installed at least 1,000 video recorders as copying machines and they all regard copying as a part of their main areas of work ie film processing, programme production, video post-production, editing. Again, only global figures for the total sales of JVA members can be indicated and these are listed in Table 5.

DISTRIBUTION

Generally speaking, distribution is handled by the producers themselves, although some book wholesalers and audio record shops also function as videogram distributors. None of these, however, is large enough to mention. There is no international distribution of videograms.

CONSUMPTION

According to the JVA out of a total sales figure of $331 million, video disc programmes exceed the sales of pre-recorded video tapes in 1984 by approximately $17 million. This can be accounted for by a uniquely Japanese phenomenon – Kara-oke. This is a system whereby people can sing to an accompaniment recorded on video disc and played in bars, pubs and cafes. However there are very few videodiscs in home use.

There were 1,669 video programmes produced in the financial year 1984/5 and interestingly, in line with much of the rest of the world, 'adult' or pornographic material is on the decline. By far the most popular areas of consumption were music and popular culture tapes which accounted for 56.8 per cent of the total market sales followed by movies and entertainment programmes which accounted for 23.6 per cent. For a break down see Table 6.

The area of major growth in addition to that of music and films is that of cartoons.

VIDEO USAGE

By December 1984, 29.4 per cent of Japanese homes possessed a video machine and by far the most popular use of the equipment is for 'time-shift' viewing. Only 1.7 per cent of all viewings were of videograms and only 6.6 per cent of video usage was for the purpose of making personal camera recordings (See Table 7).

Off air recording for group viewing at home is extremely rare although 62.7 per cent of secondary schools use their equipment for this purpose. Public group viewing of video – as in cinema type situations – does not exist at all. Schools also make very little use of videograms with only 4.4 per cent of their screenings being of such material, but their use of video cameras is on the increase with nearly 10 per cent of recorder usage being designed to make school based tapes.

THE PARALLEL MARKET AND COPYRIGHT LAW

There are many discount houses in downtown areas, one of the most famous for video equipment being the Akihabara district in Tokyo. These are not, however, parallel market establishments – these exist in other areas called *batta-ya* which sell stolen videos. The demand for such videos is very small due to the lack of warranty on such goods.

Illegal software, especially tapes called *ura-video* (which are pornographic) can be found in 'adult' shops, some bars and small hotels. As a result of this development over 120 companies have worked together to establish the Japan Video Ethics Society which is a body independent of the police or government.

The Society has a committee which views tapes and issues a seal with a serial number categorising a tape, if necessary, as 'adult level, unsuitable for minors under 18 years of age'. If a member company releases a tape without such a seal its membership is revoked. As the Society's ethical judgement is independent, there is always the possiblility that the police may have a different view and therefore take alternative action.

As for copyright protection, there are many shops that have installed videocopy systems and will copy a movie or any other tape free for the purchase of a blank cassette. Copied tapes are also available for rent. This is an infringement of the copyright law; the police, along with the Video anti-Piracy Organisation of Japan (VAPO), will make due prosecution.

In Japan, the copyright law makes provision for creative artists whose copyright has been violated to sue the person or party responsible. Unfortunately, artists very rarely discover that their rights have been violated and consequently such suits are uncommon. If the dispute is between two companies, the case is often settled out of court and the number of such lawsuits is very small. On the other hand, article 35 protects teachers from this law, stating that if a teacher has reproduced something for educational purposes, he or she is excused; but he or she may not do this 'in excess'.

Piracy is not often heard of in regard to films. But there are cases where films have been copied with the use of video cameras in the cinema. Naturally, the picture quality in such cases is poor; nevertheless, such a movie can be released as a new film video software item.

The above kind of piracy is rather popular among amateur pirates. Many do not believe that their actions are illegal. Some even claim that they are serving the public by presenting an inexpensive alternative. Many Hollywood films on videotape are copied, amateur translations of the dialogue into Japanese are superimposed as subtitles with microcomputers, labels are printed with colour-copy machines, and the video which looks like a legal, legitimate software item is sold.

Informed sources state that many small shops on the North American continent handle Japanese television programmes on video. Recorded directly from broadcasts near Narita Airport, they are copied in bulk and sent to shops for Japanese people abroad. It is estimated that about 100 shops handle these videos. Japanese copyright laws prohibit the making of copies, irrespective of use.

CONCLUSION

It is often said that Japan is a society which mixes traditional culture with high technology. The Japanese still use kanji (Chinese characters) in their ultra modern word processors equipped with LSI's. Whether the use of these ideograms has helped instil the habit of pictorial communication or not is unclear, but the Japanese are certainly a visually oriented people. Television is the most popular pastime, although there is 99.99 per cent literacy. The average person's television viewing time is 3 hours and 6 minutes per weekday (June 1984). Among younger people and the elderly (over 60s), the average viewing time has decreased compared with that of November 1983, according to 1984 NHK Research. Another NHK survey conducted in March 1985 showed that 37 per cent of the Japanese people regarded TV as 'essential'. Fifty-six per cent regarded TV as a 'convenient device, if it is there', and 6 per cent answered that 'it doesn't matter if it exists or not'. Individuals perceive their purposes in television viewing as: 'To learn what's going on in the world' (61 per cent) and 'To get information on life and leisure' (44 per cent).

Most homes in Japan have two TV sets and virtually all have radios and tape recorders so the one third ownership of VCRS in some ways seems surprisingly low. However, micro-computers have been enjoying a continuing boom over the last few years and together with the wide range of digital information processing equipment on offer it is clear that video communications will experience a golden age over the next ten years that should extend into the next century.

TABLE 1

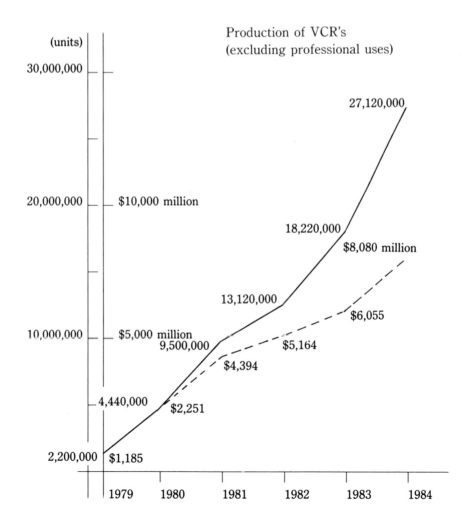

Production of VCR's
(excluding professional uses)

(units)

30,000,000

20,000,000 — $10,000 million

10,000,000 — $5,000 million

27,120,000

18,220,000

$8,080 million

13,120,000

$6,055

9,500,000

$5,164

$4,394

4,440,000 $2,251

2,200,000 $1,185

1979   1980   1981   1982   1983   1984

TABLE 2

VCR PRODUCTION

Company name	No of factories work force (Personnel)	Video type	Units produced April 84 to March 85 market share
Matushita Electric Industrial Co, Ltd	3 39,980	VHS	6,644,000 24.5%
Victor Company of Japan (JVC)	1 13,500	VHS	4,664,000 17.2%
Hitachi Company Ltd	1 80,000	VHS	3,932,000 14.5%
SONY Corporation	3 14,504	Betamax	2,468,000 9.1%
Sharp Corporation	1 19,300	VHS	2,468,000 9.1%
Sanyo Electric Co Ltd	1 20,907	Betamax VHS	1,492,000 5.5%
Tokyo Sanyo Electric Company Ltd	1 14,706	VHS	1,247,000 4.6%
Mitsubishi Electric	1 49,088	VHS	1,193,000 4.4%
Toshiba Corporation	29 64,150	Betamax VHS	1,003,000 3.7%
Akai Electric Co Ltd	1 2,074	VHS	542,000 2.0%
Home Electronics Co Ltd	6 4,516	Betamax VHS	434,000 1.6%
Nai Electric Co Ltd	1 150	1/4	0.4%

TABLE 3

BLANK VIDEOCASSETTE PRODUCTION

Manufacturer	No of factories workforce (Personnel)	Video type (Number)	Units produced April 84 to March 85
TDK Corporation	3 7,832	VHS Betamax 10,000,000	237,000,000 25.4%
Fuji Photo Film Company Ltd	1 11,000	VHS Betamax 7,000,000	191,000,000 20.5%
Hitachi-Maxell Ltd	1 2,332	VHS Betamax 6,000,000	191,000,000 20.5%
Sony Magnetic Products Inc	3 1,690	VHS Betamax 8,000,000	140,000,000 15.0%
Mitsushita Electric Components Ltd	1 10,256	VHS 4,500,000	66,000,000 7.1%

TABLE 4

INTENDED MARKETS AND THEIR RELATIVE VALUE (JAN - DEC , 1984)

Zone	No of VCR'S exported units	%	Sales $	%	Annual rate of turnover*
Asia	2,451,000	11.1	$786,000,000	12.1	104.2
Europe	4,977,000	22.6	$1,529,000,000	23.6	82.2
North America	13,380,000	60.6	$3,769,000,000	58.1	187.2
South America	45,000	0.2	$17,000,000	0.3	79.3
Africa	354,000	1.6	$111,000,000	1.7	92.7
Oceania	864,000	3.9	$271,000,000	4.2	98.6
Total	22,071,000		$6,483,000,000		Average 128.5%

*$100 \times ((1984-1983)/1983) + 1.0)$

TABLE 5

SALES OF JVA MEMBERS IN APRIL 1984 - MARCH 1985

		%
Taped video programs	$125,862,000	38.0
Videodiscs	$142,859,000	43.1
Videotapes rental	$4,815,000	1.5
Copyright revenue	$1,404,000	0.4
Production of Video software (tapes)%	$27,286,000	8.2
Production of video software (discs)%	$10,603,000	3.2
Editing, processing, and studio fees %	$9,468,000	2.9
Blank videotapes	$3,773,000	1.1
Video equipment	$3,673,000	1.1
Rental video equipment	$1,847,000	0.6
Miscellaneous	$50,000	0.0
Total	$331,640,000	100

TABLE 6

PRERECORDED VIDEOTAPE & DISC SALES

Programs	Pre-recorded video tape programs sales (Apr. 1984 - Mar. 1985)		No. of title produced		Videodisc sales (Apr. 1984 - Mar. 1985)		Total no of produced titles	
	$*	market share %		%	$*	market share %	$*	market share %
a) Business/Industry	$3,969,000	3.2	33	2.0	not available	not available	$3,969,000	1.5
b) Children/Juvenile	$18,290,000	14.5	233	14.5	$3,410,000	2.4	$217,000,000	8.1
(Cartoons)	($15,133,000)		(179)		($3,410,000)		($18,453,000)	
c) Films/Entertainment	$54,081,000	43.0	557	33.4	$9,258,000	6.5	$63,339,000	23.6
(Adult Entertainment)	($10,683,000)		(155)		($601,000)		($11,284,000)	
d) Fine Arts**	$2,278,000	1.8	72	4.3	$501,000	0.4	$2,779,000	1.0
e) Education/ General Interest	$2,074,000	1.6	172	10.3	$906,000	0.4	$2,980,000	1.1
f) How-to/Intructional	$128,000	0.1	9	0.5	$47,000	***	$175,000	0.1
g) Medicine/Science	$1,307,000	1.0	27	1.6	$47,000	***	$1,354,000	0.5
h) Sports/Leisure	$6,306,000	5.0	111	6.7	$888,000	0.6	$7,194,000	2.7
i) Music/Popular Culture	$33,810,000	26.9	425	25.5	$118,771,000	83.1	$152,581,000	56.8
j) Others	$3,619,000	2.9	30	1.8	$9,033,000	6.3	$12,652,000	4.7
Total	$125,862,000	100	1669	100	$142,861,000	100	$268,732,000	100

* ¥250 to $US1.00   ** includes "Hobby/Culture"

TABLE 7

THE HOME USE OF VCR'S IN JAPAN — DEC. 1984 —

(Multiple answers)   100% = all homes with VCR's*

Time-shift viewing
while away from
home   76.9%

Time-Shift Viewing
while watching
other channels   61.9%

Recording while   43.9%
watching the target
program simul-
taneously

Taping with video   6.6%
cameras

Viewing prerecorded   1.7%
software   *Number of samples 894 homes
                                        all over Japan. Mail questionnare
                                        method

1) Average number of blank videocassettes bought per home (w/video): 15.2
   cassettes
2) The ratio of homes that own prerecorded software: 29.9%
3) Average amount of prerecorded software per home with prerecorded software: 4.3 cassettes

By Toshitaka Kikuchi (NHK Brodcasting Culture Research Inst., 1985)

Chapter 6

INDIA

EMERGENCE OF VIDEO

Video evokes many reactions in a broad cross-section of Indian society today. Among the urban-rich, it is one of the focal points of conversation, whereas among young people of the same class, it evokes a sense of competition. It is a common scene to find young men and women hovering around video centres and libraries in the afternoons, in search of pre-recorded video tapes of some classical film or a copy of the latest unreleased film. Quite often the talk about video turns into a serious discussion on the undesirable effects it has on the studies of students in all age groups and on the morality of the nation. Video has become a new craze, a fashion, and a new means of leisure time activity. Its easy operation, continuous supply of pre-recorded video cassettes, and above all, the uninterrupted import of video cassette recorders has taken Indian men and women, whether urban or rural, by storm. It has become a phenomenon without any parallel.

Video has even shaken the confidence of technologists as it has penetrated areas which the 75-year-old Indian film industry could not and, at the same time, achieved an unprecedented success in its acceptance. It has especially bothered technologists because without any effort on their part or on the government's part, it has forced them to act as a bonded industry for transnational industries and they are forced to remain at the level of screwdriver technologists. None of them are ready to predict the direction that video will take in India.

It has provoked and touched the core of the Indian film industry, the world's largest, both financially and artistically. Efforts at various levels within the film industry are being made to fight back. Pressure has been put on the government at both the national and state levels to take stern action to stop the ever increasing 'adverse' influences of video in India. The loss of revenue from entertainment tax has further forced the state governments to take prompt action against various forms of video use.

An average person on the street makes a clear conceptual distinction between video and TV and between video and cinema. Video is not considered as another form of television, but for film viewing either at home or in public places. In many houses the living room has been separated from the video room, though in the large majority, the video room is the living room where a video cassette recorder is connected to the TV monitor. Video hotels, video restaurants, video clubs, video theatres, video rooms, video halls and even video coaches signify that video falls into a separate conceptual category as a new technology which is being integrated without being modified. In spite of having been conceived as a different audio-visual medium, it remains an extension of film viewing of Indian and non-Indian origin (largely in the English language). A few tapes of TV serials are also included in video viewing. Basically video has come to stay in India as an alternative to cinema viewing.

The majority of the interviews with users and published reports reflect this conclusion. One of the reasons that video has become an alternative to the cinema is the economics of cinema viewing and the overall increasing demand for entertainment by a whole generation of *nouveau riche* who have surfaced in post-independence India.

This analysis will attempt to explain the socio-economic and technological implications of video in India. In order to do so, it is essential to have some understanding of Indian society, economy and the technological developments that have taken place since 1947 when India achieved independence.

INDIAN SOCIETY AND ECONOMY

In the past, Indian society was divided between the rulers and the ruled. This bi-partite division of society was for the first time tempered by the British when they tried to introduce a 'middle-class' as a buffer between them and the Indian masses. However, even during the British period, more than one-third of the present India was administered by the Rajahs and Nawabs. After independence, the first task was to evolve a uniform system of administration. Efforts in this direction have led to the emergence of an Indian society with a multiplicity of languages, religions and life styles and a largely illiterate, rural poor population.

The barter and market economy operate simultaneously in different parts of the country. The so-called 'mixed economy' means different things to different classes within and outside India. The major economic changes however do not necessarily affect the entire Indian society at any given time. The national elites are, however, prone to be affected by international economic changes and video technology has invaded their lives with little effect on the rest of Indian society. Hence the video phenomenon is mostly confined to this economic class which comprises only 5 per cent of the total population.

THE INDIAN MEDIA SCENE

Mass communication is divided between 'government owned' and 'privately owned' media systems. The government owned media system includes radio, television and news and documentary films including publicity through the printed media. The privately owned media system includes cinema, a large number of newspapers, magazines and the use of the government owned media system for advertising. The latest addition to this list of privately owned media is video. The government of India ensures and regulates the quality and content of media products through censor boards, and other agencies. In this way there is direct and indirect control over the production and projection of any mass communication.

There is a large scale indigenous production of films, one of the largest in the world. Cinema hardware, as far as possible, is manufactured within the country. Film production and distribution involves a little over two hundred thousand people. It has an estimated investment of a little less than one billion US dollars. There has been a steady growth of film production in all the major languages of India. Cinema has been an urban phenomenon and a medium of popular entertainment since its inception. Out of about eleven thousand cinema halls, more than 70 per cent are located in cities and films are seen by both national elites and the common person alike.

In the case of radio and television, India is setting up radio stations from domestically manufactured hardware. Since 1982, over eight million radio receivers have been manufactured every year and it is expected that more than five hundred thousand television sets will be manufactured in the near future. About ten thousand persons are engaged in programme production and transmission.

In the last 10 years, serious efforts have been made to utilize the satellite communication technology for education and development. (Agrawal 1981; Chitnis 1976). After the successful completion of the Satellite Instructional Television Experiment (SITE) in 1976, the Indian National Satellite (INSA) became operational in 1982 for the same purpose. Today India has more than 170 television transmitters covering about 70 per cent of the population and about 100 radio transmitters cover more than 90 per cent of the population.

This report is primarily based on secondary data supplemented by data collected during research. It is important to point out that the entire video industry is privately managed and, being largely illegal, is surrounded by several underworld activities and generates fierce competition. Hence any data on actual business turnover, video production duplication, channels of distribution and source of distribution are kept strictly secret – attempts were still made nevertheless to obtain qualitative data and some estimates from the field.

All the statistics on marketing channels are drawn from published government reports or published articles. It is, therefore, clearly understood that these figures could not be verified and should be accepted at their face value – all calculations are presented in US dollars and for this purpose an exchange rate of 12 Indian Rupees to 1 US dollar has been used.

VIDEO TECHNOLOGY

Video technology appeared in India as an imported item and remains so today in one form or other. The major achievement has been that Indian industry has taken a pride in assembling the highly sophisticated video technology. At present only a small quantity of video cassette recorders are being assembled in the country, although it is expected to reach 52,000 in the near future.

In order to stimulate the manufacture of video related electronics, the Government of India's Department of Electronics has made changes in the import regulations relating to video electronics. Indian film magazines and even newspapers are carrying regular advertisements of various transnational video manufacturing companies. These advertising campaigns were a part of a well designed stategy to flood the Indian market with video related electronics. Among the companies involved in the campaign are Sanyo (Japan), now being serviced by British Physical Laboratories (BPL) India; Fisher (USA) also serviced by BPL India; Sony (Japan) being produced in collaboration with Indian companies; Hitachi (Japan); Akai (Japan); JVC (Japan); Sharp (Japan); Philips (The Netherlands) and Hotline. Many of them are advertising multiple specifications especially PAL, NTSC and SECAM.

As far as video editing, duplicating and related technologies are concerned, these are being imported from the transnational companies – a situation that existed in film technology and still continues to exist.

Some companies have started producing video cassettes in collaboration with transnational companies, like M/s Kohinoor Impex (P) Ltd and M/s Kewal Surya Commercials. Similarly a few other companies have started providing hardware systeming services like M/s Systematics (India), M/s Jain Brothers and M/s Shyam Communication Systems. In India the electricity supply is AC 220 volts (50 cycle) and television runs on 625 line PAL. However, video electronics of different specifications are available in the country including AC 110 volts which are being used with the help of transformers.

The indiscriminate import from various parts of the world of VCRs that were manufactured to meet different technical specifications has led to the presence of a large number of VCRs and cassettes that cannot be played interchangeably. This has created a problem of compatibility between various video systems. It has been reported that, 'today at least five different non-compatible formats for VCR, three for video discs, two for projection TVs ... ' are in use in India. There are two technical implications that stem from this development. The first is that a large number of VCRs will become unusable earlier than their stipulated life. Secondly, there will be a need to develop reliable systems for video-related technologies that can be applied in a universal mode to ensure interchangeability among incompatible video systems.

The chances for Indian competition in the video technology market are not good although video technology for specialised uses could be produced on a large scale. Another possibility is that India will develop a bonded industry for assembling video technology and related electronics from imported kits. While video technology will continue to improve rapidly in other parts of the world, the Indian manufacturers will be content to supply older technologies on a larger scale because human resources for repair and maintenance are available in the country.

VIDEO FOR FILM VIEWING

In less than five years, video viewing has become a part of social life. The single most important use of the video cassette recorder in India has been, and is, for viewing feature films. The majority of these are indigenous productions in more than fourteen languages.

Video viewers broadly fall into three categories: owners, renters and video parlour goers – those who pay a fee to view film on video. There are no estimates or official figures to indicate the actual number of viewers in each of these three categories. It is fairly certain that most, if not all, video cassette recorders are being used for viewing films on video. Some estimates based on the data available calculated after discounting the 'novelty effect' of video viewing are given below.

On an average, if one film is viewed on video in a household every week and the average number of viewers for each show is seven, for Bombay city the average number of viewers has been estimated at between five and six then a total of a million viewers watch video in homes everyday.

The number of renter viewers in the recent past has increased as rental prices have decreased. It is estimated that there are about a thousand video rental companies in each of the four metropolitan cities alone. In another 20–30 cities there are about 100 to 200 such companies. In each of the 400 districts in India, there are more than two video rental companies who rent two video cassette recorders a day on average. On the basis of an estimated total of 10,000 video rental companies operating in the country, it is estimated that about 600,000 to a million renter viewers watch video every day. A little over a million to two million viewers watch video in parlours.

There are an estimated 50,000 video parlours which are particularly attractive in those places where there are no cinema halls. It is indicated that the average audience per video parlour may be as high as 750 per show, almost equal to the size of a regular film theatre. It is difficult to accept this average figure but it is nevertheless indicative of the popularity of video parlours. 'Since the shows often consists mainly of blue films or uncensored films, the audience consists mainly of lower income men' writes one report. Patel (1985) has the following to say on video parlours:

'Video parlours have taken the place of theatres in many areas including cities like Bombay. They are generally located in working class and slum areas while video clubs and restaurants are for the rich. In *talukas* and villages they are an important channel for the distribution of films. Many villagers are now exposed to movies which they previously had to travel to the next town to see. Exclusive clubs and restaurants cater to all the eccentric wishes of the clientele. Video parlours generally show Hindi movies'.

Putting these figures together it is calculated that more than a billion video viewers are watching films on video every year which is proving to be stiff competition for the film industry in India. Two studies have supported this view (Agrawal and Sinha 1982 and Sudhakar Reddy 1985). As indicated earlier, video owners and renters comprise only 5 per cent of the households, which is about eight million. A survey conducted in Bombay during 1982 by Prime Time Media Services, the sole advertising concessionaries for Esquire video cassette, found that 65 per cent of the video viewers belong to the 15 to 35 years age group in which there are more women than men. The majority of these viewers belong to households with an annual income of over US$6,666, which is very high for India, and more than 80 per cent of the video owners hold top managerial positions. The remaining viewers watch video in what are now termed 'video parlours', 'video hotels' and 'video restaurants' in which video viewing is the prime activity of the visitor. Besides, there are a large number of clubs, defence personnel messes, private guest houses where 'video rooms' have sprung up for regular video viewing.

Almost all major hotels in the country make it a point to advertise their viewing facilities. They all have cable TV systems, screening films on video in Hindi and English on a regular basis. In medium range hotels, the video monitor is installed at a strategic spot in the lounge or elsewhere for 'free' video viewing.

In the semi-urban and rural areas, 'video theatres' and 'video halls' have made their mark. These are basically 'mini-cinemas' where shows are held regularly. The most pervasive in the rural areas are 'touring video companies', which are basically a one-man operation, holding regular shows for a small fee. There is no data available anywhere to indicate the number of such public places of entertainment in the country nor the number of daily video viewers who frequent them.

Video and Advertising

In the Press and Advertisers Year Book 1984, the editors observed that:

'The latest tycoon in advertising circles is 'Video'. Never in the history of Indian advertising has a medium grown with such rapidity or with such controversial effects on other media. The estimated video set population in the country today is around 700,000 and believed to be growing at the astronomical figure of 20,000 per month'.

Today a large number of pre-recorded video cassettes, especially those distributed through authorised dealers and companies, contain several advertisements in their programmes. Four companies with rights to sell video cassettes of the latest films produced in India are involved in advertising. Advertising offers within the country have mostly been received from a single Bombay-based company which controls three quarters of the total distribution of legal cassettes in India. It is reported that 'the choice of film is left to the advertiser. Rates charged are based on the number of films or cassettes bought. Video cassettes are permitted to take liquor and cigarette advertising'. Indian television advertises neither liquor nor cigarettes but all other mass media do. In this respect video has undermined the government policy in a very subtle and surreptitious manner.

The various rates being charged for such advertisements are based on two factors – the grade of the film and the length of the insertion. For example, a ten second insert in an 'A' grade film would cost approximately US$500.

The analysis presented clearly indicates that with a small incremental cost, video advertising will have greater penetration in the homes of the target population thereby increasing the conspicuous consumption of many products. It is probable that more and more advertising companies will use video for exclusive advertising of high-priced products.

The Video 'SEWA'

An interesting use of video has been observed in Ahmedabad where Self-Employed Women's Association (SEWA), a trade union for the poor, began experimenting with video for the training and self-education of its estimated 22,000 members. The experiment was initiated by the joint efforts of H.A. Bhatt, Secretary, SEWA and the late Martha Stuart of New York.

It is believed by Stuart that 'Video provides people with an opportunity to speak for themselves and exchange information and experiences without falling prey to the distortions built into the use of conventional media'. The programmes produced by the team included 'training material', 'documentation material' and above all 'presentation of SEWA activities' to be used within and outside India. Another use has been to record and show the problems of the poor to the decision makers. SEWA has shown how, with the help of a single camera and a 3/4" U-matic video cassette recorder, socially very useful needs could be fulfilled by a group of committed workers.

Video Entry and the Democratic Process

In a recent paper, it was noted that:

> VCR/VCP is also going to be a very handy for future political use.
> It will be the most potent method for carrying the message of the
> political leaders to the people. Whether it will have a higher level
> of credibility as compared to audio cassettes, needs to be examined.
> My hunch is that the moving images will have greater appeal and
> will provide high visibility for the political leaders both among the
> literate rich and illiterate poor.

At the 8th National Parliamentary Election in India the use of video was extensive. Apart from audio cassettes, video cassettes were distributed for
widespread viewing.

The effects of these video programmes on the electorate has not been studied.
But certainly, they have helped to increase the penetration of video in the
remotest parts of the country and have quickly familiarized villagers with video
technology. It is certain that, in the future, greater investment in video technology will be made by the political parties.

Wedding on Video

One of the most popular uses of video technology in India today is the video
recording of important social occasions such as birthdays, marriages, 'aran-
getrams' (graduation in the art of dance), etc. This use is, of course, restricted
to the well-to-do families in urban India since it costs about US$84 without
the cassette.

Typically, a two-man production crew is hired for this job and they shoot
the entire sequence on a 180 minute cassette. This is generally done with a
single camera and afterwards the cassette is edited and dubbed with appropriate music. Caption cards with the names of the couple and the families at the
beginning and the name of the production crew at the end are added. Very
few copies of such programmes are made and the rates for these productions
are fairly uniform throughout the country, at least in the Southern and Western
parts. The trend of video recording all such functions and ceremonies has
become widespread because of its large scale availability and instantaneous
viewing possibilities. In addition, it is a boon to Indians living abroad who can
watch all these festivities on video.

In all major cities of India, today, several one or two-man video production
units have sprung up to cater to the ever-increasing need for such productions.
It is difficult to estimate their number but it has certainly gone into four figures,
considering that most photography shops today offer video production facilities.

VIDEO: TRADE AND COMMERCE

The video cassette recorder appeared in India as soon as it was available in the world market, especially in the Western and South East Asian markets like Hong Kong and Singapore. However, its rate of acquisition has been much higher than in Third World countries and other parts of the world. Early in 1984, it was estimated that there were more than half a million video cassette recorders in India. By the end of 1985, this figure will reach a million or even more. It is estimated that about 20,000 video cassette recorders are arriving in India every month through legal channels. The estimated number of television sets in India in the same period was about five million (both black and white and colour) producing a ratio of one video cassette recorder to approximately five television sets. The calculations may not be accurate but they do reflect the rapid increase and acceptance of video cassette recorders in a country which has a largely agricultural economy and where about 50 per cent of the population lives below the poverty line. The total national investment in video cassette recorders at an average rate of 2,000 US dollars per unit (this includes a 1/2" or 3/4" video cassette recorder, a colour video monitor, at least a dozen video cassettes and other accessories like video trolleys/cable connections) is two billion US dollars. This investment is basically individual investment to which a large amount has been contributed by Indians living abroad. Children, especially sons, are expected to provide financial support to their parents and other relatives. It is this custom and the presence of a large quantity of unaccounted for money in India that have contributed to such a large scale investment in a technology that has in a way replaced the cinema going of the rich.

The method of individual investment in video can be illustrated by a case study. A young engineer who had been in the United States of America for the last five years returned home with a Japanese made 1/2" video cassette recorder for his brother at the cost of about 300 US dollars. His brother invested another 600 US dollars in buying a colour 20" video monitor assembled from a Japanese kit by an Indian television manufacturing company. A little more money was invested in acquiring other accessories. This video was brought in late 1985 and is going to be used by the buyer. Hence, the total cost is less than 1500 US dollars. If the same video cassette recorder was sold it would fetch anywhere between 900–1200 US dollars in the open market as it is a duty paid set. In 1983 the same video cassette recorder would have cost between 1500–2000 US dollars. At least 30–40 per cent of the video cassette recorders in India have been bought in this way.

In another case, the total system was brought from abroad at a cost of 2,500 US dollars after customs duty. Smuggled VCRs are of course slightly less costly and it is estimated that at least 20 per cent of VCRs are being illegally imported/smuggled into the country. An insignificant quantity of VCRs have been assembled in India from imported kits.

The trade investment in video was estimated to be 700 million US dollars in 1983. There are an estimated 40 million rental cassettes in circulation. If the cost of a 1/2" VHS three hour pre-recorded tape is estimated to be 20 US dollars, then the total investment in video cassettes is about 800 million US dollars, leaving aside other investments in manpower and other recurring costs. Investment in video is much larger than investment in the 80 year old film industry in India which will not generate more than one billion US dollars by 1990. Even though there is a continuous reduction in the cost of video, in all likelihood more money will be invested in video in the years to come.

LOSS OF FILM REVENUE

Recently Sudhakar Reddy (1985) reported general loss in the film 'entertainment tax collection' levied in India for the exhibition of any film. He has also indicated loss in film export earnings. Both these losses are directly attributed to the phenomenal growth of video in India and abroad. According to Sudhakar Reddy 'The Government has been getting substantial revenues by way of entertainment tax. But with the advent of video there has been a noticeable reduction in the cinema-going population and consequently the revenues of the Government'. Sudhakar Reddy calculated the revenue losses of the cinema entertainment tax on the basis of a survey of 100 Delhi video-owning households. If this figure is projected for the country as a whole, there is a loss of about 24 million US dollars per year if video ownership remains constant at one million. There are also revenue losses due to the 10,000 video parlours which are difficult to estimate but will doubtless be much greater than 24 million US dollars. Moreover losses are likely to increase in the future.

Several reports of the Government of India and the film industry have indicated increasing loss of foreign exchange earnings from the export of Indian films. Table 1 shows an overall declining trend in foreign exchange earnings even when there is a gain as a result of selling video rights. This reduction is both in the export and per film cost of purchase. These losses have been ascribed to illegal copying and piracy of Indian films on video. Table 2 shows that these losses have not been off-set by selling pre-recorded video cassettes of Indian films. In order to understand the full implications of video effects on revenue export losses, Sudhakar Reddy suggested 'an in depth study on the impact of commercial video on government exchequer' for formulating appropriate policies to arrest this declining trend. Others feel that these losses are due to lack of appropriate efforts by the National Film Development Corporation, the film industry and the Government of India. Whatever the reason may be, export earnings from films are declining with the appearance of video.

THE VIDEO BUSINESS

In order to ascertain the opinions and views of 'video traders' some selected persons were interviewed in and around Ahmedabad (Gujarat) in the western state of India. These interviews were conducted in the third quarter of 1985. In most cases the researcher had the confidence of and direct contact with the owners of the 'video libraries' and 'video parlours'. This was essential as many video library owners are unwilling to provide information.

Analysis shows that the video business is a growing one and people are ready to make investments in it even though competition is becoming stiffer. This is evident from the reduction in both rental fees and the price of video electronics. One thing is clear, that these businessmen have invested their money after diverting funds from other businesses and they are educated men as compared to traditional businessmen. Most of them feel that video viewing will not have any socially undesirable effect on the viewers, though there is divergent opinion as to whether video will have an adverse effect on the film industry.

VIDEO RENTAL

Video rental is very popular and widely spread in the country. Rental rates have been going down across the country and have stabilized with some variations. The major items of rental are pre-recorded video cassettes, followed by VCRs and TV monitors. Delivery and collection of the electronics is the responsibility of the rental company, except in exceptional cases where they charge transport cost. The rental of pornographic cassettes is invariably more expensive and they are rented out only to trusted clients. Rental of the newly released feature films start very high sometimes as much as 10 to 15 US dollars. Within a week or two, the rental prices come down to normal.

The entry fee for a video parlour varies depending upon the location – rural or urban – and the viewing conditions – maximum or minimum comfort. The lowest rate is less than 0.10 US dollars, where a video viewer squats on the ground, while in good parlours it is as much as 0.50 US dollars but rarely more than the regular cinema fee. In video hotels and video restaurants the cost of video viewing is included in the minimum cover fee charged by the hotels/restaurants. This is to avoid any legal complications as several High Courts have declared video showing in restaurants/hotels legal so long as no fee is charged.

In general, all video electronics brought into the country illegally are sold at a lower price. For example, a 1/2" VHS video tape recorder, if sold with a payment receipt or through an authorised dealer costs about 15 to 20 per cent more than a smuggled one. Earlier when the price difference between the national and international market was even higher energetic entrepreneurs flew to Singapore and returned with VCRs at a price of 400 to 500 US dollars and, after paying travel costs and customs, made a handsome profit. Today, this contraband market is declining.

The foregoing analysis of the video trade and commerce clearly indicates that the Indian economy has absorbed a large scale investment without any serious repercussion on the economy and is capable of absorbing much more investment in video. It is probably because of large amounts of unaccounted money, popularly known as 'black money', that such investments are not having a direct influence on the Indian economy. Moreover, another source of inves-tent in video comes from Indians living abroad, and does not directly affect the Indian economy. In the near future, video will probably divert household expenditures from consumer items such a refrigerators, air-conditioners and scooters to VCRs or colour televison monitors. It will also lead to a large scale drain on foreign exchange reserves and to increased economic dependency on external sources. But, on the other hand, it may stimulate the national economy by opening up new job opportunities for a large number of skilled men and women.

VIDEO PRODUCTION FACILITIES

There has been phenomenal growth of Indian television – Doordarshan – under the Indian National Statellite (INSAT) scheme. Recently, a second channel has been started in the cities of Delhi and Bombay. Doordarshan produces a large proportion of its programmes at many television production centres, but also telecasts feature films produced by private companies and 'sponsored programmes' produced by outside agencies. A small part of their programme needs are met by the import of foreign programmes which has been on the increase lately.

Several private companies have begun video production, though some do not have their own studios. The majority of these production factories are located in Bombay, Delhi and Madras. No information is available about their actual production capacity or level of business. Some of these companies are also involved in video copying, though the authorised companies for this purpose are Esquire with the brand name Sun Video and Surya Bharati and the National Film Development Corporation, Video Cassette Unit. As several of these companies have floated separate production and distribution compa-nies, it is difficult to calculate their actual output or distribution. It is however certain that there is far more illegal, than legal, copying.

VIDEO DISTRIBUTION

There are three levels of video distribution in the country: video retailers estab-lished by the video copying companies; advertising companies; government undertakings involved in video copying.

The regional level of distribution, though illegal, is stronger than the national level distribution. The whole distribution system, by and large, is in private hands, very similar to the film distribution network except that the movement of video cassettes is very fast and decentralised which is not the case for films.

Today, all possible means are employed for the quick distribution of pre-recorded video cassettes. Like the news in the daily newspapers, a new video film is a money spinner only if it arrives on time. To ensure the critical time factor, it has been reported that individuals often deliver the video tapes of the latest films by air. Besides the conventional modes of train and courier services, bus and truck drivers are involved in the large intricate video distribution network.

The level of business in both unit and financial terms, is unknown but some gross estimates are presented in the Video Trade and Commerce section.

VIDEO CONTENT

At present, more than 95 per cent of pre-recorded video cassettes are feature films which are either Indian, or foreign productions from English speaking countries mainly the United Kingdom and the United States of America. A few pre-recorded tapes for industrial training, and for children have been imported. However such cassettes which are used by specialised education/training institutions do not come within the normal distribution channels. Some of them are telecast by Doordarshan under the INSAT programme for higher education. Recently, some of the video copying companies have tried to market some of the popular TV serials and some popular American or British TV programmes are viewed in a few homes. By and large, however, the content of video cassettes are films which may be divided into the following categories: 1) Hindi films; 2) English-speaking films; 3) Films in 14 other languages; 4) Foreign TV serials; 5) Indian TV serials; 6) Sports programmes; 7) Pornography/adult movies; 8) Others.

The Hindi films top the list followed by English-speaking films as a majority of the video owners read, write and speak English. These are followed by regional language films.

VIDEO LAW AND POLICY

In the legal history of India, video has created unprecedented and unique problems, without any parallel even in the countries in which video originated.

CINEMATOGRAPH (CENSORSHIP) ACT

During the colonial period, control over films and film production aimed to curb nationalist sentiments and to control the 'subversive' activities of Indian nationalists. The legacy of this colonial past gave birth to the Cinematograph (Censorship) Act of 1952 in independent India. Under this Act, among other things, the government appointed a Central Board of Film Censors to grant a certificate for public exhibition of any film produced or exhibited in India. This board is expected to take steps to curb the depiction of violence and vulgarity in films. The board also has the right to refuse a certificate to films which are considered detrimental to national security and interests and to relations with foreign states.

After the appearance of video, several questions were raised both by the law-makers and by the leaders of the film industry regarding the applicability of the Cinematograph Act of 1952 to video viewing and video production. After careful consideration and a national debate

> ' ... as an interim measure and acting on the advice of the Ministry of Law, in July 1983, the Ministry of Information and Broadcasting instructed the Central Board of Film Certification and the State Governments/Union Territories administration that the public exhibition of films on video should be regulated in the same manner as that of films covered by the Cinematograph Act 1952. This implied that for public exhibition, video films must have a censor certificate and the exhibitors would have to comply with all the requirements stipulated by State Governments and Union Territories under their laws governing exhibition ie licensing of premises for screening films, show tax, entertainment tax etc' (Gupta).

All efforts of the Government of India in this respect have had little effect and even the rule that all video films must carry a separate censor certificate for exhibition has not been complied with.

COPYRIGHT ACT

The Copyright Act of 1957 was modified on 8 October 1984 'to provide for enhancement of the penalties of infringment on the lines of the Cinematograph Act 1952' in order to curb the duplication of films and video piracy. Given the nature of video technology and its preservation and viewing, it would be difficult to assess the efficacy of this act in curbing piracy and duplicating.

The film makers of India believe that the Act would not be taken seriously by the State governments responsible for its implementation. The leaders of the film industry submitted a memorandum to the Government of India suggesting 'the formulation of anti-piracy cells in all States and the constitution of an inter-ministerial committee at the Centre to oversee the implementation of the Copyright Act. The film industry has also suggested the detention of pirates under the National Security Act'. In reply the owners of video libraries and parlours and video-showing restaurants filed petitions in various State High Courts questioning the validity of the Copyright Amendment Act of 1984. The Bombay High Court has given interim orders against 'the implementation of this law on the ground of non-compliance with the provisions of the amended

Copyright Act pending the hearing and final disposal of the writ petitions or until further orders'. The battle between the film makers and the video pirates, libraries and parlours continues to be an important point of confrontation as film makers rightly feel that they are suffering from the introduction of video. Even their efforts to set up anti-piracy organisations under the aegis of the All Industry Producers Council are unlikely to be successful, as the copyright of a film is vested in the producer or distributor of the film. To solve this problem, efforts are being made to sell video copyrights simultaneously with film distribution rights. But this is also under dispute without any clear solution in sight.

In less than five years, all major states where the film industry flourishes Maharashtra, Andhra Pradesh, Tamil Nadu, Kerala and West Bengal, have enacted laws to control video viewing or have levied taxes such as the one which is imposed on public film exhibition in India.

VIDEO PIRACY

'Video Piracy' in India is of an unparalleled magnitude and should be understood in the Indian context where it largely means copying of unauthorised pre-censored films or copying of censored films by illegal means both by individuals and organised groups or agencies. There are two other forms of video piracy. These include 'counterfeiting' or authorised copying of programmes, packaged to look like the original and 'bootlegging', the unauthorised recording of a programme, performance or show without explicit permission or right to do so. Observations in the field show that a large number of video tapes are of the counterfeit type. Gupta (1985) reported that ... 'according to a report in the *Indian Express* in December 1983, the number of pre-recorded cassettes sold during 1983 was about three crores (30 million) out of which pirated cassettes accounted for 2.7 crores (27 million) or ninety per cent'. One of the possible unwitting sources of video piracy in India is the Santa Cruz Electronics Export Processing Zone (SEEPZ) located in India's 'film capital', Bombay. SEEPZ exports a hundred per cent of its items, including software such as recorded video cassettes. These pre-recorded cassettes of Indian films are 'being brought back as accompanied baggage by persons from abroad and copies made in the country which were [are] clandestinely circulated for commerical purposes. Today these pirated tapes are being duplicated on a large scale in State capitals and even in small towns' (Gupta 1985).

It is reported that several films have been pirated even before they were completed in the laboratories. One well known film maker has commented that video piracy has already negatively affected the steady growth of the film industry. It is his view that this may lead to a reduction in the production of films in India, especially of big budget films. Even the '3-D'. films produced are drastically affected as a result of video film piracy.

Video piracy is a fact not only within India but all over the world. In what can be termed the largest raid ever carried out by the Federation Against Copyright Theft (FACT), a special squad of twenty-five police officers raided dozens of shops and homes in the London Borough of Southall and confiscated over 12,000 video cassettes of Indian films and about 100 VCRs. Indian newspapers in more than a dozen languages have been full of similar reports over the last three years. A broad-based content analysis of the newspapers have indicated that these incidents are extensively reported from all metropolitan cities and states where films are produced in large numbers as well as from small cities and towns. A typical example is given below:

'*Video Cassettes worth Rs 45 lakhs (US$375,000) seized.* A large number of smuggled video cassette recorders and tapes valued at over Rs 45,000,000 were seized at the Bombay airport on Monday. an investigating team examined 32 unclaimed crates lying in the warehouse on a tip-off and recovered the 'high quality contraband'. (*Times of India*, December 12, 1984, page 11, Ahmedabad edition).

Today ' ... it is not physically or legally possible to raid all private homes in search for pirated video cassettes' (Gupta 1985). The piracy menace will continue in India, especially of Indian films, for years to come until some technological breakthrough takes place to control it.

VIDEO POLICY

The production and import of video related technologies has gone through a remarkable waxing and waning of concessions and liberalisations. An editorial on video policy captioned it 'The funny VCR policy'.

In 1982, in the wake of the IX Asian Games, the Union Commerce Ministry of India permitted the import of video tapes and cassette recorders with or without a television monitor/camera. This policy envisaged the import of video technology on a customs clearance permit given to blood relations residing outside India for more than three years. Elaborate rules were defined for this purpose and they opened up a floodgate of video imports as several million Indians live abroad in North America, Europe, South Asia and Australia. Since then, various policies have been announced by the Government of India.

While imports on an individual basis are permitted, the Government of India, Department of Electronics also encourages the manufacture of VCRs by giving licences to small scale industries within the country. The production companies have been allowed to import VCR kits in semi-knocked down (SKD) or completely knocked down (CKD) conditions for this purpose.

By 1985, several concessions had been declared by the Government of India, Department of Electronics one of which was a modification of the centralised purchase of technology. It seems however that changes in video policy have helped accentuate smuggling and the illegal entry of video technology in the country without encouraging the large scale production of video cassette recorders. Production consists of assembling imported kits which are sold at a very high price and do not therefore find favour in the Indian markets. The excise duty levied by the government on the manufacture and scale of VCRs further widens the gap between Indian and imported VCRs. To bridge this gap, in October 1985, the Government of India, Department of Electronics, decided to invite applications from entrepreneurs for the manufacture of VCRs and players. This time the applications are being invited from those units which are prepared to make sizeable investments for suitable vertical integration with an accelerated, phased manufacturing programme and also with the requisite in-built capacity to keep pace with changing technology. The new application is a composite one for industrial licence within the country and foreign collaboration, which is contrary to the earlier view of centralised purchase of technology from abroad. Specific policy related to video tapes and video cameras is yet to be fully formulated.

Another aspect that must be taken into consideration is that while there is a video hardware policy, there is no such declared video software policy. One of the reasons may be that the visual medium, like film, is a largely private sector and so the video software has been left to evolve on its own. Analysis of policy for the growth and development of video technologies reveals little concern about its production and utilisation. This aspect needs to be carefully examined if the potential of this new technology in India is to be fully harnessed.

CONCLUSION

This report is based on limited first hand data and fairly unauthenticated secondary data and there are of necessity a number of gaps. It must be considered as explanatory and the conclusions as tentative. Within these limitations an attempt has been made to bring out certain salient features and broad conclusions.

Extensive large scale investments have been made in video and will continue to be so. These investments consist largely of 'black money' (that is, unaccounted money) and the money of Indians living abroad. For this reason there have been no serious repercussions on the Indian economy.

However, one can reasonably expect long-term effects to show up in time. One such effect may be that the diversion of household resources from other consumer items will lead to a large scale drain of foreign exchange reserves and to increased economic dependency on external sources.

It may however also stimulate the national economy by offering new job opportunities for a large number of skilled men and women.

It is expected that video will widen the information gap among the population rather than bridging it, which was the original aim of all government owned communication media. While the penetration of information has been beyond wildest hopes, video will, and to some extent, already has, created new 'social groups' in the form of 'video viewers' and 'non-video viewers' or 'TV viewers'. Privatisation of entertainment, which was inherent in the class system during the colonial era, is again on the agenda. Piracy will also continue for years to come until some technological breakthrough takes place to control it. Television and particularly cinema are going to be relegated to the background and the position of video will become more secure, particularly as it has found favour with politicians who find it a most useful tool.

The chances for India to compete in the video technology market are not good. While video technology improvements will continue at a fast pace in other parts of the world, the Indian manufacturers may well remain at the level of screwdriver technologists.

TABLE 1

*EARNINGS FROM EXPORT IN MILLION US DOLLARS OF FILM
AND VIDEO RIGHTS*

Year	No of films	Earnings US$ millions	Video rights on no of films	Earnings US$ millions
1979–80	1737	10.122	–	–
1980–81	1729	12.519	–	–
1981–82	1657	12.125	24	0.133
1982–83	1281	9.591	130	0.858
1983–84	939	6.550	181	1.258

Source: Sudhakar Reddy (1985: 5).

TABLE 2

*EXPORT EARNINGS IN MILLION US DOLLARS FROM FILMS,
VIDEO RIGHTS AND CASSETTES (1981–82 – 1984–85).*

Year	Feature film[1]	Video right[2]	Video cassette[3]	Total
1980–81	12.561	–	3.750	16.311
1981–82	12.124	0.135	7.408	16.667
1982–83	9.589	0.858	6.133	16.580
1983–84	8.063	1.542	3.216	12.821
1984–85	5.781	1.298	3.216	10.295
Average:	9.6236	0.7666	4.745	15.135

Source: 'Downward Trend in Export Continues unabated', *Screen*, June 28, 1985 (a report
by V Verma).
[1] Feature Film – Earning from the shipment of celluloid prints and royalty cana-
lised through National Film Development Corporation (NEDC).
[2] Video Right – Royalty on video rights channelled through NEDC
[3] Video Cassette – Earning on video cassettes exported from the Santa Cruz Electronics Export Processing Zone (SEEPZ).

Chapter 7

HONG KONG

Hong Kong is a British Crown Colony administered by a British Governor and appointed councils of advisers and legislators. In 1997 it will become a Special administrative Region of China with a high degree of autonomy.

Currently in the first stages of an open-ended electoral reform programme, during the next decade Hong Kong will gradually become more politically self-sufficient. Localisation of the civil service will continue whilst corporate expatriate influence will remain strong and grow as Hong Kong exerts its position as the gateway to China. Hong Kong is adjusting its socio-economic and political relationship with China but has yet to find a stable position of identity.

Hong Kong's economy which is export-oriented and vulnerable to developed countries' protectionist measures has a declining growth rate. It is a free port and government policy is strictly laissez-faire with minimal regulations beyond the rule of law. Industrial flexibility and diversification will continue with increasing reliance on hi-tech skills and manufacture. Hong Kong is the third largest financial centre after London and New York.

The population is officially 5.5 million: 98 per cent Cantonese, 1.5 per cent Western expatriate and less than 1 per cent other Asian nationalities and Indian. Nominally a bi-lingual population, few are literate and fluent in their non-mother tongue.

Cinema attendances in 1984 totalled 6.24 million. Audiences are mainly in the 17–29 age group (35 per cent of the total population).

Sample TV audience Research data (1985) showed that 84 per cent of respondents watched the TVB Chinese channel the previous day, 33 per cent the ATV Chinese channel; the corresponding figures for the English channels were 8 per cent and 2 per cent.

Top ratings went to Miss Hong Kong Pageant with 3.2 million viewers. Radio audiences averaged 15 per cent for the commercial Chinese channels with 43 per cent saying they had listened to the radio the previous day.

The average household income is HK$6,228; the average personal income is HK$3,872.

The entire structure of television is under debate at the moment after a government sponsored report found the domination by TVB to be unhealthy and sugggested the re-organisation of moribund government TV production units. It is highly doubtful whether this will be implemented, though cigarette advertising is likely to be banned.

HARDWARE AND BLANK SOFTWARE

PRODUCTION

Hong Kong does not produce any VCRs. Hong Kong manufacturers have waited for the format superiority race to be settled and have steered clear of VCR manufacture.

Blank cassettes are produced, as are parts for assembly, by a number of small family businesses in Hong Kong.

It is estimated that about 50 companies are in operation, around half of which have less than 25 workers. The Trade Development Council's computer has around 40 entries (not available to this survey). Current telephone directory yellow pages list 23 manufacturers and wholesalers.

For obvious reasons, these private companies do not release commerical information relating to production of units, wholesale costs, annual turnover or discuss growth prospects of their own company. Many supply cassettes to China, others produce their own brands and supply Western brand names.

As far as format goes, Sony's HK agent, Fook Yuen, claim to have imported 0.5 million Beta-tapes (blank) in 1984, which would give them around 3 per cent of the market. The 0.1 million Beta-VCRs represent 12 per cent of the VCR market of which approximately 50 per cent were for re-export (or approx 25 per cent of all re-exports in 1984). Demand for Beta-format products is stable and not increasing thereby leaving VHS with an increasing market share. The Super-Beta format has not yet arrived in Hong Kong after its American unveiling in January 1984. The 8mm cassette format was introduced in June 1984 and the camera (list price HK$13,700) with charger in October 1984. This combined recording/viewing system is reportedly selling quite well, though Hong Kong always gives a good reception to technological innovation.

Trying to estimate the number of retail outlets where video products can be bought is almost impossible. There is no such listing or compendium.

CONSUMPTION

Hardware rentals are of the order of 10,000 units at any one time; the total number of VCRs in circulation is approximately 350,000.

Format distribution is approximately 15 per cent Beta and 85 per cent VHS with the VHS proportion rising. The Beta figure is up at the moment due to Sanyo's dumping of almost 200,000 machines.

There are no official re-export statistics showing format delineation.

Geographically, video rental patterns are split between two groups. One group are socio-economically advanced, either expatriate or fluent English-speaking Chinese and live on Hong Kong island (especially Central, Admiralty, Wanchai, Causeway Bay, Happy Valley). The second group is much poorer, living in public housing estates in Kowloon (eg Wong Tai Sin), and typically finds itself with excess disposable income since four or five members of the family may be earning and chooses to invest in video for time-shift viewing.

The average rental charges in this fiercely competitive market are in the HK$150–200 per month range, the latter price for a top-flight multi-function model like Thorn 8949 (based on JVC model). The more sophisticated models are sought by the richer user-group; the less well-off opt for simple playback models.

TV and facilities companies do not supply inventories of equipment or estimates of tape turnover. Nor do the government or armed forces reveal equipment held. Videos are in use in schools but no collated figures are available.

The commercial use of video in demonstration and/or promotional purposes is widespread throughout Hong Kong, especially with the multinationals. The Royal HK Jockey Club is already using a form of interactive video on laser disc to aid veterinary treatment. The Vocational Training Council is setting up a production unit to service a series of training centres; as yet it has no separate budget.

Educational uses are more widespread still; Hong Kong University possesses a complete TV studio with editing facilities (U-Matic and VHS). Output in 1984–1985 is up 2.5 times on 1983–1984 under the influence of younger teachers. The variety of uses includes student counselling and first year medical techniques. An inventory of A/V units listed 9,897 items (April 1985) with a book value of HK$16 million. The central teaching unit has 'several hundred' VCRs. There is a limited use of overseas software. The language of instruction is English.

The Hong Kong Polytechnic Educational Technology Unit keeps 1,700 pieces in stock including 600 videos. Around 150 VCRs are in use. The Production Unit makes videos on request for departments. The Language of instruction is English.

The City Polytechnic has an A/V unit established in 1984 with 21 cameras including a Betacam and 55 VCRs distributed throughout departments. Their centralised control system is unique in Hong Kong. All formats are available. They are researching laser disc potential and interacting teaching projects with IBM PC compatibles. Work is conducted in both English and Cantonese. Caritas has a unit established in 1980 with equipment valued at HK$1 million. Productions are made for school-leavers (aged 15–16) in their 18 day and night schools in Cantonese. Topics include Careers, Hotel Management, and Accountancy.

The Diocesan College has a 7-person A/V unit using U-Matic. The equipment is valued at HK$4,150,000 and the College has made 8–10 films (25–35 minutes) of a religious or cultural nature, and for children, for rental and purchase by Catholic groups.

The Macau Open College uses 12 British Open University courses with 6–32 videos per course showing to a potential audience of 300 students on 3 VCRs. The British Council office in Hong Kong is the largest in the world and has an A/V unit producing a range of teaching materials.

VIDEOGRAMS

PRODUCTION

There are three television stations in Hong Kong operating four channels, all commercial, two Chinese and two English.

Television Broadcasts International (TVBI), markets about 1000 hours of its 2–3000 hours of productions in 25 countries serving almost exclusively overseas Chinese communites. Material is serialised dramas, modern action programmes, Kung Fu, variety shows and comedies. Different versions are produced for individual markets; Mandarin, English, Thai, Vietnamese (in the United States and France).

Asia Television (ATV) markets 520 hours of drama showing 10 hours per week on-air.

Radio Television Hong Kong is a Government broadcasting authority which places its programmes cuckoo-like on the other four channels. Neither RTHK nor its Education TV section produce videos.

There are several production houses working either in video or on film with video transfers: Robert Chua Studios, Centro, Link Studios, Fuji Studios, Arkas Studios and Video Film productions. Working in a tight competitive market, they are not prepared to provide much information about commerical details. One industry source estimates the number of video productions per year as around 1000.

Many of these companies concentrate on TV commercials whilst others also produce documentaries. Robert Chua Productions takes a half-hour regularly on TV to present a video advertising magazine using sponsored material. At the other end of the scale there are many small Chinese operations producing poor quality videos on home-video equipment for Chinese companies.

The telephone directory lists eight Video Production houses, and 8 Video Tape Recording Services; there are many unlisted. For example, the largest copying house in Hong Kong, Esquire, has the capacity to make 550 copies at any one time, NTSC duplication, PAL and U-Matic; the managing director claims it is used by many American and European film people transferring 35mm to video.

DISTRIBUTION

There are three legitimate distribution companies in Hong Kong. Kam Distribution Ltd is owned by VCL Communications (Far East) Ltd. They are exclusive distributors of CBS/Fox Video, VCL Video, Cinehollywood, Media, China Doll, Video Classics, Video Village, Video Palace, KPS Video and dealers for CIC, Vestron, Warner Home Video, Cinema and Entertainment International Ltd is an Australian company; MGM/Embassy. WEA Records market Warner. It was impossible to obtain financial details from these companies.

Hong Kong has a host of film production companies. The two major ones, Golden Harvest and Shaws, market their products abroad, but were not prepared to give estimates. Golden Harvest arrange their distribution out of London.

Esquire (a copying house) holds the rights to distribute about 2,000 Indian films (90 per cent Hindi, 10 per cent Punjabi and Gujerati) worldwide except in India, Pakistan and Nepal. Demand is high among the Indian community which numbers about 16,000.

There are 7 distributors of Chinese language films on video, but again these companies do not give out commerical information relating to sales or turnover.

CONSUMPTION

Estimated total sales, wholesale to video clubs, average HK$0.5 million per month. Estimated parallel imports, not including adult movies, average HK$0.25 million per month. Estimated adult movies penetrating the market via corner shops average 500 titles per month.

Distinguishing between commercial and entertainment videos, it is estimated that the majority of commercial uses are for corporate clients (usually corporate promotions or information on commercial prospects), often shot on film and transferred to video for distribution.

As far as entertainment is concerned, according to one distributor, patterns of video rental in Hong Kong are the same as elsewhere; people prefer big pictures with well-known actors. Sources estimated that there were 0.25 million VCRs in Hong Kong homes; 10 per cent were used by expatriate company employees and upper-income strata Chinese who can understand English without sub-titles. The remaining 90 per cent had a video 'for status and the occasional blue movie'.

A manager of a rental company (TV and video) estimated total VCR rentals to be approximately 10,000 at any one time. This figure is subject to fluctuations, due partly to world-wide events (such as the soccer world cup) and partly during autumn and winter months because of the avid followers of horse-racing who use the playback on VCRs to study the form more closely (all race meetings in Hong Kong are televised). The same manager also estimated the total VCR population at around 350,000.

Unfortunately there are no licencing requirements nor tax or import duties and it is therefore very difficult to carry out accurate market assessments.

Even the IFPI (International Federation of Phonogram and Video Producers), in Hong Kong do not collect figures for video usage, they draw up a 'Top Twenty' based on returns from a number of video clubs. The co-ordinator says she assesses these responses partly on the size of the club and partly on whether they indulge in widescale parallel importing or not.

Within the broadly similar range of video clubs, either retailing legitimate sales or rentals or parallel imports, two other clubs stand out:

i)   Video GA GA: carrying an increasing number of Chinese language titles which began to make an impact during 1984.

ii)   Witchcraft: located in the extreme southern end of Hong Kong island next to the British army barracks, offers a range of English television programming, especially comedy material.

There is no evidence of children's videos. A legitimate distributor confided that he knew that around 500 pornographic videos per month were entering Hong Kong for sale from corner shops exhibiting blank boxes in the window.

Video retailers are not prepared to discuss their volume of business or any other commerical details a) because of traditional business attitudes; b) the high level of parallel imports, and c) fear about their tax position.

VIDEO USAGE

No market report on video usage or penetration has been compiled or made public and industry opinions vary. One distributor sees video as an expatriate habit and for the Chinese it is a status symbol. A more down market rental dealer believes that time-shift viewing of major drama serials and shows is the principal use made by large dispersed households working long and irregular shifts. Viewing pre-recorded tapes is unlikely to take off dramatically until Chinese subtitling is fully established for international films.

PARALLEL MARKET

Piracy is not a problem in Hong Kong. In 1984, 1,947 units with the value of HK$667,000 were seized. By September 1985, 3,644 videos valued at HK$1.33 million were impounded.

Counterfeiting is less of a problem because of Hong Kong's established copyright law, severe punishments and the zealousness of the Customs and Excise Copyright Division.

Bootlegging still occurs for distribution mainly in South East Asia; the main sufferers, the TV station, do not want to put financial estimates to their loss.

CENSORSHIP

There is no censorship of imported videos at all; the government takes the view that this is for home (ie private) viewing only and not for public consumption. There are no planned changes to this policy.

TABLE 1

VIDEO DISTRIBUTION IN HONG KONG

(Millions)	1982 Units	1982 HK$	1983 Units	1983 HK$	1984 Units	1984 HK$	Jan-June 1985 Units	Jan-June 1985 HK$
VCRs								
Import	0.20	566.4	0.31	940.7	0.76	2222.1	0.62	1461.9
Export	0.002	0.2	0.002	0.3	0.005	9.7	0.001	2.2
Re-export	0.06	215.3	0.10	340.2	0.26	926.5	0.32	832.6
Pre-recorded tapes								
Import	0.23	35.6	0.10	20.9	0.08	18.5	0.08	13.4
Export	0.01	5.4	0.03	10.7	0.05	13.4	0.02	8.8
Re-export	0.13	20.1	0.18	26.5	0.08	16.0	0.08	12.2
Blank tapes								
Import	5.67	319.8	6.28	356.7	15.40	688.3	9.98	407.5
Export	2.37	104.8	6.69	208.4	10.10	264.7	11.92	239.6
Re-export	4.12	226.2	4.28	235.5	8.04	333.6	5.40	184.9

Source: Trade Statistic HK Government.

Notes:
1. Does not include illegally exported tapes and machines to China
2. 1 US$ = 7.8 HK$ (pegged rate)

Chapter 8

AUSTRALIA

Australia has one of the world's most culturally diverse populations. Melbourne is second only to Athens in the size of its Greek population. Sydney has an annual Carnival that reflects the diverse nationalities and cultures that live within its environs. This diversity of culture and national origins is not, however, reflected in equal access to status, wealth or positions of political power, and racial and ethnic issues remain a significant feature of Australian society and politics.

The spread of high wages for the majority of the population makes it unsurprising that there has been a series of historical booms in cultural consumption in Australia: pianos in the late nineteenth century, books through much of the twentieth century, the gramophone in the early part of the century, radio sets in the nineteen thirties, films from the 1930s to the 1960s, television from the mid 1950s. Each boom has followed the same path: a rapid penetration of the leisure good or activity, finally stablising in a high percentage of the population enjoying that activity.

There are a total of 137 television stations in Australia. The Australian Broadcasting Corporation (ABC) operates 82 television stations, commercial groups operate 50 stations and the Special Broadcasting Service (SBS) operates 5 stations. As in radio, neither the ABC nor the SBS carries any advertisements or corporate sponsorship.

In 1981, 97 per cent of households in Australia had at least one television set, and at least 82.5 per cent of households had at least one colour television set. By 1984, 98 per cent of households in Australia had at least one television set. In 1981, the average TV viewing per household was 31 hours 48 minutes per week in the city and 32 hours 17 minutes in the country. In 1984, average TV viewing per household was 32 hours in Sydney and 34 hours 10 minutes in Melbourne. The average TV viewing per person was approximately 20 hours 20 minutes in both of these capital cities (K Windschuttle, *The Media*, p 59, Australian Broadcasting Tribunal, *Annual Report, 1984-5*).

Australia does not have cable television or pay TV. On the other hand it does have a satellite and the government is examining ways of spreading TV to those very small population pockets that do not receive a service. The large east coast commercial networks are lobbying to extend their networks into country areas and other centres via the satellite.

HARDWARE AND BLANK SOFTWARE

PRODUCTION AND DISTRIBUTION

Australia does not have any major manufacturer of VCRs. Since 1980, over 99 per cent of all home VCRs used in Australia have been imported fully assembled from Japan. The far smaller market for professional video recorders is shared between Japan and the United States. In 1984/5 total imports of video recorders into Australia amounted to $225 million. Almost all of this was accounted for by home VCRs ($220 million), with the remainder attributed to professional VCRs ($5 million). According to the Australian Bureau of Statistics, Australia has exported just over $2.5 million of VCR equipment per annum since 1983. Of this $2.5 million over $1 million is exported to New Zealand. As Australia has no manufacturing capability, these exports are primarily re-exports largely to the Pacific region.

In 1984/5 the $63 million market for both home ($57 million) and professional ($6 million) tapes was supplied primarily by Japan (approximately 70 per cent) with the Republic of Korea (12 per cent), Federal Republic of Germany (13 per cent), the United States (4 per cent) and the Netherlands as the other major suppliers. Australis has no manufacturers of magnetic tape or cassette cartridges.

Two Australian manufacturers carry out tape loading which involves cutting lengths of tape and loading these into the cassette cartridges. This is carried out primarily on demand for the specific requirements of distributors of pre-recorded software rather than directly for the domestic consumer market.

In 1984/5, the total export of tapes worth $5 million was primarily to New Zealand ($3.4 million) with a large proportion of the remainder going to Greece ($1.2 million).

Breakdown of Distribution by Company

The leading distributor of domestic VCRs is National Panasonic with approximately 25 per cent of the market share over the last 3 years. Other leading distributors are Sanyo, Sharp, Akai, AWA-Thorn, and Sony. VCR distributors are very sensitive about the release of sales statistics and little information was available publicly on the annual sales of VCR units, and market share. According to the BIS Shrapnel report, the leading distributors in 1982 were National, Sanyo and Sharp, and in 1983 National, Akai, Sanyo and Sharp. An indication of market share can be obtained from the share of each brand installed in households.

The leading distributor of blank tape in Australia is BASF. The other leading distributors are TDK, Scotch (3M), Maxell, AGFA, Fuji and Polaroid. As with VCR distributors, little information was available on annual sales of tape, and the market share of the individual firms.

CONSUMPTION

In 1985, 93.5 per cent of the VCRs were purchased by consumers and 6.5 per cent were rented; in capital cities 92.1 per cent were owned and 8.2 per cent rented; in regional areas 96.3 per cent were owned and 3.4 per cent rented. This is partially explained by the ease of access to rental locations. Adelaide has the lowest percentage of ownership (78.9 per cent) and the highest is in regional Victoria (98.7).

There are 1,711 rental outlets involved in the sale and/or rental of VCRs, not including large department stores. Of these, 894 are in capital cities and 817 are in regional districts. The top retail chain is Radio Rentals with 40 stores throughout Australia. Other major chains include Visionhire with 30 stores, Electronic Sales and Rentals with 27, and Rentlow Video with 24. The top 12 chains accounted for 236 stores amounting to 14 per cent of the total number of stores.

The history of VCR penetration shows the early (October 1983) predominance of households possessing VCRs in Sydney (21.8 per cent) and Melbourne (18.5 per cent) and the later (October 1985) dominance of regional areas and capital cities in South Australia (45 per cent) and Western Australia (44.2 per cent). The most recent overall figures (October 1985) reveal that 37.1 per cent of all households now possess a VCR. There is a slightly greater penetration in country regions with 38 per cent compared with 35.5 per cent in capital cities. The highest penetration occurs in regional South Australia with 48.9 per cent. The capital city with the greatest penetration is Perth with 47.6 per cent.

The price of a VCR in Australia ranges from about $500-800 for a VHS video cassette recorder with remote control, 14 day, 2 up to 5 event timer, up to $1,100-1,400 for a VHS video cassette recorder with remote control, HI-FI, 14 day, 5 event timer. Blank video tapes range in price from about $7-15 for a 3 hour tape.

VIDEOGRAMS

PRODUCTION

Main Television and Production Houses

There is no video software production industry as such in Australia, but there is both a television and a film production industry which have begun to release more and more material in a video format. Television and film companies are also making greater use of video as a means of filming, editing and storing material.

The main television houses are the television stations themselves. Historically the stations were required, at the time of their original licensing, to equip themselves with television production facilities.

The total revenue for film and video production for cinema and television during the financial year ending June 1985 was $410 million. It is expected that this will decline slightly during 1986 due to changes in the tax legislation. The major component was the production of TV commercials ($200 million) followed by TV series ($66 million); documentaries ($50 million); feature films ($47 million); and TV features ($47 million).

Most Film and Television is produced in Sydney (which has 56 per cent of all production companies), and to a lesser extent Melbourne (with 25 per cent of all production companies). The majority of production companies (48 per cent) are involved in the production of documentaries, with commercials (35 per cent), TV programmes (30 per cent) and Feature Films (30 per cent) being other major sources of work.

Main Facility Houses

There are no facility houses. Independent production houses have either invested in facilities themselves (eg Crawford Productions) or more usually, use the facilities available at the television stations. So, for example, JNP makes the popular drama serial 'A Country Practice' at ATN Channel 7 Sydney, using their facilities.

Main Copying House

The video duplication industry in Australia employed some 260 people in 1984 at 8 duplication facilities. In 1985, there were 12 duplication facilities in Australia, and in 1986 the industry as a whole had a level of business of approximately $25–30 million. The main function of copying houses in Australia is to make copies of masters imported from America and elsewhere. Video distributors obtain licences to import master copies which the copying houses duplicate. Most of the copying houses are situated in Sydney and Melbourne close to the main distributors.

Of the 7 major Australian production companies, the three most important are: The Grundy Organisation which is one of the largest production companies in Australia; Crawford Productions which in 1985 produced a total of 50 hours of film and TV. This was down from a level of 391 hours in 1980, and 291 hours in 1983. The productions in 1985 consisted of 3 hours of feature film and 47 hours of TV series; and Henry Crawford and Associates which produced 17 hours of television series in 1983, 26 hours in 1984, and 13 hours in 1985. In 1985, the level of business of this firm was $5.6 million.

Of the 12 Australian duplication companies the most important is The Duplication Centre. This is Australia's largest video duplication company. It opened in 1981, employing 20 people and in 1985 employed 110 people with a duplicating capacity of 7 master machines and 1,170 slave machines. In 1985, 97 per cent of its work was carried out for the domestic video software distributors, and 3 per cent for corporate video. Of this work 75 per cent was in the Beta format and 25 per cent in VHS format. The Duplication Centre had a level of business of $11.5 million in 1985, and in 1986 copied some 1.85 million tapes. The Duplication Centre accounts for approximately 35–45 per cent of all duplications in Australia.

DISTRIBUTION

In 1984/5 the Video distribution industry in Australia was worth some $85–95 million. The level of business in the industry has declined in recent years, from a figure of $150 million in 1982/3. In 1984, the video distribution industry in Australia employed 487 people. Of these 437 were employed by the Video Industry Distributors' Association (VIDA) member companies, and 50 by independent video distributors.

A number of factors are responsible for the decline in the video software distribution industry: the sale of VCRs increased rapidly between 1982 and 1985, VCR penetration increasing from approximately 5 per cent of households in 1982 to approximately 38 per cent at the end of 1985. However, the market for VCRs seems to be approaching saturation – VCR sales have dropped from a high of 700,000 in 1984 and look likely to bottom out around 300–400,000 by about 1988 with a penetration of approximately 50 per cent. This level of sales represents a basic 'replacement' market for VCRs. Because the VCR market in Australia is near saturation level, most VCR owners are 'mature owners', that is, they have owned a VCR for longer than 6 months; these owners tend to rent new releases as well as movies from the back catalogues. Mature VCR owners tend to rent only the latest movies. Other contributing factors to the decline in the software industry have been the large increase in video piracy which accounted for approximately 20 per cent of the industry (or $20–25 million) in 1985, and the banning of X-rated movies, which when legal accounted for approximately 20 per cent of the market.

The majority of video material distributed in Australia comes from the United States (approximately 62 per cent), and to a lesser extent the United Kingdom (approximately 17 per cent). Material produced in Australia accounts for only approximately 4 per cent of all titles distributed.

The distribution industry is divided into nine major companies and approximately twenty-three independents. The majors are either linked to, or are part of, large overseas distributors, mainly American. Between them they account for about 85 per cent of the market. All the majors, apart from one (Syme Home Video), are situated in Sydney. Their trade association is VIDA. The approximate share of the total market of each of the main distributors is as follows: CIC-Taft (17–20 per cent); Publishing and Broadcasting Video CEL (15–19 per cent); Roadshow Home Video (9–14 per cent); Warner Home Video (9–14 per cent); RCA/Columbia Pictures/Hoyts Video (9–14 per cent); Thorn-EMI Video (7–10 per cent); CBS/Fox Video (7–10 per cent); Syme Home Video (4–7 per cent); and Sundowner Home Video (3–4 per cent). Unlike the other majors, it is the policy of Warner Home Video to lease rather than sell to the retailers.

Approximately 23 independent distributors possess 15–25 per cent of the market. (Syme Home Video, although independent, is included as one of the majors through its membership of VIDA and close association with Disney Productions). The independents, because they are not affiliated with a major source, draw more substantially upon the product of overseas independent producers (including specialist products from Greece, Italy, Hong Kong etc). In addition, Village Roadshow, Thorn EMI and Video Classics (defunct) have all partially funded Australian productions.

CONSUMPTION

There are 2,242 retail outlets for pre-recorded software in Australia. These do not include 'racking' (the practice whereby small non-specialist commercial enterprises, serviced by warehouses, provide 'racks' of videos for rental) or direct selling to the public by a small number of department stores. The retail outlets are more highly concentrated in metropolitan regions and are more numerous per head of population in Western Australia and Queensland.

The bulk of videos, over 95 per cent, are entertainment films, of which the major proportion (in descending order) is comedy, action and adventure, family, adult, horror and X-rated.

VIDEO CRIME AND PIRACY

VIDEO SOFTWARE COPYRIGHT INFRINGEMENT

The incidence of Video Piracy has grown considerably in Australia in the last few years. It accounted for approximately 10 per cent of the Video Software industry in 1983 (or approximately $15 million at the distributor level), and as a percentage had doubled by 1985 to 20 per cent of the Video Software industry (or $20–25 million at the distributor level, and approximately $60 million at the retail level).

Australia has become integrated into an international network of video piracy that seems to be closely associated with organised crime, both overseas and in Australia. It is common for pirated videos to be found in the company of drugs and pornographic material. The majority of the pirate video cassettes appear to be imported from the United Kingdom, mainly in counterfeit packaging and labelling. Some material however is copied in Australia. For locally copied material, Australia has the dubious honour of being able to produce the highest quality pirate copies in the world, the copies being so good that it 'takes a very detailed analysis and comparison with the genuine product to distinguish the difference'.

It has been suggested that there is a close link between pornographic and 'legitimate' pirated video material, (ie, video material that is not banned): the facilities used to manufacture and distribute pornographic video tape are also used for the 'pirating' of all types of video material. Pirate copies of 'legitimate' films are often found in the company of pornographic video tapes. There also seems to have been a considerable increase in video piracy since the banning of X-rated video material in most states in early 1984. It may be that some dealers previously involved with X-rated video material have moved 'underground' to deal in pirate copies of X-rated videos, and subsequently any video material. This could account for the high quality of pirate videos in Australia.

Although we have no specific figures on parallel importing, the Australian Film and Video Security Office (AFVSO) reports that this aspect of copyright infringement is increasing at an 'alarming rate'; VIDA is concerned that it 'represents a significant threat to the investment made by distributors in the establishment and development of the local distribution industry'.

There have been many examples of pirated video movies in Australia. For example, prints of the film *Return of the Jedi* were stolen from cinemas in the United States, the United Kingdom and Canada. Subsequently video copies of this film were available in Australia before its cinema release.

Although the level of video piracy in Australia is quite high, the penalties to date have been very light. Under Federal law, until recently a maximum fine of $10,000 or a six month jail sentence could be imposed for a proven case of piracy. Even then, actual fines were much less as most prosecutions were made under civil law, and low fines were imposed. The following examples illustrate this point:

i)   A man in Perth was fined $100 on each of six charges for copying *The Empire Strikes Back, Paternity, Yellow Beard, Class* and *Trading Places*.

ii)   A man in Victoria was sentenced to seven days in jail and fined $350 for copying *Rocky II, Rocky III* and *Jaws*.

Apart from the low fines which offer little deterrent to video pirates, there is considerable difficulty and expense associated with obtaining a conviction. Under Section 126 of the Copyright Act, proof of ownership of the copyright must be established. This involves considerable delay and expense when witnesses must be brought to Australia from overseas, a problem that is multiplied when there is more than one pirated tape involved.

The Australian Film and Video Security Office (established as an independent body in October 1982), is the main body for combatting video crime. The AFVSO is one of the international branch offices set up by the Motion Picture Association of America (MPAA) in order to safeguard the interests of its members against both international and local video piracy, and is funded by both the MPAA and VIDA. Both VIDA and the AFVSO have lobbied the Australian government to tighten up the video copyright legislation. A review of audio-visual Copyright Law was set up by the Attorney General's Department in 1982, and has only recently handed down a much awaited report.

In February 1986, the Federal Government announced tougher copyright legislation. Under Federal Law, offenders can now be sentenced to up to two years in jail for a first offence; the upper limit for fines imposed in the Federal Court when there is more than one tape pirated will be increased from $10,000 to $50,000 for an individual, and to $250,000 for a company. The new legislation will also aim to make the proof of copyright in both civil and criminal proceedings easier. The government is not however considering a system of registration as has been proposed by members of the Video Industry.

THEFT OF VIDEO HARDWARE

The theft of VCRs has grown rapidly in Australia and they are now among the most commonly stolen items in domestic robberies. In 1981, in NSW alone there were approximately 12,074 VCRs stolen. By 1985 this figure had grown to approximately 21,600.

If the NSW figures are taken to be indicative of the level of VCR theft in the rest of Australia, then in 1985, some 54,000 VCRs would have been stolen in Australia.

CENSORSHIP

Because of the complex political framework in Australia, censorship can be practised at federal and/or state level.

Until 1984/85 there was no specific legislation concerning the censoring of video materials. However, in 1984/85, all states strengthened their legislation, banning the sale of X-rated vidoes. This classification was introduced in 1984 when, after much debate, the Australian Film Censorship Board decided that films and video showing explicit sex between consenting adults would be rated X. Films showing violent sex, so-called 'snuff movies' showing real life murders, bestiality or child pornography, were refused classification and are therefore illegal throughout Australia.

Following this decision, the various States have passed particular legislation to control videos.

Up to the end of 1981, more than 5,000 video tapes had been imported into Australia. However, these were not classified by the Federal Film Censorship Board, only registered as they were not intended for public exhibition. Each state was then left to deal with the video tapes according to State indecency or obscenity laws. Although there were meetings between State and Federal ministers in October 1981 to consider proposals for the uniform classification of video material, it was not until July 1983 that the ministers agreed to a uniform system of videotape classification. Under this system, imported video tapes for home use would no longer be subject to compulsory registration by the Film Censorship Board (FCB), but video tapes for sale and hire would be classified by the Board on request by the importer, distributor or retailer.

Only material that contained extreme violence (sexual or otherwise) or child pornography would be refused classification. The States would subsequently pass laws imposing restrictions on the sale and delivery of R- and X-rated material.

The 'enabling' Commonwealth legislation for the uniform classification system came into effect in February 1984. This legislation aroused considerable opposition in parliament, and as a result another meeting was held between federal and state ministers. At this meeting it was decided to replace the voluntary classification scheme with a compulsory one. In addition, the categories of material that would not be given a classification was widened to include: 'child pornography, bestiality, explicit violence against non-consenting persons, detailed and gratuitous depictions of acts of significant cruelty and instruction manuals for terrorist-type weapons and acts or abuse of hard drugs'. The federal legislation was amended to accommodate these changes in June 1984.

The Commonwealth legislation of June 1984 was confined to the Australian Capital Territory. However, the States signalled that they would introduce 'mirror' legislation by the end of 1984. In practice, this was not the case, although public campaigns were run against X-rated videos. By August 1984 hundreds of petitions had been received by the Commonwealth parliament opposing the X-rated video classification. In response to this public outcry, most of the States subsequently banned X-rated videos. Thus, rather than the States adapting a uniform system of classification of video material based on the Commonwealth model, the classification systems in the states have developed independently. There are however similarities between the various states.

SENATE SELECT COMMITTEE ON VIDEO MATERIAL

In response to public concern over the classification of video material, the Commonwealth government set up the Senate Select Committee on Video Material in October 1984 to investigate a range of issues associated with X-rated video material. This committee presented a brief and indecisive report in March 1985, the work of the committee being replaced by the Joint Select Committee on Video Material (established March 1985) which comprised members of both the House of Representatives and the Senate. The Joint Select Committee is expected to report some time early in 1986.

The video industry as a whole seems to have suffered from the banning of X-rated material. Before X-rated videos were banned by most states, they accounted for some 20–30 per cent of the retail market. At present in the Australian Capital Territory where they are legal R and X rated videos account for approximately 20–25 per cent of the market.

Apart from the loss of business to video distributors and retailers that has resulted from the banning of X-rated material, problems have been caused by the requirement for compulsory classification of video tapes by the FCB. The FCB has not been able to keep pace with the large number of video titles that have been put forward for classification. In 1984, there was an average of 650 applications per month for the classification of video tapes compared with the FCB's capacity to deal with 450 classifications per month. This has resulted in the delay between application and classification growing from two weeks in February 1984, to more than 10 weeks in January 1985, the back log growing at a rate of one month every two months. In February 1985, there was a backlog of 3,138 video titles awaiting classification.

Under pressure from the video distributors, the Federal Attorney General agreed to release for distribution all those videos which had a prior theatrical classification by the censor, subject to a statutory declaration by the distributors that the video versions of the films are substantially identical to the theatrical versions. The government also acted to boost staff of the FCB from 7 to 10. This significantly reduced the backlog of material awaiting classification, to about 1,000 titles by July 1985.

One result of the 'tightening-up' of video censorship legislation has been that a difference exists between the material classified for the cinema, and material classified for video. This has led to some films that have been shown legally in cinemas being denied a classification by the FCB for video. An example of this is the film *Rape Squad* which was released for cinema showing under an R-rating, but rejected by the censor for video on the grounds of 'gratuitous sexual violence'. Another example is the film *The Exterminator* (which had been on the market for two years prior to the introduction of the X-rating) which was refused a rating because of 'frequent high levels of gratuitous sexual violence'.

TABLE 1:
VCR's – BASIC INDUSTRY STATISTICS

Description		1980		1981		1982		1983		1984		1985	
		No.	$000	No.	$000	No.	$000	No.	$000	No.	$000	No.	$000
Imports of video recorders*[1]	Domestic VCRs	28439	16683	122144	63957	24663	112887	578950	222328	764833	295250	658148	250364
	Professional VCRs		4740	1314	5732	5005	10014	214	4206	3336	4393	3199	5000
Total imports of video recorders[1]			21423	123458	69689	29668	132901	579164	226534	768169	299643	661347	255364
VCRs sales[2]		120000		201000		533000		635000		685000		632000	
VCRs – market share by format[3]	VHS									67		83	
	BETA									32		16	
% of VCR market[4]	rent											6.5	
	buy											93.5	

Source: (1) Australian Foreign Trade Exports/Imports
      (2) 1980–1982: Video Facts and figures, Infoline, Fairfax April 1984.
           1983–1985: CESA Figures.
      (3) 1984: George Patterson Survey, 1985.
      (4) Adapted from TUB '1985 Home Video Research-Executive Summary', p 14–15.

Note: * Data for years 1979/80 to 1984/85.

FIGURE 1
PENETRATION OF VCR'S IN AUSTRALIA*

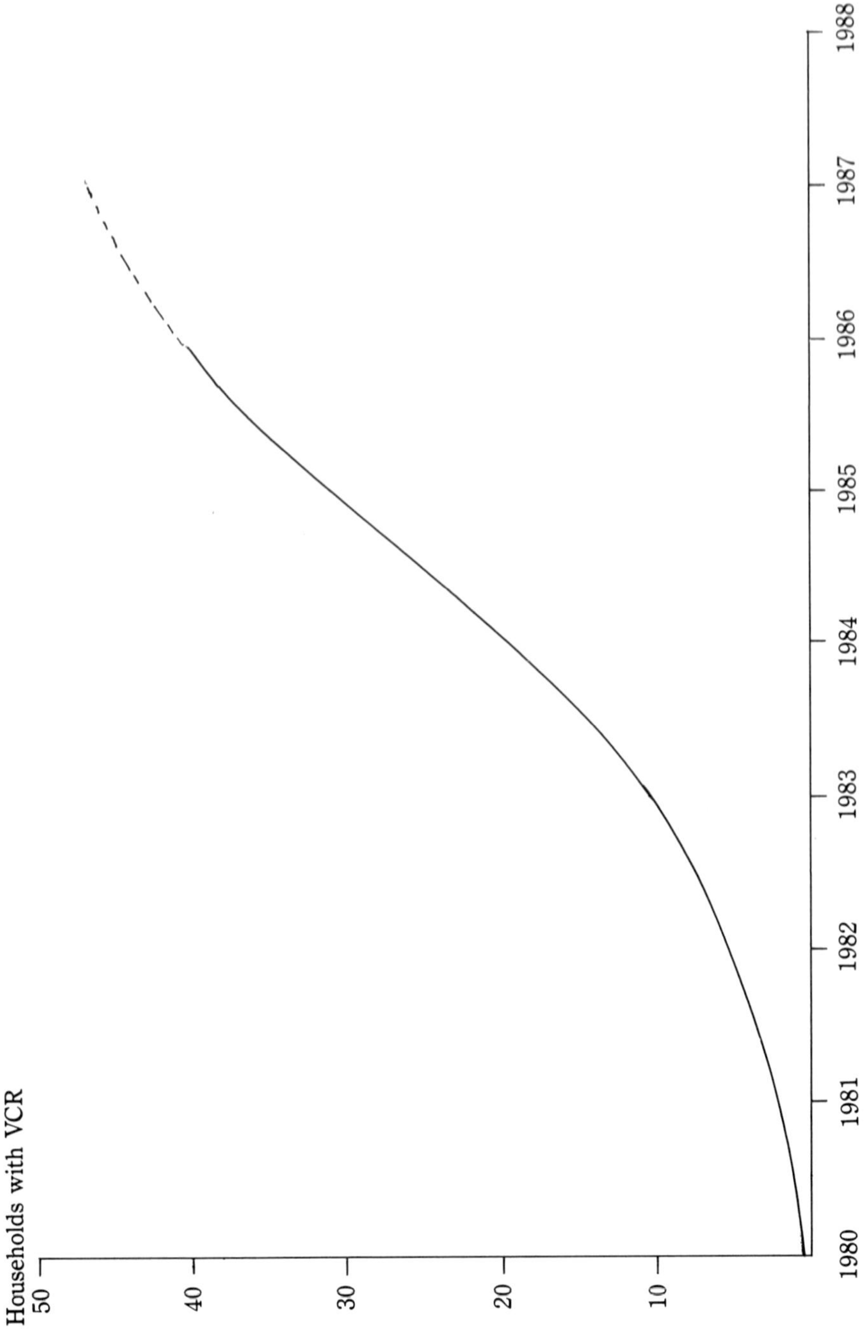

% of Households with VCR

NOTE: * Total number of Households in 1985 = 5,041,000

FIGURE 2
ANNUAL IMPORTS OF DOMESTIC VCR'S

Number of VCR's Imported ('000)

Chapter 9

UNITED STATES OF AMERICA AND CANADA

INTRODUCTION

Canada, the United States of America and Mexico, share the North American sub-continent. Canada has over 3.8 million square miles of continent while the United States has 3.6 million square miles. Each nation shares almost equally in the real estate, and maintains more or less amicable relations along a common 4,000 mile frontier. Nearly 75 per cent of Canada's citizens share a common language with their neighbours to the South. While in many other respects the two nations are quite dissimilar, in terms of their respective instruments of popular culture, Canadians are more like Americans than they would care to admit. Some critics have characterized the Canadian television broadcast services as 'de facto American affiliates' (Gathercole, 1985). It seems safe to say that, in terms of mass mediated popular culture, whatever happens to Americans happens to Canadians.

Canada's population of nearly 25 million resides in 8,857,000 private house-holds. Ninety-eight per cent of these households can receive a television signal, while 95 per cent can receive at least two Canadian stations. Colour television receivers are in 88 per cent of the Canadians' television house-holds (*Canadian Facts and Figures*, 1984). Canadians watch television for just over three hours each day, 23 hours per week.

America has a population of nearly 270,000,000 people, ten times that of Canada. Approximately 85 milllion homes in the United States (98 per cent of all households), are equipped with television receivers. Of these, 77 million households are equipped with colour receivers, and 96 per cent can receive UHF signals (*Broadcasting*, 1985). The average American household watches seven hours-eight minutes of broadcast or cablecast programming per day. Less than five per cent of that programming originates beyond the borders of the United States.

HARDWARE

Production

Canadians consume a far greater amount of video hardware and software than they produce. Canadian habits and patterns of consumption follow those of American consumers. Consumer adoption patterns of colour television in Canada and the United States illustrate the point. Similar 'S' shaped demand curves can be plotted for other communication products and services. It seems safe to say that whatever happens to the American consumer happens, or will happen, to Canadians. Indeed, the marketing and distribution sub-sector of the North American consumer electronics industry is operated on that premise.

The retail sales of consumer electronic equipment in the United States earned $34 billion dollars in 1984 (*Consumer Electronics*, 1985). The United States imports the majority of these consumer products from overseas. Nonetheless, the impact of consumer electronics on the American economy is profound.

> Even though only approximately one-third of the manufacturing value of the twelve product categories accrues in the United States, the total impact on the US economy exceeds $40 billion and accounts for almost 1.5 million full-time jobs.

Americans spent nearly 68 cents on home video hardware out of each dollar spent on consumer electronics. Table 3 charts the annual factory sales of consumer electronic products in the United States in 1984. American consumers spent approximately $5.7 billion on VCRs, cameras, and video disc players in 1984.

Americans import the majority of their home video equipment. Canadians import almost all of theirs. Three non-compatible types of home video recording and playback equipment have been used by American consumers since the mid 1970s: VHS and Beta video cassette recorders (VCRs) and players, and a Video Disc Player (VDP). The VHS video cassette format is by far the most popular of the four, controlling over 82 per cent of the Canadian hardware market. The Beta format captured 16.5 per cent of the American home video consumer market by the end of 1984 (22 per cent in Canada). Laser Disc Players (LDPs) had established an unimpressive one per cent penetration among TV households in North America (*Consumer* 1985, p 10).

A fourth 'format' of videotape recorder/player – the 8mm video format – was introduced in the American market in 1984. This new format was marketed independently by two camera companies, Eastman Kodak and Polaroid, and established an initial marketplace penetration of approximately 0.5 per cent by the end of 1984. Little more is known about this format or its acceptance by the American public at the time of writing.

126

Video Cassette Recording/Playback Equipment

The North American home video market did not really exist before 1978. Several manufacturers had earlier attempted to introduce videotape playback and recording equipment into the American and Canadian markets during the early 1970s. However, these initial efforts and formats – introduced by large companies such as CBS and AVCO, failed to create much consumer enthusiasm, and were abandoned after only brief debuts in various markets outlets.

> The first successful consumer format was introduced by Sony in 1975. Sony Betamax players were priced at $1,300 and used 1/2 inch tape cassettes .... In 1977, RCA introduced the VHS format into the United States. The RCA player had a two-hour recording capability and sold for $1,000 (*Home Video*, 1983, p 131).

Statistics compiled for Knowledge Industry Publications indicate that at the end of 1978, there were only 175,000 (VCRs), in the United States. By mid-1985, the number of VCRs had risen to nearly 19 million, and the percentage of penetration had increased to 20 per cent. A similar rate of growth was experienced by Canadians during the same period. The number of VCRs in Canada rose from just over 45,000 in 1979, to 1,850,000 by the end of 1984 (*How Many*, 1985, p 4).

As with most other consumer products, a definitive census of the VCR population is not available from any single source. Statistics that summarize annual and cumulative sales of home video hardware in the United States and Canada vary among the several sources that collect them. For example, two sources, each widely regarded as authoritative, differed by nearly one half million units with respect to their statistics on VCR ownership in the United States in 1978. By 1985, their respective cumulative statistics differed by just over four million units. Therefore, the reliability of these reported statistics remains open to question. Whenever differences were discovered among the reported statistics, only the lower of several estimates were included in this report.

But even these conservative statistics suggest dramatic growth within the home video industry. The rate of growth of VCRs in North America from 1975 to 1984, exceeded the growth rate for colour television during the similar period in its history. By the end of 1982, the penetration of VCRs into American households with television had increased to 4.7 per cent. The cumulative VCR population had increased to nearly 4 million. VCR sales for 1983 broke all previous records: American consumers had purchased over three million video cassette recorders during a single year (Harris, 1983). Manufacturers were hard-pressed to meet demand. The 11 million VCRs in Canada (1.4 million), and America (9.5 million), represented over 34 per cent of all of the VCRs in the world in 1983 (*Overview*, 1984). American VCR owners alone constituted nearly 20 per cent of the worldwide market for prerecorded or blank video cassettes (Crook, 1983).

127

The all-time American sales record set in 1983 was eclipsed the following year. More than seven million VCRs were sold to retailers in the United States in 1984 (Kitziller, 1985; 'VCR Sales', 1984). For the first time, consumer demand in the United States exceeded worldwide production of video player/recorders.

> 1984 found the supply sufficient to handle the booming demand.
> Sales were so strong there should have been severe shortages. But
> the ... demand in the European community was short of what they
> had anticipated in 1983 .... Japan's domestic market sales ... [did]
> not increase as anticipated. That allowed for additional production
> to go to the United States (Adams, 1985).

The cumulative size of the 'VCR universe' in the United States had increased to nearly five million machines.

In 1978, less than one per cent of the households with television owned VCRs. A report published in the *New York Times*, claimed that by February, 1985, Americans owned 17 million VCRs, and that VCR penetration in TV households had increased to 18 per cent. The Electronics Industry Association (EIA) projects that by the end of 1985 a total of 26 million VCRs will have been sold in the United States, for a market penetration approaching 30 per cent (Bierbaum, 1985). Estimates are that by 1990, the 'VCR universe' may increase to 40 million machines. While the total number of VCRs in Canada is much smaller than the figures just cited, the percentage of penetration is nearly equivalent. Two million Canadian households with television owned VCRs by the end of 1984 and this amounted to a rate of penetration of 25–30 per cent.

HARDWARE MANUFACTURE AND DISTRIBUTION

All VCRs and VDPs sold in the United States for home use during 1984 were imported from Japan or the Republic of Korea. No VCRs were manufactured or assembled in the United States. Packaged finished units were imported and sold by manufacturers or shipped to American companies that had purchased these products on a private-label basis. For example Hitachi supplied RCA-brand VCRs, and captured 16 per cent of the market (*TV Digest*, 1985, p 10). Matsushita supplied Panasonic's product line, and captured 14 per cent of the market. Sony, also the manufacturer for Zenith product lines, controlled 6.5 per cent. Sanyo supplied Sears and also manufactured equipment under the name of Fisher. Sanyo had, by 1985, captured 12.5 per cent of the market (*TV Digest*, 1985 p 10).

VCRs were sold under 32 different brand names during 1983–84. Although there are fifteen manufacturers in Japan who make VHS and Beta VCRs, five companies accounted for 75 per cent of production in 1984 (Callahan, 1985). Table 6 summarizes the activities of the Japanese manufacturers.

Of the two VCR formats [VHS and Beta] VHS, pioneered by JVC in 1976, is overwhelmingly popular, with a worldwide market share in 1984 of 80 per cent, a five percentage-point increase over 1983. The eleven member group of VHS manufactureers is dominated by Matsushita and JVC, its subsidiary (50.3 per cent owned by Matsushita). In 1984 Matsushita and JVC together accounted for over two out of every five VCRs sold worldwide.

The incompatible Beta format, developed by Sony in 1974, has been taking a declining percentage of total sales every year. In 1984, we estimate that the Beta format was down to a worldwide market share of less than 20 per cent, and we expect it to drop to close to ten per cent by 1988 (Callahan, 1985).

Distribution of VCRs and VDPs are very similar to the system used for the delivery of television receivers to consumers. Manufacturers and importers of home video equipment use one-step or two-step distribution systems, or some combination of the two. In the two-step system, the manufacturer or importer sells VCRs and VDPs to an independent wholesaler/distributor, who, in turn, sells directly to the retail outlet using either a directly employed sales force and/or manufacturers' representatives. Larger retail accounts are increasingly serviced directly by the manufacturer outside of conventional marketing procedures.

Economic Impact of Home Video Hardware. VCRs are the second largest of the four home video product categories, and second also among the major consumer electronic product categories. VCRs had a direct impact of $1,258 billion on the American economy.

In 1983, the sale of these products generated more than $2.5 billion in business and almost 94,000 jobs. While this economic impact was spread throughout all sectors of the economy, [...] more than 35 per cent of the total economic impact took place in the retail and wholesale sectors; VCR sales supported over 35,000 jobs in those two sectors alone. VCR sales also have a large impact on the transportation sector ($119 million), and construction sector ($94 million) (Little, 1985).

It is estimated that in 1983, VCR selling prices declined at both the wholesale and the retail levels. These declines were the result of several marketplace phenomena, with their origins among overseas manufacturers as well as within the domestic market. Manufacturers began to produce less costly units, price competition increased, and promotional sales were held to move excess stock that had built up during the previous year. Consequently, average retail sales for VCRs fell by twelve per cent, from approximately $740 per unit to approximately $650 per unit in 1983. The average retail price of LaserDisc players remained the same at approximately $400 per unit.

VIDEOGRAMS

The home video sub-sector of the United States mass media industry resembles a broadly shaped triangle whose base is formed by the 20,000 retail operations. Approximately five hundred television and motion picture producers provide the materials that retailers sell or rent to consumers. An infrastructure of wholesalers and home video distributors intervenes between the retail store and the programme supplier. Andre Blay, Chief Executive Officer of Embassy Home Entertainment, described the production – distribution subsystem thus:

> The network consists of approximately 30 independent businesses [wholesale operations], that purchase from the over 40–50 suppliers. [Because] a lot of wholesalers have multiple locations, we ship to about one hundred destinations. So there are thirty or forty business units that control 100–110 shipping outlets that go to the 20,000 or so retailers. In addition to that, there are a few retailers that we ship to directly. We have one [retail customer] that has branches up and down the entire state of California.

Home Video Programme Suppliers. The 'business units' identified by Blay produce and/or acquire from others the home video materials that they sell to distributors (Harmetz, 1984). More than 80 per cent of the products distributed for home video consumption are products previously produced and distributed through theatres, cinemas and network television broadcasts. Programme suppliers have not as yet become involved in the business of renting cassettes to consumers, and make no additional money from retailer rental activities. Programme suppliers failed to anticipate the rental phenomenon when they made their initial market analyses. They have since attempted to compensate for the fundamental oversight by demanding higher wholesale prices and surcharges.

Whether the programme supply company 'produces' or 'acquires' the majority of its home video inventory depends on the size and background of the organisation. Major motion picture producers often strike copies 'in-house' from recent productions, or from materials stored in their libraries, and sell these prerecorded video cassettes to distributors. In addition, these 'majors' often supplement their inventories by purchasing the distribution rights for titles produced by smaller 'independent' producers.

These smaller 'independents' often lack both the capital and the extensive libraries of the major producers. While they may produce some of the titles listed in their inventories, the independent producers more often buy the home video rights to titles produced by even smaller production companies who, in turn, need these 'advances' to launch their productions (Horowitz, 1983).

There are currently 494 American programme suppliers who conduct business in the worldwide home video marketplace (Miller, 1985). However, not all share equally in the revenues provided by the home video consumer. Approximately 250 of the 'Home Video Programme Producers' included in the 'Knowledge Industry Yearbook' maintain company inventories of less than seven titles. Moreover, many companies, like Wooden Boat Publications Inc, carry only speciality titles that appeal to a limited audience (Miller, 1985). The bulk of the programme supply business belongs to twelve major motion picture studios. Statistics gathered by Paul Kagen Associates indicate that 'of the top 12 suppliers last year [1984], eight were motion picture studios that combined held 83 per cent market share' (Schneider, 1985).

Home Video Distributors. Wholesalers and distributors (hereafter referred to as 'distributors'), serve as conduits that suppliers use to pass on their library holdings to retailers and, ultimately, to consumers. Miller (1985), lists 208 home video distributors operating within the United States. Nearly 30 per cent of the distributors listed in the *Home Video Marketplace* describe themselves as suppliers as well as wholesalers. Four of these supplier/distributors are, in addition, major forces in the motion picture industry.

> MCA and Warner Home Video use the expert services of their in-house record divisions to distribute their home video products. CBS/Fox Video and RCA/Columbia Pictures Home Video each have access to major record distribution divisions within the infrastructures of their parent corporations (Seideman).

By comparing the descriptions of each of the remaining 'supplier-distributors', listed in the Yearbook, one can conclude that these types of programme suppliers provide rather specialised video materials to specialised audiences. Individually, these companies have little influence in the retail market. Their collective influence is not much greater. These tentative conclusions, however, cannot be supported by evidence. Nonetheless, it appears that at least one-third of the distributors (and perhaps more), control a relatively small proportion of the market. As is the case with suppliers, a relatively small number of distributors dominates the market both in terms of inventory and revenue. One report indicates that of the 208 distributors only about 20–30 are 'big league distributors, and two of these, Commtron Corporation and Sound Video Unlimited, control about 18 per cent of the market between them' (Seideman, 1984). Interviews were conducted with two executives of Sound Video Unlimited for this project.

The Canadian distribution network mirrors the system for video distribution in the United States. The major programme suppliers maintain offices in one or both of the two major Canadian centres for programme distribution,

Toronto, Ontario, and Vancouver, British Columbia. The Home Video Board of Canada represents eight American suppliers and distributors: Astral Video; CBS/Fox Video; Walt Disney Home Video; MCA Video; Media Home Entertainment; MGM/UA Video Enterprises; Paramount Home Video; RCA/Columbia Home Video; and WEA Music of Canada (*Who's Who*, 1984). Serving a function akin to the Motion Picture Export Association of America (MPEAA), the Home Video Board acts as the spokesman, policeman and lobbyist. It negotiates wholesale prices for its members and determines the credit limits offered to Canadian retailers. The board also operates its own security division that investigates allegations of video piracy. In 1983, the security division obtained the confiscation of 18,000 illegal copies of American programmes (Devins, 1984).

Home Video Retail Organisations. The home video industry meets the consumer at the retail counter. The number of retail shops has increased dramatically in North America during the last seven years. The network and scope of retail activities is presently more extensive in the United States, due to the size of its population and the extent of penetration of VCRs in households with television. What follows is a brief description of these retail activities.

The Canadian retail industry resembles the American retail network in structure and method of operation, albeit on a somewhat smaller scale. The largest national retail chain in Canada is National Video, an American company with headquarters in Portland, Oregon.

There were fewer than 4,000 stores in the United States in 1978. Sale of pre-recorded video cassettes was accomplished mostly via mail order and catalogue types of sales operations.

By 1983, 10,000 or more video speciality outlets sold or rented pre-recorded video cassettes to consumers (Crook, 1983). One year later, the number of speciality stores in the United States had grown to more than 14,000. Ninety per cent of these retail stores were run by single store operators (Kerr, 1984). By the end of 1984 there were 15,000 video software speciality outlets across the country (*Video Industry* 1985). Industry estimates indicate that there are at present more than 22,000 video software speciality stores in the United States (Schneider, 1985). It has been estimated that there are approximately 5,000 retail/rental stores in Canada (Simandl, 1985).

Retail operations in both countries have their origins in direct – mail companies and mass merchandising chains. These nation-wide companies sold both hardware and software. Mass merchandisers, however, were unwilling to maintain the full range of software available for sale to consumers. Smaller entrepreneurs quickly seized a marketing opportunity, and created small video retail shops that carried larger inventories.

As the number of video-cassette recorders purchased by consumers increased, so the demand for pre-recorded materials grew. The size and complexity of home video retail operations changed, simultaneously, in two directions: 'bigness' and 'smallness'. Speciality stores gradually increased their inventories, while store owners increased the number of outlets. Local and regional chain stores started to eclipse the local market. Industry representatives foresaw chain stores as the outlet of the future (Wharton, 1985).

At about the same time that regional chain stores were increasing their size, another group of entrepreneurs was trying to capitalise on the interconnected marketing notions of ubiquity and convenience. Small home video concessions, sometimes little more than automated vending machines, were installed in gas stations, convenience stores, and restaurants. The inventories of these small scale retail operations were maintained by rack jobbers – individuals who leased shelf or floor space from other store owners. In rural and outlying areas, rack jobbers provided consumers with their only source for home video software and/or hardware. In urban areas, these small 'video stalls', thrived on an income provided by 'impulse buyers' who, in all likelihood, had come to the market for another product altogether.

By 1984, blank as well as pre-recorded video cassettes were rented or sold in book and record stores; in grocery and convenience stores; in mass merchandising department stores (Target stores in 22 states); and even in cinemas. By the end of the year, large chain and mass merchandising companies entered the home video software retail market.

> The average number of titles per store is 1,578, while the number of inventory units averages 2,321 .... The average [merchant] owns 4.6 stores. He or she has 3.2 full-time and three part-time employees.

Retailers in the United States and in Canada are joined together in two national organisations. Membership in the Video Dealers Software Association (VSDA), numbers approximately 5,000 local speciality stores as well as regional and national chain stores in the United States. The Video Retailers Association of Canada maintains a membership of approximately 200 members.

Distribution

Inter-Industry Relationships. The emergence of home video provided a financial boom for programme suppliers who happily added another exhibition window to the storefront of North American mass media. But for other operators in other sub-sectors of the entertainment industry, home video represented an intrusion that portended smaller profits from advertising, programming and exhibition. Doomsayers in the 1940s–1950s predicted that television would decimate theatre attendance, and indeed, cause the financial ruin of the entire Hollywood motion picture industry. Nothing, as it turned out, could have been further from the truth. Similarly dire predictions have been proffered about home video's financial impact on the entertainment industry's *status quo*. Some argue that the flexibility of home video technology and the convenience offered to the consumers is 'stealing momentum and dollars away from the other tech-nologies' (Seideman, 1983). Not all members of the industry agree on the intensity with which this larceny occurs, and one consumer advocate charac-terized this debate as 'nothing more than a falling out of thieves' (Geller, 1984).

Release Windows. Perhaps the best way to examine the effect that home video has had on the other methods of programme exhibition and distribution is to look at the timetable used by suppliers to schedule the release of their products. Release dates for each window are carefully planned by suppliers in order to maximise profits at each stage. Figure 1 indicates the various 'release windows', available to programme suppliers. The figure also charts the 'life-time' of a feature film as it passes through each window. In 1979, the timetable was arranged into the following pattern: 1. cinema showing; 2. second cinema showing; 3. network television; 4. pay cable; 5. home video and private exhi-bition (Cahill; 1983). Figure 1 illustrates how that release pattern has changed over the past five years. First run at the cinema still leads the timetable. At present, films are released on cassettes to consumers in Canada and the United States four to six months after they open in cinemas. A film that fails to draw good box office receipts will probably pass through the video 'window' earlier in its release cycle. Films are available on cassettes six months before they are allowed to be shown on pay cable. Network and national television syndi-cation are last. Release patterns change as revenues from each window change. Likewise, an individual title's progress or itinerary through the various windows may change as its anticipated revenue profile shifts. By the end of this decade, it will probably not be unusual to see a simultaneous release at the box office, PTV and home video.

Although home video revenue has increased the revenues of the major Ameri-can motion picture programme suppliers, this may have been at the expense of cinema owners in the United States and Canada. The home video market has had a negative impact on the revenues available to 'blockbusters' during their second releases to cinemas. 'Consumer expectation of feature film releases in the video cassette format combined with the steadily increasing sales of VCRs has dashed the whole reissue programme' said James R Spitz, Presi-dent of distribution for Columbia Pictures (Groves, 1985). Theatre owners worry that the release time between cinema showing and subsequent licens-ing to home video may be shortened, causing further erosion of their profits.

At present, the cinema and home video audiences are drawn from different demographic pools. The median age of the core filmgoer in the United States is 18-25 years, somewhat younger than those who generally purchase home video software and hardware (see Table 7). In fact several cinema chains have tested the possibility of selling video cassette copies of features currently playing on their screens. The results have been favourable to both parts of the industry.

Home video and other mass culture technologies have made their presence known to television broadcasters in several ways. Thirty per cent of the American television households have a VCR and nearly half have cable television. Viewing feature films on video cassette takes up leisure time that might otherwise have been spent watching broadcast television. Subscription television and pay-as-you-view services have combined with home video to reduce the audience for direct television broadcasts. For example, 750,000 American television households currently have satellite receiving apparatus (similar figures were unavailable for Canada). As a result the three American television networks, accustomed to a combined domestic audience share of 90 per cent or more since the mid 1970s, captured just 74 per cent in 1984 (Zoglin, 1984). Precise figures were not available to show how the 'defectors' spent their leisure time. These 'defections' occurred, however, during a period of increased penetration of alternative entertainment technologies and in a nearly inverse proportion (Maisel, 1982).

Home video technology allows the consumer to manipulate the otherwise fixed programming schedule of local and network television broadcasts by recording a programme at one time and viewing it at another. Indeed 'timeshift viewing' is the way in which video hardware is most used in the home. Television network operators would like to believe that time-shift viewing increases rather than decreases the size of the audience (Ranger, 1985). However, some research suggests that many programmes recorded off-air may never be seen by the user of the hardware. Levy determined that:

> On average, 3.31 recordings were made by each household during the diary week, and, excluding pre-recorded cassettes which had been rented, borrowed or bought, the average household played back 2.42 programmes .... There is some evidence to show that upwards of 40 per cent of all recordings are never played back; the tape is used to make new recordings, automatically erasing the first programme (Levy, 1983).

In addition, time-shift viewing allows the viewer to scan rapidly through advertisements using the fast-scan technology of the hardware. Research by the AC Neilsen Company in the United States and Canada, found that about half of the commercials in a taped programme get 'zapped' by the viewer during playback. One advertising company estimated that 'at the current rate of VCR growth, the loss of commercial viewing will be almost one percent by late 1987, which could translate into a $200 million loss in advertising revenue' (Zoglin, 1984).

Pay cable system operators worry about the extent to which home video may have diminished the market for pay and subscription cable television programme services throughout North America. Knowledgeable Hollywood executives argue that pay cable channels, such as HBO – despite their head start – may lose out to video cassettes but only in the long run. According to Valenti, 'it will devastate the post-theatrical market' (Harmetz, 1984). Of the three pay services in Canada, none have reported a profit during the last

135

four years ('A Switch-Off,' 1984, p 68). Studies conducted by A C Neilsen, on the other hand suggest that home video penetration is higher in households that already subscribe to one or more pay cable services.

Ultimately, home video use may actually stimulate the growth of pay and subscription services. According to Brian Wenham, Programme Director for the BBC, pay television and home video can be complementary rather than mutually exclusive:

> In a nutshell, the answer to those who fear that the penetration of VCRs would automatically chop the legs off new services trying to get established on cable or on satellite, is that there would seem to be little cause for fear. The VCR is a secondary tool. What it does best is to re-fashion what others put before it. A new film service, on cable or on satellite, would therefore be meat and drink to it, as would blocks of programming offering sport, film, classics, ballet, pop and opera. No video store can in the end match the deter- mined programme provider either in range or in cost. To take the simplest example of the film service: you do not need to offer many attractive films in a package that might come out at 8–10 pounds a week to underprice the totted up costs of all those trips to the video store and you offer too great a savings to bother' (Ogan, 1985).

The Hollywood entertainment industry has become increasingly dependent on the revenues brought in by its home video activities. 'A major film can gener- ate $10–20,000,000 worldwide in home video revenues; an average film-on-video can garner $4–5,000,000,' said the executive vice president of RCA corporation (Terry, 1984). Studios estimate that by 1988, worldwide theatrical releases of films and television programmes may account for no more than 50 per cent of a producer's gross revenue, down from 80 per cent in the mid-seventies. Revenues earned from worldwide home video sales in 1983 suggest that the prediction may be quite close to the truth of the matter. In 1983, the motion picture industry estimated that worldwide cinema showings accounted for approximately 63 per cent of its revenues.

During that same year, worldwide home video distribution provided less than ten per cent of the revenues while free television and pay cable operations in the United States and Canada provided entertainment producers with approximately 27 per cent of their incomes (Pollack, 1984). But the gap between entertainment spending in video-cassette sales and rentals, and traditional cinemas is narrowing. Each year the percentages shift in favour of home video operations.

> In 1984, American Film Marketing Association (AFMA) compa- nies earned approximately $375 million from the foreign sales of motion pictures for theatrical, television and home video exposure

.... Foreign theatrical sales ... accounted for 52 per cent and television (including cable), 16 per cent (Hollinger, 1985).

Anticipating this shift, some producers are already beginning to carve out their niche in the home video sector. 'Walt Disney Home Video', for example, expects within a year to earn 20 per cent of its revenues from titles produced exclusively for home video release (Melanson, 1984).

In the words of Wolf Schneider, of *The Hollywood Reporter*, the home video industry is 'booming', and can expect to earn sales and rental revenues of $3.3 billion in 1985, 'more than three-quarters of the total domestic box office revenues', according to the Fairfield Group.

> Pre-recorded video cassettes sales are one of the more remarkable sales stories of at least a decade. Hitting a stride of 5 million in 1982, units sales leaped to 11 million in 1983, are expected to hit 18.5 million this year, and are projected at 36.5 million in 1985. Average [wholesale] prices dropped from $30 in 1983, to $24 this year and are expected to plunge to $18 in 1985 (Roth, 1984).

Programme suppliers alone made $754 million in 1984, when more than 25 million videocassettes were sold to distributors (Schneider, August, 1985; September, 1985). Analysts predict that double that number will be sold in 1985 (Schneider, 1985). Estimates are that this increase will give wholesalers $925,000,000 (Bierbaum, 1985). Predictions now forecast a $4 billion market in 1986 (Schneider).

1984 was the homevideo's first 'billion dollar year, in terms of the retail value of [pre-recorded] videocassettes' (Bierbaum, 1985). Sales of pre-recorded video cassettes to American consumers will provide retailers with $1.5 billion in revenues in 1985, approximately 33 per cent of worldwide revenues (Terry, 1984). That estimate, if realised, will amount to a 50 per cent increase over last year's sales of 22,000,000 units, for wholesale revenues of $660,000,000 (Boss, 1985).

Pricing and profits. In 1978, video cassette sales and rentals provided retail store owners with little more than a subsistence income, and did not exist at all as a source of revenue for Hollywood. By 1982, a typical film earned eight per cent of its revenue from the sale of cassettes and discs, according to Wertheim and Company, a New York investment banking house. In 1983, the figure jumped to 13 per cent (Harmetz, 1985). *The Mean Season* earned $4 million during its cinema release in the United States. That amount of revenue is not the mark of a successful box office release. *The Mean Season* was subsequently released for home video distribution, and earned $4.8 million from an initial sale of 60,000 units (Schneider, 1985). New World Video, for example, projected gross earnings for 1985 of $36–41 million, a projection almost equal to the 1984 earnings of its parent company, New World Pictures. An estimate of $1 billion in wholesale video cassette revenues by 1990 is not considered unrealistic by industry observers (Pollack, 1984).

Producers often sell or 'licence' the right to distribute their programmes and films. Separate 'licensing agreements' are sold for each 'exhibition window'; cinema showing; broadcast television; pay cable; home video (see Figure 1). Producers often underwrite production costs with the revenues provided by these licensing agreements. Licence fees are based on an estimate of the programme's earning potential in each exhibition 'window'.

Home video licensing fees have risen dramatically during the past three years, illustrating the increasing sensitivity of programme suppliers toward the profit potential of home video.

> A few months ago, US and Canadian home video cassette rights to the movie *Silkwood* were sold for about $1.5 million. That record was soon broken when similar rights to *Santa Claus – The Movie* sold for $2.6 million. The rights ... were sold ... although the movie has yet to begin production. By comparison ... an average of $400,000 was paid for such rights in 1982, and about $500,000 last year' (Harmetz, 1985).

Even films with middle-range budgets are routinely securing home video licensing agreements worth $1,000,000, and sometimes considerably more (Bierbaum, 1984). This was the profit scenario sketched by two industry spokesmen:

> If you sell 20,000 copies of a poor film and each retail outlet rents it ten to fifteen times, that's 300,000 people to make a success for everybody concerned ... another media couldn't handle those 'numbers' (*Video Industry*, 1985).

According to Dick Kelly, marketing consultant for Cambridge Associates,

> ... Sales of 5,000 can be great, if [...] there has been very low cost in making the product. If a producer can get $39.95 for a cassette, then after duplication costs and low royalty fees that producer can earn between $7 and $11 per cassette before promotion costs ... and can I sell 5,000 with a video consumer base of 16 million? Yes! (*Video Industry*).

The prices that retailers must pay for pre-recorded video cassettes are established by the supplier. The broad range of prices that seems to exist among supplier products reflects not so much consumer popularity of individual titles, but rather a 'fundamental divergence of views on pricing and marketing among the companies that produce videocassettes' (*Video Producers*, 1985). Whether lower prices can lure consumers into buying rather than renting the units is a question not yet fully resolved by the industry. Although members of the home video industry are not uniformly split into clearly identifiable camps on this issue, the sentiments and opinions represented by the two poles of the pricing debate can be generalised.

When end-of-year figures for 1982 sales made it clear that most of the home video business would be done in rentals, programme suppliers considered several options that they believed could maximise their profits. They would have preferred a two-tier pricing schedule – one for rental, another for retail sales; but a provision in the copyright law of the United States prevented it. Instead, the suppliers decided to push prices even higher, in effect cutting themselves in for a share of rental income (Block, 1984).

Retail store operators and their allies argue that exorbitant retail prices 'suggested' by programme suppliers actually inhibit sell-through to consumers. Only about 15 per cent to 20 per cent of the revenues of most video outlets is derived from sales (Pond, 1983). A spokesman for the Electronics Industry Association (EIA) commented, 'Until Hollywood gives us a break and lets the law of supply and demand take over, this will continue to be predominantly a rental market' (Bierbaum, 1985). Most retailers argue, understandably, that if suppliers would lower their wholesale prices consumers would be more likely to purchase pre-recorded materials. Retail sector industry analysts maintain that lower prices could stimulate

> ... impulse buying, and greatly stimulate both the supplier and the retail portions in the industry .... The retailer now lives in the never-never land of trying to turn a movie enough times to equal the cost of buying it. If he sells it, he recovers his costs instantly (Video Producers, 1985).

Marketing stategists for Paramount Home Video tend to agree with these findings. Paramount concluded in 1982 that the home video market was, potentially, a retail market, requiring only more aggressive retail pricing to become a reality. 'We did research two years ago', said Robert Klinginsmith, executive vice president, 'that showed that $19.95 was the point where 88 per cent of the consumers said they would buy a tape' (Video Producers, 1985). The 'sell-through' statistics for titles priced at $25 were almost as good, and provided impetus for Paramount's '25/25' marketing activities during the 1984 Christmas season. Paramount offered consumers an opportunity to purchase any of its twenty-five titles for $25. The promotion resulted in the sales of 1.3 million video cassettes, 'three and one-half items more than we needed to sell to break even at higher prices' (Video Producers, 1985). Paramount executives believed that lowering the wholesale prices of its titles would still allow for an acceptable margin of profit. According to Rich Frank, president of Paramount's Television Group, the wholesale price for a $39.95 video cassette is $25.00. Paramount's cost ... for the tape, reproduction, packaging, wrapping and shipping ... is $12 ... I have to pay the creative participants out of the $13 that is left, but our profit is obviously more than 50 cents (Harmetz, 1984).

The result of Paramount's efforts to increase consumer purchases of its products were immediate. Although Paramount's library accounted for only 1.5 per cent of the nearly 2,000 videocassettes released in 1983, Paramount had 16 per cent of total sales.

Other major programme suppliers were not totally committed to the Paramount philosophy. Executives at Embassy Home Entertainment, for example, believe that lower prices, like the $24.95 price charged by Paramount, will not increase volume as much as it will cut into the profit margin. They believe that a lower price may be effective once a title has reached saturation point within the market.

The [wholesale] prices are way too high .... The figures are well known. It costs us $6 to manufacture a cassette that we sell for $50. That's economic exploitation, not economic value. And the only reason we're doing it is because the retailer is pre-empting us from sharing in the rental income that he is legitimately collecting from the consumer. Added surcharges protect the supplier from that loss of income. I maintain that the consumer will benefit by having somewhat higher rental, but significantly lower sale prices, which means they will have a choice between buying and renting. Today there is no choice (Blay, 1985).

Other members of the home video industry maintain that lowered wholesale prices would not appeal to the consumers at all, but rather, to the retailers. The argue further that consumer purchase decisions are not necessarily price motivated. According to Richard Kelly, president of Cambridge Associates, a marketing company in Stamford, Connecticut,

One school of thought says that if you lower the price, you will only give the stores cheaper rental inventories .... If prices are cut in half, sales have to be quadrupled before profits are matched. (Video Producers, 1985).

Individual wholesale prices established by the suppliers seem to reflect their opinions as to whether a title will sell or rent at the retail level:

If they believe a cassette will flourish only as a rental item, their concern is how high a price retailers are willing to pay. By contrast,

> if a cassette has potential for high sales to VCR owners, the producer
> may slash prices in an effort to inspire high volume (Video
> Producers, 1985)

Most of the major suppliers believe that the majority of people will watch a title only once. Most are unwilling to lower prices on anything other than 'collectibles' and 'cult films' (described below). Also, there seems to be a perpetuating tendency among suppliers not to lower prices, unless all others do, thus diluting the competitive advantage (Video Producers, 1985).

So far, the major programme suppliers have been willing to lower the suggested retail prices for their cinema titles, but only on a limited basis. Fluctuations in home video wholesale prices tend to be associated with special promotional packages, designed to steal numbers from the ranks of the broadcast audience. The Christmas holiday period and the summer months are both lucrative periods for the home video industry. Commercial television network programming schedules in the United States are usually given a short respite from the 'ratings race' during these periods. Accordingly, programming during these times tends to be particularly uneventful. Each of the major suppliers has announced plans to offer special Christmas promotional packages in 1985. These packages will provide reduced wholesale prices for popular video titles, and are expected to double the sales volume for the same period in 1984 (Bierbaum, 1985). Pre-orders based on 1985 Christmas promotions will probably peak at record high levels, estimated to be approximately $44,000,000 in wholesale revenues and approximately $77,000,000 in retail sales (Bierbaum, 1985).

Embassy Home Entertainment was one of the home video suppliers that announced its plans for a Winter Promotion in September. Embassy announced that the wholesale prices for its twenty-five most popular titles would be lowered to under forty dollars, a strategy that had earlier been successful for Paramount. However, Embassy executives acknowledged that early responses to the promotion indicated that 'sell-through' to customers would be out-paced by sales to retailers attempting to extend their rental inventories. Embassy quickly modified its promotional strategy, and encouraged retailers to 'replace old rental copies or stock up for future use during promotion', and targeted stores that weren't carrying titles at the time of the promotion. The company hoped to sell 100,000 units with this winter sales promotion.

When considering the 'pricing debate', it is important to remember that suppliers sell to retailers, not consumers. While the number of VCRs owned by consumers has increased dramatically during the past decade, increases in the number of retail centres have been even greater. Thus, the majority of the pre-recorded tapes sold to date have been 'pipe line fill' sales, sales made to fill the inventories of newly established retail operations (*Billboard*, 1985). Thus, the average number of video cassettes sold in most markets may be more closely related to the number of stores than to the number of VCRs within each region of the market. If the supplier wants to estimate the market's ability to provide revenues to a supplier, perhaps the supplier should divide the VCR population by 1,000, the national ratio of retail centres to VCR households (Bierbaum, 1984).

Intra-Industrial Relationships. A rather intricate web of financial arrangements, licensing conditions, and limited partnerships often connects many suppliers who might otherwise be predisposed to be competitors rather than partners. A detailed accounting of these relationships is not possible here. Several examples may, however, illustrate the point. Embassy Home Entertainment is the subsidiary of Embassy Communications, a company that produces network television programming, and serves as a distributor of syndicated television programming. Embassy Communications was recently purchased by the Coca-Cola Company, a transnational organisation that also owns Columbia Pictures International (CPI). A subsidiary of CPI is involved in a limited partnership with Radio Corporation of America (RCA), in a company named RCA/Columbia Pictures Home Video. Home Box Office (HBO), a subsidiary of Time-Life, Inc, is the dominant pay cable operation in the United States. HBO has entered into a contractual agreement with Orion Pictures International in an effort to get HBO-produced films into the international theatrical and video market place, as well as onto the shelves of United States video retailers. 'HBO is also partnered with Columbia Pictures and CBS [Columbia Broadcasting System] in TriStar, which has been a source of home video product for Columbia and CBS' (Melanson, 1984). According to a report in *The New York Times Magazine,* 'One of the largest [theatre] chains in the US, UA Theatres, has bought heavily into cable systems .... Wometco, a major theatre chain in Florida, has bought subscription television systems in three states (Harmetz, 1982).

Under present methods of operations, distributors are not completely in charge of their destinies. The financial welfare of each distributor dangles rather precariously above a web of credit stretched beneath their activities by the supplier. Suppliers allow distributors a certain line of credit and terms for payment. Credit limits are determined by the supplier's assessment of the distributor's net worth, credit history, and strategic value to the supplier (Blay, 1985). The key to the problem is the capital – intensive nature of the prerecorded video business.

> Large distributors handle from 3,000–5,000 retail stores. An average [pre-recorded] tape costs $40, and a large distributor can carry an inventory of 2,000–3,000 titles. Wholesalers have to lay out $120,000–$200,000 per title, times 2,000–3,000 titles carried if they choose to keep only one copy per title in the inventory. Costs, they say, can rapidly soar into the tens of millions of dollars .... To worsen the problem, only about one third of the titles he carries [current releases and recent theatrical blockbusters] are actually working to pull in bucks and pay off debts (Seideman).

Distributors must work from within a framework of wholesale prices established by the suppliers. The positive economic effect of lowered wholesale prices is often offset by the distributor's need to augment his inventory in order to service an increasing number of retail outlets. Current gross profit margins for the distributors run within a range of 12–20 per cent (Seideman, 1983). Because suppliers have been hesitant to increase credit limits, distributors can only maintain or increase their net profit margins by minimising their inventories, or minimising their costs. The latter tactic usually results in a reduction of services offered to the retail organisation by the distributor. The consequences of either tactic is reduced sales or rental volume at the retail counter.

The retail subsector of the home video industry has undergone significant changes both in the number of stores competing for consumer dollars, as well as in the nature of retail outlets themselves. The arrival of mass merchandisers and the evolution of national video chain stores had made it increasingly difficult for stand-alone shops to remain in business. Competition has been fierce among the smaller retail stores. The failure rate is quite high (although exact statistics were not available). Video speciality stores in North America are bonded with other forms of home video retail operations, albeit loosely so, through membership in trade organisations. Most American video software retailers belong to the Video Software Dealers Association (VSDA), while their Canadian counterparts belong to the Video Retailers Association. Neighbouring retailers have had to cut profit margins in an effort to remain competitive (Kerr).

According to a spokesman of F. Eberstadt and Co, 'Our speculation is that retailing is going to shift away from the 'mom and pop' stores to the larger chains, and new formats for video cassettes are evolving as the market grows. It's really a whole new medium.

Large retail chains were reluctant to enter the video cassette sales and rental market before 1983. A relatively small VCR universe, the high price of pre-recorded video cassettes, and the consumer preference for renting rather than buying pre-recorded materials were reasons cited for mass merchandiser reluctance (Seideman, 1983). The video cassette market failed to provide what mass merchandisers most wanted – a product that sold fast and created a large volume of customer traffic. According to Cy Leslie, Chief Executive Officer for MGM/United artists Home Entertainment Group, 'the problem is the complication of rentals. Among other problems, rentals reduce turnover to such a low rate that the volume-dependent department store chain can't support a rental programme'.

Entrance into the marketplace by companies such as U-Haul, Safeway, Target, and a score of other mass merchandising and grocery stores will change both the nature of retail operations as well as the nature of the software sold or rented to consumers (Wharton, 1985). The initial tendency of mass merchandisers to carry only high-volume software will have a negative impact on the profits of smaller speciality stores by cutting into sales and reducing profit margins (Kerr, 1984). Several analysts have turned to the example provided by the recording industry for a forecast of what may happen to home video speciality stores as mass merchandisers expand their involvement in home video software and hardware activities:

> Estimates are that in the rack-jobbed mass merchandised record industry, 50 per cent of the sales are through giant department store chains. It seems to be the case, insofar as the record industry is concerned, that the speciality stores sell the catalogue, while the mass merchandisers sell the hits. 'And the hits', claimed MGM/UA marketing vice president Bill Gallagher, 'can be worth up to 80 per cent of a supplier's gross sales' (Harmetz, 1984).

HARDWARE/SOFTWARE CONSUMPTION PATTERNS

THE DEMOGRAPHICS OF HOME VIDEO

There is a general paucity of information about the home video consumer. In relation to the millions of dollars spent annually on the production and marketing of materials by the home video industry, very little has been spent in an effort to learn about the consumers who buy or use the products. Marketplace researchers working for hardware manufactures have, indeed, committed considerable money, time, and energy to the study of the consumer. However, most of the summary data that has resulted from all of this 'marketing research' has done little more than compartmentalise consumers into a number of 'purchase potential' catagories. When analysed, the data provide only a very general measure of the consumer's ability to pay, but not necessarily his or her inclination to buy or rent one product rather than another.

Hollywood seems to have very little time for research. When asked to predict a title's potential revenues, corporate eyeballs roll skyward to conjure up educated 'best guesses'. These 'guestimates' are usually based more on recollection, and less on prediction; and in Hollywood, a reputation for accurate guesses can elevate some-one to the status of corporate potentate.

The success of the industry so far has been based on the tendencies of its leaders to look into the future – through a rearview mirror. Change, either in terms of programming content or relationships with other sectors of the entertainment industry, has traditionally been anathema to the motion picture industry. Small wonder, then, that home video took the telefilm production industry completely by surprise. Numerous industry leaders have suggested that the future of home video, at least from the point of view of the producers, will be in the cultivation of the software retail market. Successful development of a retail market for home video software depends, in turn, on continued expansion of the number of VCRs in American (and worldwide) households.

Several studies that attempt to identify those who purchase video cassette recorders and players in demographic terms have been conducted. A recent study concluded by the Electronics Industry Association provided a rough sketch of the average home video hardware 'family' (Table 7). EIA researchers analysed the questionnaires returned by nearly 13,000 respondents who report owning 2,939 video cassette recorders, (a 23 per cent penetration). Of the total number of VCRs identified by the study, 29 per cent were owned by two-member households; 32 per cent of the VCRs were owned by younger adults, ages 20–39 years (EIA Colour Television, 1985). These findings were echoed by a research study compiled by Frost and Sullivan Inc. (Home Entertainment, 1985) and the Fairfield Group, Inc. (Video Hardware, 1985).

The consumer of home video software can be categorised as belonging to one of a number of more or less discrete groups: those who own their own home video hardware, and purchase their own software; those who own their own hardware, but rent the majority of the software; those who rent both the hardware and the software (Home Entertainment, 1985). A discrete software consumption pattern is beginning to form within each of these groups (Harmetz, 1983).

Of the three groups, those who own VCRs will be more inclined to purchase video software. In terms of diffusion, the consumers who bought VCRs during the first nine years of home video's development in North America can be generalised as early or 'first wave' consumers. 'The early purchasers of machines tended to be single member households, upwardly mobile, which meant that they used their machines for a quick release of pleasure, as opposed to something long-term' (Blay, 1985). For Blay and other suppliers, 'quick release of pleasure' reflects a consumer demand for entertainment program-ming. Over 83 per cent of the total dollar volume of pre-recorded software has been spent by consumers to rent or buy general entertainment program-ming. 'Quick release' is further implied by the ratio of software rental to purchase volume. The revenues derived from rentals to Canadian consumers are greater than those in the American market. Over 95 per cent of the retail volume in Canada is created by rental (Devins, 1984). Software rental is more often provoked by impulse than by pre-determined needs. Further study is called for with respect to consumer purchase/rental motivations. Nonetheless, the increasing number of video software rental racks located in grocery stores, service stations and other convenience shops suggests that attempts by wholesalers to appeal to the impulsive nature of the North American consumer have been successful.

Home Video Hardware: Uses

The first home video format introduced in the American marketplace was dropped into the murky waters of copyright law. In October 1981, the United States Court of Appeals for the Ninth Circuit in San Francisco ruled that it was the manufacturers and retailers of home video recorders who were liable when consumers recorded copyrighted material. Although the matter was ulti-mately resolved by the United States Supreme Court (with a favourable finding for the home video hardware industry), the interim legal uncertainties had a dampening impact on the promotional strategies of manufacturers and retailers. VCRs were promoted and sold on the basis of their abilities to record 'home movies' of family activities.

Notwithstanding that home video recorders were produced with antenna and cable input receptacles as well as channel tuning mechanisms, the fact that the hardware could be used to record broadcast and cable programming 'off-air' was never actively promoted by the manufacturers. Consumers had to work that out for themselves.

Recording television programmes for viewing at a subsequent time had been the primary function of most VCRs purchased by consumers in North America. Neilsen surveys of Canadian home video users found that 75 per cent considered time-shifting as the primary purpose served by the hardware (Canadian VCR Use, 1985). A similar finding was made a survey of American VCR owners. Time-shift viewing served several purposes. First, time-shift viewing gave the comsumer greater control over the programme schedule, allowing him or her to watch news, sports and entertainment programming at a time different from its scheduled broadcast (Ogan, 1985).

> Daytime network soaps (serials) still hold the number one position in percentage of total VCR recording in the home, with motion pictures in second place .... The diaries established that there was more household recording of primetime programming and more recording of programming while the viewer was watching another channel (time-shifting), than before .... The study revealed a large increase in recording of network shows, and a decrease in that of independent and PTV [shows] ... *All My Children* was the most recorded show, however the programme is available for taping 20 times per month (Denis, 1984).

The study suggested that time-shifting created a new market for the broadcast advertiser. It was discovered that the audience created by time-shifting recording and playback was younger, and more upwardly mobile than was the audience for the original day-time broadcast. The survey also concluded that the types of programming recorded for time-shift viewing changed with the seasons. More 'off-air' programming was recorded during the fall and winter periods, periods of new programming and increased competition among the three commercial networks. The commercial networks lapsed into their repeat schedules in spring and summer. Accordingly, time-shift viewing of pay and subscription cable programming increased. Secondly, time-shift viewing allowed the consumer to watch a number of programmes broadcast simultaneously by different programme services.

More recently, a second function – television displacement – has emerged, as more and more pre-recorded titles become available from which to select an evening's entertainment. The percentage of individuals purchasing or renting pre-recorded cassettes increased, nearly doubling to 70 per cent (Neil-sen's VCR, 1984). In areas of limited media diversity, the VCR tends to be used for the showing of taped films rather than time-shifting (Ogan, 1985).

> Nearly 57 per cent of the VCR owners who had purchased their machines within the previous year indicated that the availability of pre-recorded materials was an important factor in the purchase decision (Harmetz, 1984).

Patterns of Home Video Software Consumption

Video cassette recorders in the home have transformed the experience of watching television. Home video has made the viewer a more active participant, more actively engaged in programme selection. Moreover, home video recorders have made the relationship between the user and the software more print-like and less television-like. The new video technologies allow the user to browse through video materials much as one might browse through a book.

Of the greatest importance to the producers and suppliers of video programming is the fact that home video has whetted the appetites of its users for greater quantities and different types of programme fare. This anecdote appeared in a recent edition of *The New York Times*:

> 'What did you get?' said one man to another.
> 'The *Philadelphia Experiment*', the second answered.
> 'Why?'
> 'Another guy was about to get it.'
> 'Closing time,' said Mr Medwick, 'is like closing time at a bar. People get desperate, and they'll go home with anything'.

In 1983, most cassettes that were rented or purchased by consumers were repackaged films. 'My customers want to rent a movie that's still playing in theatres', said one Los Angeles retailer. 'The movie can be garbage, but they still want to be able to say, 'it's still playing in theatres, and I already saw it on tape' (Harmetz, 1983). Feature films made up 86 per cent of home video revenues in 1984. Recent releases provide up to 70 per cent of the pre-recorded videocassette sales and rental business, but make up only 30 per cent of the total number of titles a distributor has to carry (Seideman, 1984).

> While the top ten is the top ten everywhere, there are regional differences. Billy Dee Williams and Diana Ross are popular video stock in Detroit (large black population); *The Godfather* is popular in New York City. 'That's the closest thing to a family home movie,' said Morowitz of Video Shack (Harmetz, 1983).

147

'Of the top 10 best selling videocassettes ... only two, *Jane Fonda's Workout*, and *The Making of Thriller*' were *not* films released to cinemas within the last seven years' (Pollack, 1984). Music videos accounted for less than 2.9 per cent (Kerr, 1984, p42). In the American market, music videos have been popular only in isolated instances. Vestron sold 850,000 units of *The Making of Michael Jackson's 'Thriller*', priced at $29.95 retail. No other titles have been able to surpass that retail sales record. Ranked second is RCA/Columbia's *We are The World* which sold 225,000 units. In 1984, several programmes sold 100,000 units, and many more reached the 'gold' plateau with 20,000 units or $800,000 in needed retail sales. A few more earned 'platinum' awards with the sale of 40,000 units for $1.6 million retail sales (Schneider, 1985). Industry experts like Robert Blattner (RCA/Columbia Home Video Press), agree that concept pieces sell better than pure concerts (Schneider, 1985).

The present share of pre-recorded video software dollar volume controlled by music video titles hovers at just under three per cent. It is estimated however, that by 1988, films should hold only a 50 per cent share, with music videos taking at least 15 per cent of the total sales and rental dollar volume. (Bierbaum, 1984; Kerr, 1984; Melanson, 1985). Music videos provided $40,000,000 in sales in 1984. Analysts anticipate that earnings will increase to $1.25 billion by 1988 (Terry, 1984).

'Each new medium creats its own form of programming. Just as early television borrowed from vaudeville and Broadway, later developing its own type of programmes, home video will borrow from the old and create the new' (Terry, 1984). Industry experts believe that music videos will be one source of programming that can be used to replace the dwindling supply of feature film titles available for pre-recorded cassette sales and rentals.

> The rising number of VCRs is spawning an industry of original programming for the home video market. Tapes featuring self-improvement, instruction, music, original comedy, and children's programming are flooding the market. Industry analysts estimate that original programming accounted for ten per cent of the $900 million in gross revenues in 1984. A number of experts expect it to total 25 per cent of sales by 1990 (Ames, 1985).

The current volume of sales in each programme content category may, in fact, reflect availability more accurately than popularity. Suppliers, until recently, have released existing inventory, and have been unwilling to produce materials specifically designed for the home video market. When they have produced for home video, the programme contents have been little more than timid copies of mass entertainment programming.

According to a spokesman for Embassy Home Entertainment, while 'how-to's' make up but a small percentage of the video cassette market at present, (approximately 2.7 per cent), 'there is an iceberg out there ... and it's going to surface and surface big'. Eicher believes that the market for original 'How-to's' will probably double over the next year, 'primarily through the increased involvement of publishers and chains of bookstores – where original programming sales can really take off' (Bierbaum, 1984).

According to marketing analysts at Embassy Home Entertainment,

> The second wave of VCR purchases will herald the wave of potential customers for 'How-To' types of programming .... It may require 40 per cent penetration before this market evolves, and there is still a likelihood that it won't happen. We happen to believe in it because it does manifest itself in the publishing industry in terms of how people spend their free time. People are interested in being better people, citizens (Blay, 1985).

Star presence seems to be the one factor that consistently contributes to increase the sales potential of an instructional video; the only way these tapes will get attention. So far, stores have been reluctant to stock instructional programmes. Even Jane Fonda's workout was a hard sell at first.

Not everybody is as enthusiastic about the likelihood of a boom in the sales of the original or 'made-for' programme materials. According to Eric Doctorow of Paramount, until 'the retail base becomes more aggressive and understands the importance of merchandising for sale, it's going to be very difficult to crack the sales barrier with them' (Bierbaum, 1984). A spokesman for Vestron Video indicated that most instructional videos reached retail sales of not more than 5,000 units.

> 'Anything more than that is considered successful. If you reach 20,000, you're very successful, at 30,000 you have a moneymaker, and if you reach 100,000 you're home free' (Bierbaum, 1984).

> While exercise tapes and music videos are big sellers, the average tape rarely sells more than 10,000 copies – far below the 40,000 units that a popular film sells (Ames, 1985).

At a recent seminar for Homevideo Production convened at the University of Southern California, participants cited a range of production budgets for original materials at approximately $40,000–$50,000.

The videocassette industry started with pornography, but the proportion of X-rated material has dropped dramatically, from 25 per cent in one store in 1981, to 18 per cent in that same store in 1983 (Harmetz, 1983). The national average total dollar volume share for adult materials is presently 13 per cent. The figures are somewhat higher in urban areas than in rural and outlying regions of the country.

VIDEO SOFTWARE SALES AND RENTALS

In terms of total retail dollar volume, nearly 85 per cent was derived from software rentals in 1984. As was mentioned earlier, Canadian rental figures are somewhat higher. The rental-to-sales ratio has actually increased since 1982.

> According to a 1982 Neilsen home video survey, 70 per cent of those who own VCRs rent films on cassettes, and 24 per cent purchase pre-recorded materials .... Instructional material, music videos, and children's cassettes have a somewhat higher sales percentage, but renting, rather than buying, is clearly the norm (Video Producers, 1985).

The rental market caught Hollywood napping. The main reason why retailers rented, was because they couldn't afford to stock more than two copies of a cassette. The suppliers soon found that they couldn't do anything about rentals. The predilection of suppliers for higher wholesale prices perpetuated a consumer inclination to rent rather than purchase programming that, for them, had little, if any extended utility. Many within the industry, both from the production as well as from the retail subsectors, argue that the future of home video is in retail sales, not rental. Success in the retail sales market means, among other factors, lower prices. 'Homevideo is not a rental business. And as long as you regard it as a rental market, you won't be a part of the business that is going to be as strong as anything in the entertainment industry' (Bierbaum, 1984). Although there have been some isolated instances where retail centres have emphasised retail sales over rental, most of the calls for change have not moved beyond rhetoric.

The Fairfield Group, a video consulting company, reported that there were 150 million cassette rental transactions last year (1984). A videocassette that can be purchased for $80, can be rented overnight for $2 to $5. Only 1 in 10 is sold to consumers. The other nine are sold to retailers who rent them out. MPAA president Valenti said that eight million cassettes were sold in 1983. (Harmetx, 1984). Twenty five or more rentals a month for each cassette of a popular film are fairly common (Crook, 1983).

The factors that promote sale rather than rental of a title often include not only the retail price of a title, but also its format and genre. Price is often a secondary consideration.

CONCLUSION

In order for the software retail market to flourish, VCR ownership must expand into the second wave of consumers and usage patterns. The second wave population is comprised, among others, of households with four or more members (adults and children), whose head-of-household will be in the 40–49 age group.

The second wave of consumers will probably consider the VCR as an essential rather than as an electric toy or novelty.

According to industry experts, sociologists and consumer analysts, the second wave of VCR consumption and use is about to wash over the United States. It will probably occur in Canada within the next few years. Rather than being undiscerning or compulsive users of the technology, the second wave of users will have learned to use it in a way that's best for them. The second wave of home video users will most probably be comprised of consumers who initially put aside the purchase of home video hardware so that other needs could be satisfied. '... family, education, raising children, buying their first mortgage, buying all the goods necessary to outfit a house ... you can think of a thousand reasons to delay purchase of a VCR' (Blay, 1985).

Researchers have as yet not clearly defined the factors that will drive the second wave consumer to the hardware marketplace. While the popularity of entertainment programming will doubtless continue across both categories of consumers, the programming needs of the second wave will probably be broader. Home video hardware will be used to satisfy instructional as well as entertainment needs, and will be used to fulfill the more individualised needs of household members. The arrival of second wave consumers in the home video marketplace may be implied by the data pertaining to children's programming. Nearly 17 per cent of 1984 video software dollar volume in North America was derived from the sale and rental of children's programming, music videos, and 'how to' (instructional) programmes, up nearly 85 per cent from 1982. The dollar volume of total software sales and rentals of children's and non-entertainment programming has increased steadily since 1981. These programme types are more often purchased rather than rented by consumers.

TABLE 1

PERCENTAGE OF BASIC CABLE, PAY CABLE, AND HOME VIDEO PENETRATION IN UNITED STATES TELEVISION HOUSEHOLDS BY DESIGNATED MARKET AREAS (DMAs), MAY-JULY, 1985*

DMAs	TV homes (millions)	Cable in TV homes	Pay in TV homes	Pay in cable homes	VCR in TV homes	VCR in cable homes	VCR in pay homes	VCR but no cable
1-10	26.6	37.3	25.1	67.3	30.3	36.1	39.8	26.9
11-20	11.2	41.9	25.9	61.8	24.2	28.4	33.5	21.1
21-50	18.9	47.7	28.2	59.1	20.1	23.6	28.9	17.0
51-100	16.7	50.0	27.1	54.1	18.0	21.4	26.9	14.6
100+	11.8	54.8	26.0	47.4	17.7	20.4	26.4	14.4
U.S.	84.8	45.1	26.4	58.3	23.1	26.4	32.0	20.4

*Sources: A. C. Neilsen Company; *Video Week*

TABLE 2

SUPPLIER REVENUES AND COMMAND OF HOME VIDEO MARKET-PLACE, 1984 (IN THOUSANDS OF DOLLARS)

Supplier	Revenues	1984 Market Share %
CBS/Fox Video	128,000	17.0
Paramount Home Video	115,000	15.0
Vestron Home Video	84,480	11.0
Warner Home Video	64,512	8.4
Disney Home Video	61,440	8.0
RCA/Colombia Home Video	58,368	7.6
MGM/UA Home Video	44,544	5.8
Thorn EMI/HBO	34,560	4.5
Embassy Home Ent	31,488	4.1
All Others	102,912	13.4

Source: *The Hollywood Reporter* ; *Video Week* ; *TV Digest*

TABLE 3

AFMA SALES BY COUNTRY AND MEDIA PERCENT OF TOTAL, 1984

Market	Theatrical	Television	Video	Total
Europe				
United Kingdom	6.38	2.17	9.08	17.73
France	4.99	0.15	5.08	10.22
Federal Republic of				
Germany/Austria	3.97	1.23	5.14	10.34
Italy	3.94	6.58	0.22	10.74
Spain	3.03	0.04	1.29	4.36
Other Countries	7.42	0.29	5.49	13.20
Total	29.73	10.46	26.30	66.49
Latin America				
Mexico	1.19	0.13	0.05	1.37
Brazil	0.19	0.08	0.01	0.28
Venezuela	0.78	0.01	0.01	0.80
Other Countries	3.18	0.21	0.01	3.40
Total	5.34	0.43	0.08	5.85
South and East Asia				
Japan	4.90	2.35	0.78	8.03
Other Countries	4.20	0.19	0.11	4.50
Total	9.10	2.54	0.89	12.53
Other				
Australia	5.58	1.56	3.76	10.90
South Africa	1.64	0.21	1.06	2.91
All Other Countries	0.74	0.43	0.15	1.32
Total	7.96	2.20	4.97	15.13
Total 1984 sales	52.13	15.63	32.24	100.00

*Source: *Daily Variety*

TABLE 4

1984 PERCENTAGE OF RETAIL VIDEO SOFTWARE VOLUME BY HARDWARE FORMAT*

Format	American percentage	Canadian percentage
VHS	72	76
BETA	14	22
LASER	4	0.5
CED	14	1.5

*Source: Statistics Canada; Variety; Devins;

TABLE 5

GROWTH AND PENETRATION OF NORTH AMERICAN HOME VIDEO, 1978-1984 (IN THOUSANDS OF UNITS)*

Year	TV house-holds	America 'uni-verse'	VCR pene-tration	TV house-holds	Canada 'uni-verse'	VCR pene-tration
1978	73,300	175	0.2%	-	%	
1979	73,900	575	0.8%	-	45	%
1980	76,400	1,100	1.4%	-	228	%
1981	77,800	1,900	2.4%	-	228	%
1982	82,000	3,860	4.7%	-	569	%
1983	83,000	9,000	11.0%	-	1,303	%
1984	84,800	16,000	23.0%	8,857	2,001	22.5%

* Sources: Home Video and Cable Yearbook, 1982 1983; Electronics Industry Association; Broadcasting

TABLE 6

WORLDWIDE SHARE OF MAJOR JAPANESE VCR MANUFAC-
TURERS, 1983-1984 (THOUSANDS OF UNITS)

Manufacturer	1983 Prod	% Share	1984 Prod	% Share
Matsushita	5,150	28	6,655	24.5
JVC	3,100	17	4,665	17.2
Hitachi	2,000	11	3,945	14.5
Sony	2,150	12	2,500	9.2
Sharp	1,500	8	2,470	9.1
Share by format				
VHS	13,360	75	21,775	80.3
Beta	4,610	25	5,349	19.7

TABLE 7

DEMOGRAPHIC PROFILE FOR U.S. OWNERS OF ELECTRONIC
PERIPHERALS

	VCR %	Home computer %	Video game %	Basic cable TV %	Pay cable TV %	Video disc player %	All U. S. house-holds %
Household size							
One	17	10	8	20	16	15	23
Two	29	22	17	32	28	28	32
Three	21	20	23	19	21	19	18
Four	20	28	29	18	21	18	16
Five or more	13	21	23	12	14	19	12
Income							
Less than $10,000	9	8	10	15	9	17	24
$10,000-$14,999	8	8	11	13	9	13	14
$15,000-$24,999	21	20	24	25	24	23	24
$25,000-$39,999	31	33	31	27	30	20	23
$40,000 and above	31	31	23	20	27	26	16
Age							
Under 10	20	15	21	17	20	18	21
30-39	32	40	42	26	34	25	22
40-49	20	25	23	18	21	25	16
50-59	16	14	11	17	15	15	15
60+	11	6	4	22	10	16	26

N = 2,939   1,639   3,164   4,339   2,545   201

TABLE 8

SELECTED SALES OF MUSIC VIDEO RECORD, 1983 – PRESENT

Title	Units sold	Price	Supplier
The Making of 'Thriller'	850,000	$ 29.95	Vestron
We Are The World	225,000	14.95	RCA/Columbia
Video Rewind	200,000	29.95	Vestron
Title	Units sold	Price	Supplier
The Complete Beatles	200,000	59.95	Vestron
Do They Know It's			
Xmas	130,000	9.95	Vestron
All Night Long	125,000	14.95	MusicVision (RCA/Col susid)

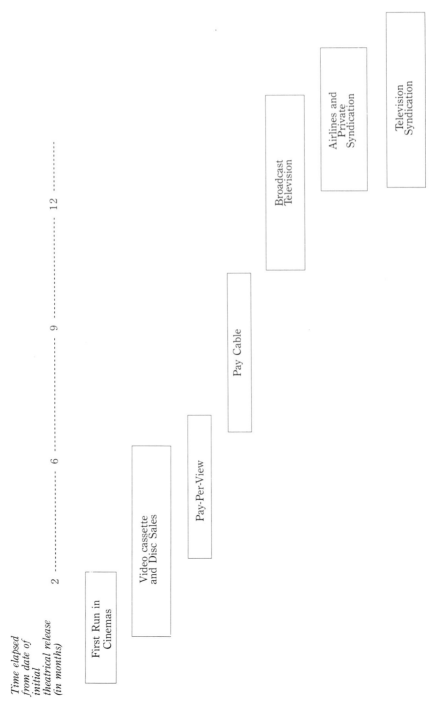

FIGURE 1
EXHIBITION WINDOWS (1984)

*Time elapsed
from date of
initial
theatrical release
(in months)*

2 — 6 — 9 — 12

First Run in Cinemas

Video cassette and Disc Sales

Pay-Per-View

Pay Cable

Broadcast Television

Airlines and Private Syndication

Television Syndication

FIGURE 2

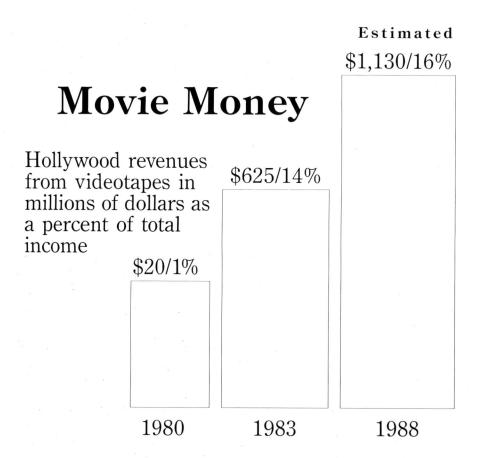

Estimated
$1,130/16%

Movie Money

Hollywood revenues from videotapes in millions of dollars as a percent of total income

$625/14%

$20/1%

1980   1983   1988

Chapter 10

THE GULF STATES, JORDAN AND EGYPT

Several media have made an impact on the developing world since mass communication has been perceived as a means to promote national development. Following what has been called the 'transistor revolution', radio has been the most cost effective medium, because it reaches large numbers of people both quickly and inexpensively. More expensive than radio for the broadcaster as well as for the individual viewer, television has proved an effective development tool when used to achieve specific ends, even though the majority of television programming in the Third World entertains rather than educates.

One common advantage of the broadcast media is ease of control; they originate from central production and transmission complexes where those responsible can influence the content of news, education and entertainment.

The home video cassette recorder (VCR) introduces an entirely different dimension to home entertainment. This seemingly neutral consumer item has altered the broadcasting establishment in some Third World countries to the extent that television stations no longer provide all that viewers see. The acquisition of a VCR implies the purchase, renting or borrowing of programming on cassette and as a result the owner has control over what is viewed. VCRs in effect, give owners the ability to become their own television station programme directors. This means that VCR owners are no longer limited to the programmes offered by domestic television – whether organised by a government, a public corporation, or the private sector.

Certain factors in both the developing and the industrialised world influence the percentage of VCR ownership. Some of these factors are:

– *Level of income* Countries with high per capita Gross National Products (GNP) have high VCR ownership. As one might expect, Kuwait, with a 1982 GNP of $19,610, has a much higher VCR penetration than does Egypt, whose 1982 GNP was $670 (*The World Bank Atlas*, 1985).

— *Expatriate workers* Large numbers of Middle Eastern and Asian expatriates working in the oil-rich Gulf states bring VCRs home during visits or when completing assignments. Most Gulf countries do not tax consumer electronics goods, thereby making them much less expensive than in the worker's home country.

— *Limited television programming* Where only a few channels are available for certain periods of the day, people are more predisposed to purchase VCRs in order to satisfy their own viewing tastes. In the small number of countries where there is no television broadcasting, VCRs are the only means of enjoying the medium.

— *Controlled television news and entertainment* Where governments, private broadcasters, or public corporations present heavily controlled news and entertainment, viewers acquire VCRs in an attempt to gain control of what they see.

— *Political activity* VCRs may also be used as a means of communicating political points of view.

While these are by no means the only factors affecting the acquisition of home video cassette recorders, they provide the basis for a discussion of the impact this consumer device is having in the Arab states.

Not all countries in the region could be studied and this report concentrates on the Gulf states and two individual countries. The Gulf states have played a vital role in the use and spread of VCRs in the region. It was in this region that the machines were first acquired in large numbers. Jordan has been chosen for particular study as a country which represents an intermediate stage between that of the wealthy Gulf states and of the second country in this study, Egypt, where expatriate workers in the Gulf have imported substantial numbers of machines. While poor in comparison with the Gulf states and Jordan, Egypt is the largest producer of film and video tape material in Arabic.

ELECTRONIC MEDIA

There are obvious pitfalls in generalising about any geographical area. Yet common factors in the Arab states, including the development of television are important to an understanding of the role of video cassette recorders and the programming used with them.

The Arabic language is an important cohesive force in the region. Although an Algerian speaks an Arabic which differs from that of a Yemeni, the two can communicate in the neo-classical form of the language. The Egyptian film industry, active since the late 1920s, made the Cairene dialect universally understood, even before television became widespread in the Arab states.

There is also some international television viewing in the Arab states. During hot, humid weather, television and FM radio signals travel beyond line-of-sight, or 'tunnel', in the Gulf, Red Sea, and Suez Canal areas. A viewer in Dhahran, Saudi Arabia, may view as many as 12 different channels, ten of which are non-Saudi signals.

In all Arab states television is operated either directly by the government or through a quasi-government corporation, usually one that reports to the Ministry of Information.

Television broadcasters receive little or no formal scientific feedback from the audience. It is not the practice of these broadcasters to undertake research providing information about programme preferences or research exploring the uses of television among viewers. Most reliable research data comes from surveys commissioned by manufacturers in search of information about consumer brand preferences or from Western international radio broadcasters gathering audience estimates.

Most Arab television systems carry advertising. However, advertising income provides only a small portion of the systems' operating and capital revenue. Governments provide most of the financing for television broadcasting.

Many Arab states have a second television channel, which may cater for Western expatriates or the Western tastes of their own citizens. There is a great deal of television programming imported from the United States and the United Kingdom.

In the Arab region television is extremely popular. During the hot summer months people become more home-bound and television plays an important role in leisure activity. The medium is ideal for the Arab culture with its strong family ties and tradition of entertaining family and friends at home. There is little competition for television in some countries where there are often no nightclubs, few cinemas and little live theatre.

Every country in the region uses the CCIR 625-line standard, even though they do not all use the same colour system. The Gulf states, except Saudi Arabia, use the German PAL, while other countries such as Egypt and Syria transmit colour via the French SECAM system. (See Table 1 for television and VCR data on the Arab countries included in this study).

Finally, some Gulf states have extremely high VCR penetration rates.

THE GULF STATES

Kuwait, Saudi Arabia, Bahrain, Qatar, the United Arab Emirates and Oman share historical, linguistic, economic, and political backgrounds to an extent that makes it possible to examine them collectively. With enough in common and sufficient motivation to co-operate in areas such as defence, telecommunications, fiscal planning, and broadcasting, they formed the Gulf Cooperative Council (GCC).

In these countries consumer electronic equipment is inexpensive because there is little or no tax on such imports. High disposable income among citizens and resident expatriates provides the thriving retail electronic business with a steady stream of customers.

In Kuwait and the United Arab Emirates fewer than half of the population are citizens; expatriates from other Arab states (mostly Jordan, Lebanon, Egypt, and the Yemen), Asian countries such as India and Pakistan, and some Western countries make up a substantial, although temporary, part of the population.

English is widely used as a second language in the Gulf states. This is due in part to the close association these states, excepting Saudi Arabia, had with the United Kingdom up to the late 1960s. These states, excepting Oman, have second television channels devoted mostly to foreign-made English-language programming and they are the countries which constitute the world's most active per capita home video market.

THE BEGINNING OF THE VCR EXPLOSION

As early as 1968 a small number of residents of Saudi Arabia who travelled frequently to Europe, Japan, and the United States brought back half inch reel-to-reel Sony video tape recorders, used at that time by educational institutions and industry. Although crude by modern VCR standards, the recorders did allow owners to tape monochrome programmes directly from television for later playback. Most of the materials recorded were Egyptian and Western films shown occasionally on the Saudi Arabian government channel.

Saudi Arabia is the only Arab country with no public cinemas. Since the 1950s a small industry has been allowed by the government to rent 16 mm projectors and films to families for home entertainment. This was an expensive and cumbersome undertaking; video tape was a way of viewing films without renting or purchasing a projector. Most people in the kingdom already had a television set and, they reasoned, all they needed was a video tape recorder to attach to it.

The reel-to-reel machines did not become popular. They were difficult to service locally, people had trouble threading them, and there was little available material, other than that taped off-the-air. Those with an interest in home programming were ready for something new.

In 1972 an American working for the Sony dealer in Riyadh began to import and sell three-quarter inch U-Matic video tape machines. These, however, were manufactured for the American industrial and educational market and used the American 525 line system. Many were sold in Saudi Arabia and could be operated there when linked to multi-standard (525/625 NTSC, PAL, SECAM) sets marketed almost exclusively at the time by Sony. These machines were more reliable then the reel-to-reel models and they were easier to operate. It was also possible to obtain some pre-recorded material for them, despite the obvious disadvantage of one-hour U-Matic cassettes. By 1974, after the 1973 price increase of OPEC oil, the number of Western and Asian companies in the kingdom had increased. These organisations understood the problems of keeping workers content when not on the job in a country where most did not have families with them, where there is no public entertainment, and where alcohol is forbidden. Television programmes and films on tape were thought to be an important part of keeping workers happy and motivated under difficult working conditions.

Some of these programmes found their way to the homes of Saudi Arabia with U-Matic machines. U-Matic material became available locally from other sources: internal cable systems both in new hotels catering to business travel and in new health care facilities such as the King Faisal hospital in Riyadh.

The U-Matic tape standard was successful for the Japanese manufacturers who adopted the format, but it was primarily intended for the business rather than the home market. In the meantime, video tape technology improved so that machines using smaller, slower moving tape could be used. The first success was Sony's Beta format introduced in the region in the mid-1970s. Saudi Arabia, Kuwait, and the United Arab Emirates were better markets during this period because their oil-based economies were accelerating faster than those in Bahrain, Qatar and Oman.

The Beta and later the VHS format VCRs were an immediate success in the Gulf States. First, a large percentage of the local and expatriate population could afford them. Second, they recorded and played back colour, and Gulf television stations had converted to colour by the late 1970s. Third, seemingly overnight a wide variety of taped material was available.

Some VCR owners recorded programmes off-the-air for playback at a later time. But the advantage of taped material obtained from a source other than television is that it is not usually censored. Western television programmes, Western feature films, Egyptian films and television programmes, and probably pornographic material were available.

Social and economic conditions contribute to the appeal of taped material for home use in the Gulf. Most social events are family centred; people usually entertain family and friends at home rather than going out. The working day is short (usually from 8:30am until 2:00pm six days a week), thus leaving abundant leisure time. Finally, the excessively warm and humid climate keeps the relatively affluent in an air conditioned environment for a large part of the year. Sohair A Barakat profiles the interest Kuwaitis have in VCRs, an interest not unique among Gulf states.

> Kuwait is probably the video land of the world. Tax-free sales of video recorders, and the sale or rental of video cassettes, are a booming and very profitable business. Video watching is becoming a daily habit for increasing numbers of people. A favourite topic for conversation among friends, as well as for press comment, is the latest tape titles available for rental and/or the new features of the latest recorder models available in the market. To some extent,

most of these developments are to be found in other Gulf states. But Kuwait is a pace-setter among her neighbours (1983).

VCR PROGRAMMING IN THE GULF

What was at first the informal acquisitions of VCR programmes by individuals who brought pre-recorded cassettes back from abroad or copied tapes of family members or friends quickly became rather formalized. The business opportunities of selling or renting material were immediately obvious to Gulf residents already involved in the electronics business. Money was to be made not only by supplying the home market, but also by supplying material to hotels, to companies with large numbers of expatriates, and even to crews on oil tankers.

Ministries of Information had difficulty in keeping up with the rapid proliferation of VCRs. They were aware of the phenomenon but did not realize how rapidly VCRs would spread and did not anticipate the innovativeness and determination of owners in obtaining video material. By the time ministries came to enact rules regulating the type of material permitted locally, it was too late. It is difficult to view every tape legally imported; it is impossible to censor what has already entered the country illegally.

VCR OWNERSHIP

When machines started appearing in the late 1970s they were purchased by the more affluent. VCRs were a new gadget to add to television and home audio equipment. As prices decreased, more middle-income families purchased machines and some families with one machine purchased another. The second VCR was important for duplicating material owned by others or rented from video shops. Many second machines were of a different standard; VHS owners often purchased Beta machines and vice versa.

Japanese manufacturers quickly sensed the direction of the Gulf market and sets capable of handling multiple television colour standards were imported through local agents. This way an owner could play any tape which might come into his possession. Several companies make multi-standard VCRs, but JVC has been successful in the Gulf with models such as the HR-7600MS. This five-system machine will play PAL, two SECAM systems (the Arab states and French standards) and two NTSC systems – 3.58 and 4.43 mhz. It is of course much more expensive than the one-system set, but the high disposable income in the area that allows many to afford higher priced VCRs must be borne in mind.

A check of retail stores in Bahrain in August, 1984, and in Kuwait in February and March, 1985, showed that most machines for sale are dual standard. They can play PAL as well as ME SECAM (Middle East SECAM standard) tapes. Having the option of playing tapes of both standards is particularly important in the Gulf because tapes from Egypt tend to be SECAM (the colour system used in Egypt) and most Western films and television programmes are PAL (the system in the United Kingdom from which about half of the Western material originates).

Prices of VCRs have dropped since 1982, particularly for the less well known brand one-system machines without remote control. Many citizens of the Gulf States purchasing VCRs in the late 1970s or early 1980s now have second generation units capable of being operated with hand-held wired or wireless remote control units. In March, 1985, it was possible in Kuwait to buy a VCR without remote control capable of playing both PAL and SECAM ME tapes for about $350.00, a price most people can afford in Kuwait.

The number of VCRs in the Gulf can only be estimated. Even if accurate figures of machines imported by each country were available, they would not accurately depict the number of VCRs in that country. The reason for this is to be found in the labour market in the Gulf. There are large numbers of expatriate workers from other Arab states and from India, Pakistan, and Far Eastern countries. An estimated one-third to one-half of VCRs sold in the Gulf are taken out of the country when workers return home.

Machines are also commercially smuggled to other countries. VCRs find their way to India and Sri Lanka by the traditional means of Gulf-Asian trade, the Arab sailing boat called a dhow. Yemeni workers in Saudi Arabia bring back VCRs; those without the opportunity to purchase machines to bring home can simply buy them in Yemen. There is a well established truck route from the Red Sea port of Jidda to Yemen and specialised VCR smugglers take them from near the Saudi Arabia-Yemen border in four-wheel drive trucks to distributors in urban areas.

The percentage of homes with VCRs is more easily determined because some survey data are available. In 1982 Kuwait's Pan Arab Research Centre, a Gallup affiliate, undertook survey research on behalf of VCR manufacturers to determine brand and format preferences as well as to learn something about how people used VCRs. The research was done in both Kuwait and Saudi Arabia and indicated that more than half of all homes with television sets also owned video cassette recorders.

> In 1982, 52.7 per cent of Kuwaiti homes with television sets owned VCRs, just over 20 per cent owned more than one machine. 1981 was the most important year for VCR purchases – 28.2 per cent said they purchased units during this year (Pan Arab Research Centre, 1984, October).
>
> In 1982, 61.4 per cent of Saudi Arabian television homes owned VCRs. About 17 per cent owned more than one machine. Also, in Saudi Arabia 1981 was an important year for VCR purchases – 27.6 per cent said they first acquired machines this year (Pan Arab Research Centre, 1984).

In late 1984, another survey was done and preliminary results show that the percentage of ownership has increased dramatically. In Kuwait 85 per cent of television homes have VCRs and it is anticipated that by the end of 1985 the market will be saturated (Sami Raffoul, personal communication, Kuwait, 9 Feb, 1985).

Bakhaider (1981) found in his survey of VCR usage in Jidda, Saudi Arabia, that all 120 respondents owned machines. In Gulf homes, a VCR is as common as a refrigerator.

Based on available survey data, discussions with media experts, and personal visits to Gulf states, the following figures are estimates of the percentage of television owners with VCRs in the six Gulf States.

1985 VCR Ownership
Television owners with VCRs

COUNTRY	%
Kuwait	85
Saudi Arabia	75
Bahrain	60
Qatar	70
UAE	80
Oman	55

Regulation of Video Cassette Programming

Retail businesses in the Gulf operate informally. Most states abolished all taxes after the increase in oil income in 1974, so tax records are not available on imported goods. There continues to be smuggling of contraband goods, via long and difficult-to-police coastal areas and desert borders. Video cassettes occasionally enter this way, but it is not the way most programming reaches the Gulf states.

Most of what is imported comes in legally with approval from the Ministries of Information. Egyptian and Western 'family' films come in this way, but 'adult' material or programming thought to be against prevailing political or religious beliefs enters without government knowledge. It only takes one video cassette, a master copy, to produce sufficient material for the market.

American and European distributors of films and television programmes have all but ceased business in the Gulf. The same material that they would supply to video shops for sale or rent enters both legally and illegally from Europe and Asia. There is little recognition of international copyright conventions and master pirated copies of the latest Egyptian and Western films find their way to duplication houses from Europe and Asia. Singapore is known to be the most active piracy centre for video material supplied to the Gulf. Some material is smuggled into the Gulf on an informal basis.

Video cassette smuggling is best illustrated by the example of a joint British-

American television film supposedly re-constructing an event in Saudi Arabia which was shown on independent television in the United Kingdom and on American non-commerical public stations. The Saudi Arabian government objected to the film because it was not an accurate depiction of either the event or of Saudi Arabian culture.

The night it was shown in the United Kingdom the film was taped directly off-the-air and flown the next morning to Saudi Arabia's Eastern Province where is was duplicated and distributed. This example indicates the ease with which material to which a government objects may enter Gulf countries as well as other Arab states. Airport customs officials usually open luggage looking for contraband but a Beta or VHS format tape can easily pass undetected in a pocket. Moreover, it only takes one cassette to supply an entire country; the master is used to make copies commercially and those with second-generation versions informally copy them for friends and family.

In 1985 a double-cassette video recorder made by Sharp of Osaka, Japan, made its world debut in the Gulf. The machine capable of duplicating tapes using only one machine and believed to have been manufactured for a dealer in Saudi Arabia, was not well received in Western Countries where film industries and governments alike are attempting to stop video piracy. The double-cassette VCR is an ideal device for the Gulf states and its development points to the Sharp Electronics Company and their Middle Eastern distributors' sensitivity to that market (Watts, 1985).

Governments have enacted rules hoping to stem the spread of material thought to be undesirable. Ministries of Information play a central role in policing video material and they work closely with the customs service to monitor imported material. Realizing that private video importation and ownership are impossible to control, they have concentrated on video rental shops. Most Gulf states now require lists of tapes for sale or rent and some indication that they have been approved for public consumption. Security personnel and Ministry of Information officials often make unannounced visits to video stores in an attempt to ensure that no undesirable or banned material is for rent.

Saudi Arabia enacted a Video Bill in February, 1980. It provides specific guidelines for those eligible to own and operate a video store: citizenship and age (a Saudi Arabian citizen over 18 and not enrolled in school); location (on a main road with a visible entrance, not near a mosque); and licence (including a security check by the intelligence service). The regulations further stipulate that women are not allowed to enter video rental or sales stores (Bakhaider, 1981).

Not all Gulf states have specific rules under which video stores operate. For example, it is relatively easy to regulate the 75 video retail stores in Bahrain because it is a small country. Saudi Arabia presents a different problem because of its size, location, and wealth. It is not always easy to exclude politically undesirable, anti-Islamic, or pornographic material.

Available Video Material

The focus of this report is the English- and Arabic-language material. However, the video market consists of several sub-populations that use VCR programming in other languages. The service industries in these countries employ large numbers of Indians and Pakistanis. Speakers of Hindi, Urdu and south Indian languages import Indian films on cassette in these languages and some video stores specialise in serving Asian communities.

There are also large numbers of workers from Thailand, The Republic of Korea and the Philippines. Some service industry and construction workers from South East Asia came in the late 1970s during the construction boom. Kung-Fu type films popular in South East Asia originally were brough to the Gulf for this group, but because many are dubbed into English for a world wide market they are the source of video rental material for a cross-section of Kuwaiti residents.

By the mid-1980s English and Arabic-language video programming in The Gulf states had become more sophisticated, of higher technical quality, and more readily available. From the late 1970s until approximately 1982 almost anything available on the market was consumed. At first, most tapes were of programmes recorded directly from television systems in the United States, the United Kingdom and Egypt. All a pirate needed was an American or British contact who had a television set and a VCR and was willing to tape material and forward it. In 1980, a BBC spokesman said, 'we learned of one organisation which taped the entire BBC output every evening and flew it off by private jet next morning to an Arab country' ('Thieves who steal your TV shows', 1980). Tapes of American and British television programmes seen in hotels and private homes often contained commerical advertisements, promotions for other programmes, and even evening newscasts. It was not until later that video distributors started paying attention to the technical quality and the editing of video material.

Tastes for video programming rapidly became more sophisticated. Viewers wanted more recent material, particularly first-run Western and Egyptian motion pictures. VCR owners also wanted tapes of higher technical quality; the third and fourth generation material on the market was becoming tedious to watch.

It is difficult to provide accurate data on all aspects of the Gulf video market because the governments do not require the type of formal reporting procedures common elsewhere. The majority of video material for sale or rent is pirated, ie, the producers and artists receive no renumeration from those consuming the material.

Piracy of American films is so rampant that the cassettes of new features often reach Kuwait via Singapore before they are released theatrically in the United States (Borsten, 1984).

At least 80 per cent of video offerings are pirated. In 1982, almost 4 billion blank video cassettes were exported from Japan to the Arab states; an addi

tional 10 million came from the West. In 1984 the Middle East had an estimated 1,300 pirate tape outlets grossing an estimated $50 million (Campbell,
1984).

In 1983 video pirates in the Gulf discovered a means of increasing income:
they sold advertising time on pirated copies of first run films. Commercials
for cigarettes, automobiles, soft drinks, and watches are edited into some films
on tape, but this is unlikely to become a thriving business even in Saudi Arabia
– which does not carry advertising on television. The newer machines with
remote control devices permit easy 'zapping' or fast forwarding of the tape
to avoid advertisements.

Television and VCR viewing

There are many reasons for which people purchase VCRs and then acquire
tapes to be shown on them. Adwan's (1985) study of Kuwait and Qatar indicates that one of the main motivations for viewing video cassettes is
dissatisfaction with what is offered on national television. Respondents said
that programmes were unsuitable, boring, frequently repeated, and generally
did not meet their needs.

Pornographic Material

There has always been a market for 'blue films' in the Gulf. These were shown
privately when 16mm projectors were the only means of seeing such material.
Large numbers of home VCRs and the ease of smuggling tapes, either per-
sonally or commercially for wide distribution, expanded the market. The
number of pornographic offerings in the Gulf is not large, but there is demand
for such material.

Travellers visiting airports in Europe or the South and East Asia know that
pornographic tapes may be purchased in airport tax-free shops. These are
imported in various ways, and the pirate video companies also distribute pornographic material through video stores.

Some stores provide this type of material openly; others are more circum-
spect. In the Gulf those wishing to purchase or rent a pornographic tape usually
ask for and receive a tape marked with the name of a well known film or television programme. The store tells the renter or purchaser that the tape has
a false start: that is, the tape does begin with the film marked on the label,
but at a designated number of the VCR counter the actual pornographic films
starts. This system helps avoid detection should a tape be examined at customs
upon entering the country or in occasional spot checks by Ministry of Information officials at video stores.

Some residents in Kuwait have complained to the Ministry of Information
about the amount of pornographic material available on the market. In early

1985 a family in Kuwait rented a cassette of the film *ET* for a children's party. By mistake, the shop gave the family the pornographic *ET*. The tape began with the opening scene from the actual American movie but then switched to the pornographic version. In an April, 1985, a study conducted in Kuwait by the Arab States Broadcasting Union's Arab Centre for Audience Research found that 18.5 per cent of respondents said they watched video material for 'sex thrills'. This does not mean that the material was necessarily pornographic, but it indicates that films and television programmes with sexual themes are popular and have a potentially 'great negative effect on the general values in the society' (Adwan, 1985).

JORDAN

The unique political and economic situation in Jordan has had a great impact on VCR ownership. The country itself has few natural resources and little industry. The West Bank with its light industry and fertile agricultural area continues under Israeli occupation following its capture during the 1967 war.

At least half of all Jordanian citizens are Palestinians – former residents or children of residents of what is now Israel. The other half of the population traces its origins to Bedouin stock. The 3 million residents of this kingdom have benefitted indirectly from the post-1973 Gulf oil boom, for the Gulf states continue to provide financial support to the Jordanian government to offset the loss of the West Bank to Israel. Moreover, large numbers of Jordanians work in the Gulf and expatriate salaries returned to Jordan have helped supply funds for Amman's commercial and residential building boom.

JORDANIAN MEDIA

Jordan is rich in media. Local and imported English- and Arabic-language newspapers and magazines are available. There are several public cinemas, some of which cater for Egyptian workers and others to those wanting to see Western films. In addition to local English and Arabic radio stations, Jordan television operates two national channels, one featuring mostly imported Western television programmes and films. Israeli and Syrian television are also received in Amman and in other urban centres.

VCRS IN JORDAN

Jordan did not experience a VCR explosion similar to the ones described above. This is due primarily to lower per capita incomes in Jordan, more available television and cinemas offerings, and high – because of import taxes – local VCR prices. Jordan does not have the same type of high-volume retail electronics stores as The Gulf states. Consequently, the first VCRs came to urban areas, mostly to the capital Amman, from the Gulf or from Europe with the returning of vacationing residents. These early VCR owners had little pre-recorded material at first and machines were used initially for time-shifting.

From 1978, when the first VCR arrived, to 1980, there was no government regulation of pre-recorded cassette material. Residents could import whatever they wished, but this changed when a department of the Ministry of Informa-tion dealing with film censorship was also put in charge of cassette material (Kefay, 1983).

The period between 1980 and 1983 was the most important one for VCR imports and for the proliferation of cassette material, because it was during this time that large sums of money entered Jordan from the Gulf. After 1983 the Gulf recession had an impact on economic fortunes in Jordan and slowed the growth of the VCR market.

VCRs and the Jordanian Cinema

One of the main differences between the conditions of the VCR industry in the Gulf states and in Jordan is the long-established Jordanian cinema busi-ness. Several families with cinemas in Lebanon and in Palestine prior to 1948 moved to Jordan in the 1950s and built cinemas. Some specialised in Egyp-tian films and others showed mostly American and British films with Arabic sub-titles. When television came to Jordan in the late 1960s cinema attendance decreased somewhat, but families of all economic levels regularly went to cinemas because they offered material not available on television. By 1980, cinema attendance was down dramatically, primarily because of the prolifera-tion of VCRs (Samir Seikaly, personal correspondence, Amman, Jordan, March 18 1985).

From 1983 onwards, some cinema owners in Amman decided that they must take steps to compete with the shops supplying rental cassette material. Most cinemas had fallen into a state of disrepair because income had decreased. Furthermore, going to the cinema was no longer fashionable – middle- and upper-income families did not want to attend because to do so indicated that they did not own a VCR, a status symbol. Even the large number of Egyptian films failed to attract audiences because they too were available on cassette.

The solution for some owners was to go into the video rental business and to refurbish older cinemas and even build new ones. The modernised Rainbow Theatre and the newly constructed Philadephia Cinema in Amman are exam-ples of an attempt to revitalise the cinema business. Some of the new or modernised facilities are multi-purpose and can be used for live bands, plays and concerts. Yet, competition from VCRs may prevent these establishments from surviving. Pirated material is on the market before first-run Egyptian and Western films are in cinemas and cinema owners are essentially power-less to do anything about it. Although the following example deals specifically

171

with Jordan, it illustrates a problem pervasive throughout the Middle East where cinemas are in competition with VCRs.

The Seikaly family has been in the cinema business since 1943, moving from Palestine to Jordan in 1948. The family were film distributors until 1954 when they built their own cinemas. Business was good until 1978 when the VCRs first arrived and in 1981 the family moved into the video rental business, albeit temporarily. To begin with, they purchased and imported 10,000 blank VHS and Beta tapes at $15 each. Six months later the price of tapes dropped to $6. Because they lost so much money on the blank tapes and because video rentals were so competitive, the family sold its shops, deciding to return to the cinema. The new $1.4 million Philadelphia Cinema is their newest and most expensive investment in Jordan. The intention was to attract customers by showing films which could not be obtained on cassette.

During the first part of 1985 Samir Seikaly signed a contract with an Egyptian film company for the exclusive Jordanian rights to an Egyptian film entitled *Huna Qahira* (This is Cairo) starring Mohammed Sobhi, a popular actor/singer. The contract stipulates that if any pirated versions of the film appear on the Jordanian market before 15 March 1985, the distributor pays the Seikaly Cinema Company $50,000. This clause was to protect Seikaly against the eventuality that Egyptian film companies sold the VCR rights at the same time as the cinema rights, thus making double the normal fee.

On 2 March 1985, the film was released by the Ministry of Information censorship office to Samir Seikaly. Although the film was locked in a vault for safe-keeping, video cassettes of *Huna Qahira* were immediately available in Amman's video rental stores. Philadelphia also booked a film entitled *Body Rock* for an exclusive showing, but pirated video cassettes were on the market two weeks before the scheduled showing. (Samir Seikaly, owner Philadelphia Cinema, personal communication, Amman, Jordan, 18 March 1985).

The Jordanian video revolution also has financial repercussions for the government. The average price of a single cinema ticket in Amman for a first-run film in one of the new cinemas is $4.80. About half of this is government tax. Video cassettes are inexpensive to rent, particularly considering the cost of the cinema ticket. Several viewing plans are available through the hundreds of video stores in Jordan. The standard scheme involves joining a club for about $20.00 which entitles the member to several film rentals. Thereafter, a cassette costs approximately $1.50 for 24 hours. If the tape is something worth keeping, a copy may be made using the VCR of a friend or relative.

VCRs and Television

The development of VCRs in Jordan has affected Jordanian television (JTV) in two ways. First, the two Jordanian channels rely on commercial advertising to help meet operating costs and advertisers believe that fewer people are viewing television and more are watching programming on VCRs. Thus, television income is at best stagnant. Second, some material JTV would like to show has already been circulated on video tape. In 1983, the JTV programme director approached the American Broadcasting Company (ABC) in New York to determine whether he could purchase the television film *The Day After*. Upon returning to Jordan he notified ABC that JTV was no longer interested in showing the film because pirated versions were on the market and that a substantial portion of the population had already seen it (M Kheir, Programme Director, Jordan Television, personal communication, Amman, Jordan, 14 January 1984).

Government Regulation of Videograms

Jordan, like many other countries, was slow to recognise the effects video tape would have on both Jordanian media and society. The problem is not one dealt with only by the Ministry of Information. Cassettes entering the country are identified by customs officials who either allow them to enter or hold them until they can be viewed by members of the Censors' Council, a body functioning under the Ministry of Information Press and Publications Office.

Video rental establishments in Jordan must have a licence from the Ministry of Information's Press and Publications Office. In March, 1985, there were 430 shops in the country, 4 having been closed during the first quarter of 1985 because they were found to be renting 'undesirable material'. Despite its efforts, the Censors' Council cannot view in its entirety all of the video cassette material entering Jordan legally. Between 1982 and 1985 the 4 members of the censoring body viewed 20,000 cassettes. The criteria for rejecting cassettes: a) sexual activity unacceptable to an Islamic society; b) excessive violence; c) anti-religious material; and d) films and television programmes depicting Israel in a positive light (Issa Jahmani, Director, Ministry of Information, Press and Publications Office, personal communication, Amman, Jordan, 17 March 1985). The Ministry of Information is concerned about pornographic and other types of undesirable material, but officials realise that they are essentially powerless to prevent it entering the country (Michael Hamarneh, Under-secretary, Ministry of Information, personal communication, Amman, Jordan, 17 March 1985).

EGYPT

Egypt is very different from the wealthy Gulf states and Jordan. This country's 45 million people reside in the Nile Delta, in the Nile Valley, and along the Suez Canal, a small arable area on which the largely agrarian economy depends.

The country is rich in history and tourism is an important industry. After the July 1952 revolution, Gamal Abdul Nasser, a man from a modest rural background, expanded Egyptian radio and started television as a means of helping to promote political and national development.

EGYPTIAN ELECTRONIC MEDIA

The Egyptian Radio and Television Federation is an important part of the government's Ministry of Information. An estimated 12,000 people are employed in the radio and television complex, a landmark on the Nile in Cairo. From here Radio Cairo, a name by which the radio services are generally known, originates eight domestic programmes plus an extensive international short-wave service. Television started in 1960 on the eighth anniversary of the July 1952 revolution. There are two national colour television channels providing information, education, and entertainment, mostly during the late afternoon and evening with a lengthier schedule at weekends.

Twenty-five years of television has popularised the medium and a remarkable number of people own and watch television sets. Nasser wanted as many people as possible to have access to television and one way of accomplishing this was to assemble sets locally. Colour sets are, of course, much more expensive than monochrome ones, but still it is possible for an Egyptian family of even modest means to own a second-hand monochrome set. A television set is more than a status symbol to poor families – it is a way of bringing the world beyond Egypt into the home and of entertaining those who otherwise could not afford to seek entertainment outside the home. A 1983 survey commissioned by Egyptian television provides the only available contemporary data on set ownership and usage.

- About 60 per cent of the population, 27 million people, watch television.
- The average number of people per set is 6.4.
- Viewers watch an average of 3 hours and 49 minutes per day.
- Peak viewing time is between 7.00pm and 8.00pm.
- Sundays and Fridays are the two most popular days for viewing (Middle East Advisory Group, 1983).

Egypt remains in many ways the artistic and intellectual capital of the Arab states. It is also the region's largest producer of Arabic television and film material. Egypt has a long tradition of artistic expression, and the Egyptian cinema industry dates from the late 1920s. Egyptian films are seen throughout the Arab states, while Egyptian video taped music, drama, and educational programmes from state-run television are seen on virtually every Arab television system.

The Economy and VCRs

One of Egypt's main exports is labour. Tens of thousands of labourers, skilled construction workers, teachers, and physicians work in other Arab countries, mostly in the Gulf states. They either bring or transfer back to Egypt between $3 and $4 billion per year (Critchfield, 1984). After completing an overseas tour or during home visits, Gulf workers bring back electronic equipment either not available or prohibitively expensive in Egypt. Until about 1980, colour television sets were brought back; after 1980 workers brought back VCRs. Because large numbers of Egyptians working abroad are from rural areas a substantial number of imported VCRs are used in small villages.

VCR prices in Egypt are high because the machines, like all luxury consumer goods, are highly taxed. Workers bringing back VCRs from the Gulf pay 100 per cent customs duty on them, but this is still much cheaper than purchasing a machine in Egypt. In the Gulf, the very latest Japanese dual-standard (PAL/SECAM) remote-controlled models are available and these are preferred to the older machines imported locally. However, some of the Gulf equipment finds its way to the electronics shops in Cairo and Alexandria. They are brought to Egypt by workers who have previously imported another machine; the second is sold to a dealer.

Video Cassette Recorders

Egyptians have not had the money to acquire large numbers of VCRs nor because of an abundance of television programming and cinemas, have they had the motivation.

In Cairo and Alexandria, there are video clubs and video rental shops with the usual pirated Western films and television programmes and Egyptian films. Egypt does not have as many video stores as Kuwait or Jordan because of the low percentage of VCRs and the fact that those possessing machines cannot afford the $0.75 to $1.00 daily rental fees to spend on home entertainment.

There is probably less private copying of tapes in Egypt than in the Gulf or in Jordan because there are fewer people with more than one VCR. The popularity of Egyptian video material outside the country is an advantage to the domestic cassette market.

> The flow of recorded cassettes in and out of the country follows a rather strange pattern. There is a huge demand in other Arab countries for cassettes produced in Egypt. At the same time, cheap editions of programmes originally made in Egypt and reproduced abroad are smuggled back into the country to avoid copyright and other dues as well as censorship regulations. The rule is to have such cassettes erased if and when they are seized. TV serials which

use Egyptian talent, even when they are produced abroad, are also popular (Aboubakr, 1983).

The censors have a fairly liberal attitude in Egypt, but even so in Cairo video material is one means of circumventing Ministry of Information censorship decisions. *The Witness Who Witnessed Nothing* is an Egyptian play recorded on video tape and popular throughout the Arab states. The play has still not been shown on Egyptian television because it is considered to be unsuitable, but it is available in Egypt and in other Arab countries in video shops ('Middle Eastern story-tellers give way to videos', 1985).

Egypt will not have the economic base to support a high percentage of video cassette recorders for some time. However, the country will continue to be involved in the production and consumption of video material. Because of decreases in OPEC oil prices and production the economic growth experienced between 1974 and 1982 in the Gulf states has at best levelled off. This means fewer Egyptian workers will be employed in the Gulf and thus the flow of VCRs from that area to Egypt will decrease.

Conversely, the flow of software, Egyptian plays and films on cassette, will continue to be toward the Gulf. Despite some successful attempts to market television plays made in the Gulf, most popular video-taped offerings are Egyptian, whether they are made in Cairo by the state-run television organisation or by Egyptians producing material in Europe or in other parts of the Middle East.

Video: Culture and Communication

It has already been noted that banned films circulate freely, although unofficially, on video tape, despite government attempts to censor material thought to be offensive to citizens or politically unacceptable. Increasingly, however, material considered to be political rather than cultural in nature is seen in homes with VCRs. Some tapes of religious and political figures circulate among a small group of people interested in learning about opposition political movements. These are usually crudely done and present little more than people talking directly to a video camera. On the other hand, cassettes of professionally produced satirical plays are in demand because they extend this Arab art form to a wider population. Abdul Hussein Abdul Ridr is a Kuwaiti producer, writer, actor and comedian best known in the Gulf as a political satirist. His biting humour is popular in Kuwait where the Ministry of Information subsidizes some of his productions. Perhaps his best known production is *Bye Bye London*, a satirical comdey about Gulf Arabs in London. Allowed to circulate freely in Kuwait, it is banned in Saudi Arabia but is available on the underground video tape market.

Similarly, *The Keeper of the Keys*, a musical featuring the Lebanese actress/singer Fairouz is only available on the illegal market because it contains an unmistakable political theme.

VCR: IMPLICATIONS FOR DEVELOPMENT

There are two views on the effects VCRs are having on attempts to use television for development purposes. One view argues that the freedom the machines bring viewers is detrimental to development because they have, in effect, decentralised television in countries with high VCR penetration. Now, certainly in the Gulf states, VCR owners, rather than the government, have control over what viewers watch. For example, in Saudi Arabia, since the first broadcast was aired in 1965, programming has on the whole reflected the Ministry of Information's philosophy of what people should see. However VCR owners may now obtain almost any tape either legally, from government-approved video stores, or illegally, via the video tape underground. As a result, Bakhaider (1981) found that 73 per cent of his Jidda sample watched less Saudi television after acquiring a VCR. He concluded that the VCR '... has had a negative influence upon the Saudi Arabian television network because it has detracted from the latter's public following, the amount of time it is viewed, and its economic importance'.

The other view is that VCRs are having a positive influence in countries with large numbers of machines because they allow owners the freedom to see what they want when they want to see it. This 'freedom of choice' view argues that the individual, rather than the state, knows what is best for him/her. Those espousing this position also note that VCRs are the best means of supporting specific national development programmes. VCRs are being used in some educational institutions and health facilities to teach new techniques and to change behaviour. Yet, in the home, where almost all VCR material is consumed, families are not watching educational programmes; they are viewing entertainment programmes imported from Egypt and the West.

Arab television programming supports the government in power and reflects that government's development priorities. However, broadcast television also presents material unavailable on tape: sports, special entertainment, and public affairs programmes. Television, when the occasion demands, provides a unifying national video experience. Nevertheless, VCRs are a major force in home entertainment.

TABLE 1

ELECTRONIC MEDIA IN THE GULF STATES, JORDAN AND EGYPT

Country	TV system	TV% of household	VCR% of TV owners	Year
Kuwait	625-Line PAL	25.8	85	1983
Saudi Arabia	625-Line SECAM	26.4	75	1983
Bahrain	625-Line PAL	32.7	60	1979
Qatar	625-Line PAL	50.9	70	1979
UAE	625-Line PAL	9.3	80	1983
Oman+	625-Line PAL	4.3	55	1983
Jordan	625-Line PAL	6.8	20	1983
Egypt	625-Line SECAM	15.0	3	1983

+ Oman is the only Gulf state without two national television channels.
Source: Intergovernmental Conference on Communication Policies in the Arab States; Working Document, Khartoum 19–25 July 1987, Unesco.

TABLE 2

SOURCES OF VIDEO CASSETTE MATERIAL

	Source	Percentage
Kuwait		
	Exchange with friends	31
	Recording from TV	30
	Rental	26
	Purchase	13
Qatar		
	Exchange with friends	32
	Recording from TV	20
	Rental	31
	Purchase	17

Source: *Research on Video Programmes in Iraq, Kuwait, and Qatar.* Arab Centre for Audience Research, Baghdad, Iraq, April 1985, p 11. Data are based on 200 interviews in Kuwait and Qatar.

TABLE 3

VIEWING HOURS PER WEEK

Number of VCR Viewing Hours Per Week	Kuwait %	Qatar %
1 to 4	37	51.5
4 to 8	34	37.5
8 to 12	9	12.0
12 to 16	11	10.0

Source: *Research on Video programmes in Iraq, Kuwait, and Qatar.* Arab Centre for Audience Research, Baghdad, Iraq, April 1985, p 17. Data are based on 200 interviews in Kuwait and Qatar.

Chapter 11

POLAND

The world history of video is short and in Poland the medium has been developing since the end of the 1970s. It was then that the first Polish videotape recorder, MTU 10 appeared, and was followed by MTU 20. They are used mainly by state educational institutions. Today there are 170 MTU 10 units and 198 MTU 20 units in schools. Unfortunately, equipment is complicated both to use and to service and there was practically no software to accompany it.

In 1980–1981 the political and social climate was favourable to the mass production of information and all available equipment was used to this end. It was also hoped that visual as well as spoken information about the activities of the independent trade union would be available to the population through the national TV network, since negotiations concerning the access of independent political organisations to the electronic mass media were already in an advanced stage. All kinds of printing shops flourished, usually small ones, utilising copiers, and based on both imported equipment and more primitive home-made appliances. The next stage in the development of this information process relied on audio cassettes and although the years 1980–81 were not the peak of video production, it was then that there appeared small groups of video-fans, sometimes students, who organised the public showing of films. Such groups were however marginal to the extensive state cultural activity.

Within the State sector culture is often one of the casualties of economic or political crises. The number of books published in this period declined sharply as did the number of cinemas. In 1965 there were 3,935 active cinemas; in 1981, only 2,158, in 1982, 2,089, and in 1984, 2,061; the annual ratios of film-viewers per 1000 population were 5,492 in 1965, 2,788 in 1981, and 2,467 in 1982. 1983, the year which brought a certain increase in the number of cinemas, witnessed the growth of cinema-going to no more than the 1955 levels with a slight increase in 1984 to 3,457. Television was therefore undoubtedly the main supplier of cultural and entertainment shows in the whole decade of the seventies. The numbers of TV viewers were steadily increasing. In 1965 there were 2,077,800 TV sets (65 per 1,000 population); in 1979, 7,7808,000 (218 per 1,000 population); and in 1983, 8,542,000 (233 per 1,000 population); in 1984, 8,765,000 (236 sets per 1,000 inhabitants). The number of colour TV receivers now exceeds 2 million.

The programming policy in the 1970s provided quite a broad selection of productions from all over the world both on television and in cinemas. According to some estimates, Poland, next to Yugoslavia, seemed to be most open to the outside world in respect of the content of its TV programming. In 1980, 502 foreign films were imported for screening in cinemas and the structure of these imports is noteworthy: 187 items from the socialist countries and 315 from the rest of the world. Television programming also diversified. Although the products of mass culture – Western commercial productions – did predominate, artistically valuable programmes were also present. Also, whilst Western commercial programmes usually appeared some time after their first showing, the delays were not significant, and in certain cases all efforts were made to present a given programme to the Polish viewer in the same year of its world appearance.

In 1982, there was a sharp reduction in this broad repertoire. This is best illustrated by the data concerning film imports. Over a period of two years the number of imported films dropped from the 502 items in 1981, to 256 items in 1983. There were also changes in the structure of imports: 163 films from the socialist countries, and 93 from other parts of the world; in 1984, 280 films were imported – 143 from socialist countries and 137 from the rest of the world. Television programmes suffered the same reduction. Precise data are not available, but the decrease in the share of commercially successful items was quite evident; most of the programmes imported from the capitalist countries are no more than repetitions of previously transmitted material. Television has also introduced many often repeated serials addressed to their fans rather than to the audience at large; cheaper documentary and educational films have taken the place of feature films which are more expensive to import.

The reduction in the size of the TV repertoire was an inevitable result of the financial difficulties suffered by the national TV network. An over-generous financial policy up to 1981 led to a need to reduce financing radically and to do this programming increasingly utilised items which did not require dollar expenditure (or other convertible currency).

There were of course other factors which influenced the poverty of the TV repertoire, and the programmes of all other media in Poland during this difficult period. Some authors, directors and producers did not wish to co-operate with state TV and others were not allowed to do so.

The mass media audience reacted to this situation. Research shows that a large number of viewers no longer watched TV programmes. The number of newspaper readers also dropped. The circulation of the national press and magazines was especially hard hit, while there was a certain growth of interest in local newspapers which recorded an increase in circulation. Under these conditions, video provided an alternative for those who wanted to construct their own programmes, with the emphasis on cultural and entertainment values, rather than overtly political values. It may be argued that the difficult political situation favoured the development of video, by creating a specially powerful demand for this medium, because video was independent from the State controlled programming, development and distribution. Nor was it illegal.

VIDEO HARDWARE

Researchers into the video phenomenon have not yet reached agreement concerning the number of video recorders in Poland today. The international magazine *TV World* in its April 1985 issue features a chart of TV and Video in the world, which shows Poland, the only socialist country for which figures are given, as having 400,000 VCRs. Unfortunately, the editors of the magazine did not answer the letter in which we inquired about the source of these estimates. According to most Polish specialists in this field, the above figure seems to be an exaggeration. ZAIKS, the Polish organisation controlling the application of copyright legislation, puts the number of video recorders in private hands at about 200,000. Other sources quote even lower estimates; the management of the Kasprzak TV and Radio Equipment Company suggested only 100,000 machines. Nevertheless, it is possible to find arguments in support of the estimate quoted by *TV World*. The national representative sample research conducted on a group of adult citizens (over 14 years of age) by the Public Opinion Research Centre of Polish Radio and TV, in May 1985, showed that 2.7 per cent of those questioned had a video recorder at home. Since the sampling method excluded the questioning of two people from the same household, we can reasonably accept that the above figure also describes the number of households possessing video-equipment. As the number of households in 1985 was approximately 12 million, calculations show 324,000 video recorders in private ownership.

There remains the question of the number of video recorders utilised by various institutions. The school network has approximately 2,300 pieces of video equipment of various types. Undoubtedly, quite a significant number are utilised by Roman Catholic institutions. However, no data is available, partly because the equipment may be owned by parishes. If we accept the simplified assumption that every parish has one video-recorder at its disposal, the total number in the hands of the Church would be 11,000. Another potential user, the higher schools, has no aggregate data, while the Ministry of Higher Education has not devoted any funds from its budget to the acquisition of such equipment. It is quite probable that video equipment is being utilised in other fields of social and economic life, especially in some industrial branches, but no data is available at present. It is also known that new specialised hospitals and clinics availing themselves of international assistance (for example, the Child Health Centre) are in possession of considerable numbers of video recorders, used to record more complex surgical operations. Thus, it is perhaps in these fields that we could find the 70,000 recorders completing the number of 400,000 quoted by *TV World*. In January 1986, estimations still vary from 200,000, according to the Polish Press agency to 500,000 on the basis of more scholarly approximations.

While assuming this estimate to be an approximation of the total number of VCRs in Poland, we shall consider the problems of individually owned units. If our calculations are correct, 324,000 recorders in private hands means that there is one video recorder per 37 households, and bearing in mind that the possession of such equipment is typical for city-dwellers, this would mean that approximately one in 20 households in the cities possesses a recorder. Finally, taking into account the number of TV sets, it appears that there is one video recorder for 26 operational TV sets.

The dynamics of this phenomenon are interesting. We must also be satisfied with estimates in this case, since so far only one study has been conducted on a national sample. Again, our considerations apply to video recorders in private hands. According to the estimates from the first half of 1983, the number of video-recorders was no higher than 30,000. Although estimates for the same period in 1984 vary between 20,000 and 50,000, we may assume that there were about 40,000 units in private hands. If we remember that the figure for May 1985 is 324,000 we note a tremendous growth (13.5 times as many) between the first part of 1983 and 1984, and 8.1 times between 1984 and 1985.

Forecasts of future growth can be constructed on the basis of data on the dynamics of individual imports – provided by the Central Tariffs Bureau. Though the aggregate data concerning total imports of video equipment is quite low and does not confirm our estimates based on the national sample, the high growth rate is worth noting. Individual imports of video equipment in the first quarter of 1985 were five times higher than in the same period in 1984. Moreover, individual imports tend to increase in the second and third quarter of the year, so one may expect very high growth for the whole of 1985. If we assume that the number of privately owned videos at the beginning of 1986 was between 1,700,000 and 2,200,000 units (which would mean the ratio of 6.8 or 5.6 households per recorder), Poland would then find itself somewhere between the Federal Republic of Germany and the United States in the world scale, according to the data for the beginning of 1985. Such a rapid advance however, does not seem feasible because of a number of obstacles.

VIDEO AS AN ECONOMIC PHENOMENON

Video recorders can be bought in Poland only with convertible currencies. This is so even at PeWex, the State enterprise selling imported goods, which charges relatively high prices. Licensed private businesses work on the same basis, though charging slightly lower prices. Individual non-licensed importers selling

VCRs also prefer convertible currencies. They usually require PeWex vouchers with the nominal value of one dollar, which in effect comes down to payment in foreign currency (payments in PeWex vouchers is legal, while dollars are legally banned from private transactions). Deals in Polish zlotys do occur from time to time, but in this case the sum of payment is related to the current extra-legal price of the dollar. At the beginning of 1985, the price of video recorders in zlotys on the 'grey market' was between 300,000 and 450,000 zlotys, ie 460 to 700 dollars at the black market exchange rate. In December 1985 the price range varied from 180,000 zlotys (280 dollars) to 540,000 zlotys (850 dollars).

It should be explained that while it is legal in Poland to possess foreign currencies and to use them for payments to selected State institutions and other licensed firms, the exchange of foreign currencies between individual citizens is forbidden. Foreign currencies may also be held in private accounts at State banks. Private citizens may acquire foreign currencies either through gainful employment abroad (both legally and illegally), or through the network of extensive family and social relations. Large numbers of Polish citizens leave the country annually in order to find temporary employment abroad or to conduct various business transactions consisting mainly in buying goods that are in short supply at home and then re-selling them, often also for hard currencies. According to the calculations of the Finance Ministry, Polish citizens possess from 2 billion to 6 billion dollars – depending on the season of the year.

At the beginning of 1985, the PeWex price for the video-recorder JVC HR 120E was 760 dollars; Sony Beta SL-ZGPS, 815 dollars. At the end of 1985, prices varied from 449 dollars for NV 6464 Philips to 1,359 dollars for Panasonic NV 180E6 with camera. Individual video recorders or personal computers may be purchased abroad at much lower prices than the sales price at home. Thus, individual imports of video recorders have an assured sales market at home, and are a safe investment for a Polish traveller abroad. PeWex recently reacted to these developments and differentiated, and in some cases, lowered, the prices. The price for the cheapest available VCR at the end of the year was 450 dollars.

In July 1985 the Sony video recorder was being sold for 830 dollars, but the price of JVC was lowered to 576 dollars, and the newly introduced NECK video recorder could be bought for 399 dollars. At that time PeWex offers became, in certain cases, competitive with the offers on the 'grey market', but only for a while since the 'grey market' now once again offers lower prices than the State shops. The domestically produced (although in small numbers) Kasprzak video recorder has a 'combined' price tag: 230,000 zlotys plus 200 dollars, which amounts to 560 dollars. However, private importers are in a position to cut their prices further. This is favoured by the special position of video recorders on Western markets. This usually reliable equipment can be bought much more cheaply secondhand and particularly in the Federal Republic of Germany. In 1982-83, the Panasonic, Akai, and Sony (NV 332, NV7200, VS-1, VS-2, SL–C6E) which had an original price tag of 600 to 850 dollars, were available secondhand for 150–430 dollars. This mass purchasing of used equipment by Polish tourists in the West, fits perfectly into the marketing strategy of electronics firms in the country concerned, since it enables them to introduce new lines of equipment on the usually well saturated home market.

Clearly one of the obstacles to the development of video in Poland, is the relatively limited number of people who are able to purchase a VCR. These are estimated to be approximately 750,000.

On the other hand in a situation of economic crisis the more affluent Poles have many more zlotys at their disposal since the goods they might wish to purchase are not always available. Moreover, since they fear a decline in the value of the zloty their spending is high. The demand for video equipment, considered by many as standard household appliances for middle classes in the future, thus stems to a large extent from the excess of money in the hands of the population in relation to domestic goods and services. Many think that economic stabilisation in the future will halt this rush towards new technologies, for which many buyers find only limited use. This question is also related to the problem of the availability of video software.

The stabilisation of the internal market would, in fact, lead to a return to normal practices, a decrease in personal expenditure and a return to a more rational purchasing pattern. Thus the video recorder seems to be one of the articles purchased largely as a result of the current crisis, and is not perceived as an immediate need by the average citizen.

In the face of such a complicated situation many decision-makers assume an attitude of passive observation in relation to the development of video in Poland. On the other hand, there are those who believe that a more positive and determined policy towards video is essential. In view of recent discussions it seems that the arguments of the realists are starting to gain the upper hand. In July 1985 there were discussions about future 'video-isation' of the country, and the economy has started to make its preparations for such developments.

THE DOMINANT VIDEO HARDWARE TECHNOLOGIES

The stock of video equipment possessed by the Polish population at present is a mosaic of various types manufactured by firms from different countries. At first, video recorders were mostly purchased by the affluent, usually those who had long-term contracts abroad. These buyers mostly acquired the products of well known firms, without major concern about current trends on Western video markets. Sony and Philips products (Betamax and V-2000) predominated. The first licensed company importing video to Poland (mixed Polish-German company Konsumprod S. A.) sold the quality video recorder Grundig V-2000. A change occurred in 1984 as a result of the increasing domination of the VHS system on the Western market. Due to this change, soon registered by individual importers for the 'grey market' in Poland, the VHS system became dominant in sales, accounting for 85 per cent of all operating recorders in 1984. Another mixed capital company, ITI (International Trading and Investment) which emerged as a result of an organisational split in Konsumprod), introduced Japanese Hitachi equipment.

It should be noted that cheaper, lower quality equipment has been increasingly popular on Polish markets. The buyers do not have sufficient knowledge of technological differences, and are therefore attracted by the most readily available product.

BLANK VIDEO CASSETTES

Poland does not produce video cassettes. The State enterprise ORWO plans to start production but not earlier than 1987 – until then, PeWex is the official importer of video cassettes. They are not very expensive and are gradually becoming cheaper, but can be purchased only with convertible currencies. In 1983, the price of blank cassettes was approximately 13 dollars whilst the information provided by the PeWex enterprise in July 1985 indicates a further reduction of prices: a 120 minute cassette costs 8 dollars; a 180 minute cassette 10 dollars; and a 360 minute cassette, 15 dollars. At the end of 1985 the cost of a 240 minute cassette was between 5 and 6.5 dollars.

Cassettes are also imported by private individuals. The Central Tariffs Bureau registers only a part of these imports (19,000 cassettes in 1984); the growth dynamics are very significant – between the first quarter of 1984 and the same period in 1985 the number increased by eight and a half times. In the 'grey market' in 1983 cassettes sold for 10 to 12 thousand zlotys (15 to 18 dollars), in 1984 for 6 to 8 thousand zlotys (9 to 12 dollars) while in 1985 the grey market registered the following prices: 180 minute cassettes at 6 thousand zlotys (9 dollars); 120 minutes at 4.5 thousand zlotys (7 dollars). At the end of 1985, a 180 minute cassette cost 4 thousand zlotyz (6.25 dollars). At present, blank cassettes are available on the official market (for hard currencies) and on the grey market (for hard currencies and zlotys).

PRE-RECORDED VIDEO CASSETTES

The distribution of pre-recorded video cassettes is a State monopoly. This results from the Cinematography Bill of 15 December 1981. However, until July 1985, the Central Cinematography Board and its subordinate institutions had taken no part in this field. The developing video market was therefore based on individually owned cassettes imported from abroad, and to a very large extent on pirate recording activities.

All the official measures taken in this respect were of a marginal character and related mostly to the question of video libraries. In the meantime the Polish subsidiary of ITI with headquarters in Panama, was granted a licence to produce pre-recorded video tapes in 1984 and is the only company to produce and sell them. The licence was granted for co-production with a Polish enterprise and the utilisation of its equipment. As a result of this arrangement ITI, in co-operation with P.I. Interpress, produced the first Polish video cassette which offered the programme of a well known Warsaw cabaret. The cassette was sold publicly, through press advertisements and the price at the end of 1984 was 110 thousand zlotys (171 dollars at black market rates). The company is also producing other cassettes about cookery. In December 1985, the private music shop in Warsaw offered pre-recorded cassettes, mainly video-clips, for 8.5 thousand zlotys each (13 dollars) for 180 minutes.

All other market activities are essentially illegal and assessment of the size of this market and the range of the cassettes appearing on it is quite impossible. ZAIKS, the Polish organisation safeguarding the observation of copyright legislation, estimates that two-thirds of the operating cassette market is illegal. Illegal copying activities are mostly conducted by small home-production operators in possession of two recorders. Their daily output usually amounts to three 180 minute cassettes. The prices obtained on the black market stabilised at the end of 1985 to 1,000 zlotys (1.6 dollars) for one hour. The copying operators do not usually supply the matrix (original) cassette; their activities are limited to copying cassettes supplied by the customer. Law enforcement in relation to such cases is very difficult and investigations are centred on mass dealers. The police sometimes uncover such cases but the illegal copiers usually omit the opening identifications, which makes the discovery of original sources difficult.

There are also illegal cassette producers who identify themselves. Niezalezna Oficyna Wydawnicza, 'NOWA' (the Independent Publishers) distributes films withheld from public screening by censorship. Examples of such films are – *Przesluchanie* (The Interrogation) directed by Bugajski; Western films such as *The Squaring of the Circle,* which appeared in domestic underground distribution only 3 days after its first screening in London; and other Western films which were banned, such as *Doctor Zhivago, 1984, Animal Farm, The Deer Hunter,* and even the James Bond series. Cassettes registered by NOWA cost 12,000 zlotys (1985 price) which equals 18 black market dollars (according to the author's information).

VIDEO LIBRARIES

In 1983, the mixed capital company Konsumprod S. A. filed a request for licensing a system of 8 video libraries in major Polish cities. This application was rejected by the authorities. Nevertheless, in the same year the administrative authorities in certain cities, including Warsaw, issued permits to open video libraries but because of legal doubts most permits were soon recalled. The existing libraries are uncertain about the future, and their managers are shy of any publicity.

In July 1985, the state enterprise Przedsiebiorstwo Dystrybucji Filmow decided to open video libraries in five cities: Warsaw, Katowice, Szczecin, Gdansk, and Krakow. These new libraries jointly received 1,000 cassettes. The price of borrowing a cassette for 24 hours is 500 zlotys for individual customers, and 1,500–3,000 zlotys for institutions. The offers of these State rental shops are not attractive, compared with private offers. They supply only the home production, plus one foreign film (Attenborough's *Ghandi*). Rental shops in Krakow offer mainly sensational, science fiction and children's programmes. The technical quality is poor and the number rented varies from 30 to 80 monthly. The customer must be officially registered and pays a deposit of 12,000 zlotys (18 dollars) per unit. The lending of cassettes through private contacts has often been conducted on commerical principles. In 1983, the price of borrowing a cassette for 24 hours amounted to 6–15,000 zlotys in 1984, and in 1985 the price fell to 1,000 zlotys.

VIDEO CLUBS AND OTHER PUBLIC SHOWS

As early as 1979 in Katowice and in the years 1980–1981 in many other cities, video shows which were then described as video clubs were organised. This kind of activity flourished, especially in the second half of 1982, and in later years assumed in most places (outside Warsaw) the character of open public shows. The 'club' character of these performances, with audiences theoretically limited to members, solved many legal problems concerning censorship and copyright protection. Clubs of this type emerged mainly in the colleges and in the premises of various youth organisations, but with increasing frequency they developed in the new housing areas of the cities, the inhabitants of which found it difficult to travel to far-off cinemas and theatres in city centres. Everyone who happened to be in the college building or a given city district culture house could easily find out the hours of the shows, and attend after buying a ticket. Posters advertising these shows soon appeared on city walls, but this was regarded by the authorities as a violation of the 'club' character.

Warsaw was left behind in the field of public video shows, since the Ministry of Culture and art residing in the capital disapproved of the public character of such presentations. Nevertheless, they continued to be organised in various clubs under the heading of promotion of new technologies in the media, etc. The changing character of such video shows is well illustrated by the numerical characteristics compiled in 1984. The data was collected from the city of Krakow.

1 May 1983-20 March 1984

1 The costs of the show (price paid by the organisers to the owners of equipment)	10–20,000 zl	5–10,000 zl
2 Ticket price for one film	200–300 zl	80–150 zl
3 Number of viewers per video screen	60–200	30–60
4 Technical conditions	mostly black and white	colour

The following data covers Warsaw student clubs in the years 1984–1985:

	1984	1985
1 Ticket price	150 zl	100 zl
2 Number of viewers per screen	150	50

The supplier was expected to lend and deliver the video recorder with the proper number of screens and cassettes; to service the equipment; and then read a translation of the dialogue of the film if it was in a foreign language. The data presented above shows that all these activities gradually became cheaper and the tickets are now in the same price range as cinema tickets. The systematically decreasing prices and simultaneous improvement of the performance quality disproves the press opinions about the excessive exploitation of the market by private video entrepreneurs. In the middle of 1985 the first official video cinemas appeared. At the end of 1985 the status of video agent was officially approved. The agent offers video show services to tourist centres, cultural centres etc. He provides his own equipment and services and has a right to about 70 per cent of returns.

The organisers of these shows and the video entrepreneurs were obliged to submit their programmes to the Board of Censors, and they were also required to prove that they were not violating the rights of the authors and producers. Some of them had such proof. Behind the scenes, one can detect a certain softening of the censorship regulations – there were usually no difficulties in obtaining permission for 'club' shows of 'soft-porn' films, which are described in the language of censorship as 'erotic', in opposition to 'hard-porn', which the censors classify as 'pornographic'.

Public Preference

It is possible to formulate tentative opinions about the preferences displayed by the public. It must however be noted that because of the lack of any general policy on the introduction of video into Poland, no alternatives to the screening patterns of the Western countries were offered, ie the greatest emphasis at first being placed on films of a pornographic or 'Karate' type. The suggestion that video play the role of a medium to supplement and assist the cinema network was voiced much too late in view of the fast, spontaneous development of this medium. However, one must observe that, as in Western Europe, the interest of audiences in the films featuring pornography and violence is approaching saturation point. The audiences, and especially the audiences of 'club' shows, expect new material of a more artistic quality. According to A Gawe's estimates in 1984 the preferences of the audience for various types of shows were the following: erotic films – 35 per cent; adventure, war stories etc – 30 per cent; Karate films – 20 per cent; science fiction – 10 per cent; musicals – 5 per cent. The five most frequently watched films in 1984 were: *Emmanuelle 1, Caligula, The Return of the Jedi, E.T., Rambo.*

The management of ZAIKS has the following estimates for the preference of video audiences: (1985)

> Adventure, war films, etc – 60%
> Video-clips, etc – 20%
> Erotic – 10%
> Other – 10%, including political films – 3.4%

According to the opinion of the above quoted sources, approximately 10 per cent of the films currently in video circulation would be stopped by censorship.

VIDEO SERVICES

Video activities performed at the specific order of a customer will be described here as services. We include under this heading the trans-recording of cassettes, which are covered by copyright and production legislation, as described above.

The brief survey made among the individual VCR owners in Krakow, in 1985, shows the following tendencies in the private use of video:

a) privately owned video recorders are divided equally between those of Japanese manufacture and those made in Western Europe.

b) most of the VCRs in use were individually imported from the West, mainly from the Federal Republic of Germany, Berlin and Austria. Only about 10 per cent were bought in Poland for zlotys.

c) pre-recorded cassettes were obtained, in descending order of importance, by copying a programme borrowed from friends, by individual import from abroad, or by time-shifting television programmes.

d) preferred programmes are video clips, erotic and science fiction films, and sensational and sports programmes.

e) the predominant motives for purchasing a video recorder and developing a private collection of cassettes are: a disaffection for Polish TV programmes; entertainment; and interest in new films.

> f)   all users collect their own video cassette libraries, accumulating, on average, about 35 units.
>
> g)   all users are developing contacts with 'friends' who are also video-enthusiasts. One user contacts, on average, 7–8 such 'friends', and two modal types of network emerge: the limited video-user's circle – 4–5 people; and extended circle – 10–20 people.
>
> h)   all users report that their video-viewing is also a social activity which includes groups of close friends and neighbours.
>
> i)   the main problems perceived by video users are:
> - the lack of open rental systems;
> - high prices on the black market;
> - difficulties in the purchase of equipment and cassettes.

Video services are subject to licensing by local authorities and it is difficult to observe a developed market for this type of service. The pioneers in this field had to create the market themselves through intensive promotion and one of these pioneers was the mixed capital company Konsumprod S.A. which offered and promoted various services in 1983. The range of services included the production of commercials; the recording of important domestic events such as wedding ceremonies, family reunions, as well as recording congresses; and test performances of actors. This latter service was designed as an economy device to save the cost of expensive film tests. With the agreement of Polish television, Konsumprod also recorded certain TV programmes, mainly sports events, for the use of Polish people working abroad. For domestic customers, the company offered combined services consisting of the recording of a family event and then the organisation of several shows – an important factor for those who did not possess their own equipment.

These types of services are continued nowadays by the new ITI company which emphasises the production of commercial programmes for both Polish and foreign customers such as airlines, and firms participating in international affairs. Licences for such activities are being issued outside Warsaw. For example, in Krakow five such licences were issued by July 1985; here the services consist mainly in recording family events and the preparation of video materials for training in various enterprises.

OTHER USES OF VIDEO

The programme for introducing video to schools as a teaching aid, though advancing rather slowly, seems to be the most serious plan of video utilisation. The programme is piloted by the Ministry of Education and so far three major regions have been selected: the highly urbanised district of Poznan, and the rural regions of Nowy Sacz and Zamosc. The long-term plan foresees the supply of video recorders to all schools in these regions in order to assist the teachers of (mainly) natural sciences and technical subjects. The contents of the programmes are being prepared by the Institute of School Programmes but work is still at an early stage. The school system overall has approximately 2,000 video recorders, most of them operating on tape, but there is a general lack of appropriate programmes. Nevertheless, some money has already been devoted to the development of the scheme, including certain sums in hard currencies, which will enable the Ministry to acquire further domestically produced video recorders (for which payment partly in hard currencies is required).

One of the youth organisations, the Union of Rural Youth, has also declared an interest in the popularisation of video in villages, but no tangible results have been observed so far.

Video recorders are also used by the Catholic Church. Apart from the recording of religious services and ceremonies and the presentation of films of a religious and artistic nature, the Church authorities plan to establish parish video libraries for practical advisory services.

PROGRAMMES OF VIDEO DEVELOPMENT

Plans are now being drawn up to transform the spontaneous and unorganised development of video in Poland into a more orderly process. Official sources proclaim the necessity of the popularisation of video, maintaining that in a socialist country this new technological achievement which arouses so much popular interest deserves the support of the state.

We are now at the stage of studying particular models and of designing plans. Video has been assigned two basic functions. Firstly, it is expected to supplement and reinforce the cinema network. An increasing interest in cinema has been observed recently, but since there seems to be little prospect of major new investment in large, costly cinema halls, the modest space requirements of video viewers can in a way solve this problem. Secondly, video is expected to make an important contribution to both the regular school system and to permanent education. The Open University, which is to be established in a few months' time, serving the needs of the working population of various ages, will utilise video tapes as an important teaching tool.

The popularisation of video must rely on the general availability of recorders and cassettes for Polish currency and at moderate prices. Therefore the Kasprzak enterprise plans to start production of its own video recorder adopting the VHS system, with an annual output capacity of 10,000 machines, beginning in 1986. If the equipment is to be widely purchased, the price should not exceed 100,000 zlotys (about 150 dollars), and this will not be easy to achieve. The state company ORWO is preparing the production of video cassettes and the first output can be expected in 1987.

The problem of recorded software will depend on future legal regulations. In 1986 Parliament (Sejm) is expected to pass a new Cinematography Bill to resolve a number of problems connected with the relations between the production and distribution of films and of video. More concern is expressed with finding a solution to the problem of the State monopoly over the import of cassettes. Two possible solutions are being considered: either the State will act as the only distributor with the possibility of sub-licensing other firms; or it will limit itself to controlling the kind of materials already in distribution. The Bill will also regulate the payment of copyright charges.

The presence of the pre-recorded cassettes on the zloty market depends on production capacities. These capacities are at present about 2,000 cassettes a year. However, there are plans for the purchase of equipment which will increase the capacity tenfold, and the 20,000 cassettes implied will constitute the first stage of development. The target of 100,000 is thought to be close at hand, and at this level of production there should be a profit margin and possibilities for export. The issue is quite urgent, since for example, the enterprise Polski Film, promoting Polish film productions, has already received requests from potential buyers willing to purchase video cassettes of Polish cinema productions.

In July 1985, practical solutions to the problems of video libraries were considered. So far cassettes have been very scarce; market observers say that in order to meet demand, the libraries need 200,000 copies. The attainment of this target depends entirely on the production capacities of the national industry. Thus it seems that during the next two years the owners of video recorders in Poland will have to rely on private loans. However, it is difficult to say whether a system of private video libraries will be allowed to operate. The authorities seem to be in two minds about this question and the licences already granted may very well be withdrawn. There are also rumours that the owners of private video libraries will be required to pay for their licences in convertible currencies. All this provokes much anxiety for if economic measures prove too strict, there is a real danger that all lending activity will recede underground, at least until the State-run libraries become fully competitive. This kind of development might result in a situation where the market is dominated by productions banned through censorship. Such programmes tend to be either political or violent and brutal.

The present plans are that state video libraries will charge very low fees for cassette lending (the target is 50 zlotys for 24 hours, the original charge being 500 zlotys). The realisation of this ambitious plan depends entirely however, on having a sufficient number of cassettes in the state libraries' stocks. Otherwise there is little chance of success.

Another problem may be the attractiveness of programmes offered by the state libraries. The Polish cinema board is in possession of a number of attractive items, and some successful material has been selected for video-copying. On the other hand, the import purchases are bound to be very modest in the immediate future and in this field, State libraries will probably fail in competition with private lending schemes. At the end of 1985 the private operating rental system in the 'grey market' is offering more attractive programmes for lower prices. Financial decisions at the central level are awaited, but expectations should not be too high in view of the lack of foreign currencies.

CONCLUSION

We have characterised the present stock of video recorders in the hands of the population in Poland as largely influenced both by the economic situation – purchases of durables as a form of investment – and by the lack of attractive TV programmes. Another factor should also be taken into account: video is a 'private' medium utilised at home, in family circles. This fits in very well with the present tendencies prevailing in Polish society, where most social relations tend to be limited to a close circle of family and friends. The possession of video equipment is usually accompanied by the process of establishing contacts with other video owners which facilitates the exchange of pre-recorded cassettes. Many people who decided to purchase video equipment found out that as a result they entered into new and hitherto unknown circles of those who lend or exchange cassettes. These circles tend to be closed to the outside world. Many comparatively affluent individuals questioned by the author had difficulty in identifying those of their friends who were owners and utilisers of video. It is this kind of secrecy that leads to conclusions about the limited scope of video technology on a national scale. Moreover the same representative sample study which allowed us to calculate the number of video recorders as 324,000 also shows that only 5.1 per cent of individuals questioned (ie 1.4 million persons) could point to friends who possessed video equipment.

Another paradox of the Polish video situation which also contributes to the limitation of the circle of receivers, consists in the very restricted access to pre-recorded cassettes; this means that home video collections are poor and the equipment is often in need of repair. However, this situation is slowly changing, and the utilisation of video is bound to become increasingly popular. Further reductions in prices, the availability of recorders and cassettes for Polish zlotys will make video accessible for those groups of the population who do not accumulate foreign currencies but nevertheless have a fairly high standard of living. This category should be estimated at no more than 2 million households. If video recorders do not become available for zlotys at a price of approximately one and a half times the value of a colour TV set, demand in the private market may soon be saturated.

This does not mean that the 'club' reception of video programmes will not be on the increase. This form will probably remain the basic one for the utilisation of video equipment in the years to come. The level and quality of equipment owned by various clubs and culture houses is close to the one possessed by the average household, the difference being perhaps only in the quality of the TV set or the size of the cassette collection. The people who frequent the clubs are attracted not only by the facilities but also by the opportunity to meet friends. If the development of video were to be channelled through the clubs, this could lead to the revival of this form of social reception of cultural values. However, this will depend on the contents of club video cassette collections. The successful clubs will be those which find access to new and foreign material. If the public clubs are not able to provide attractive programmes, video fan clubs may develop in private houses; this is possible aiming young people or in the suburban housing areas. Even now there has emerged a group of people who manage private libraries, lending books from their private collection – which seems a useful service in view of the crisis of public libraries in many parts of the cities. This kind of activity may also be extended to video cassettes, especially in those city districts where neighbourhood relations are lively.

However, all the prognoses may turn out to be wrong. We are now facing very serious decisions concerning the form of video in Poland. These decisions are expected in the near future, and the rapid development of video proves that the situation may change quite radically in the coming years.

Chapter 12

UNION OF SOVIET SOCIALIST REPUBLICS

'Don't we have the right to assume that television will give rise to new technology and will bring about new means of expression which we cannot
even imagine now?'

Réné Clair.

Video has become commonplace in the Soviet Union. True, people still invite
each other to see home and club video-programmes as they did to watch TV
in the early days of its development, but video is no longer exceptional. It is
both a new form of cultural leisure and a source of knowledge and progress;
the number of foreign-made video tape recorders in the USSR is over 2 million.
But the development and spread of video technology is unbelievably rapid and
is giving rise to a new subculture and means of communication; this video
boom has taken some public institutions as well as law-makers, and theorists
in culture, information and communication, by surprise.

In their attempts to come to grips with the specific character and functions
of video, different researchers suggest completely different approaches. Theorists and practical workers in 'electronic journalism' raise the problem of the
new aesthetics of television: something which supposedly appears on the basis
of magnetic tape video recording technology. It allows the wide use of the
depictive-expressive techniques of cinemas within the limits of the methods
peculiar to a 'live' telecast. 'Now it is quite obvious', underlines M Goldovskaya,
art critic and producer, 'that video tape recording has brought about a wide
range of previously inaccessible artistic possibilities which are very important
for telecasts of all types and genres, that its role in transforming TV from a
'transport' means into a screen art is exceptionally important'.

In their turn, researchers and publicists viewing video in social, cultural and
everyday life situations see it as a factor of knowledge, information, cultural
development, ideological and aesthetic education and entertainment, a factor
which may help solve a problem of great social importance – the problem of

leisure. It is beyond doubt that the rapid development of video may be conditioned by the fact that it has advantages over the traditional means of communication, and that it has shaped a definite social need.

Free choice of time and repertoire gives rise to a new aesthetic quality, a new character of psychological perception. At home for example, it is possible to view a video film repeatedly, reflecting upon it, to stop a shot, to see the film in sections over a long period of time and so on. Video helps to solve the problem of 'difficult films' – masterpieces of world cinema which did not find large audiences, and in this sense it may be considered as a school of aesthetic education. Video provides a possibility of restoring some lost public values – for example, by exerting influence upon children with the help of 'films of youth'.

The entertainment, cultural and recreational functions of video are so evident and vast that many researchers did not notice, at first, the major possibilities which this phenomenon offers for ideology, information and propaganda. But, due to the nature of the video-screen, even a documentary is perceived as entertainment, and that is why there are few psychological barriers to the acquisition of information. The video picture is memorised in a leisurely fashion as if unrelated to the spectator's will. Audio-visual stereotypes directed towards subliminal perception are firmly fixed in the consciousness of the mass audience.

The social and public importance of video lies in two facts: the first, that the audience, traditionally provided with political and artistic information from a number of sources, has received another one, effective and particular; and the second, thanks to new technology, that a sphere of communication has become available to population groups which formerly had no access to it, given the existing means of distributing information and culture.

The genie has been let out of the bottle. How will he behave: will he be become an assistant, a servant of those who have opened the vessel, or will he be an uncontrolled and evil element? Video has attracted the attention of workers in different fields: politics, sociology, culture and mass media.

VIDEO AND TELEVISION

The USSR is the first socialist, multinational state in the world. It covers 22.4 million square kilometres of which about 25 per cent is in Europe and over 75 per cent in Asia. The population on the 1st of January 1985 was 276.3 million.

Experimental video-tape recording on Soviet TV began in 1954 and since 1960 has been used at TV studios throughout the country. For a long time it was used for the preparatory recording of a 'live' telecast with the aim of editing it later and for preserving programmes to be used repeatedly. By the middle of the 1960s the technique of videotape recording was widely, but not creatively, used and it had little influence on the development of TV. Bulky, immobile equipment, the need for high illumination, problems of arranging magnetic tape 'by eye' were obstacles to the use of video-tape recording in television.

The newsreel-documentary serial *Our Biography* directed by G. Shergova, was an important stage in the development of Soviet TV. It was shown in weekly parts from November 1976 to November 1977, and was devoted to the 60th anniversary of the Great October Socialist Revolution. Film crews engaged in making the serial used a new kind of mobile reporting TV station of a new vintage with colour TV cameras and compact video-tape recorders. The films of the serial were arranged with the help of video-tape recorders equipped with computers which allowed matching to a precision of 1/25 second ie one shot.

The development of portable video-technology provided new possibilities for TV in the 1980s. Side by side with mobile TV stations mounted in buses, (MTS) Soviet TV crews use complete sets for television journalists which include a hand colour TV camera weighing up to 8kg and a video-tape recorder with an autonomous supply unit.

When video-tape recording was first introduced on Soviet TV a magnetic tape 50.8 mm (2 inches) wide was used. The first mobile video-equipment was supplied with a tape 25.4 mm (1 inch) wide. New video-cameras and cassette video-tape recorders make a single unit and are designed for a tape 3/4, 1/2 and even 1/4 inch wide. There is no world standard for the format of video-tape recording, and although this may indicate a trend in further miniaturisation of video-technology, at present it considerably hampers the exchange of video-programmes. Undoubtedly, the proposals on unification of TV standards submitted in 1982 to the International Union of Cinematechnology Associations (ICUA) by RCA, Matsushita, Hitachi, Ikergami concerning the adoption of a telecasting standard for recording on a tape 12.7 mm wide, as well as those proposals made by Sony, Matsushita, Victor, Hitachi, Philips on the introduction of a single standard of video-recording on a tape 7–8 mm wide and 10 MCM, deserve attention.

The video hardware used today is, in the opinion of Soviet specialists, not only the complete electronic equivalent of cinema hardware, but it has also a number of advantages. It is fairly comfortable, silent, portable, mobile and transportable; video-tape, as compared with cinema film, may be used repeatedly. It makes video-programmes more efficient. Modern video hardware makes it possible to carry out shooting by several cameras simultaneously, at different angles, with long shots and close-ups and so on; to arrange the pictures in the process-shooting as well as to choose and arrange the material just after shooting, to pre-view the material, to make picture by picture arrangement on stationary equipment, to obtain combined shots in the process of shooting or arranging, and to obtain special electronic effects.

All this suggests that very soon video film in all its genres will become a basic type of preliminary fixed TV programmes and will take a key position in telecasting. At the same time, there are fears that video-tape fixed programmes, reducing TV to 'home cinema', threaten to destroy in TV audiences that specific faith in telecasts which has been created by the simul-taneity of this type of communication – the wonder of seeing actual up-to-the minute life at a distance. That is why there are those who think that in future there should be combinations of video-films and direct telecasts on TV screens.

TECHNOLOGICAL AND ECONOMIC ASPECTS OF VIDEO

Over 2 million foreign-made video-tape recorders used in this country represent different firms and trademarks (Sony, Hitachi, Matsushita, Philips, Akai, Pana-sonic, Grundig and others). The greater part of them are sold through 'Commission shops' in which the price is decided upon by the shopkeeper. In the last 3 to 4 years the prices of foreign-made video-tape recorders has dropped from 4–5 thousand to 1.5–2.5 thousand roubles. A considerable number of video-tape recorders have been sold through the 'Vneshposyltorg' shops.

There are some tens of thousands of Soviet-made video-tape recorders in public and individual use. At present, three enterprises produce video-hardware: Complex in Novgorod, Pozitron in Leningrad and Electronika in Voronezh.

The cassette video-tape recorder Electronica BM-12 (priced at 1200 roubles), produced in Voronezh, is in greatest demand. This recorder meets the level of world standards. It has 26 integral schemes, 10,205 resistors and conden-sors, 164 transistors, 5 magnetic heads and is designed for high-abrasive tape. Electronica BM-12 weighs 10 kg, it is operated with the help of a micro-computer and has a timer for setting and calculating the time to record a chosen TV programme. The recorder makes it possible to speed up or slow down a review of recordings and to stop at a given picture. The complete set of Elec-tronica BM-12 includes a video-camera. The recorder does not need any adapting device for the reproduction of a recording on Soviet-made TV sets. Electronica BM-12 provides high quality recording on ordinary serial video cassettes of BK 180-type.

The unreliability of the video-heads and some high-precision mechanisms has repeatedly been a subject of criticism in the press but despite this, Elec-tronica BM-12 is in great demand (and in short supply), thanks primarily to its low price.

The number of video-tape recorders produced yearly by the Soviet elecronic industry does not exceed 30,000. It is planned to increase the level of annual production to 60,000 by 1990 but even this will not satisfy the demand. Until recently video cassettes were also in short supply. Now Soviet-made cassettes are freely available. The price of a 3 hour unrecorded cassette BK-180 is 43 roubles and, a pre-recorded cassette with a full length feature film is 75 roubles. The relatively high prices of Soviet-made video cassettes may be accounted for by the fact that they are manufactured on the basis of a Japanese-made tape which must be bought for hard currency. The cost of a state-made record-ing of a full length film is so high – 32 roubles, that it encourages a holder of a video-tape recorder to turn to a 'private trader' who asks 15 roubles for such a recording. The hire prices are high too, from 2 to 5 roubles per day. For the same price one may hire a TV set for a month, or to go and see 6–10 films in a cinema. A drop in prices of video cassettes and hire-services is expected soon, since the USSR Ministry of Chemical Industries intends to start production of its own tapes.

Video Usage

The potential of video in achieving state aims and tasks, in carrying out a purposeful cultural policy, in the intensification of the international exchange of information and cultural values, is undoubtedly vast and not yet fully realised. However, the specific character of video becomes most obviously apparent in public and individual use, since it satisfies the cultural and ideological needs of both small groups and individuals. The specific character of video production increases the importance of the subjective factor. The consumer of video information has considerably more possibilities to formulate the content and repertoire of programmes and voluntarily chooses the time, place and frequency of their performance. The possibilities of video combine the advantages of audio-visual means of communication with those of printed journalism, in particular of illustrated magazines, or rather they 'remove' the limitations inherent in other audio-visual means, by driving away the 'forced character' of television programme consumption (time, sequence, volume, rhythm and so on). In this sense, video may be regarded as an important element of personal freedom in the field of communication. Thus it is obvious that 'domestic video' has great prospects and all aspects of its development should be considered.

VIDEO SOFTWARE

Films for Soviet TV are produced at practically all TV and cinema studios in the country to special order. In 1984, the cinema studios released 127 such films; in 1985–1986 their number was considerably greater. The work of film-makers is directed by the production-creative association Ekran set up in 1968 within Central Television. The association has studios producing feature films, documentaries, musicals and cartoons; it also co-operates with film-studios when making television films for central television.

There is a new tendency to establish special units for making video-films at cinema studios. For example, the Central Studio of documentary films has established a unit which produces newsreels and popular science films for TV. It has also started production of pre-recorded video cassettes for public and individual use – plays, concerts, practical advice programmes on the cooking of national dishes, car driving, car servicing, and so on.

The leading producer of video software for public and individual use is one of the associations of the State Committee for Cinematography of the USSR (USSR Goskino) – *Soyuzkinofond*, which has a special department engaged in making copies of video-films. *Soyuzkinofond* puts out 500,000 video cassettes of VHS/SECAM system – 12.7 mm (1/2 inch), and it is planned to double production by 1990.

The best works of Soviet cinema are recorded on cassettes. These are feature films – from the serious, including historical films, to pure entertainment. 'In my opinion', says Valery Markov, the director of *Soyuzkinofond*, 'it is quite natural for a man to see first of all those films which have been made in the world where he lives, and hence which reflect its realities'.

As the *Soyuzkinofond* catalogue for 1986 shows, the four hundred films recorded on its video cassettes are arranged into 10 groups: 1 – historical-revolutionary films; 2 – military-patriotic films; 3 – historical films; 4 – films portraying present day life; 5 – screen versions of works of fiction; 6 – adventure films; 7 – fairy-tales and films for children; 8 – science fiction films; 9 – musicals and comedy films; 10 – foreign-made films.

The press and the public appreciate the choice of the films as well as the fact that both popular old films and quite new films, not yet released on cinema screens, are recorded. There is nevertheless a negative aspect – the video cassette repertoire of the *Soyuzkinofond* is actually the same as that of the cinema. The number of original video-recordings of musical shows, circus performances, plays and so on is very small at present. 'The number of classical works is not enough. And they should have started with the works of Charles Chaplin, Walt Disney, Réné Clair, Federico Fellini, not the 'Angelique films' writes the newspaper *Nedelya* (Week). 'There is a danger that hits will prevail'. It is felt by some that an effort should be made to copy cinema films, presented at international film festivals, and 'to buy the best works offered by the world video-cinema'.

Today USSR Goskino plans to put out cassettes with about 100 programmes of Central Television and also to make about 60 independent original programmes every year.

Thus, the state aspires to influence the development of video; viewing it as a new and effective instrument of ideological and aesthetic education, as an important factor in spreading and shaping cultural policy.

FOREIGN POLICY

Much is being done to make video a medium for information in foreign policy and to measure its possibilities for the development of international relations. The Novosti Press Agency (APN), established in 1961 as an information agency of Soviet public organisations, directs the production of video software addressed to foreign audiences. At the end of 1985, the Joint Editorial Board of Video Information was set up within the APN structure. (Material concerning the activities of APN is compiled and summarised by Eugeny Y Dugin,

Doctor of Philology, Dept of Journalism, All Union Institute of Higher Qualifications for Workers in Mass Media). Its task is to make, either independently or in co-operation with foreign TV companies, video-films and video-clips covering various aspects of Soviet life, advocating ideas of peace, friendship and co-operation between the USSR and other countries. Recently a serial about the Soviet Republics has been released. The video-films about Georgia, Armenia, the Ukraine, Tadjikstan, Moldavia and Estonia were made in co-operation with Bulgaria. Hungary, the German Democratic Republic and Poland all of whom contributed to producing video-films about Kazakhstan, Siberia, Dagestan, Azerbaijan, Byelorussia and Lithuania. APN and 'Interpress' (Poland) have jointly produced the film *To be or not to be* featuring the work of the 'Workers of Science and Culture for Peace Congress' which was held in Warsaw.

Video-clips about important political events can be a useful form of international co-operation. For example, all APN video-programmes covering the work of the 27th Congress of the CPSU were shown on TV screens in the socialist countries. Copies of the best films were sent to Africa, Latin America and Western Europe. APN programmes are systematically used by tele-studios in India, Cuba, Egypt, Democratic Yemen, Kampuchea and other countries of the world. Co-operation has been established with the TV organisations of Malaysia, Singapore, Morocco, Colombia, Mexico and others. The exchange of video-information between APN and TV companies in capitalist countries has been introduced.

The number of countries to which APN sends it video-software is continually growing. The agency constantly perfects its forms and methods of disseminating information on foreign-policy by the use of video. One such promising form is the showing of video cassettes at briefings, press conferences for journalists at APN and so on. A video-tape recording which featured the results of the meeting of the Soviet and American leaders in Geneva was shown in Algeria. Video films about the 12th World Festival of Youth and Students which were part of the Quiz *Do you know the USSR?* were also very popular with Algerian audiences.

Video-programmes about Michail S Gorbachev's visit to France were shown to local journalists in the APN information centre in Delhi, in the International Centre of India and at the International Trade Fair in Delhi. Reviews of video-material on Soviet-American political relations took place in the German Democratic Republic, and at a number of videotheques. The video entitled *A Threat to Europe is a Threat of the World*, made by APN, was an important element in the work of the meeting 'Workers of Art for Peace' held in Vienna. Many public organisations in Austria requested and received copies of the film for further copying and demonstration.

Video cassettes are also shown through diplomatic channels. Recordings of important political events are often shown at official receptions in Hungary, Yugoslavia, Romania, Ghana, Kenya, Egypt and other countries. In Austria, for example, the video recording of Mickhail Gorbachev's presentation of the political Report of the CPSU Central Committee to the 27th Party Congress was shown to the diplomatic corps.

In view of the increasing interest in Soviet video software, the APN Board of administration has taken a decision to provide all its representatives and bureaus abroad with video hardware by 1987.

Besides APN, other Soviet organisations are establishing mutually beneficial relations with various foreign organisations. The foreign trade association 'Sovexportfilm' has signed agreements to co-operate with the export-import organisations of Bulgaria, Hungary, the German Democratic Republic and other countries on mutual rights to choose and to show feature, popular science, documentary and cartoon films recorded on video-tape. Exchanges of video-programmes are many. For example, the first video cassette hire centre, opened in Czechoslovakia in July 1986, offers films made in Czechoslovakia as well as foreign films, including Soviet ones. The creative team 'profile' set up at the Barrandov film studio will be engaged in making video-programmes to be shown in Czechoslovakia.

Mutual purchases of video-software are made by 'Sovietexportfilm' and the Hungarian export-import organisation Ofotert. The Orion plant and the Video-ton enterprise in Budapest produce video-tape recorders under Japanese licence.

Wide co-operation in the production and distribution of video software has been established with the Bulgarian Cinematography Association where the production association Bulgarvideo is also engaged in the distribution of programmes among video-clubs and for individual use.

At present, with the aim of systematising and regulating all these activities, the possibility of bringing video software of the member countries of the CMEA under a single standard, of concentrating the production of video hardware in one of these countries and of unifying technical requirements, is being considered. All these measures may contribute considerably to a wider international co-operation in the field of video – a prospective means of spreading knowledge and culture.

SOFTWARE USAGE

The most common form of public and individual use of video software in this country is videotheques (centres which hire out video cassettes), which were set up in the autumn of 1985 in Moscow, Leningrad, Kiev, Vilnius, Rostov-on-Don, Kaliningrad, Novorossisk and Voronezh. The videotheque network belongs to the USSR Goskino, which announced that by the end of 1986 there will be videotheques in 25 cities: Tallin, Minsk, Odessa, Kharkov, Alma-Ata, Dushanbe, Tashkent, Frunze, Yerevan, Tbilisi, Sukhumi, Bsku, Novosibirsk, Omsk, Perm, Sverdlovsk, Ufa, Kuibyshev, Gorky, Cheliabinsk, Vladivostok, Khabarovsk, Kazan, Kishinev, Riga.

These videotheques are centres where state and public organisations, as well as individuals, may hire cassettes. At present their repertoire includes over 500 titles of video films in a number of copies. All the films are divided into four categories. The first includes historical-revolutionary films, political films, films for children and young people. Such films as *Battleship Potemkin* (Goskino), *Chapaev* (Lenfilm), *Peter I* (Lenfilm) are included in this first group. The cost of hiring a 2 hour cassette from this category is 2 roubles per day.

The second group consists of films which have most contributed to the development of Soviet and world cinema; films raising complex problems of social life. The cost of hiring a film from this category is 2 roubles 50 kopecks.

The repertoire of the third group includes concert and variety programmes, circus performances, sports-casts, those home-grown films which are most popular with the audience, plays, and films made in socialist countries. A cassette of this type costs 3 roubles a day.

Films produced in capitalist countries are in the fourth category and the cost is 5 roubles per day.

Video-salons, set up in some cities on the basis of videotheques combine the functions of a hire-centre and a viewing room. In Moscow, a video-salon in Arbat Street has a viewing room for 40 viewers and small rooms for 2–4 customers. In spite of the rather high cost of the tickets – from 50 kopecks to 1 rouble 40 kopecks, which is equal to the ticket price in a high-class cinema – the number of prospective customers is always rather large since the latest feature films are shown there, very often before they are shown on cinema screens. The USSR Goskino intends to open 100 new viewing rooms for which experimental video-projecting equipment made in Japan and Italy has been purchased; video-equipment with 19 mm tape gives a good picture on a screen 3m (9 feet) across.

Without doubt, videotheques and video-salons are a prospective form of the consumption and use of video-software. At present, however, they cannot satisfy all public and individual needs. That is why 'video-lovers' resort to the services of 'businessmen' . The lack of interesting recordings on hire makes a video-tape recorder an instrument for making easy money. This situation gives birth to a number of ideological, economic and legal problems connected with the production, functioning and use of video.

VIDEO AND THE LAW

Video is gaining strength as a cultural and social phenomenon, but there are a few unfortunate consequences. A number of trials connected with unlawful activities in this sphere have been covered in the newspapers and the legal aspects of the problem are of great interest to numerous owners of video hardware and to the public at large.

The law is based on moral principles, and a conscientious, honest owner of a video recorder, acts according to the law, even, if he or she is not fully aware of all the legal niceties – notes a Doctor of Law, Professor I M Galpenin. One of the violations of the law connected with video is the collection of payment by private persons for the viewing of a video programme. This is prohibited and involves administrative or criminal responsibility. Under Soviet law, a private person is not allowed to provide entertainment for profit.

Owners of video recorders collect cassettes, borrow them from their friends, make copies, exchange cassettes and so on. These actions are not punishable. But the gaining of unearned profit should be guarded against, for it is both immoral and illegal.

Soviet law is a good barrier to works of poor taste propagating the cults of violence and cruelty, humiliation of human dignity and sex perversions. The list of prohibited imports includes videocassettes which may harm the political and economic interests of the country, state security, public order and its citizens' health and morals.

Video cassettes featuring cruelty and violence as such are not banned from distribution but those featuring cruelty and violence which incite abuse of the basic principles of morality and humanism are prohibited.

As early as 1923, the USSR signed the Geneva Convention against pornography. Under article 228 of the RSFSR Criminal Code and similar articles of the other Union Republics, the production, distribution or advertising of pornographic works as well as their sale is punishable by a maximum prison term of 3 years or by fines up to 300 roubles with confiscation of the works. Video tapes with indecent, cynical pictures of sexual acts are pornographic products. The showing of pornographic video cassettes, whether for money or free of charge, to a large audience or to a narrow circle of people, is a criminal offence.

The press has printed material from trials connected with the distribution, advertising and selling of pornographic video tapes. The court decision to institute criminal proceedings against a certain citizen, as the newspaper quotes, said: 'Being in possession of foreign-made video hardware and video cassettes with porno-films, the accused distributed and advertised the contents of these films and showed them to other people'.

In deciding such cases in court the statement of a competent expert in the arts is taken as evidence. Pornography is indissolubly connected with obscenity; in the Commentary to the Criminal code, pornography is defined as 'obscene publications cynically picturing sexual life of people ....' But notions and appraisals in this field, as experts treating the legal aspect of the problem emphasise, change with time. 'Criminal punishment is imposed for the distribution of pornography proper but not for any deviations from usual standards of 'moral' permissibility. Subjectivism, approximation, judging by one's personal predilections are inadmissible here'.

The problem of protection of copyright in the field of video is even more complicated. There have been no expert elucidations of the problem in the press. Meanwhile, the question of the existing restrictions provided for by copyright should be discussed by the public at large since its practical application at present is of concern to everybody.

From the legal point of view, there is no difference between the distribution of sound recordings and video recordings. The number of cassettes of musical hits made by 'amateurs' is, many people believe, considerably larger than the number of 'industrial' cassettes of the same hits, which are under the control of Copyright agencies. In accordance with common sense, nobody tries to tackle the problem since the possibility of uncontrolled distribution lies in the very nature of magnetic recording which indicates the artificial character of the term 'video-piracy', coined, undoubtedly by firms but not by law-makers. Obviously the prospect of wide uncontrolled distribution of software should be taken into account when drawing up a contract for the original recording of works of music or video-films.

Legal norms in the field of video are a complex question which is not yet fully settled by the laws in force. Thus it is necessary to regulate legal relations in the field of video in order to achieve a harmonious combination of public interests and the rights and legitimate interests of individuals.

CONCLUSION

The need to expand video technology was raised at the 27th Congress of the Communist Party of the Soviet Union when the main directions of the country's expansion in the coming years were discussed. This means that from 1986–1990 solutions to the problems of video in the Soviet Union will be sought on a state-planned basis. At this level a higher quality of decision may be expected and new trends in the expansion of this medium of communication and of culture may appear. Goskino USSR faces the specific problems of re-working the new video systems, cinema-television technology, holographic cinema, vario- and poly-screens.

The prospects of video expansion are characterised first and foremost by the fact that the video tape is the first revolution in technology since the invention of electronic television, and has far from exhausted its possibilities in the field of television. In 1967, when the first models of light weight video-cameras had only just appeared, a British journalist Robin Day noted that 'the disappearance of cameras working with celluloid is only a question of time.'

The video magnetic tape has become not only a means of conserving television programmes, but has changed the very character of the creative process of telecasting. The new possibilities offered by video tapes continue to extend the spectrum of television's artistic expression, to enhance its specific nature, and to contribute to its transformation from a mere 'means of transport' to an independent and special form of screen art.

Thanks to the simplicity and purity of the tape and its reproduction, video is begining to break into the realm of cinema. In a range of specific fields the substitution of a video screen for a cinema screen has begun, and undoubtedly this trend will broaden with the expansion of video techniques. A preview of the films competing in the XXXVIII International Congress and Festival of Scientific Cinema, in September 1986 in the Leningrad Picture Theatre,

'Rodina', was mounted on a video screen. Since all the competing films which had been shot in traditional cinematic fashion had been transferred to video tape, it was possible to examine a frame more carefully, stop the picture, change the speed or bring shots of the films stills straight from the screen to the participants of the Congress.

The remarkable prospects of video are connected with its extension as a new and effective channel for ideological and aesthetic education, as a method of spreading culture and of shaping cultural policy, as a means of scientific research activity, as a form of education and learning. If, at the present time, video is employed by several scientific research institutes, hospitals, faculties of journalism and institutes of the creative arts, schools, sporting organisations, leisure and cultural centres, then in the course of the next five years, it follows that a massive increase in the practical applications of video-- techniques may be expected; video will become the main element in the processes of learning and discovery, training and leisure. The idea of one New York firm to set up a 'Video-encyclopedia of the 20th century' which, according to the journal 'US News and World Report', has already incorporated material on 2,217 of the more important events of the century and prepared them for use in schools, has aroused the interest of the Soviet press. 'We connect the further expansion of video with its introduction into schools, higher education, houses of culture, enterprises and factories, sport complexes', writes an APN correspondent. 'There it will be possible to show specialised programmes; for example, how to work electronic calculating machines, or safety techniques, or the demonstration of various sporting techniques'.

There is no doubt that the educational and cultural-recreational functions of video will lead to the further expansion of the network of videotheques and viewing halls. Many small and middle-sized cities have taken the initiative and are organising hire pools and viewing salons for themselves. The local press reports that three video salons and a video cassette hiring point are being opened in Nalchik (Northern Caucasus). This lead is being followed in other cities of 200–300 thousand inhabitants. But, obviously, the spread of video could have its greatest social and cultural impact in small settlements without theatres, concert groups and so on.

The mass adoption of video serves not only to strengthen and add to the cinematic systems, but also in the organisation of micro groups which possess common educational, creative, local, and other interests. Video offers considerably greater possibilities for satisfying the interests and expectations of these micro-groups than, for example, cinema; its strength being in the intimacy of its nature, its active character in shaping a repertoire to the objectives of the communication process; and, to the viewer, a greater diversity of already existing programmes. Used by individuals, video fulfills the role of home cinema, of a new form of family leisure, and may prove to have a special influence on relations between generations and on the psychological climate in the modern family. The increase in production of video equipment and the lowering of prices will undoubtedly bring about the further spread and democratistion of video.

At the same time, it would be very limited to treat video simply as a 'family medium', a way of spending leisure time, and to develop its meaning and perspectives only from this point of view. Of course the entertainment and cultural-recreational function of video is important – it is possible that it is precisely this that lies at the base of its original nature. At the same time, to perceive video as essentially a source of entertainment, an escape from the daily cares of life, would be not only a limited treatment of its possibilities and functions, but a conscious attempt to shut out the existing problems of contemporary society; to escape from the problems of life and existence of mankind into the illusionary world of video. Video is beginning to be actively used by international and national organisations for the exchange of information, for comparing ideas and learning about other cultures. Video should become one of the instruments of mutual understanding in the fight for peace; a review of new ways of thinking, for this has become absolutely necessary in the nuclear age if we are to preserve the world in which we live.

Video will not take over or change other methods of communication; it adds to traditional methods of spreading information and culture. The establishment of video as an integral part of the communication system leads to a changing of the other elements, a partial re-allocation of function, a change of correlation.

In turn, in accordance with the principles of systems analysis, the changes effected by video in the media – television, the press, radio, cinema – must be seen in terms of the evolution of a newly developed element entering into the system; that is, of video itself. Therefore, in the not too distant future, a new level of quality may be expected in the expansion of this interesting, informative, cultural and social phenomenon, the full potential of which is as yet the stuff of which dreams are made.

Chapter 13

YUGOSLAVIA

There has been a rapid expansion of radio and television in Yugoslavia in the last 15 years (the most rapid in the world, after Japan). The demand for radio is satisfied while television is approaching that point. Yugoslavia has approximately 23 million inhabitants living in 6.2 million households with an average of 3.6 members. The number of registered and unregistered (portable) radio sets is equal to that of households, while the number of TV sets is almost so (5.5 millions). It is estimated that there are approximately 1.5 million colour TV sets. Television programmes are produced by 8 RTV centres and broadcast on two channels in colour (the PAL system) with the daily schedule lasting for approximately 15 hours on average. Programmes are televised in the languages of every region (republics and provinces) of the country.

Information programmes constitute 20–30 per cent of the schedule whilst cultural and entertainment programmes constitute 30–50 per cent. Over half the information programmes (judged by length) are newscasts, while the cultural-artistic and entertainment programmes comprise films, TV serials, programmes of general entertainment, folk songs and children's programmes in almost equal proportions. About 500 feature films and a large number of documentaries are shown annually. Almost half the foreign films come from the United States (the largest group offered and at the lowest prices). About half the TV serials and dramas are of foreign origin (American, British, French, Italian, Soviet, Czechoslovak, GDR, etc). The most popular programmes are films, TV serials, plays, sports events (telecasts), with the major news bulletins being watched by about 70 per cent of viewers (the potential audience numbers approximately 12 million inhabitants). The cinema network and cinema-going is declining.

Year	Number of cinemas	Number of cinema-goers (in 000)
1963	1,629	116,885
1973	1,512	86,317
1983	1,293	86,500

On the basis of this data one may conclude that in Yugoslavia two processes have provided the basis for the development of video: the rapid expansion of television; and the crisis, or stagnation, of the cinema. It should also be added in this connection that the move from the initial period of largely unselective television viewing which lasted 3–5 years to more selective viewing in the late 1970s was fairly rapid (according to audience research using a model group).

In recent years, the economic crisis contributed to this state of affairs as well as a decline in the quality of TV programmes which was caused both by the economic crisis and other factors.

Although these factors alone have been quite sufficient to create the space for a video breakthrough, there are also some more specifically Yugoslav factors. Firstly, the Yugoslav population is very open and receptive to innovation in general, and to technical and technological ones in particular. Though this phenomenon is a general characteristic of new, dynamic societies undergoing a process of a rapid (revolutionary) demographic, cultural, social, political and economic transformation, the people of Yugoslavia have always reacted more quickly in the acquistion of innovations than their social organisations and institutions. This is particularly significant for the development of video in that the change in viewing patterns in general, has been more extensive than in other societies with similar characteristics and degrees of development. Thus in the last five to ten years the Yugoslav population have tended to give up going to the cinema, have been more selective in watching a rather poor television system, and have been steady and quick to accept all the new developments which affect the quality of life – if necessary making great efforts and even sacrifices.

HISTORICAL DEVELOPMENT

All these factors have been sufficient for the breakthrough of video technology, but the speed at which developments took place was unexpected. The first video recorders in private use emerged around 1975. By the end of the 1970s there were several hundred video recorders; at the beginning of the 1980s about 10,000 and at the end of 1985 almost 250,000 (our estimate). In that year, however, it became evident that developments were slowing down and expansion came to a halt. The so-called 'boom' period came in the years

1982/83. This fast and wide expansion of the video market in Yugoslavia was generated by a very important single factor, which is the existence of, and the impact exerted by, two large migrant contingents of the population abroad – we are referring to the economic migrants and their descendants (about 3 million people residing in the United States, Australia, Canada) and people working on a short term basis abroad (about 600,000 with almost 300,000 additional family members in the Federal Republic of Germany, Austria, France, Sweden, Switzerland). This factor indicates the openness of the country towards the rest of the world and the unlimited two-way traffic of foreigners and Yugoslav citizens.

According to estimates of the *Mladost* newspaper dated 21 October 1985, there are between 300,000 and 500,000 video recorders in Yugoslavia and the role of the migrants in the development of video was complex:

a) They gave the initial impetus to the development of video as they were very quick to discover and utilise the advantages of this new communication media for the recording of significant events or situations at home or abroad – weddings, 'Slava', birthdays, funerals, holidays, parties, etc. The cassettes could then be exchanged;

b) They searched for, and were supplied with, tapes of Yugoslav TV programmes;

c) They encouraged the RTV organisations to begin the production of video recordings of the performances of popular artists;

d) They supplied the domestic market with approximately one half of the existing recorders and cameras – in two thirds of the cases in accordance with Government regulations.

One major factor in the rapid expansion of video in Yugoslavia is therefore the need expressed by large groups of citizens, both at home and abroad for this new media which they use to maintain and strengthen family links. The state neither helped nor hindered this process through its regulations. Indeed, it did not formulate any particular policy in the area. However, in the period 1980–1985, the customs regulations concerning Yugoslav citizens abroad did change several times, particularly with regard to citizens returning home. These changes contributed to an increase in the import of video hardware and of blank and pre-recorded cassettes. The possibilities for illegal imports are also great because strict customs control is virtually impossible at peak periods, (eg religious and official holidays and particularly when the tourist season is at its height). When relatives and friends are thus supplied, a large quantity of video begins to circulate on the 'black' or 'grey' market (through direct arrangements, advertisments in the newspapers, magazines or special press, on the local radio, sales through commission stores in the social sector, etc).

Foreign citizens represent the second channel for importing video hardware and software to Yugoslavia. Foreign tourists (nearly 6 million in 1982) are primarily responsible and it is well known that they import video equipment in unknown quantities, and then sell it. Another (also large) group is made up of foreigners who are in Yugoslavia on a temporary basis, such as business people or diplomats or the personnel of commercial firms and of course several thousand foreign students. Some observers consider that the role of this channel in supplying the market (in Belgrade and big cities in particular) is the most important one. It also has to be borne in mind that official control and repression in this sphere is slight and almost of no practical significance.

The third, and in practice the only, legal and legitimate channel for supplying the market with video equipment is to stock goods received on consignment ie sales of video equipment produced abroad. Yugoslav work organisations authorised and registered for the trade of foreign goods are agents for virtually all the significant producers of video equipment in the world and sell their products in practically unlimited quantities.

In view of the fact that every citizen may have a hard currency account with an unlimited deposit potential and given that no-one has to justify the funds in the account, it may be estimated that there are approximately 3 million private hard currency accounts totalling about US$8 billion (October 1985). This is very significant, though its actual share in the expansion of video ranks third. Its specific significance lies in that it introduces quality video hardware and software (the latest models of Sony, Panasonic, JVC, Hitachi, Philips, Saba, Grundig, etc). Sales through consignment stores, however, lag behind due to unavoidable and rather high customs duty of 43 per cent.

The fourth possible channel is the domestic production of video hardware. Although Yugoslavia has a developed electronics industry (of a medium size) which covers a broad area of professional electronics, small computers and colour television sets ('Iskra' of Kranj, 'Elektronska industrija' of Nis, 'Ruid Cajevac' of Banja Luka, 'RIZ' of Zagreb), a periodic display of interest in video has not produced concrete results. The reasons for this are to be found with different priorities and problems caused by the economic crisis. There is no doubt, however, that sooner or later domestic production will develop. For the time being only pre-recorded cassettes are produced (the Belgrade RTV and Sarajevo RTV). Blank cassettes made from imported BASF and ORWO tapes are produced by a workshop at Brcko. The significance of this is best demonstrated if prices of cassettes are compared: a cassette made at Brcko costs about 900 dinars (US$2.99) while the price of a blank cassette in the market is 2,500–3,000 dinars (US$8–10); the RTB sells a pre-recorded cassette at a price of 10,000 dinars (US$35) while its production cost is about 1,999 dinars (US$6), etc. There are, of course, other channels which supply the market with video hardware and software in the 'grey' or 'black' market. Airline staff and other professions are also significant importers.

EFFECTS OF VIDEO

This rapid expansion of video varies both geographically and socially. Belgrade has the largest number of video recorders and the most lively market (due to the concentration of the factors of expansion). In Belgrade there are 25 video clubs (privately owned) which constitute the major basis for the video turnover. It should be remembered that the capital has 1.5 million inhabitants, sophisticated communications with the other parts of the country and the world, numerous foreign embassies and foreign companies, frequent international gatherings and a large number of migrant workers. One third of the population is in the higher than average socio-economic bracket and 30–50 thousand citizens and foreigners belong to the so-called elite. Belgrade thus occupies the leading place with regard to the volume and intensity of video communication. However, when certain aspects (for instance video art) are considered, advantages can be attributed to other centres, for example, Ljubljana where the Second International Video Festival was held recently (at which a Yugoslav was awarded the prize for the best visualisation).

Other big urban centres, above all Ljubljana and Zagreb, as well as smaller towns in border areas with local border traffic (Koper, Maribor, Rijeka, Split) and urban centres of the migration areas (Livno, Mostar, Krusevac, Bitolj, etc) rank second.

The third place is occupied by a broad area of rural settlements and small towns scattered in the less developed south and southeastern parts of the country where video communication is increasingly a way of entertaining and linking families separated by migration. Thus, for instance, in the small Bosnian town of Donji Vakuf there is a video studio 'Aida'. Its free of charge catalogue offers 500 hours of recorded material consisting mainly of concerts, sports, cartoons and 1920s and 30s comedies.

With regard to the country's official regions video is most developed in Serbia and Croatia. Slovenia and Bosnia Herzegovina follow, then Vojvodina and Montenegro, whilst video is least developed in Macedonia and Kosovo. This distribution does not necessarily reflect the level of socio-economic development of the Yugoslav republics and autonomous provinces but rather the extent to which the factors contributing to the development of video are present.

VIDEO USAGE

A study of video users has produced the following results:

a) Institutional users are not numerous; they are about 10 per cent of the total. They are as follows: schools; scientific and artistic institutions; military institutions and internal services; sports clubs (professional ones in football and basketball in particular); health institutions (screening and analysing of operations and new procedures); and industrial organisations. The degree of utilisation of video hardware is rather low (in schools it is slightly higher) while the mode of utilisation is elementary and displays little inventiveness. This finding raises a very important question about the systematic and organised spread of video culture.

b) Collective users are small in number. Only a few instances of collective watching have been recorded, such as those organised by the Catholic church and some cultural-artistic clubs. There are almost no gatherings at which people pay to watch video films as in Poland and other Eastern European countries.

The predominant form of video use in Yugoslavia is for private or family group viewing. Group viewing most often takes place within the family or within a circle of friends and acquaintances with whom informal social ties are maintained. In this respect, video no doubt plays a positive role as it often enriches what has become exhausted, superficial, formalised and repetitive communication.

The programmes viewed become the subject-matter of discussion in the same circle while impressions and information are afterwards spread in the next circle of contacts. Individual use of video is often for the purposes of time-shift viewing.

The demographic and socio-professional structure of video users comprises almost all the existing categories (universal popularity and spread) but with an unequal frequency. Men are more often both owners and watchers of video than women probably because women rarely watch sports and pornographic films or war and other films with scenes of violence. As far as age range is concerned, the younger generations dominate (25–40 years), but there are video fans in almost all the age groups. With regard to socio-professional status, the majority of video users belong to the category of people with at least secondary school qualifications from all backgrounds having a source of extra earnings with centrist socio-political (prevailingly self-management) opinions. In terms of property ownership, they cannot generally be considered wealthy and with regard to their value systems and interests they express a technical-specialist rather than humanist-intellectual orientation. In Belgrade there is no residential concentration of video fans but rather an irregular territorial dispersion.

AUDIENCE PREFERENCES

Content preferences vary greatly depending on demographic and socio-cultural characteristics. These preferences are concentrated and ranked as follows:

I   Domestic films
II   Foreign box office hits
III Other films not presented on television
IV   Other films not presented in the cinema

V   Documentaries and cartoons

V I   Pornographic films (recently of declining interest after an initial period of great popularity)

This list was made on the basis of the turnover of the video lending clubs. However, at this point it should be added that the total structure of preferences also comprises (a high rank) individual material of a personal or family content and time shifting of TV programmes.

The Yugoslav 'top list' of films (published in the *YUVIDEO* review 21 October 1985) is as follows:

1   *Oci u oci sa smrcu* (*A View to a Kill*)
2   *Rambo II* (*Rambo First Blood Pt.2*)
3   *Put za Indi ju* (*Passage to India*)
4   *Cotton Club*
5   *Snezana i sedam patuljaka* (*Disney's Snow White*)
6   *Policajac iz Beverli hila* (*Beverly Hills Cop*)
7   *Prohujalo sa vihorom* (*Gone With the Wind*)
8   *Otac na sluzbenom putu* (a Yugoslav film, the Cannes Festival winner)
9   *Radovan III* (Yugoslav)
1 0   *Krav rata* (Yugoslav)

In addition to the limited domestic production of video cassettes, legal and illegal imports, primarily from the countries with the PAL TV system, represent the major source of videograms for the Yugoslav market. The highest imports are from the United Kingdom, Denmark, Holland, Federal Republic of Germany, Singapore, Kuwait. Customs duty is 500–600 Dinars (US$2) per cassette imported legally. However, pre-recorded cassettes are rather expensive in the United Kingdom and for this reason many of them are pirated TV programmes.

VIDEO EQUIPMENT

The diversity of video equipment is very wide as there are no regulations or standards, no domestic production and imports are chaotic. Almost all machines available on the world market are obtainable in Yugoslavia, but the latest and most expensive video hardware is relatively rare and limited to the video clubs and a few individuals. The cheapest hardware is also relatively rare with the result that the middle range of video recorders dominates. Video cameras are not numerous (approximately 2 cameras per 100 video recorders). All three systems (PAL, SECAM and NTSC) are available but VHS dominates (70 per cent recorders). Panasonic (Blaunpunkt) and JVC (the largest number of recorders) dominate the VHS system followed by the cheaper models produced by Fisher, Sharp, Orion (fairly recently) and finally Hitachi and other producers.

The Beta system which has 10 per cent of the world market represents 30 per cent of the market in Yugoslavia and is available from Sony and its licensed partners (Dual, ITT, Graetz, Nordmende, Saba, Telefunken). There is a very small number of V2000 systems.

Video clubs of various types, mostly privately owned, make up the major part of the video infrastructure in Yugoslavia. These clubs are registered at local bodies of administration (communes) and established by individuals who invest a significant amount of their own resources (ranging from 5 to 25 million Dinars (US$2,000–10,000), work, inventiveness and risk. Thus, '... Thanks to private initiatives we have climbed into the last carriage of the train of the technological revolution ...' (R. Zelenovic, editor of the *Yuvideo* review). The basic role of these clubs is to lend and copy cassettes. All the clubs are involved in these activities which are fairly well remunerated (up to 30,000 dinars (US$100) daily if it is well organised). However, they are rarely established on a professional basis (only about 5 per cent of clubs are professional) and most are a secondary or part-time occupation. In Belgrade and other centres the more developed and better equipped clubs offer a broad repertoire of services.

The way in which video clubs are organised and the volume of business varies widely from simple, modest clubs to complex, developed ones. Some have regulated their organisation and business by statutes. Some publish monthly bulletins containing information about new films, which are despatched to all the members. In addition to servicing the general public, the clubs also offer service to their members who enjoy certain privileges (lower hire prices, small services free of charge, assistance in the maintenance and servicing of video hardware, etc). The largest clubs have over 1,000 members. The membership fee can be paid monthly (1,000–2,000 Dinars; US$3–7); about 2,500 Dinars for three months, with or without an obligation to contribute (usually) two blank cassettes. The hiring of cassettes, and films, costs 200–400 Dinar (US$0.50–1.00) per day, depending on whether a film is an older one or a 'hit'; whether it is a domestic or foreign film, with sub-titles in translation or in the original language only, etc. The copying of a customer's material costs about 1,000 dinars (US$3) for every hour. All these prices do, of course, increase with inflation and the figures presented are for October 1985. Some of the clubs deliver cassettes ordered by telephone and most clubs offer an average of over 1,000 titles.

Although video clubs are assumed to constitute the infrastructural basis of the market in Yugoslavia they are not the only operators in this field. There are also numerous individuals with both domestic and international activities as well as certain public institutions and organisations. A significant role is also played by the press. Almost all newspapers and magazines, particularly those for the young, supply information about video. In Belgrade there is a specialised *Yuvideo* review with a circulation of 90,000 and the Zagreb *Trend* review provides comprehensive information.

The Yugoslav market is closely tied to the international video market in many diverse ways. For example, some ten Yugoslav families in the opal mine Coper Pidi in the middle of the Australian desert have jointly bought a video recorder and have a contact in Belgrade who records popular songs and other TV programmes and despatches them to Australia by air. There are many firms in the world entitled 'Jugo video', 'Jugo media' and the like, which offer video services in addition to the sales of other Yugoslav products (drinks, speciali- ties, newspapers, books) and other business in general.

Cases of individual initiatives are numerous. A resident of Munich purchased 35 domestic films from *'Yugoslavia film'* at the price of 300,000 DM, with the exclusive right to distribute these films in the German language area, so that his cassettes (at a price of 129–199 DM) can be purchased in the Federal Repub- lic of Germany, Austria and Switzerland. A Yugoslav businessman in Sydney, Australia, with the same type of arrangement, sells cassettes of popular songs, the price of which ranges from 70–80 DM to $50 in Australia and the United States of America. The Department of Records of the RTV in Belgrade has entered this market with its recordings of the very popular 'Hit Parade'. The RTV of Sarajevo offers its programme *Koncert Lepe Brene u Mostaru* (the Concert of Beauty Brena at Mostar). The matrix on a U-Matic professional cassette is sold to overseas countries at a price of US$2,500, while the Depart- ment of Records of RTV in Belgrade distributes almost all cassettes for the family video recorders in Europe. However, this break-through of Belgrade TV and Sarajevo TV to foreign markets, with Yugoslav customers, has still not produced the anticipated results, because private middle-men are quick to find ways of obtaining cheaper pirate software with little risk of prosecu- tion as there is practially no restraining legislation. Programmes by Yugoslav authors are pirated by private individuals as soon as they are broadcast on television. In some cases, programmes are stolen by those employed at the television offices. Not only can modern copying equipment together with com- puter printers reproduce the high quality opening identification for a video cassette but a poor copy can be enhanced.

Joint ventures with foreign partners, on a shared profit basis, would be one solution to the problem mentioned above. Agencies for the protection of copyright should, of course, participate in such projects. Prices would then be competitive and the quality better than that of pirate productions. There are other original solutions such as the *'Video Estrada'*, a firm run by three Yugoslavs in Dusseldorf. This firm records its own one hour programmes of popular songs for the price of $600 and promises that the programme will be sold only to one purchaser in any given country. The only condition that the customer has to agree to is to purchase 12 programmes out of the 24 recorded annually. In addition, the firm provides the printed credits and the packaging. They expect that such favourable conditions will attract customers from all over the world and sell programmes in at least ten countries.

It is, of course, no wonder that so many producers and middle-men appear in such an unregulated state of affairs. Thus, for instance, the concerts of the Yugoslav Podium's stars (Beauty Brena and Miroslav Ilic, etc) are recorded

under a strict control by their managers and cassettes are then sold successfully during their tours. Such phenomena are quite understandable, since
television in the countries in which large contingents of Yugoslav migrants
live, does not offer many possibilities for entertainment (many migrants do
not know the language well) and certainly does not satisfy the migrants' needs.
Special programmes intended for foreign workers are often broadcast once
a week only. At the same time, a video recorder has become almost a status
symbol of a migrant worker. In the Federal Republic of Germany, for instance,
it is possible to purchase a new video recorder of an older generation for less
than 1,000 DM so that the majority of Yugoslav workers possess one or two
of them. Video recorders may also be borrowed. However, as far as software
is concerned, the situation generally has been bad. The channels of supply
for the Yugoslav market abroad have been, and still are, insufficient and inade-
quate. In the Federal Republic of Germany, 'Yugo-media' distributes to some
twenty libraries from which Yugoslav workers may obtain not only video cassettes but also music cassettes, records and books. However this is insignificant
as compared with about 1,000 Turkish and almost the same number of Italian
video-libraries. It is then no wonder that there are exchanges of cassettes. For
example Yugoslav migrant workers may trade their unrecorded cassettes for
those recorded by Yugoslav owners of video recorders.

Unfortunately the competent Yugoslav organisations have not yet entered
the video business either in the domestic or in the international and potentially stronger market. Film organisations including the Belgrade 'Centar films'
and the Zagreb 'Croatia films' as well as other organisations have expressed
the intention of engaging in video production but so far without any significant results. *'Yugoslavia film'* has contracted several arrangements with
Australia and the Federal Republic of Germany but it is a poor beginning.
Yugoslav TV centres have the best chance for a rapid expansion, but their
activity is, in fact, insignificant bearing in mind the possibilities they possess
(a rich fund of recorded serials, dramas, music, entertainment, children's
documentary programmes, etc) for both the domestic and international
markets.

VIDEO REGULATIONS

In order that video in Yugoslavia might further expand and develop its undoubtedly positive and significant potential, it is essential that there are social
regulations in the broadest sense.

Earlier experience has shown the speed with which technical innovations
are accepted in Yugoslavia and this makes it all the more necessary to formulate a policy for the development of the new communication media and for
video in particular. The lack of such a policy has already caused serious
problems and damage.

Video is already fairly developed, but there are no legal provisions governing this activity. The lack of social initiative and the insufficient activity on the part of institutions and work organisations in the social sector has led to the emergence of video operating exclusively within the framework of *private ownership*. A law passed in January 1985 now governs all private business activities in this area and all of them should be in conformity within the provisions of the law by the end of the year. Before this, a work licence for a video club was issued by the competent communal bodies along with an authorisation for providing audio-visual services, but without any closer specification. In autumn 1984, the Town Committee for the Economy of Belgrade turned to the Yugoslav authors agency for an opinion on 'whether and under what conditions, a person can be engaged in the video cassette lending of domestic and foreign pre-recorded cassettes and whether and under what conditions they can be engaged in copying pre-recorded video cassettes by their personal work as an occupation'. The agency's legal department's answer was categorical: as video club owners do not pay authors' fees their activity is contrary both to the copyright law and the Law on the Film Industry as well as to international instruments to which Yugoslavia is a signatory such as the Berne Convention on the Protection of the Rights of Authors of Literary and Artistic Works. This assessment ends by noting that the matter under consideration is not legally regulated. So an analagous implementation of the Law on the Film Industry is in question here. However, member states of the Berne Union and other states consider that the problems arising with regard to video cassettes are similar to those of the record industry. The International Federation of Phonogram Industries added the word 'videogram' to its name. This is significant because the rights of the producers of phonograms (and now of videograms) were regulated at an international level by the provisions of the Rome Convention of the Berne Union countries as early as 1961. A condition of the convention was a specification of the provisions in each domestic legislature. So far, Yugoslavia has not ratified the Rome Convention so that there is a legal void not only in the sphere of video but also in the sphere of records and audio cassette production within which there are also twelve producers working with foreign licences.

The buying up of film rights for Yugoslavia falls under the competence of the *'Yugoslavia-film'* a business association of film distributors. In *'Yugoslavia-film'* the opinion prevails that the future of video in Yugoslavia is a matter for the film industry not for private individuals. They point out that film lending can be done by those possessing a legal permit and add that the video-clubs' repertoires often comprise the films considered unacceptable for showing in Yugoslavia by the Programme Council of *'Yugoslavia film'*. In interviews the video-club owners say that they are not against purchasing cassettes via the *'Yugoslavia film'* or even in department stores. They have been very flexible and even suggested varying models for their own self-management in association with the social sector and institutions. If no solution in this direction is found, if one respects only the legal provisions, which forbid, from December 31st 1985, the copying of cassettes, the situation will be even more

221

aggravated. It is impossible to believe that a very developed video business will cease. It will simply recede and become an 'underground' operation. 'Secret' clubs with non-professional equipment will flourish instead. There will also emerge even worse chaos and insecurity and damage for the society as a whole. It is therefore absolutely necessary to undertake urgent, provisional legal and other measures so that permanent solutions can be found in accordance with the character of the Yugoslav socio-economic and political system to ensure the significance and development of video communication in the country.

Chapter 14

HUNGARY

> By definition the video approach to culture serves not only large masses
> but minor groups, [...] Inherently, it is the basis of the regional visual culture
> from a technical point of view. It touches off a new quality of democratic
> folklore.
>
> Csaba Pogany

In Hungary, in 1984 about 120,000 adults had video recorders in their homes.
It is estimated that there were about 72,000 privately owned sets. This figure
surpasses all earlier predictions which is taken from data collected by the Mass
Media Research Centre in 1984 from a sample of 10,000 people. The sample
was representative of those aged 18 and over. The participants were asked
about the means of mass communication they owned or had access to, and
about listening, reading and viewing habits. The systematic collection of data,
which has been going on for more than a decade, makes it possible to observe
changes over time and to describe the spread of the new technologies.

Ten years ago in Hungary only a few institutions had video recorders. Privately owned sets began to be brought into the country four or five years ago,
and the number brought in has increased substantially in the past two years.
In the early 1960s during the initial phase of the television era it was a popular
custom to watch TV with friends, acquaintances, neighbours or at institutions
or restaurants. Now that there are one or more TV sets in almost every home,
these seem distant memories, although hardly more than two decades have
passed.

Today we are witnessing the development of a new popular movement. Many
people now visit friends or neighbours in order to see a film or video
programme, which can be seen neither in the cinema nor on Hungarian TV.
Out of 100 adults questioned, 6 answered that their acquaintances had video
recorders. On the basis of this, the number of adults who have the opportunity
to watch video films may be estimated at 470,000. Among people under 18,

the number is probably higher, especially if we take into account possible access to the sets of various educational establishments. An extensive social life and an increased interest in the new technologies among young people accounts for the fact that 15 per cent of our 18–19 year old interviewees have acquaintances with video sets. This new technical marvel, which has become quite common in the West, should be considered as an important factor, an integral part of the lives and entertainment of several hundred thousand Hungarians. From the number of video sets and the proportion of those who have access to them, conclusions may be drawn as to the size of the social group affected by the video recorder.

The number of regular viewers of video films can be estimated at 200,000. This number includes the owners of video recorders and the members of their families. If it is estimated that the owner of a video recorder together with friends and friends of their children adds up to about 10 persons. The number of those having access to video recorders may be approximately 700,000. In other words the minimum number of people with the opportunity to watch a video set is 670,000 but the actual number may be as high as 800,000 to 900,000. Thus, a large number of people may be able to watch different films or TV programmes recorded on video cassettes independently from the television broadcast schedules.

This is by no means a small social group ready to promote its own interests at all costs and it is clear that there is a large popular demand for access to video films other than those recorded by television. In a year or two we ought to be cured of the infantile disorders attached to the use of video equipment and thus able to avoid any permanent damage which might hinder the spread of the new device on a national scale. In time, video may surely be expected to fulfil several purposes and prove useful for society as a whole.

1984 was a turning point in the domestic use of video equipment. Among other things the production of video recorders, and the lending of pre-recorded cassettes and recorders began, while the duty on VHS sets was significantly reduced. The acquisition of VCRs is not easy, so they should be regarded as highly significant family investments. Who can afford this luxury?

About one third of the sets are to be found in Budapest, one third in country towns and one third in smaller communities. Those who have video recorders represent 2 per cent of the adult population in Budapest, 1.8 per cent of that of the country towns and 1.2 per cent of adults in smaller communities. The national average for video sets is 1.5 per cent.

In 1984, 98 per cent of adults had radios, 96 per cent television, 18 per cent colour television, 53 per cent tape recorders, 33 per cent portable sound systems and 40 per cent record players. Of the total number of adults 1.5 per cent had video recorders, 8.5 per cent of those having colour TVs and 10 per cent having colour TV with a decoder.

In Hungary today, approximately every tenth inhabitant has the chance to watch a programme recorded on a video cassette using a video recorder, and every twentieth person has an acquaintance who owns a video recorder.

The majority of the video sets in private ownership serve either as substitutes for, or as additives to, television and they also provide an opportunity for the individual to import films from abroad. The use of video radically alters the habits associated with television. This new means of mass communication, which is the first real challenge to traditional television, is exercising a tremendous influence despite its limited presence.

DOMESTIC VIDEO PRODUCTION

The production of TV sets goes back to the 1950s in Hungary. Besides satisfying domestic needs, colour television production is also export-oriented.

Two large electronics companies are planning to start producing desk video recorders, and both are co-operating with Japanese companies. In the first phase, all components and assembly units will be manufactured and supplied by Japanese firms, and only the final assembly will be done in Hungary. In the second stage, the principal mechanical and electro-mechanical assembly units will be supplied by the Japanese firms, the remaining parts will be produced locally and final assembly done in Hungary. In the third stage, only the high-tech mechanical elements and some semi-conductors will be imported, and everything else will be done in Hungary. The annual production capacity is envisaged to be 50,000 to 100,000 units, a rate which would satisfy home demand and open up export opportunities. As a first step, the Videoton company put 1,000 video recorders on the market at the end of 1984.

A third company Hiradastechnikai KTSZ (Cooperative of Telecommunication Engineering) is preparing to produce Panasonic video cameras on the same basis. This company has been making video mixer consoles for some time. They are, however, a poor match with amateur and semi-professional video equipment due to the technological problems of the different systems. For this reason, an institute of public education developed a video mixer and effects unit and supplies it to institutes of public education at cost price.

In the domestic production of video cassettes, one company entered into an agreement with the Magna company. So far, only the assembly has been undertaken in Hungary and the current price is approximately 500 Fts for a 180 minute cassette.

Overall, the development of domestic production has been progressing very slowly and uncertainly, whilst imports show a steady growth.

DISTRIBUTION OF VIDEO RECORDERS AND CAMERAS

Experts estimated the number of video recorders in the country to be between 50,000 and 80,000 in 1985. This number is growing very rapidly and yearly growth is about 20 to 30 per cent. If favourable measures were to be taken this figure might be doubled. One such measure could be the launching of the domestic production of video recorders – this has been the intention for many years – in co-operation with certain Japanese firms. Another factor might be the stepping-up of national imports. So far, however, private importation seems to be the most reliable source. A considerable proportion of this is semi-official (eg buying articles in hard currency shops for hard currency of unauthorised origin etc) or illegal (video recorder coming into the country without paying the levied duty and then being sold through private channels).

The territorial distribution of video recorders within the country is fairly even. Most sets are located in the capital, Budapest, as well as in the major towns of the counties, but there are video recorders in several villages, and the owners are not always the centrally backed educational centres, but in quite a few cases private individuals. Assessments reveal that half of the video recorders in the country are privately owned.

When surveying the various kinds of video systems, we will start with colour television sets and monitors. The Hungarian production of colour TV sets is high and has satisfied demand so far, although there is sometimes a shortage. For this reason colour TVs from the West are available especially as they are of a higher quality and provide a better service than the Hungarian ones. Approximately one fifth of all television sets are colour sets.

Institutions have preserved a great many imported video cassette recorders which began to come into the country in the early 1970s. These machines have become obsolete, because their recordings cannot be played elsewhere, unless they have been copied (we refer to the 1/2" Sony, the 1/4" Akai, the Philips VCRs etc). The first U-matic video recorders also date from this time and the majority of them are still functioning (Sony VO 2850, VO 3800, VP 1230 etc) In the early 1980s a number of Betamax sets were imported and they are also still operative.

In 1983, the Government took a decision to standardize the introduction of the VHS system. As a result, the duty on VHS video recorders will be reduced and units manufactured by the state will be of the VHS type. Since the state system and the lending services deal almost exclusively with VHS cassettes, private imports are also of VHS systems. The variety of systems reflects the wide choice on the Western market, but Hungarian buyers generally prefer Japanese brands (Panasonic, JVC, Hitachi, Sony etc). The Hungarian video market used to be several years behind the Western market but this is no longer so and the latest models appear quickly in Hungarian shops. For example, the compact VHS, the Hi-Fi VHS and the 8mm video camcorders are all available. The cost however is 6 to 8 times higher than it is in the West.

TV and Video Standards In Hungary the state-run television relay stations broadcast using the SECAM (E) system and the tranmission is through the OIRT channel distribution. There are two broadcasting channels. The video recorders in circulation in Hungary are dual standard (PAL and SECAM), as are TV receivers. Dual standard sets of Western origin, however, have to be re-tuned, as they are of the DDR-SECAM system, where the picture-sound distance is 5.5 Mhz. All systems of hardware are available.

There are approximately 30 different VCR models (mostly VHS) in Hungary. This high number is due to a lively second-hand market. Firms dealing in second-hand goods sell privately imported material. As these companies (whether they are co-operatives or run by the state) do not register the turnover of video sets separately, there is no data about the number of sets entering the country in this way. In the past year or two private video boutiques have appeared. They sell Western equipment which has been privately imported.

Video sets rarely turn up in the retail trade for there is no continuous, regular supply either from imports or from domestic production. Since 1983, there have been minor quantities of Siemens and Panasonic video recorders in the metropolitan department stores of the two big chains (Centrum and Skala). In 1985, somewhat larger quantities of recorders arrived in these department stores, but the retail sales will amount to a maximum of 3 to 4,000 units throughout the year.

In the legal domestic trade, the largest proportion of the sets is bought by public institutions. Private customers prefer buying their sets during their trips abroad. Because of the high import duty, the illegal or 'parallel' market plays an important role, although turnover is kept down by the fact that there are difficulties in getting equipment serviced and malfunctions are quite frequent in video sets.

In the hard currency shops of the Intertourist network, some video recorders (mostly Siemens and JVC) can be bought fairly regularly, but sales are low, because people without hard currency accounts cannot buy such expensive articles and those with such accounts can choose from a larger and cheaper range of goods, if they have their equipment supplied by the Quelle chain.

PRICES

The price of video units is very high in Hungary. The prices of the most common video recorders and turntables are 60 to 100 thousand Fts, the average income for from 12 to 20 months. The Panasonic video recorder, which can be bought in the Federal Republic of Germany for 1,400 marks (25 thousand Fts approximately at the official rate) can be bought in Hungary at about 70 thousand Fts whether in a second-hand shop, the 'Skala' department store or in a private boutique. A Hungarian citizen can buy and import a video recorder from Vienna for 40 to 45 thousand Fts. This includes customs and travelling expenses. It should be remembered that the majority of consumer goods are much cheaper in Hungary calculated at the official rate of exchange, than in Western countries.

The high prices result from the fact that there are no regular commercial imports nor any competitive domestic production. In the Federal Republic of Germany, the import sales tax and the retail profit margin are added to the wholesale price of the Panasonic video recorder for example. The price in Hungary, however, of the same recorder is increased in the first place by the addition of duty and a very high sales tax. A further increase results from retail profit margins and the private importer's profit. The private importer tends to spend the hard currency he or she is allotted for the journey, or hard currency purchased on the illegal market on the kind of goods that can subsequently be sold at home at the highest price. Calculations show however that the state makes a larger profit than the private importer on a video set brought into the country. Duty and the sales tax combined are greater than the private importer's profit margin.

CUSTOMS DUTY

Since 1 December 1984, customs regulations have made a distinction between imports for private use and imports for sale. Fifteen per cent duty is to be paid on VHS sets imported for private use and thirty per cent on sets for sale, just as on any other article (with the exception of personal computers) regardless of the purpose for which they are imported. In other words customs regulations favour imports for personal use, but maintain the high price levels in Hungary, which in turn influence the prices of domestically produced units and those of the small number of sets imported commercially.

IMPORTS

The decisive factors in the supply of video are the legal and illegal forms of private imports. Commercial imports play an insignificant role even if imports debited to hard currency owned by citizens (Intertourist, Quelle) are included. Only blank cassettes are imported regularly on a commercial basis. The two department store chains generally acquire imported video recorders through a direct exchange of goods (eg the Centrum chain supplies Japan with furniture in exchange for Panasonic NV-730 sets). This type of trading saves hard currency but makes the sets rather expensive since the Hungarian articles which are traded are usually priced very low indeed.

In the future, imports from socialist countries are foreseen as playing a significant role and in particular the Soviet Panasonic and the Philips-Tesla machines. The possibilities of importing from socialist countries, however, are somewhat uncertain at present because production in the Soviet Union is not very high because of technological and quality problems and a low capacity which has yet to be developed. There is moreover a large internal buyer's market. Further, it may well be that even imports from socialist countries will have to be paid for in hard currency.

EXPORTS

Apart from a small number of pre-recorded music cassettes supplied by Hungarian Television to Hungarians living in North America, there are no exports of video products. Many experts think that Hungary might successfully export software. Hungarian video recorders may very well be sold on the Comecon market, but as they are manufactured in large part from components bought with hard currency it would be unwise to produce in large quantities before the possibilities for exports have been assessed.

The principal forms of video distribution in Hungary at present are: central allocation, state-run trade, private trade and the illegal or 'parallel' market.

So far the state run trade has imported four thousand video recorders to be sold in retail shops, and it seems no increase in this number is intended. The import quota for firms meets about half the demand of the population.

Private import is the most important source of video equipment. The majority of video recorders and cassettes for which demand is highest enter the country in this way and reach the consumers through the mediation of state-owned shops. In certain cases there is a hire purchase system, particularly for television sets.

The illegal or 'parallel' market plays an important role in the prohibited sector of the horror/sex/pornographic market in pre-recorded cassettes.

VIDEOGRAMS

Until the beginning of 1985 only one programme had been copied in Hungary in commercial quantities – the jubilee concert of the Benko band by Pannonia Filmstudio. However with the expansion of the network of rental services, the production of pre-recorded cassettes began in 1985. As production is expected to supply only the rental network for the time being, cassettes are made in small series. The Television and MOKEP are planning for a larger production capacity in the next few years. At present the biggest copying shop is functioning in MOKEP's rental base, the 'Videotheque', where 60 to 70 cassettes can be produced in one shift. The following institutions will have a major role in cassette production, according to the government resolution of January 1985: Magyar Televizio (Hungarian Television) MOKEP (Company for Moving Picture Sales and Distribution) and MAFILM (Hungarian Film Producers).

In 1985, a number of specialised rental services were set up, supplied by independent copying shops. For example, a co-operative named 'Kollazs' supplies software to the Hungarian Chamber of Commerce (Magyar Kereskedelmi Kamara) and to the 'Reflektor' Publishing house of the Central Committee of the Hungarian Socialist Workers' Party (MSZMP KB Reflektor Kiadoja).

The production of illegal pre-recorded cassettes is well organised and fairly extensive in relation to the overall volume of video in Hungary. The larger illegal networks copy video discs smuggled into the country primarily from the Federal Republic of Germany, whereas smaller ones copy films of television broadcasts recorded in some Western country. The illegal networks thus provide both copying facilities and rental services. Once the legal rental service has been expanded the importance of the illegal copying shops will decrease but they will no doubt continue to produce material which is 'foreign to the ideas of socialism' or 'offends good taste'.

The hiring of software is the accepted norm. A small assortment of pre-recorded cassettes (music and adventure films) is legally available in private shops at the price of 2,500 to 2,900 Fts and in the second-hand shops of the BAV company (Commission Store Chain) at 1,700 to 2,000 Fts. In the retail trade, until early 1985 only the first Hungarian recorded cassette, that of the jubilee concert of the Benko band could be bought for 1,700 Fts. In the rental shops of the Television and MOKEP there has been a larger volume of sales since the second half of 1985. Counting on the interest of public institutions and schools in the first place, they sell domestic television and cine-films as well as films for the wider public. Cassette sales are expected to go up in both volume and variety within the framework of Videotheque, MOKEP's lending service. As far as we know the illegal rental services do not sell cassettes.

DISTRIBUTION OF USERS

Educational establishments should be mentioned first among the user institutions. About half of the one thousand VHS video recorders made by Videoton were made available under favourable conditions to the country's secondary schools with the result that nearly all secondary schools now have basic video facilities.

The other important users are the companies directly or indirectly engaged in production for firms, research institutes and other establishments that use video equipment. This is one of the ways in which video use supports production and sales.

Public education also took an important step forward when it acquired the other half of Videoton's reduced-rate Akai video recorders. In fact, all the major cultural centres now have video recorders, and a number of programmes worthy of a wider circulation have been compiled. It should be remembered here that in many cases the headquarters of local cable television are also cultural centres.

The companies offering video services so far have themselves been institutional users of video and the customers have also been mostly institutions. Recently private individuals have been offering these services at rather high prices. It is here that video appears as a luxury item rather than a medium for the distribution of information.

There are few examples of the collective utitilisation of video. Because of the high price owners tend to guard their possessions very carefully, which means that video equipment is not often used for collective purposes. At the moment there are no groups of video fans, in which members have video sets of their own. This reflects a technical lag and a shortage of facilities. The first video clubs are just being formed.

It is rather difficult to draw a picture of the individual use of video facilities. Because a significant proportion of the privately owned video machines came into the country illegally, and because possession of such facilities still presents a kind of challenge, nobody boasts about having one.

Relying on information from private sources, the conclusion may be drawn that a significant proportion of the private users cannot resist the spectacular 'hot' Western programmes and keep (and swap) sex, pornographic, horror and karate films. As video cameras are owned by only a few private users, the creative application of video techniques has hardly had a chance to develop. There are some attempts to make tapes but they are usually no more than imitations of the more stereotyped television broadcasts, which do not seem to offer much variety. Moreover the private use of video cameras tends to reveal the deficiencies of amateur film-making.

The state-run lending service of pre-recorded video cassettes is trying to improve the situation, but the interests of borrowers usually centre on cheap, phoney materials.

Main Fields of User Interest

Public organisations are primarily interested in video material which corresponds to their particular interests. They also try however to meet other expectations because of the scarcity of the facilities. For instance, they go well beyond the boundaries of using the video facilities strictly for technical purposes. They provide programmes for company get-togethers, for celebrations, the documentation of the life of the organisations, marketing, advertisements etc. In some cases the public education headquarters may be a company or a co-operative. For this reason all institutions are interested in video recordings of entertainment, music, educational and other popular video material.

Public education can be interpreted very broadly, and nearly all video material, which is associated with recreation, may be classified under this category. Yet in the video libraries of public education, Western commercial materials represent the majority of the titles, or are at least in the heaviest demand, as opposed to the much more modest presence of indigenous instructive materials.

It is rather difficult to obtain a general view of the individual use of video. The information gathered from indirect sources indicates that people are most interested in the following types of video: sex, pornography, horror, cartoons, adventure films, as well as pop music and disco programmes.

ENVISAGED AMENDMENTS TO VIDEO LAW

Following the development of the wide-scale use of video a number of amendments, extending existing copyright law to video, were introduced. They have not however clarified the situation concerning the use of video. Some more comprehensive arrangements, in addition to the latest amendments that were made public at the end of 1986, are being prepared.

The adjustment, specification and extension of the copyright laws to cover the area of video have been only partially implemented. In practice, and with a few exceptions, the regulations pertaining to films are applied. The more significant exceptions are:

-   if a video version of the film is made, the creators of the film receive additional fees;
-   television programmes or video films may be copied for private non-profit making purposes if the authors' fees (8 per cent) are paid when paying for the cassette. In this way the authors' fee is incorporated in the price of the blank cassette.

The production or propagation of video films without permission is an offence against press regulations in the case of smaller quantities; and in the case of larger quantities or repetition, it is an offence against press regulations which also contravenes the Penal Code.

The unlawful copying, selling and public presentation of the works protected by copyright is also forbidden. In both cases, the police are responsible for taking action and the sanctions are fines or confiscation.

The legal situation in Hungary with regard to video is typically transitional. Both the up-to-date and the obsolete are present in the current regulations. Attempts to make the measures coherently uniform started in 1984, but this is a very slow process and it is hindered by the efforts of specialised fields and institutions to protect their interests. Preparations are being made to issue a new law on information with a view to modernising the management of the press, and a new measure on the management of video activities is to be made public in the near future. Fully regulated video practices however are some way away. Offences so far have been dealt with leniently and the application of sanctions has been inconsistent. In such a situation the illegal market may flourish.

GOVERNMENT POLICIES

The state supports the spread of video – though it attempts to counter undesirable developments (so far with little success). Efforts are being made to provide video hardware and acceptable software domestically and all types of video activities can count on some official or semi-official backing. This is where the Orszagos Kozmuvelodesi Tanaco (National Council of Public Education) should be mentioned, because it has been spending heavily on backing the development of video technology in public education – accessible due to the Soros Foundation's allocation to the Hungarian Academy of Sciences. So far video purchases in the order of 15 million Forints have been made, financed by this Foundation.

State support exists jointly with free market conditions. For example, the domestic production of video units is encouraged although the manufacturers receive no help and the only possible source of video acquisitions at present is private import mediated by the state.

Chapter 15

WEST AFRICA

Studies on the mass media and the flow of information and communication in Africa are made difficult by a lack of data and the absence of reliable surveys; information is at best, fragmentary, incomplete and sometimes contradictory.

Neither the public authorities, academies nor mass media professionals have systematically studied the phenomenon created by the penetration of video equipment and programmes into African countries: much less have they been able to analyse what is at stake or the implications for the development of communication and for society.

When the first video recorder appeared on the African market in 1978, the cost of this new technology was extremely high. While television was no longer considered a luxury in many urban homes, video was looked on as an expensive toy. Yet within only three years a market developed and sales figures rose. It is true that the video recorder was seen as a logical complement to television, which in the African market is currently enjoying an unexpected boom. This is the result of a buoyant international market which is dominated by a few companies and the increasing transnationalisation of both equipment and programmes.

The appearance of video on the market has led to the domestic consumption of audio visual material replacing to a large extent the cinema, for the myth and the magic of the cinema, already undermined by television, are still further challenged by the advent of video.

The absence of reliable data might suggest that the African video market is negligible, but in reality there are clear indications that the demand for both hardware and software has been steadily increasing.

The existence of a fairly affluent and entertainment-hungry elite, together with a sudden demand for recorded images, seems to be the cause of the video boom, as witnessed by the increase in the number of video recorders.

Statistics on the video market in Africa should be analysed with prudence.

Frequently supplied by the public authorities, they are the result of partial or incomplete surveys. The increase in the number of sets is usually under-estimated, given the large number of sets smuggled in from Europe, North America and other countries.

An increase of 70 per cent was recorded in the export of Japanese equipment to African countries in 1982. Despite language differences, legal problems and high import duties, Africa has now become an important market. The Japanese export drive to Africa illustrates the way in which certain countries are directing their sales strategies to the less structured and less controlled markets of the Third World in general and Africa in particular.

It is important to note that the statistics available in African countries are often subjectively used and vary widely in reliability according to whether they are provided by public authorities, manufacturers, media professionals, international organisations or private bodies.

GENERAL TRENDS

In order to understand the situation of the video market in Africa answers must be found to the following questions: Who are the owners of video recorders? What kinds of programmes do they watch? For how long? What are their expectations?

The answers to these questions should also enable us to evaluate the initial effects of video on the development of communication in particular, and on society in general. At present, the effects are often harmful, as the sudden upsurge of video has created a growing and still uncontrolled market which suffers from the 'juvenile ailments' of failure to respect copyright (illicit commercial exploitation of pirated programmes) and a flood of pornography and violence. These are the first consequences of the arrival of video.

The second set of consequences relates to the debates about the new world information and communication order. Although Africa is still technologically weak, the combination of the vast reservoir of human resources and the steadily increasing population of the continent may well make it an important market for video and institutional television in the near future.

All communication experts are aware that the crucial issue for video is that it should be used to serve the needs of a society. Until now Africans have been content to watch a few thousand North American programmes disseminated by a few thousand Japanese sets. As products of a cultural industry, neither programmes nor equipment are 'neutral'. They are products, despatched mainly from rich to poor countries, and they have a substantial influence on the ideas, values and life styles of the consumer populations. Foreign programmes frequently present aspects of the consumer society which bear little relation to the poverty of African populations. For these reasons, video still further accentuates the imbalance in the international network of the cultural industries.

Furthermore, video should not be merely a form of entertainment. It can

be given much more ambitious scope, through judicious use in vital development sectors such as education, training and the socialisation of communities.
   The growth of video in Africa gives rise to two questions:

–   Can the video explosion be controlled? Will it follow its present blind course,
    or, on the contrary, can it be harnessed to meet the growing need of develop-
    ment projects?
–   What will be the specific influence of video on other means of communi-
    cation, for example, radio and television?

It is however, too early to look for answers to these questions for two reasons.
Firstly, this is a very complex and diversified field in which the situation is
changing very rapidly; secondly, at the international level video is a part of
the whole range of new means of communication such as direct television satellite broadcasting, cable television, telematics, the video-disc, and image
syntheses by computers. All these are new technologies which are central to
the 'audio-visual revolution'.
   The Côte d'Ivoire, Gabon, Nigeria, Senegal and Zaire are studied below,
although the diversity of national situations in these countries, tends to high-
light the difficulties of a regional approach to the question of video in Africa.

HARDWARE

There are no video recorder production or assembly plants in Africa and the
sets in use are imported from Japan, the United States or Western Europe.
Furthermore, since there is no national production, only international distribution (import-export) has been studied. The small size of the market is
illustrated if we look at the case of Gabon.

GABON

There are three main distributors:

CFAO – Electro-Hall, sole representative of the Japanese Company SHARP
distributes VCRs imported from Japan, through a purchasing office in Paris.
   In 1984, the number of VCRs sold was 544 whereas in the first eight months
of 1985 sales reached 474. Prices varied between $1,140 and $1,350 depending on the exchange rate of the yen, the currency in which orders are paid.
   CECA GADIS – Electro Centre imports the following makes of VCRs:
Thomson from France and JVC (HRD series) from Japan through a Paris based
agency. In 1984, they sold 280 VCRs and the price for a mono-system was
$1,275 whereas the multi-system cost $1,770.
   SOMATEM is the sole representative of imports from Philips (France) and

in 1984, 430 VCRs were sold. In the first eight months of 1985 sales reached 488. The price was $1,350.

SOFTWARE - BLANK

All blank video-cassettes sold in Gabon are produced by Sharp. Their price ranges from $16 for a 60 minute tape to $32 for a 240 minute cassette and 5,576 tapes were sold in 1984. This figure increased to about 9,000 in 1985.

HARDWARE IN THE FIVE COUNTRIES

The growth in the number of video recorders in West Africa has varied from country to country. For example between 1981 and 1985 Senegal saw an increase of approximately 150 per cent whilst Nigeria saw an increase from just under 50,000 machines to 1,500,000. See Table 1 for the comparative figures.

By 1985 however the percentage of homes in each of the five capitals, owning a video set did not vary to any great extent. Dakar in Senegal registered the lowest figures (1.9 per cent) whereas Libreville in Gabon with 2 per cent more than Lagos had the highest with 3.8 per cent.

Liable to tax and customs duty representing 70 per cent to 100 per cent of the purchase price (depending on the country), a video set varies in price from 1,500 to 2,000 dollars, which is the equivalent of ten to fifteen times the minimum monthly wage in two-thirds of the 50 member countries of the OAU.

Because of these prohibitive prices, customers buy on credit, thereby paying 20 per cent to 40 per cent more than the list price.

There are no rental facilities in the five countries studied.

In 1985, of the three formats used 90 per cent were VHS (JVC, National, Hitachi, Panasonic, Telefunken, Philips, Sharp), 5 per cent Betamax (Sony, Toshiba, Sanyo) and 5 per cent V2000 (Radiola, Grundig, Schneider).

According to the information provided by the distributors and the public authorities in the five countries studied, the institutional market is considerably larger than the domestic one.

We have no precise information on the breakdown of the institutional market but the information available shows that most of the equipment is concentrated in secondary vocational training schools and in the universities.

Next in order of importance are: community groups (cultural and religious associations, clubs), inter-governmental and non-governmental organisations, television stations.

In domestic use about 71 per cent of owners record television programmes while watching them. Sixty per cent record television programmes in their absence and 51 per cent watch pre-recorded programmes. Forty-two per cent of owners spend up to 6 hours a week watching video, 30 per cent spend eight to 12 hours a week, 19 per cent spend 19 to 22 hours a week and 9 per cent more than 22 hours a week.

BLANK VIDEO CASSETTES

Sales of blank cassettes have increased at a greater rate than those of VCRs between 1981 and 1985 with Nigeria again constituting by far the largest market. See Table 2.

VIDEOGRAMS

Production

National production is chiefly by the public television broadcast authorities which are:

Côte d'Ivoire: Radiodiffusion Télévision Ivoirienne (RTI)
Gabon: Radio Télévision Gabonaise (RTG)
Nigeria: Nigerian TV Authority (NTA)
Senegal: Office de Radiodiffusion Télévision du Sénégal (ORTS)
Zaire: Office Zairois de Radiodiffusion Télévision (OZRT)

Since July 1985, cassettes have also been produced by Altervision, the Agence d'Images du Groupe Panafricain de la Communication, which has its head-quarters in Dakar. The average price of a pre-recorded cassette is between 50 and 70 dollars.

National Distribution

Whereas the emphasis was originally on sales, in the last three years distribution firms have been introducing a variety of rental facilities. This is justified firstly by the very high cost of new cassettes; and secondly because customers prefer to hire several programmes for a single viewing rather than buy one cassette for frequent viewing. This new market trend has encouraged the creation of video clubs.

There are three ways of hiring cassettes in the five countries studied: individual hire requires a deposit of 75 to 100 dollars a year plus four dollars for each film hired. A lump sum of between 125 and 150 dollars a year secures up to four films each week.

Sale/exchange: the customer may exchange a film for a new one for a fixed charge of between 15 and 20 dollars.

International Distribution

Video Clubs are linked by contract to the following large distributors based in France or the United Kingdom: VIP, Régie Cassette Video (RCV), Rene Chatmau Production; Video Filipachi; Gaumont; VGC; Panafrance; Alpha video.

These European firms usually make their distribution networks available to the large American film companies. Films made by the eleven largest Hollywood companies have been shown in video clubs in Libreville, Abidjan, Kinshasa, Lagos and Dakar.

Video cassette rentals have shown a steady increase but only Nigeria and Zaire have more than doubled their market size. Table 3 gives the figures.

Consumption

The data collected from a questionnaire sent to two video club managers in each of the capitals to discover the most popular cassettes can be broken down as follows:

Entertainment Films: 85% sub-divided as below:

	%
Detective	30
Adventure	20
War	10
Science-Fiction	10
Political	7
Kung Fu	7
Musical	5
Western	4
Drama	4
Others	3
Childrens' Films	7
Sport	5
Other (performing arts, documentaries)	3

The above does not take into account films recorded from the television programmes which include the following:

-   films (detective, war, drama, childrens' films) generally made available by

French producers (TFI, Antenne 2, FR3 and SFP) and British producers (BBC, Visnews), under co-operation agreements;
- documentaries (road safety, hygiene, cooking, sport);
- plays (local productions);
- sports events (national sports events or competitions retransmitted live – by satellite from France – football, tennis);
- religious programmes: national events, the Pope's visit to Africa.

A study of video usage was conducted between 1981 and 1984 and in order to attempt to construct a profile of the typical Africa video user a survey of 300 people in the five countries was carried out. The figures (see Table 4) reveal that the typical VCR owner is male, aged between 25 and 50 years, with a relatively high income (over 900 dollars a month). He belongs to the socio-professional category of higher management or exercises a liberal profession in a large town.

The success of video in Africa can be attributed to a combination of factors of which two should be mentioned here. Television programmes do not always respond to popular demand and television is in any case restricted to urban areas and a small minority of those enjoying political and economic power. The programmes are usually censored and frequently dull. As a result, the public uses video as a substitute for broadcasts on the national channels, since with video, groups and individuals can make up their own schedules.

National film production is severely handicapped by a lack of financial, material and technical resources and by the barely concealed stranglehold of foreign monopolies over national distribution networks.

COPYRIGHT AND PIRACY

One of the main drawbacks of the rapid development of video in Africa is that it has created an unregulated market. Unprepared for such rapid growth, countries have not passed legislation either to protect film-makers and actors, or to combat various forms of piracy.

Not only is it difficult to supervise strict application of copyright laws, but many governments do not consider such supervision to be a priority. Furthermore, countries may feel disadvantaged by any strengthening of copyright laws, since they are not in a position to develop a two-way trade in cultural products protected by copyright.

In other words, countries which are primarily consumers of imported video programmes may consider the application of international copyright conventions as an obstacle to the free use of audio visual material.

The five countries studied are signatories to the Berne International Copyright Convention, and three of them (Côte d'Ivoire, Gabon and Senegal) have ratified the agreement on the creation of l'Organisation Africaine de la Propriété Intellectuelle (OAPI)' which came into force on 8 February 1982.

Articles 24, 25 and 26 of this agreement relate to the protection of cinemato-graphic works. In spite of this, distributors, retailers and the public authorities agree that the 'parallel market' is more developed than the legal one.

In view of the prohibitive prices of pre-recorded programmes, a relatively organised parallel market has grown up which has links with foreign coun-tries (France, United Kingdom, Belgium and the United States) and is involved in illegal copying and piracy.

Prodigious technological advances have produced more sophisticated media. An increasing number of Third World countries are displaying an interest in the vast possiblities opened up by the communication explosion. Yet a small number of industrialised countries and transnational corporations have a monopoly in advanced communication technologies (satellites, telematics, com-puters, cable television, direct satellite broadcasting, video recording, video discs etc).

It is in this field that the gap between the industrialised and the developing countries makes itself most noticeable, and the consequences are likely to be harmful.

In addition to being technologically dependent, developing countries do not have the capabilities for absorbing and mastering highly specialised technolo-gies. The choice of technology is often imposed by transnational corporations in the light of their own commercial interests, which do not correspond to the needs and life styles of the people involved.

Technological domination has economic ramifications which are all the more important in that communication has become a key sector in international trade. In addition, the communication industry is characterised by concentration and increasing transnationalisation: 75 per cent of the market is controlled by some 80 transnational corporations, all from the industrialised countries.

The arrival of video in Africa has been followed by an invasion of imported programmes which reflect foreign cultural models, with the attendant risk this implies for local cultural values. After cinema and television, video serves as a medium for the dissemination of uniform and homogeneous models of a stan-dardised culture industrially produced and based on accepted ideas.

VIDEO AT THE NATIONAL LEVEL

The acquisition of a VCR requires such a prohibitive investment that few people can afford one. In spite of its remarkable development, video still affects only a small ruling class, an elite which is drawn from among high officials and executives in the private and semi-public sectors. Given the nature of socio-economic structures, rural and marginalised groups (who represent a large part of the population) do not participate directly in its use.

The use of the new mass media remains the privilege of the groups which dominate political, economic and cultural life. There is, therefore, a great danger that this privileged minority will serve as a vehicle for models of behaviour which conflict with local socio-cultural and religious values.

It is true that this elite represents a small fraction of the population, but it is the fraction in power, the fraction that leads the way in intellectual and aesthetic fashions, disposes of an appreciable part of the national income, and is sufficiently geographically mobile to be influenced by the foreign press and to be interested in new ideas and theories in vogue.

The fundamental question is whether the new communication methodologies can and will be put to good use by governments in the interests of the community at large.

VIDEO AT THE INTERNATIONAL LEVEL

Communication is a worldwide industry and needs ever-increasing infrastructures. The growth of the communication industries has led to concentration in the areas of the collection, storage and dissemination of information and cultural products and it is difficult to imagine a free pluralistic flow of informational and cultural products in an industry dominated by a small number of transnational corporations.

Indeed, one may foresee a strengthening of the transnational cultural industries which produce standardised works for international consumption. At the international level, new communication structures are emerging which reflect the lifestyles, values and models of a restricted number of societies and which spread such consumption patterns throughout the world. This represents a serious task to be confronted in the creation of a balanced flow of international information and communication systems. For the moment the flow is only one way, from the countries which are rich both in financial resources and in the experience of cinematographic production, to countries which confine themselves to providing a public.

The new media, including video, provide the cultural menu for millions of people throughout the world. Their scenarios are based on set patterns of interpretation and identification symbols. The films marketed by the multinational film coporations are becoming more and more easily available. Many of them, often stereotyped, induce imitation and passivity in the consumer public of video-spectators.

External domination has been rejected in the political field and inequalities denounced in the economic field. Can one possibly admit their survival in the highly sensitive field of communication?

ONE-WAY INTERNATIONALISATION

With video there are ever greater risks of dependence and the strengthening of the one-way flow of cultural products from the centre to the periphery. International communication structures show that the developing countries are now the main importers of cultural products, which they buy from the industrialised countries.

Almost all film programmes come from the studios of the major American film companies: 20th Century Fox, Columbia Paramount, MGM and Universal Warner.

These multinational film companies produce and distribute, for mass consumption, products which have a strong influence on the consumer nations, even in cases where these nations have rich, age-old cultural heritages of their own.

BUILT-IN CULTURAL ALIENATION

With the arrival of video, Africans are consuming an ever-greater number of informational and cultural products originally produced for the populations of industrialised countries. It is particularly in the field of video that there emerges the danger of cultural domination, with its attendant threats to cultural identity.

Video first came to Africa at a time when the worldwide leisure industry was expanding rapidly. While growth was chiefly in the rich countries; it also spread to the urban areas and to the privileged social classes of the developing countries. The relatively rapid growth of the electronic media can produce harmful effects. For example, the continuing increase in informational and cultural products can create uniform attitudes in the groups which are most exposed to them. As with television, the introduction of new media in traditional societies has almost always disrupted cultural practices, lifestyles, social aspirations and economic patterns. In the case of the electronic media, the process of modernisation is seldom free of irreversible upheavals and foreign cultural products sometimes bring with them negative influences which disturb the social order.

It is also obvious that the cultural industry plays an important role in shaping the consumer mentality, and that it exercises an increasing influence on other attitudes.

Ultimately, however, the penetration of North American and European programmes into African homes seems to be due to the real fascination exerted by these products and an enthusiasm for the cultural content of programmes which show some of the more attractive aspects of industrial societies.

The result is that local creative artists, writers, musicians, playwrights, scriptwriters and producers take second place to imported products or to local imitations of foreign cultural material which is gradually imposing standardised international patterns of a mass culture.

As regards video, what is at stake is not only the spread of the video recorder as an electronic gadget, but also profound changes in lifestyles, social relationships and work. The cultural scope of video will not be limited to art and

literature, but will extend to all fields, economic, social, scientific and technological. Above all, the danger is that it may serve as a vector for a standardised
culture.

TABLE 1

TOTAL NUMBER OF VCR SALES

	1981	*1983*	*1985*
Côte d'Ivoire	15,000	41,000	118,000
Gabon	11,000	35,000	41,000
Nigeria	49,000	650,000	1,500,000
Senegal	9,000	16,000	23,000
Zaire	11,000	31,000	85,000

TABLE 2

NUMBER OF BLANK CASSETTES SOLD

	1981	1983	1985
Côte d'Ivoire	120,000	410,000	503,000
Gabon	100,000	210,000	308,000
Nigeria	580,000	3,800,000	10,000,000
Senegal	11,000	130,000	190,000
Zaire	115,000	201,000	305,000

TABLE 3

NUMBER OF VIDEOGRAMS HIRED

	1981	*1983*	*1985*
Côte d'Ivoire	39,000	46,000	69,000
Gabon	29,000	35,000	57,000
Nigeria	90,000	980,000	3,100,000
Senegal	19,000	28,000	36,000
Zaire	17,000	49,000	95,000

Chapter 16

SOUTHERN & EAST AFRICA – BOTSWANA, ZIMBABWE, KENYA

This report gives the findings of research conducted on the use, the spread and the potential of video in Botswana, Zimbabwe and Kenya. Botswana and Zimbabwe are both frontline states in the critical Southern African region. Botswana is directly in South Africa's economic sphere of influence and video is widespread in South Africa. Both Botswana and Zimbabwe are members of the Southern African Development Co-ordination Conference (SADCC) which is an organisation of Southern African states formed to reduce economic dependence on South Africa. The Secretary General of SADCC is the former Zimbabwean minister Simba Makoni and SADCC is based in Gaborone, the capital of Botswana.

Zimbabwe is the most recently independent African country and has a diverse, multi-ethnic population. It has good infrastructure but lack of foreign currency is a major problem. High expectations of an improved standard of living on the part of the majority has resulted in high government expenditure. Zimbabwe has a sophisticated middle class and is a country where video could develop but there are economic factors which are likely to hinder this development.

Botswana has no television network and potentially video could provide an entertainment and educational service for a section of the population.

Kenya is an East African country with a population of 17.4 million people. The country became independent in 1963 after a popular uprising by the Kenya Land and Freedom army (known as Mau Mau). Kenya is a *de jure* one party state. Agriculture accounts for 33 per cent of GDP, manufacturing 13 per cent, other industries 9 per cent and services 45 per cent. GNP per head is US$420.

BOTSWANA

Botswana was formerly the British protectorate of Bechuanaland and became independent in 1966. It is land - locked and the Kalahari Desert covers most of the country. In 1983, the population was estimated at 990,700 of which more than 100,000 live in the capital, Gaborone. The country which is sparsely populated considering its land mass is relatively wealthy with natural resources, such as diamonds and the GNP is high for Africa. Basic commodities and luxury goods sold in Botswana are mostly imported from South Africa.

However, Botswana's proximity to South Africa puts it in a precarious position, both economically and strategically. The Botswana currency, the pula is tied to the South African rand and so economic instability in South Africa affects Botswana adversely. An example of this is that when the Johannesburg stock exchange was temporarily closed in August 1985, major foreign exchange transactions were suspended in Botswana. Earlier in 1985 Gaborone was attacked by South African Defence Force raiders as warning against giving refuge to South African exiles. Thus, although Botswana appears to be economically and politically stable, it is affected by the apartheid policies of South Africa and their ramifications.

VIDEO AND THE ESTABLISHED MEDIA: ENTERTAINMENT PATTERNS

Botswana has one radio station, Radio Botswana which broadcasts in the official language English and the national language Setswana which is spoken by the majority of the population. The director of Information and Broadcasting in the Ministry of Presidential Affairs and Administration is responsible for Radio Botswana. There is no television network although one is planned. According to one expert, 60 per cent of Radio Botswana's broadcasting time (119 hours) is taken up by music. Radio Botswana has video equipment and the only editing suite in Botswana but these are not used because of lack of skilled personnel.

Owners of television sets can receive two television stations, SABCI (of the South African Broadcasting Corporation) and BOP TV (the television network of the Bantustan Bophuthatswana). The latter broadcasts in both English and Setswana, the language it shares with Botswana. These stations can be received in parts of the country because of an overspill and in Gaborone because of transmitters maintained by the TV Users' Association. The association has 400 paid-up members and they estimate that there are approximately 5,000 television sets in Gaborone. This has led to the association threatening to switch off the transmitter if more people who own television do not join the association. The system used is 625 UHF.

There is very little cinema outside the capital. In Gaborone, there is one cinema which shows British, American and South African films. There are concerts and occasional theatre performances. The South African musician Hugh Masekela is resident in Botswana where he has started a music school.

The poor quality of programmes on SABCI and BOP TV (the former is heavily controlled; the latter likes to give the impression that it is independent but is still influenced by the South African authorities) and the lack of other forms of entertainment has led to a recent increase in the use of domestic video.

VIDEO ECONOMICS

Imports of Television Sets and VCRs

It is impossible to give precise figures for the number of television sets and VCRs imported into Botswana because neither commodity is given in a separate category in the customs statistics. It should be noted that Botswana is in a common customs area with South Africa, Lesotho and Swaziland and that goods imported within the common customs area are duty free. VCRs and television sets in Botswana are mainly imported from South Africa and because there is no duty to pay, they are relatively cheap. Goods can be imported from other countries but duty has to be paid (physical 15 per cent and *ad valorem* 35 per cent).

Production and Distribution

VCRs and blank cassettes are not manufactured in Botswana. One company, Interelectronics assembles components (television and VCR) from the Federal Republic of Germany but on a very small scale. Since there is no manufacturing of VCRs and television sets in Botswana, there is no major distribution. The following firms are responsible for the importing and sale and/or hire of VCRs: Felix, Vision Hire, Holly Radio, Freshaire and Bash-O-Vision. The majority of VCRs imported and sold or hired are VHS and the average price of a VCR would be 1,000 pula (500–550 US dollars).

Consumption

A report on small business enterprises published in 1984, estimated that there were approximately 5,500 TV sets and 1,100 VCRs in the country, mainly in the south-east. However, since the TV Users' Association estimated in September 1985 that there were 5,000 TV sets in Gaborone alone, the number of VCRs may also have increased.

About 20 per cent of the market for VCRs is rental and the rest is sales.

Rental is predominantly Gaborone based. Rental of a VCR is approximately 85 pula a month (about 40 US dollars). Vision Hire offer a three month contract which includes the hire of 15 pre-recorded tapes.

It is estimated that about 80 per cent of the market is home viewing and approximately 20 per cent institutional. The predominant usage is for viewing pre-recorded cassettes.

VIDEOGRAMS

There are no production houses and there are no major distributors. There are a small number of video shops which hire video cassettes, mainly imported from South Africa. The video shops are in the cities, mainly Gaborone, Francistown and Lobatse.

Sixty to seventy per cent of the cassettes hired are films/entertainment and 30–40 per cent are children's programmes. There is a market for pornography but it is impossible to assess its importance – at a maximum, 12 per cent of the entertainment category.

COPYRIGHT AND PARALLEL MARKET

There is little observance of the copyright laws and illegal recordings are distributed. The most common distribution is that of tapes illegally recorded from British television.

VIDEO AND NATIONAL DEVELOPMENT

Some government departments have video cameras, recorders and monitors and have attempted to produce their own material on a very small scale. Andrew Quarmby, Adviser to *Tirelo Setshaba* (Help the nation), has attempted to collate the work done by different ministries and government departments and to keep a check list of the equipment different ministries have in order to standardise. Quarmby believes that VHS is most suited to Botswana's needs but the 3/4" U-Matic have been donated to the National Health Institute and Radio Botswana. Officials in the following departments who felt that video did have a part to play in the development of their area were interviewed.

Tirelo Setshaba

Tirelo Setshaba is a community youth project administered by a department in the Ministry of Presidential Affairs and Administration. Students in Botswana who have completed their secondary education and wish to proceed to higher education have to apply to *Tirelo Setshaba* for a one year community service placement in the rural areas before starting a course at university, polytechnic or college.

Tirelo Setshaba has made four educational videos of original material and four videos of plays presented in Botswana. It has a small library of video cassettes available to educational institutions.

Ministry of Education

Of the Ministry of Education's five teacher training colleges, three had video equipment installed in 1984/5. The remaining two colleges are shortly to receive video equipment. The main use of video in the colleges will be for microteaching. However, Ulla Kann of the planning section of the Ministry, felt that if proper training were given, it would be useful for the Ministry to produce its own material for use in schools. One senior secondary school has been equipped with a VCR and monitor and the Japanese government is donating further video equipment to Botswana for installation in secondary schools. However, at present, only imported material can be used and much of this is not suitable for Africa.

The Police

The Police have video equipment, but have made only one film which was for promotional purposes and was shown at the Botswana Trade Fair in 1985. The equipment is housed at the Police College but only the VCR and monitor are used on a regular basis when imported films are shown, mainly for training. The Police Commandant would like the police to make better use of the equipment and to produce videos for training cadets and teaching road safety in schools but they cannot do so because they have no personnel trained in video production. Given this situation, they prefer to rely on overhead transparencies and slides rather than make amateurish films.

The University

The Educational Resources Centre at the Univeristy and PEIP – a primary education project based at the university – also have a range of video equipment which is used primarily for micro-teaching.

CONCLUSION

Video is in its infancy in Botswana. The domestic market is expanding, partly because of lack of choice in entertainment, but also because VCRs are in a price range which the employed middle class can afford. The poor quality of many of the programmes of SABCI and BOP TV is a further reason for the mushrooming of video shops.

Although little has been achieved in the institutional/governmental market up to now, there is a place for video in national development, providing there is a clear policy for the implementation of video and proper training is given in video production and maintenance.

ZIMBABWE

Zimbabwe became independent in 1980 after a liberation war against minority settler rule. It is a potentially wealthy country but income is unevenly distributed and urban unemployment is rising. It was seriously affected economically by three years of drought but had a good harvest in 1984-5, thus avoiding the threat of famine and bringing in foreign exchange from exports. Politically the country is divided into two regions.

In terms of assessing the control of video hardware and software, the most important factor is lack of foreign exchange. Unlike Botswana, Zimbabwe has strict foreign exchange control regulations: firms must apply to the reserve bank for foreign currency allocations and individuals are granted permission to import goods only if certain conditions are satisfied. This affects the importing of televisions, VCRs, video cassettes, other video equipment and spare parts. Government expenditure is high in Zimbabwe, especially on education which has been greatly expanded since independence.

VIDEO AND THE ESTABLISHED MEDIA

Both film and video production are in embryonic stages in Zimbabwe. The ministry which can be said to have the major responsibility for film is the Ministry of Information which has a film adviser and which also has the main film production unit – Production Services. However, Production Services has no video equipment. It produces films (mainly 16mm) for the ministry's mobile rural film units which show films throughout the country to up to 200 people at one sitting hence its reluctance to make videos. The films produced are educational and informative (Production Services was a major propaganda weapon for the Smith regime during UDI) and Production Services is also commissioned to make films for other ministries. However, at present, work has been suspended at Production Services while the unit is investigated by government auditors following allegations of fraud. Hence, film is a sensitive issue in Zimbabwe.

There is no major film production in Zimbabwe but because of Zimbabwe's excellent climate and scenic conditions major foreign film companies have made films in Zimbabwe, most notably Cannon who made *King Solomon's Mines* in Zimbabwe in 1985 and are now making a sequel. The Ministry of Information is encouraging foreign companies to film in Zimbabwe because they bring in foreign exchange and provide employment. However, major disadvantages are that the films they make have an ideological bias which is unsuitable for a country which is officially declared to be in a transitional period towards socialism, the work they provide is only temporary and because there is no strong unionisation, local workers and extras are paid low wages. A film/media workers' union is now being set up to negotiate wages and the foreign companies do provide some small degree of technical training for Zimbabweans.

One major project is a proposed French/Zimbabwean co-production on the liberation struggle – *The Struggle for Zimbabwe*. This project has been beset with problems and although some of the script has been completed, it has not yet gone into production. Part of the agreement is that the French should provide training in film for Zimbabweans and should loan or donate equipment to Zimbabwe. This was also problematic because it was not known whether the equipment would suit the needs of future Zimbabwean film makers.

The development of film in Zimbabwe is also of interest to the Ministry of Youth, Sport and Culture which is a relatively new ministry, being an amalgamation of the previous Ministry of Youth, Sport and Recreation and the culture division which was moved from the Ministry of Education. The culture division of the ministry sponsored the first Southern Africa Regional Film Conference which was held in Harare in August 1984 and at which film makers were able to articulate their needs and aims in order to suggest a direction for the policy-makers.

ENTERTAINMENT PATTERNS

There are two major film distributors and a number of independently owned cinemas. The films shown are predominantly British and American although occasionally seasons of European (foreign language) films are held. African films are not usually shown on the main circuit although they are sometimes shown in the independent cinemas and by independent groups. In 1984 and 1985 one of the major distributors, Monte Carlo Theatres, held so-called Foreign Film Festivals (in fact, every film shown on the major circuit in Zimbabwe is a foreign film). In these festivals, embassies and high commissions were invited to submit films which were then adjudicated. During the 1984 Southern Africa Film Conference a season of African films was shown at the National Gallery. Although this innovation was welcomed the choice of venue was criticised because it meant that the audience was a small elite.

Rock and jazz concerts are held in the main cities and are well attended. The theatres are mainly oriented towards the white population and their plays are seen by a minority, although there are occasional visits by theatre companies from other African countries. Rural and urban drama projects are being encouraged, some of them sponsored by the Zimbabwe Foundation for Education with Production (ZIMFEP). The university also has an active drama group.

Film of the Month Committee

This is a newly formed organisation set up by members of the university which is in Harare. Its main aim is to show films with progressive content which would not otherwise be shown in Zimbabwe. The committee has held a lunch-time African film week and in its regular monthly slot it has shown films from Cuba and the Democratic People's Republic of Korea. It is envisaged that schools and colleges will be invited to screenings and the committe is seeking to encourage non-academic university staff to participate. At a later stage, they hope to work with Zimbabwean film and video makers.

Film and Video

The managing directors of the two main cinema chains, Rainbow Theatres and Monte Carlo Theatres, have both expressed concern about the growth of unlicensed video clubs. They claim that films are being seen on video before they reach the cinemas and before they have been passed by the censors. Video clubs are able to avoid paying copyright which the cinema distributors cannot do.

The growth of video clubs also means that the government is unable to control the content of films people see. For many years films in Zimbabwe have been predominantly American with an emphasis on sex and violence. Even 'quality' films such as *Amadeus* have been advertised in terms of 'sexploitation'. The government's aim is to encourage the showing of those films which do not glorify crude sex and violence or denigrate women or have an avowedly pro-Western bias. In October 1985 two American films, *Rambo-First Blood II* and *Gotcha* were withdrawn from the cinema circuit in Zimbabwe after the Soviet Embassy had protested to the Ministry of Information over the films 'which it found offensive and likely to harm relations between Zimbabwe and the Soviet Union'. Video allows people to see films of which the content opposes the government's ideological stance and hinders attempts to educate the population to be more aware of films such as those shown by the Film of the Month Committee.

COPYRIGHT AND CENSORSHIP

Zimbabwe has a censorship board which censors those films which come into

Zimbabwe and can ban films which are considered to be undesirable by the board. The chairman of the censorship board, Dr Jackson Chirenje has said that his board has no evidence that films not passed by the censors are being shown on video. He has stated that, 'as for video clubs and cinemas, we have our own way of monitoring which I am not prepared to divulge' but has admitted that 'we have no mechanism of inspecting private homes'. A survey conducted by *The Herald* newspaper in February 1985 found that there were at least 20 video clubs operating in Harare with an average membership of 200. On joining, members had to give 4–6 pre-recorded tapes to the video library of the club. The two legal video distributors in Zimbabwe claim that their tapes are being copied and then are used to join the illegal clubs. Pirated tapes from British television are also believed to be circulated widely.

The Copyright Act in Zimbabwe is generally agreed to be ineffective and new legisation is to be introduced to cover all areas of copyright. The Minister of Information has stated that video clubs 'will have to be legalised and royalties paid each time a cassette is leased out' but appropriate legislation has not been passed to bring this into effect.

BROADCASTING

The broadcasting authority is the Zimbabwe Broadcasting Corporation (ZBC) which has four radio stations and one television channel. The corporation is a parastatal unit for which the Mass Media Trust in the Ministry of Information is responsible. Newspapers are also owned by the Mass Media Trust, through Zimbabwe Newspapers. There is a certain amount of government control over what is broadcast or published and over senior broadcasting and newspaper appointments.

VIDEOGRAMS

Production

There are no major production houses. There are seven organisations, including the Zimbabwe Broadcasting Corporation and two Government ministries, which produce video on a small scale. Both Howard Kramer of Central Film Laboratories and Lee Allen of Film Com emphasised that finance for video and film is a major problem. Videos which are made independently will not always find a buyer and the number of videos and films being commissioned is decreasing.

Distribution

There are two national companies which distribute imported video cassettes
but not the software recorded in Zimbabwe.

Consumption

A distinction has to be made between the video cassettes produced in
Zimbabwe by the production houses or individuals and the cassettes imported
and distributed by Rainbow and Libra.

It is extremely difficult to categorise the content of the cassettes produced
in Zimbabwe but a *rough* estimate would be 50–58 per cent Business/Industry;
40–45 per cent General Interest/Education/Instruction and 1–2 per cent Entertainment.

Of the cassettes imported and distributed through video shops, approximately
80–85 per cent are Film/Entertainment; approximately 15 per cent Children's
and 0–5 per cent other categories.

VIDEO ECONOMICS

Video Hardware and Blank Software: Distribution

There is no production of video hardware in Zimbabwe, nor are there any
national wholesalers or distributors. Government departments and businesses
can import VCRs and other video equipment (if import licences have been
granted) from the United Kingdom, other European countries or South Africa.
Central Film Laboratories will advise on equipment and order it for government departments where clearance has been given. Some agencies and
government departments have received equipment from donor agencies.

Individuals can import VCRs if they have obtained 'no foreign currency
involved' import licences. This usually means that they have to prove that they
have legal external funds. They have to sign a declaration stating that they
will not attempt to sell the VCR for two years. However, despite these
safeguards, there is a lucrative market for VCRs in Zimbabwe. VCRs are advertised in the local press and a VCR changes hands for 2,000–4,000 Zimbabwe
dollars (1,200–2,400 US dollars) and a VCR + colour TV set for approximately
6,000 Zimbabwe dollars (3,500–4,000 US dollars). These figures should be
compared with those for Botswana.

Blank video cassettes are generally not retailed in Harare or the other major
Zimbabwean cities. They are imported by firms and individuals either with
a licence or on return from a country where they are retailed. They are advertised for sale in the local press on rare occasions. The price varies but will
probably be 30–40 Zimbabwe dollars (20–28 US dollars).

British distributors advertise colour television sets, VCRs and video cassettes in the Zimbabwe press to attract those with external funding who can obtain the necessary import licences. The leading format is VHS although Beta is also imported.

Consumption

From July 1984–June 1985 the following number of television sets were licensed:

Black and White	76,587
Colour	9,151

It was impossible to obtain figures for the number of VCRs imported but clearly private ownership of VCRs if more likely to be among those owning colour television sets. There is very little hire of hardware. Video cameras etc are hired to independent film makers on a small scale. The dominant use of VCR's is for viewing pre-recorded cassettes.

Community Video: Workers' Groups

The Zimbabwe Film and Video Association was formed in 1984 after the regional film workshop. Among its objectives are the following:

- To encourage wider appreciation of film and video in the Zimbabwean context for both cultural and training purposes;
- To promote interest in the development of locally made films and videos;
- To provide a forum for the public display and discussion of film and video in general and Zimbabwean film and video in particular;
- To research and develop means for wider public display and more effective usage of locally made films and videos.

Since the association was formed only a year ago, its objectives are still fairly nebulous as can be seen from the above. However, it has organised the following events:

- Showings of films and videos by Zimbabwean film and video makers at the National Gallery;
- Copyright Seminar – provided assistance to the Ministry of Information and the Ministry of Legal and Parliamentary Affairs for its organisation;
- Inter-Ministerial Video Seminar – organised jointly with Training Management Bureau of the Ministry of the Public Service;

– Anti-Apartheid Film Festival – organised jointly with the Cultural Department of the African National Congress.

The first three events were largely successful and received wide support. Criticisms of the Anti-Apartheid Film Week were that there was minimal discussion and that the venue was the National Gallery where only a small audience could be reached. However, the executives of the association are aware of these criticisms and hope to hold future events which reach more people.

VIDEO AND NATIONAL DEVELOPMENT

Video is mainly used in ministries and the public sector as a training aid. The main problem is that adequate training in how to use video has not been given to those who have access to video and so it is being underutilized.

CONCLUSION

Video has a role to play in national development in Zimbabwe and in community groups. However, progress in these areas is being impeded by lack of a clear national policy on video and by lack of finance, especially foreign currency. In the meantime, foreign films whose content is often contrary to the Government's ideological stance and alien to African culture are both made and shown in Zimbabwe. Video primarily exists, at present, as an alternative form of entertainment to television and film, offering video cassettes of mainstream Western films for the minority who can afford this form of entertainment.

KENYA

The Voice of Kenya is the state radio and television network under the Ministry of Information. There is one television channel and two national radio channels. Regional radio channels also exist on a small scale.

HARDWARE

Production

There is no production of video hardware or unrecorded software in Kenya. VCRs are imported from Europe and the Middle East, mainly Saudi Arabia.

Distribution

VCRs are sold by authorised dealers in local electrical and television shops although sales are also made privately. The average price of a VCR and colour television set would be 20,000–25,000 Kenyan shillings (US$1,235–1,563). VCRs are also imported by those with access to foreign currency and by those who work or who have relatives who work in the Arab states.

TELEVISION AND VCR OWNERSHIP

TV World (April 1985) estimated that there were 100,000 television sets in the country. Statistical information compiled by the IFPI gives the number of VCRs in Kenya at the end of 1985 as 20,000.

Figures for television ownership can be compared with those for other East African countries, eg 106,000 for Sudan and 7,500 for Tanzania. Tanzania, although it has access to the Arab states through its ports and migrant Tanzanian workers in the Middle East, has no mainland television network and until 1985 had strict import controls and taxes on televisions and VCRs.

VIDEOGRAMS

Pre-recorded software is mainly imported from the United Kingdom, Japan and the Middle East.

Video cassette libraries are a growing phenomenon in Kenya, especially in Nairobi and the coastal region of Mombasa (where there is strong Arab and Asian influence). Piracy is widespread. Library cassettes are obtained through duplication of master tapes. Illegal recordings of television programmes are imported from the United Kingdom and the Arab states.

In mid-1985, because of concern about piracy and the infringement of copyright regulations, the Kenyan government imposed a tax of 2,000 Kenyan shillings (US$123) per annum on video cassette libraries.

VIDEO AND THE ESTABLISHED MEDIA

Film

Kenya has a national film corporation and trains personnel in most areas of film production. It has a small-scale film industry but the Kenya Film Corporation does not work in video.

Until recently Kenya has welcomed foreign film production and major productions have been partly filmed in Kenya because of its fine locations, climate and good processing facilities. However, a dispute between the Kenyan

Ministry of Information and Universal Pictures, the producers of *Out of Africa* may cause the Kenyan government to reassess its policy of allowing foreign film production in Kenya.

Film and Video

Cinemas are financially disadvantaged compared with video cassette shops and libraries. Cinema owners are required to pay for a municipal licence, a trade licence, a performing rights licence, to pay import duty on film and to pay sales tax and entertainment tax. Prior to 1985, video cassette outlets only paid for a trade licence and after mid–1985, paid for a trade licence and paid a new tax.

The rise of video in Kenya has resulted in a fall in cinema attendances. Mkangi estimated that in 1981 Mombasa cinemas were earning 37 per cent less than in 1978.

Video and Culture

As in many other African countries, video is considered to be an alien influence which helps to import foreign values. Mkangi states that because most of the imported cassettes are in English and Hindi, fears have been expressed that video will downgrade KiSwahili and the Kenyan national languages.

However, video is now well established as a form of entertainment in Kenya and it is unlikely that critics will be able to halt what they see as its adverse cultural influence.

Chapter 17

BRAZIL

Any research into video in Brazil immediately encounters two fundamental problems; piracy and the involvement of multinational corporations. The Brazilian video cassette industry is an imported industry and the shelves of videoclub shops are almost exclusively filled with foreign, or rather, American titles.

The domestic presence on the market is dependent on the protective measures adopted by the Concine (National Cinema Council). However, piracy or clandestine operations (contraband) continue to increase creating a *de facto* situation for which it will be difficult to find a legal solution as the Government, domestic producers and multinational distributors desire.

The estimates presented in this report were checked with professionals and producers who work in the Brazilian video field and represent a reasonable consensus. On the basis of these data, projections have been made with regard to activity and movement on the video hard and software markets.

A considerable amount of work in this field had already been carried out by *The Brazilian Video Guide* (*Guia do Video no Brazil*).

The State has a monopoly of TV and radio stations, granting concessions to individuals or groups who present the appropriate application. Over the last few decades, the government has established a client-orientated policy and set up a network of stations which contribute to its own survival. The pro-government tendency was its strongest at the beginning of the 1970s.

At that time, the television networks were beamed through a microwave infrastructure provided by the State (through its telecommunications agency EMBRATEL), which made it possible for programmes and messages to be broadcast 'live' to each Brazilian State. This possibility catered for various interests. From the government point of view, its voice could immediately be heard throughout the country and this combined very well with government plans for national integration and centralisation.

Brazilian industry, encouraged by promises of an 'economic miracle', seized the opportunity to create, through publicity, a nation-wide market for its products. Advertising campaigns produced in the Rio de Janeiro – São Paulo nexus were given air-space throughout the country to the detriment of regional programmes and of small local advertisers. This network was fundamental to industry's conquest of the domestic market. The idea of a network, in which the affiliates put out programmes produced on a production line is quite attractive to regional producers who have practically no production costs since they are shared amongst them all. Television series and TV journalism were, and still are, the most important sectors for maintaining network audiences.

Within the general picture, it may be said that an average of 80 per cent of programmes watched by viewers at a national level come from a world other than their own, reaching in some regions almost 100 per cent. There are 16,100,000 homes with TV corresponding to 57 per cent of all Brazilian households which possess 22 million television sets (12 million black and white, 10 million colour). Average viewing time was calculated in 1982 to be three and a half hours a day.

In March 1985 the 'New Republic' removed the restrictions on broadcasting stations imposed by the former regimes. Today censorship is barely visible with respect to moral matters and freedom of speech in politics on both radio and TV. However, there are still no programmes for people to express their own needs and points of view; this really would demonstrate effective community participation in the communication process. The self-censorship of the broadcasting stations which bow to economic interests, has come to replace state censorship.

VIDEO HARDWARE

Production

Video cassettes arrived in Brazil in the middle of the 1970s legally imported by TV stations (U-Matic format) or brought by travellers (VHS and Betamax). The professional market was not weakened when Sony launched in 1984 two U-Matic models (players and recorder/player) assembled at their factory at Curitiba. The products were manufactured at prices that were prohibitive for the ordinary consumer and were technologically backward in terms of their use by TV stations. A few years later, production of these models was suspended.

The first domestic video cassette was introduced in March 1982 and was made by Sharp. The model chosen – VC8510 – was as modern in its time as the imported models. Later introduction of other models, in the same year, by Sony with the Betamax SL-5000 and Philco who opted for the VHS PVC-1000 (with Hitachi technology) came to stimulate the market which was beginning to expand.

For 1985 it is calculated that between 40 to 50 thousand units were manufactured – the number being increased by Mitsubishi's entry into the Brazilian video market.

In the four cases (Sharp, Philco/Hitachi, Mitsubishi and Sony) the technology is imported and developed on Japanese models. The case of Sharp exemplifies the multinationals' strategy: their subsidiaries in Brazil form part of a group of more than 30 companies using domestic capital to manufacture television sets, sound equipment and calculators, among other items.

According to data supplied by CACES, the government agency responsible for import and export, total elements imported for video cassettes reached over 55 million dollars by 1985:

July-December 1984 – US$23,245,588
January-July 1985 – US$32,579,701

As with everything relating to video in the country, contraband takes the greatest slice of the market. Although it is estimated that there are about 400,000 video cassette players in Brazil, the figure is an estimate for it is impossible to establish the number of sets smuggled in up to the present. The figure given was obtained on the basis of interviews with manufacturers, advertising agencies, owners of videoclubs and tape hiring agencies. There is general agreement that the participation of domestic manufacturers is less than 25 per cent since just one firm, Sharp,|has 60 per cent of the market|.Moreover the division between the various types is extremely unequal: 90 per cent of sets are VHS and scarcely 1 per cent Betamax (curiously concentrated among the Japanese community).

Manufacturers estimate a potential video cassette market for 1986 of more than 2 million. Since market growth has been so rapid (almost doubling in the past two years) new manufacturers are coming onto the market. At the present time they offer buyers the choice of four quite sophisticated models. In Manaus, some ten years ago the government set up an industrial and commercial development area: the Zona Franca or Free Zone. Their objective was to turn the region into an industrial centre which, besides encouraging the growth of the region, would also create employment for local people. For this reason, it established imports of electronic components and by means of tax incentives encouraged the setting up of assembly plants. All travellers to the region are entitled to buy imported equipment tax free at prices well below those of domestic products and similar to the price of smuggled videos. There is however a ceiling, at present 600 dollars per person, but that has not prevented video cassettes from being the main attraction in the shops of Manaus throughout 1985.

The growth of the domestic video cassette industry, the Manaus Free Zone and the impunity afforded smuggled products gives rise to an optimistic outlook for 1986 (Sharp has 3 factories in Manaus, Sony 2, and Philco 1).

One of the curious aspects of video cassette smuggling in Brazil is that it

formed the basis for the present market for video clubs, and even for legislation and technical standards. At the end of the 1970s, the VCRs reaching Brazil
had colour systems of the American NTSC pattern. They were then adapted
so that they could record, in colour, programmes put out on TV on the official
PALM system. Thus a hybrid system – called N LINHA – was created.
Videoclubs in their turn came up with films which were almost all imported
and for the NTSC system. This led to a parallel circuit since in order to watch
hired films, VCR owners had to have sets that could receive the NTSC system.
The solution was to alter TV sets which were fitted with a device which allowed
the three systems to function: PALM to watch TV programmes without VCR;
N LINHA to watch programmes recorded on imported VCRs and NTSC to
receive video originally recorded on NTSC. The result was a total confusion
which made the systematic distribution of products almost impossible. When
the domestic industry introduced its video cassettes in 1982, the market structure was already established, and producers had to adapt to the market. For
this reason all Brazilian videos have a switch which allows the copying of tapes
and recording on the PALM and NTSC systems but with video output always
on PALM. In this way the TV monitoring device does not need to be adapted
further. Any set can be used with VCR, giving the buyer a saving of about
50 dollars – the price of adaptation.

The contraband trade has not suffered from this change because an adapter
that leaves them in the same position as domestically produced equipment.
Thus today the N LINHA system no longer exists and all the products on
the market record and copy PALM and NTSC on TV in PALM. This eliminates
any problem regarding programme exchanges since the NTSC system is used
by almost everyone.

SOFTWARE

Production

The software market is expanding and this encourages the production of blank
video cassettes. It is estimated that annual sales in Brazil have reached close
to 1.6 million units, with the contraband sector taking about 60 per cent of
the total. In 1986, it is expected that there will be an overall growth of 25 per
cent.

Among those who operate the market legally there are three different groups:

- Brazilian companies which manufacture cartridges and import tapes.
  PLAJET
  VAT
  V TA

- Companies backed by foreign capital that import all material and simply assemble cassettes inside the country.

    BASF – 50 per cent of the domestic market

    3M (Scotch) – 20 per cent of the domestic market

    Fuji – 10 per cent of the domestic market

- Companies backed by foreign capital which sporadically import blank cassettes.

    TDK

    Maxwell

    Kodak (uses TDK material)

Brazilian companies, together with the foreign companies which import complete cassettes, take the remaining 20 per cent of the domestic market, which means roughly 1 million units a year (the total with contraband added on is 1.6 million).

The financial value of the market in tapes in Brazil, excluding contraband, is about 10 million dollars, in terms of sales. With respect to the import of material (tapes, cartridges) import quotas authorized by the government give figures of 7 to 8 million dollars.

Because of the restrictions imposed by Brazilian law, it is difficult to obtain these import quotas which means that companies import only once or twice a year at the most. There is a certain amount of protection for domestic manufacturers in this area. Import by foreign companies is restricted or strictly scheduled. For example, Fuji imported about 600 thousand dollars worth of material in 1985 despite having applied for 800 thousand dollars worth. The difference did not receive the approval of CECEX the organisation which deals with these questions.

Domestic manufacture is also protected by high rates of taxation on imported cassettes:

- import duty: 45 per cent
- IOF (Financial operations tax): 25 per cent
- Customs fees
- Freight

To avoid these costs, foreign manufacturers import the material and assemble the cassettes in Brazil. In this way, the cassettes come to the consumer at a viable price – around 9 to 10 dollars per unit.

The greatest competition is still provided by contraband which takes 60 per cent of the market. Nevertheless, this volume is diminishing with the entry of new domestic brands into the market. There is also the high value of the dollar with respect to the cruzeiro. A blank imported cassette costs 8 dollars contraband, only 10 to 20 per cent less than the domestic product, which allows large buyers – the companies – to deal in legal products.

However, the price that manufacturers and assemblers are paying to gain a position in the market requires a reduction in profit margins, for as soon as their prices are substantially above contraband prices, the latter return to fill the gap.

In 1986, the government introduced new regulations to control the sale of blank tapes by adding to the manufacturer's price a Merchandise Circulation Tax in an attempt to prevent the seller from avoiding payment of such tax. The consequence was a final increase to the consumer of around 10 per cent.

The format of blank video cassettes being manufactured is important. About 90 per cent follow VHS norms, U-Matic accounts for 9 per cent and Betamax for 1 per cent. The main buyers are TV companies, video clubs, video hire companies and institutions. The Brazilian home user on average buys less than two cassettes a year.

Distribution

When the first video cassettes arrived in Brazil, especially at the beginning of the 1980s, there was practically no software or programmes on tape: people either recorded TV programmes or brought original tapes from abroad. Then came the birth of the videoclubs, where members brought 5 original titles as the membership fee for taking part in these exchange schemes – apart from this there was a monthly subscription to pay. These video clubs soon became profitable in that they began to produce extra copies to which they gave brand names without any kind of authorisation. In this fashion there grew up the so-called 'video pirates' and, together with the videoclubs and video hire companies, the unchecked piracy which led the way in the establishment of video in Brazil.

Law 5,988, dated 14 December, 1973, regulates copyright in Brazil, whereby producers, directors, screenwriters, musicians and other like parties involved in audio-visual products are protected. Within the framework of this law a video tape is construed as a support medium for a cinematrographic work, and cannot therefore be copied or commercially marketed, even when apparently no profit is to be obtained. This provision appears on the tapes jointly with the trademarks.

According to UBV (Brazilian video union) the pirate market in Brazil is estimated to involve more than 10 million dollars a year, as a result of the videoclub members' 'monthly payments' and tape rental. Out of this amount, the government receives no taxes, authors' and distributors' copyrights are not paid, and the public is actually cheated by the poor quality of successive copies and badly translated subtitles.

From the legal point of view, the only protection against piracy is the Copyright Law and Concine's resolutions. In order to enforce such protection, distributors created the UBV, a non-profit organisation whose purpose is to co-ordinate the protection of film producers' copyrights and the distribution rights on video films, both domestically and abroad.

The pirate video market is basically concentrated in São Paulo, where more than half the video clubs and rentals are located. North American distributors are wary of entering such an unprotected market in view of the very large investment involved: legal tapes demand their own wrapping, stamps, etc. How can a market be supported when from one legal original hundreds of illegal copies are created?

At present only 300 legal titles are registered in Brazil, compared with the two thousand owned by the average video club. Pursuant to Resolutions 97, 98 and 99/83 issued by Concine legal tape must be packed in boxes showing an image of the movie on the face, and carrying a stamp obtained from Embrafilme. This stamp is given once the petitioner proves he or she is the holder of the movie's copyright or distribution rights. The following legal procedure applies:

a) Copyright verification;
b) Registration with Embrafilme;
c) Application for the respective stamp from Embrafilme, to include the film's registration number, descriptive information, and number of copies;
d) Delivery of the master to a laboratory for making of copies;
e) Delivery of the invoice for services rendered by an accredited company for making of the copies, giving the exact number of copied tapes and submission to Embrafilme together with the tapes in question;
f) Embrafilme seals and returns the tapes to the distributor.

This process is slow and very bureaucratic. It is ill-adapted to the market needs of a business which reflects the latest trends and novelties.

The market is currently facing a problem: there is a need for legislation as demanded by both domestic and foreign producers and distributors, but the cost implied by such legislation would make the reproduction of films far too expensive, forcing the vast majority of the companies involved (video clubs and rentals) out of business and discouraging the consumer market.

To give an example, a legal business pays about 12 dollars for a blank tape. Pirates who purchase a large number for about 5 dollars each do not pay the 20 to 25 per cent tax levied for copyright, nor the 17 per cent laid down by the ICM Law (Goods Circulation Tax).

Thus, the daily rental of a pirate film costs a third as much as a legal one: forty cents as opposed to a dollar twenty cents.

Currently the pirate market places close to fifty thousand copies a month on the market, while Embrafilme seals between three thousand and three thousand five hundred a month.

Taking into account the cost of the contraband virgin tape (5 to 6 dollars) and the recordings (an average of 3 dollars each), we can surmise that after eight rentals of the tape ie in less than a month, the cost of the investment has been absorbed. The legally sealed copy costs, after taxes, a total of 40 dollars (five times more than the pirate tape) with the additional disadvantage that it can not be re-recorded. The return is thereby much slower.

In Brazil, there are almost 700 videoclubs and rentals, and about 15 companies are involved in making copies and sub-titles, both official and pirate, some having up to 50 duplicating sets available. Videoclubs have more than a million tapes in stock; some of the larger ones may have up to fifteen thousand.

In addition the purchase of copyright for a foreign film must be paid in dollars and in advance, which implies an impossible initial investment for Brazilian videoclubs and rentals.

The possibility of introducing legislation which will little by little empty the videoclub shelves of pirated products has been discussed. Nevertheless, the speed with which new businesses open and the constant supply of new films, make this solution to the problem that much more difficult.

The director and owner of Videoclubs do Brazil (the largest in the field with dozens of units all over the country), states that a solution to this matter cannot fail to take into consideration certain variables inherent to the Brazilian context: 'all foreign distributors we contact to do business with Brazil ask despicable prices, payment in advance in dollars .... With this kind of payment requirements, they will never be able to do business within the Brazilian market, unless more feasible proposals can be negotiated where all involved can obtain a fair return, including those representatives involved in reproduction of tapes in Brazil ... paying in advance three million dollars (the amount required to use the Metro, Warner or other like names), aside from a percentage on tapes sold, is hardly attractive. A more fair arrangement is necessary, something more in keeping with the Brazilian trade system, paying later by installments'. In short, a legalisation process would produce a contraction of the market possibly resulting in the disappearance of most Brazilian companies in the video business.

There is a market reserve for domestic films pursuant to resolutions 97, 98 and 99/83. Twenty-five percent of releases and copies should be Brazilian. These resolutions cannot be complied with since, according to the videoclubs, there are not enough domestic movies to meet demand.

Another aspect which affects the movie industry in Brazil in general, is mentioned by the Director of Globovideo: 'For a good Brazilian film to be produced, it costs 300,000 dollars, as in the case of *Avaete* made by Zelito Viana, using the whole of the small Brazilian promotion structure. Negatives are imported with 300 per cent tax, while the master (inter-negative) for *Amadeus* for example was imported with 5 per cent tax. These two movies are going to dispute the market at the same time and *Amadeus* can be bought for thirty thousand dollars without any development of the domestic movie industry and without giving employment to anybody'.

The main legal distributors in the country engaged in the video business are:

- CIC Video – exclusive distributor for Paramount and Universal Pictures in 'home-video' for 30 countries;
- FJ Lucas – European film distributor;
- Globovideo – distributes practically all Brazilian films;
- VCL – distributor of independent Brazilian and foreign productions;
- MACDATA – distributes films by the 'Os Trapalhoes' group and some international films;
- NETWORK – distributes for independent producers;
- VIDEOCAST – ex-pirate, engaged in distribution of European films;
- NACIONAL Video Producoes – also ex-pirate, operates within the same area as above.

Almost 80 per cent of the titles found in the video clubs and rentals are of American origin followed by some European productions mainly in the pornographic area. The general preference is for adventure, drama, comedy and children's films. Brazilian videoclubs differ from those in many other countries in that pornographic videos make up 5 per cent of their stock.

Some types have larger circulation at certain times. At the time of the Falklands/Malvinas war, war movies were most popular and during the arrival of Halley's comet, science fiction took the lead.

As a result of the extent of piracy in this business, there are no accurate surveys of the market proportion held by each video category or type. A survey derived from catalogues of the main rental companies shows the following:

	%
– Industry	–
Children	10
– Entertainment	67
– Arts	1
– Education	–
– How To (instructional)	–
– Medicine	–
– Sports	–
– Musicals	20
– Erotic	2

This is the average proportion found in videoclubs and rentals, but some specialise in certain fields such as education, medicine and business management, aside from numerous programmes produced for internal use and not for distribution.

There is just one video rental club specialised in education: Videoarte do Brasil, associated with the São Paulo Teaching Centre Syndicate which brings together owners of private schools.

Videoarte rents out educational programmes to more than 300 schools, has seven thousand titles on catalogue with instruction classes and video films covering all areas related to 1st and 2nd grade education. Associated schools rent three films a week on average, attaining a total of more than four thousand orders per month.

In 1986 Globovideo (a company associated with the Rede Globo TV network) intends to enter the educational market with 'packages' to be sent monthly to the schools on a rental basis.

In both cases, the programmes for the most part have already been aired on television in educational projects, television courses, etc. At the moment the volume of video productions specially conceived for school instruction is small, but growing.

Many schools purchase video equipment for internal production (recording and small programmes), mostly in the VHS format. Communication Schools (65 in the country) have video studios, some in the U-Matic format on account of legislation, and their equipment is used for student training.

In either case there is no distribution mechanism and the productions are used only within each institution. Their volume therefore is impossible to determine. On the basis of data provided by Videoarte do Brasil, the schools that use video number in the hundreds, but the data is inaccurate and estimated. One of the manufacturers, Philco, is trying to expand this market supplying equipment at lower prices than the stores, and selling directly to the schools.

Consumption

A 1983 survey carried out with videoclub clients produced some interesting results with respect to tape-consumers. According to the report, almost 60 per cent of purchases were made on the recommendation of friends, relatives and acquaintances. Nevertheless trade magazines do have a considerable influence amounting to 36 per cent, a very high rate considering that these publications have been in circulation for a very short time. Newspaper advertisements accounted for 8 per cent of the video cassette purchases.

With respect to the reasons for such purchases, the following answers were given:

	%
– watch films	87.5
– record TV programmes	63.5
– personal recordings	24.0

To the question 'how do you use video cassettes?', the following answers were given:

		%
–	recording TV programmes	56.3
–	videoclubs	45.8
–	video-rental	44.8
–	personal recordings	18.8
–	swapping films among friends	15.6

This survey, now three years old, called attention to the existence of a large number of consumers who are capable of making their own recordings, that is, are owners of video cameras, which represented 20 per cent of consumers.

In view of the growth of videoclubs and rentals and the domestic production of video cassettes, recorders became somewhat more accessible to middle class people.

The hardware market operates basically on the sale of equipment. Few companies engage in video cassette recorder or camera rental, the large clients being the hotel business.

In commercial broadcast TV, video now occupies a space which two years ago was non-existent. Some independent producers are producing weekly programmes different in both form and content from regular commercial TV productions. The innovation is that certain attitudes and the language of the announcers are not 'perfect' and would be absolutely forbidden by the quality standards of the big broadcasters. They are however the rule in the programmes by the 'Olhar Electronico' group, 'TV Viva', and with the announcers Goulart de Andrade and Fausto Silva.

In the case of televised journalism, the creative influence of these producers can be felt; lighter and less costly video equipment make these productions more agile and has paved the way for an ever-increasing number of groups 'making TV outside TV'. Some example are: parts of Rede Globo's 'Globe Reporter' programme are produced by Manduri 35; the 'Olhar Electronico' group is responsible for production of TV Gazete de São Paulo's '23 Horo' and Olho Magico; Goulart de Andrade created 'Perdidos na Noite' and 'Conexao International' and 'Xingu', among others, produced by Intervideo; Gazeta Mercantil, a newspaper, makes 'Critica e Autoritica' for the Bandeirantes network, focussing on political debate.

The journalism departments in the broadcasting companies started using lighter equipment for internal production at the end of the 1970s (the ENG system). This equipment which is mobile and easy to operate (technical adjustments are almost automatic), is of sufficient technical quality for broadcast transmission.

This simplified cheaper equipment together with the use of video cassettes has led to the appearance of a series of minor broadcasters all over the country. Almost all of them use U-Matic equipment since Betacam sets are not yet widespread in Brazil.

The use of video by the business sector is growing at an annual rate of 20 per cent insofar as *production* of programmes for use is concerned. These enterprises have 15 per cent of the country's video market, and purchase almost exclusively Brazilian equipment in order to maintain legal ownership. Several yearly seminars and courses on the use of video cassettes in a company environment have been organised, and some have been published in books or articles.

One factor that has contributed to the proliferation of video for corporate use is to be found in the tax incentives for the professional training supplied by the companies, pursuant to Law 6297/75. This law authorises companies to discount from their Income Tax, double the amount of an investment accompanied by training, including the purchase of equipment. Video cassette manufacturers have stressed this sales point with very positive results.

Since the authorities have not given this sector much priority in the last few decades, libraries, especially public libraries, have not yet entered the electronic age. Corporate libraries are speedily arriving at computerisation, while the others have not even reached the audio-visual age. They are no more than book warehouses.

In 1985 the São Paulo Cultural Department proposed a project still under discussion to place one video cassette system per public library in São Paulo, with the purpose of creating an informal exhibition circuit to serve as a medium for cultural activity within the various communities. The initial project has plans for 400 to 500 video cassette units.

INDEPENDENT VIDEO PRODUCTION

One sector in which video is creating a state of euphoria is that of independent production. Dozens of groups all over the country are engaged in producing programmes ranging from video-art to the recording of wrestling matches. Though the content is different, they have one point in common: individual or group expression through video, which is completely absent in the mass communication media.

Though access to the broadcasting companies and videoclub shelves is limited and is the privilege of a few, the number of shows, festivals and exhibition halls is constantly growing. Nowadays every national cinema festival has a video section denoting the trend in the film industry towards using video instead of 16 mm film for short films and documentaries.

In 1985 there were video showings in festivals held in Brasilia, Salvador, Rio de Janeiro, São Paulo, Curitiba, Porto Alegre and Belo Horizonte.

The Olhar Electronico group in 1984 published the Brazilian Video Catalogue in an attempt to determine the magnitude of independent video production.

Nevertheless, the productions by groups working directly with popular movements, schools, institutions or Church groups, were not present in that catalogue, which mainly included experimental and documentary programmes made by video companies and producers.

Video has characteristics which make it particularly interesting to certain groups involved in developing cultural activities and social participation. The recent proliferation in Brazil of groups working through video is due not so much to the appearance of a new communications technology, but to the possibilities offered by the liberal political situation in Brazil.

The victory of the opposition parties in the 1982 elections in the large urban centres was followed by a general relaxation of mass communication media censorship, though such censorship continued to exist at times of social tension. Simultaneously, self-censorship developed within the broadcasting companies. State censorship therefore gave way to another type arising from the economic crisis, which has resulted in such a high rate of unemployment that professionals do not wish to jeopardize their jobs in the communications companies by taking political risks.

The work of a professional within these companies has certain defined boundaries, in spite of all the possible contradictions and liberties that may be taken. The fear of unemployment has created a decisive pressure so video is quite a promising alternative for professionals, being structurally outside those limitations. This may explain the considerable number of graduates from communications schools who, disappointed by the restricted job market and its limitations, work in video.

The emergency measures adopted in April 1984, at the time of voting for a constitutional amendment for direct presidential elections, silenced practically all radio and TV broadcasting. Even when these measures are taken as an isolated event, what was observed is of considerable interest. In the absence of television analyses of the polls taken, coverage of the polls was carried out by several video groups. This coverage includes sounds and images showing the rallies from the point of view of the participants, rather than from specially built platforms that only give general overviews of the action without any statement from the participants themselves.

The political and social transformations the country is experiencing, its economic crisis and foreign debt, constantly generate movements seeking to debate subjects that the communications media fail to air. Therefore, with the relative political relaxation, the video groups can act freely, without repression, and fill the gap left by TV broadcasters through superficial or partial treatment of popular movements. Evidently the penetration and broadcasting power held by video is much smaller than that of television, but video does reach an organised willing public and on many occasions is inserted in well-defined and systematised broadcasting and discussion projects. Certain groups associated with trade unions, local associations, schools, and the like, offer promising broadcasting space for their products. As an example, a video, made on the occasion of the creation of Worker's Union in August 1983, by various video groups, was finished a few days after the meeting ended. The following month about eighty orders for copies were placed by unions from all over the country, although there was no publicity or distribution mechanism. Though much is disjointed and disorganised, this demonstrates the expectation created in the labour union movement, through this kind of production. In the last

275

few months many unions have purchased equipment for video production, since they are aware of the flexibility this communication medium offers and its value when the need is for swift and specific information.

Video is also used by popular groups in 6 complementary ways:

1) Self-orientated – recording parties, individual 'performances', for internal exhibition by those groups. There is no interest in screening outside the group.

2) The recording of events or happenings of interest to the group without editing, with the simple objective of keeping a memory alive for later use.

3) Editing rough material, 'cleaning up' material with the idea of getting out some sort of documentary based on original recorded material. There are a great number of these group productions, normally a sequence of speeches and action shots without much elaboration.

4) Planned documentaries.

5) Original scripts, including fiction, where the final result is a video with a narrative structure and a more highly-polished finish, because it is possible to exercise greater control over recording variables. Groups producing fiction are few, principally because of the esoteric nature of the message they are trying to put across. This has been one of the main topics of discussion among producer groups.

6) Showing pre-recorded tapes coming from other popular groups (when possible), hired from the films available in video clubs or recorded from TV, especially with regard to literary activities, critical discussion or matters of cultural interest.

In 1984, the ABC Centre of Popular Memory Studies, which is linked to the Methodist Institute of Higher Education, organised the First National Meeting of Popular Video. For 3 days (14–16 September) almost 50 video groups and producers who had been working with the popular movements had their first opportunity to get to know each other and to discuss forms of organisation.

Awareness of the absence of information among themselves resulted in the decision to publish the bulletin *Video Popular* and distribute it to everyone with an interest in popular communication – 2,000 copies are printed.

The fragmentation of the groups led to the decision to organise an association at national level. The name 'Associacao Brasileira de Video no Movimento Popular' (Brazilian Association of Popular Movement Video) was officially launched in March 1985. Beside courses, exhibitions and publishing *Video Popular* the association organised a Second National Meeting in October 1985.

The Association has at present about 80 individual producers or groups interested in popular video. Taken together, they represent a volume of production of almost 200 titles. Besides this, all groups have a large quantity of unedited recorded material, usually unedited versions of events of interest to the different popular groups in the country. The catalogue being prepared by the Association is the only systematic classification of this material and was published in 1986.

The question of programme circulation is linked to the type of performance presented by each group. Those that have greatest circulation among certain social groups, circulate their material without any great difficulty, reaching thousands of viewers during the course of a year. Nevertheless, for less well-organised video groups the problems of distributing programmes outside their area are great: there is no distribution circuit. Church organisations, associations and individuals have nowhere to hire videos produced by popular groups that might interest them, because video clubs have no time for these productions, at least for the moment. Everyone recognises that discussion of these aspects of distribution is of fundamental importance. At various festivals (Video Brasil, Bahia and FestRio) the question has repeatedly been raised.

Chapter 18

PERU

One of the characteristics of Peruvian society is the concentration of economic and political resources in the capital city. This phenomenon also manifests itself in the communication sector which primarily serves major urban centres. In 1982, television reached only 25 per cent of the population. Today, the state channel has been extended to reach 60 per cent coverage.

In Lima there are 845,000 TV sets or one receiver for every five persons. For the country as a whole, there is one receiver for every 20 persons.

During the past few years, an acute economic crisis and a neo-liberal policy has liberalised imports, reduced fiscal spending and salaries and given rise to a dollar economy and the concentration of resources. For instance, 10 per cent of the population appropriates 52 per cent of net income and 2 per cent absorbs 28 per cent. A large proportion of the under-employed and peasant population account for 23 per cent net income. Thus, only a small proportion of Peruvian society has the resources to purchase video recorders. This has encouraged the institutional use of video, since individuals are generally unable to purchase the technology.

The current government has not yet set clear guidelines for the communications sector. The private sector regulates itself in terms of percentage of national programming, censorship, and a code of ethics. It has also put pressure on the government so that the state channel no longer accepts advertising.

There are five TV stations in Peru; a governmental one (Channel 7) and four private ones (Channel 2, 4, 5 and 9). Channels 4, 5 and 7 are networks operating at a national level. Channels 2 and 9 cover only the Lima Metropolitan area. The government channel (7), achieves the most widespread coverage via satellite (INTELSAT). The colour system is NTSC.

Peru is one of the thirty-one countries of the world in which broadcasting systems are privately owned and are exclusively financed by advertising, although there have been periods of State intervention. For example, in 1969, within the context of a set of reforms that also covered the press and the education system, the State bought 51 per cent of TV enterprise stocks. The experiment lasted until 1980, when TV stations reverted to their former owners.

During the current decade Channels 2 and 9 have appeared and have contested the market dominated by Channels 4 and 5. This new situation of rising competition within the TV industry has resulted in the broadcasting of new programmes, many of them political. Thus, after some years of stagnation there is a renewed dynamism in the industry, as a result of the competition. The situation has also led to the censoring of controversial material. Furthermore, the private character of TV channels and their dependence on advertising and on the political authority has also limited innovative programming.

Television is therefore mostly for entertainment and the tendency, verified by Tapio Varis, is toward an increased flow of imported programmes: in 1972 the imported programming reached a level of 60 per cent, in 1980 it was 70 per cent and in 1985 with the new channels it reached 75 per cent. Half of these programmes came from the United States and in many cases are old TV series acquired at low cost. However if audience preference is analysed it will be noted that from the 9 highest rated TV programmes, five are produced locally, and the two with top ratings are a comic programme *Risas y Salsas* and a soap-opera *Carmin*, both Peruvian.

National production is considerably influenced by the lack of government policies in this area. This situation has resulted in a generalised shortage of national productions because the television channels do not consider them to be profitable.

During 1985 only about 20 per cent of total transmissions were national productions.

The increase in imported programming was noted by Tapio Varis in 1973 and by Livia Antola and Everett Rogers in 1982 (see Revista Chasquie, CIESPAL No 9 - January - March, 1984).

This trend however will vary significantly in Peru as recent governments have begun to enforce Law Decree 190.20 which was originally formulated in 1974. According to this law, television channels are required to devote 60 per cent of their transmission time to national production. While this might appear to be a nationalistic policy intended to promote local production, it has more to do with problems of foreign exchange and a high rate of inflation which has increased the cost of imported programmes (see Chasquie No 9, CIESPAL). Thus, the major channels (4, 5) have now stressed local production and the minor ones (9, 2) which have relied chiefly on foreign programmes no longer benefit from cheaper imports. The 60 per cent ruling would mean significantly expanding local production to fill in the 204 hours of broadcast time per week.

Actual production is in the hands of the channels themselves or related companies. New companies have emerged to co-produce material with the channels. For instance, Channel 5 (PANTEL) is affiliated with PROPAN and CINETEL, the former being dedicated to news programming (*Buenos Dias Peru, 24 Horas,*

Buenas Noches Peru, Panorama, Pulso) and the latter to tele.1ovelas (soap operas) and action series (*Carmin, La Casa de Enfrente, Gamboa*). In the case of Channel 2, Imatic is involved in some productions.

Although all publicity is required to be of national origin, it is often produced abroad using foreign actors. Publicity accounts for 20 per cent of total programming time.

HARDWARE AND BLANK SOFTWARE

Although Law No 24,000 of 1984 favours organisations involved in social communication by exempting imported equipment from duties, the law is only now (October 1985) being applied. There have not been any major imports over the past few years. This is understandable, since the import tax has been as high as 165 per cent, over and above the free on board (FOB) price. Another factor to be considered is the economic crisis affecting the TV channels.

Non-commercial Video

During the last few years the use of video has spread at both the governmental and non-governmental levels.

There has been much valuable experience gained at the governmental level. The work done by the 'Centro de Servicios sobre Pedagogia Audiovisual' (CESPAC) for the agriculture Ministry should be mentioned. It has specialised in rural training and has produced more than one thousand programmes. Likewise, ALEAVISION from the Education Ministry has been responsible for producing literacy programmes.

At the same time a number of universities, institutions and non- governmental development agencies have incorporated video into their programmes. Among these the Catholic University has a Tele-education centre (CETUC) and the University of Lima is also producing videos through its Department of Communications. In addition, non-governmental organisations like 'Video Centro', 'Centro de Informacion y Desarrolla Internacional de Autogestion' (CIDIAG), and 'Videoteca Alternativa' are using video in their social programmes.

With the purpose of gathering together all these experiences and others, in other Latin American countries the Centre of Transnational Culture from the Institute for Latin America (IPAL) is in the process of establishing an exchange network.

Video Red (Video Network in English) will collect information from independent broadcasters, who use video for development, education and popular organisation projects. It will work as a Latin American Co-operative and its members will send IPAL a copy of its productions and receive a monthly service including all the productions obtained by IPAL. Each Video Network member may acquire a production at the cost of a blank cassette plus a small charge for equipment maintenance and operation as well as for mailing costs (the service is also available to groups outside Latin America). In this way, a widespread co-operation network is being created for grass-root groups and independent producers all over Latin America.

At an institutional level, the market is supplied by Carsa SA, representing Sony, Matsushita Electric del Peru SA, representing National Panasonic, Philips Peruanua SA and RCA.

1/2" Video The 1/2" video recorder market is not considered very important by the electronic equipment companies (eg Carsa SA or Matsushita Electric del Peru SA). The prohibition on imports in 1984 left Carsa SA with no stock since in the past it carried a small line of video recorders. Matsushita SA was left with 250 units.

According to the head of Carsa SA, the firm has not sold more than 5,000 Betamax units over the past few years. This is attributed to the high cost imposed by import duties which make video recorders a luxury item.

This is true for the Sony SL2000 for which the FOB price is US$625 and the selling price in the stores is US$1,773. As a result, most of the video recorders in Peru have been smuggled into the country at a cost of US$800 and it is impossible to estimate the total number of these units. According to Datum SA there are 50,000 video recorders in Lima. Carsa SA confirms this estimate. Rental houses put the figure as high as 150,000. A closer estimate might be that of 70,000 video recorders in the entire country of which 85 per cent have been imported illegally.

Contraband in the flow of 1/2" tapes is extensive. However, since the local currency suffers from the high dollar rate even contraband items will become expensive and this may stimulate the sale of non-recorded tapes.

VIDEO CLUBS

There are 35 video rental stores in Peru. The market is small and stores come and go. The more stable outlets for video are usually found within existing businesses such as supermarkets (Wong Sa) and drugstores (Deza). Geographically speaking, they are located in commercial zones which serve the higher economic strata of Peru: San Isidro, Miraflores, Chararilla, Rinconada, San Borja.

According to estimates by proprietors of video rental outlets, there are 150,000 video recorders in Lima (an unrealistically high figure) and the stores rent an average of 100 video tapes a week, a figure reflecting the small size of the market. Rental procedure involves leaving a deposit and paying a sum of one US dollar per tape, a price which may in some cases be even lower. About 70 per cent of all videotape offerings are in English and most of them are American productions based on well publicised films already screened in

Peru. These are generally purchased in Miami and are of very poor quality. It is nearly impossible to obtain original versions of a video tape.

The majority of productions fall into the category of entertainment. In second place there are children's films followed by horror films. The pornographic video market is relatively small and relies on newspaper advertising to reach the consumer.

VIDEO USAGE

Instituto Nacional de Teleducacion (INTE) is part of the Ministry of Education and is responsible for State programmes in tele-education. Despite having well equipped facilities, its full potential in tele-education has not yet been realised. A circuit for videotapes among schools has been established using 75 VHS National (Panasonic) recorders donated by the Japanese government. Due to a lack of programming, these facilities are underutilised. INTE's budget of $200,000 (US) allocates no funds for production.

Centro de Servicios de Pedagogia Audiovisual (CESPAC) initiates its activities in the context of the 1975 agrarian reform to provide informal instruction to a large peasant population. CESPAC is politically autonomous and by 1982 had extended its activities to the marginal urban population. Its production equipment includes: 1 multicopying module, 10 recording modules, 5 editing machines, 2 audio machines, 1 dubbing machine, 1 illumination module. The equipment is worth US$4,000,000. For diffusion purposes CESPAC has distributed 130 monitors and Beta playback machines. Their 1,200 productions are grouped under the following headings:

a) Agricultural Technology
b) Animal Husbandry
c) Resources for Production
d) Mechanisation
e) Health and Housing
f) Fisheries

Centro de Produccion Audiovisual Alfavision was created within the framework of the national multisectoral literacy campaign of 1981–1985 and since 1982 has been involved in production and diffusion. There is a 20 per cent illiteracy rate in Peru and during the past 3 years video has been used to raise literacy among 300,000 people. The success rate has been low due to the fact that programmes reach only a fraction of the target population. Alfavision counts on 25 diffusion modules (one vehicle, monitor, recorder). During this period Alfavision has made 70 productions with facilities which include 3/4" recorders and editors. It also has printing equipment for the production of supplementary leaflets. All of this equipment is valued at US$120,000 but due to recent funding cutbacks activities have generally been curtailed.

Empresa Minera del Centro – CENTROMIN PERU is the Peruvian mining company which has its own television system. Once a system dedicated to producing and distributing educational material, it has offered canned programmes since 1983 which are obtained from the TV channel in Lima. In spite of this, programming is selective as it avoids violent material and publicity. The estimated viewing audience is 350,000 persons per day. Its centre is in La Oroya and there are affiliates in several other mining cities.

Centro de Teleducation de la Universidad Catolica (CETUC) is located on the campus of the Universidad Catolica. It is primarily involved in educational promotion and extension. Since 1970, the CETUC has had a video archive consisting of its own productions which have not been marketed due to their high cost. It has organised national film, video and radio festivals for five consecutive years.

Universidad de Lima, with the financial support ($430,000) of GTZ and the Ministry for Technical Co-operation of the Democratic Republic of Germany, has a programme in communication sciences. Contributing its own funds, the University of Lima has built a TV studio, laboratories etc worth $800,000. These facilities are used primarily for educational purposes or for productions supporting other university faculties.

Chapter 19

COLOMBIA

HARDWARE AND BLANK SOFTWARE

Colombia has a substantial network for the production and commercialisation of professional and domestic video, but has not yet developed a full video industry.

Equipment and magnetic tapes in 1", 1/2" and 3/4" formats are imported both legally and illegally. Legal imports are through representatives of the main international manufacturers which, in order of importance in market share, are Sony, Ampex and Panasonic.

In video transmission there are 3 'programmers', which have the most complete digital production and post-production equipment, namely: RTI, Caracol and RCN, which have a mobile unit for outside broadcast work.

The domestic market for video recorders, is dominated by smuggled goods: Colombia is often called the 'paradise of video smuggling'.

In August 1985, it was estimated that there were about 400,000 video recorders operating in the country, 50% of which entered the country illegally.

The import restriction measures enacted by the government in 1983, brought strong reactions from private enterprise and now this import line has special tariff treatment.

TELEVISION AND VIDEOGRAMS

Television is transmitted via three channels. The first, Channel 7, has mixed programming: commercial and cultural-educational. The second, Channel 9, was born as a strictly commercial channel, but has slowly started to introduce educational and cultural programmes. The third, Channel 11, is strictly a cultural one and is totally state controlled but financed through advertising.

There are at present 66 producers registered by Inravision. They were licensed under the legislation in force, but due to strong competition and the economic problems of the television industry only 25 are fully operational.

PRODUCERS

Commercial programming in Colombia is controlled by TV production companies; hence, there are no independent producers, except for the 4 enterprises listed below. The rest are small, family businesses which render services to private persons.

In order of importance, these producers are:

1) Provideo Created at the beginning of 1981 as ECOS producers, Provideo has production and post-production equipment and is located in large premises which it rents to smaller producers such as Colvision and Proyectamos.

2) Televideo With production and post-production equipment, it provides services for Teleantiquia (regional channel) and Audiovisuales (belonging to the Ministry of Communications) and other small producers.

3) JJB TV

4) Mastervision

Main Duplicators. For many years the piracy of films from Venezuela, Panama and Miami was the dominant element in the domestic video market. However the process of legalisation began with the confiscation in November 1984 of 8,000 tapes and the closure of the most important rental firm, 'Batimovie Club'.

In May 1985, six months later, 4 legal companies for video duplication were formed: Cine Video, Magnum Video, Videotec and Videco.

These four companies copy and reproduce a large number of films for which they have paid royalty or copyright fees to international production companies. The most important is Cinevideo, linked to Colombian Movie (multinational of film distribution in Colombia) accounting for 47.4 per cent of the 118 titles already available in the market.

According to the Journal *Documento Cinematografico* Oct–Nov 1985, there are about 1,700 to 2,000 rental firms in Colombia and they work either with legal or pirate films and their market of commercial sales is similar to the one existing in the United States.

DISTRIBUTION

Programmes

In Colombian television there is no distribution system of pre-recorded national programmes, since programming companies – as sole producers – commercialise their products through space concession with Inravision. The business structure of the big companies such as RTI, Caracol and Punch, (to mention just a few) is such that commercial operations include production, editing and post-production in studio and on location, selection and purchase of foreign material and the production and post-production of commercials. Since there is a production monopoly, the distribution processes are minimal because there are no intermediaries or beneficiaries to enlarge that process.

Foreign programming may be selected and obtained by programmers. Contracts for these programmes are made through the legal representatives that supply all the other Latin American chains. The same holds true for non-commercial (educational and cultural) programming.

Duplicating Firms

Pirated video, comes in order of importance, from: Venezuela, Panama, and Miami in the United States. Legalised video is provided by international distributors: Paramount – Cinema International, Universal Studios, Viacom, Vill and Ziv and also by the national commercial producers and distributors: Cinevideo, Magnum, Videotec and Videco.

Cinevideo: is in charge of distributing products directly to rental companies or to the commercial branches of the two companies that also work with a legal product. Up to date, it has 56 titles, which have been distributed in packages of 8 or 10 titles.

Videco has authorised representatives in the existing Video Clubs. As can be appreciated, Cinevideo with 47 per cent of total titles, controls the sales tariff, although it does not own rental premises.

CONSUMPTION

Duplicating Firms

In terms of the number of rental stores and of the average turnover of tapes per month (12,000 according to figures provided by Cinevideo) after Brazil and Venezuela, Colombia is the third most important Latin American video market.

Video piracy and smuggling have reached such dimensions that it is impossible to establish absolute figures for the number of existing titles.

Nevertheless, it is possible to assert that adventure films and children's programmes are the most popular.

All the 118 titles of the incipient industry of legalised video belong to the entertainment category, distributed as follows:

Action	54
Comedy	19
Children's	10
Drama	15
Suspense	15
Science Fiction	2
Musical	3
Total	118

The top ten titles in the Colombian market during Oct – Nov 1985 were:

1. *Cross-Creek*	Thorn-Emi	Martin Ritt
2. *Los reyes del Sablazo*	Aries-Argentian	R Sofovich
3. *La culpa la tuvo Rio*	PSO	Stanley Donen
4. *Gremlins*	Warner Bros	Joe Dante
5. *Amadeus*	AMLL	Milos Forman
6. *Dona Flor y sus 2 maridos*	Embrafilme	Luis C Barret
7. *Padre e hijo*	Orion	Paul Newman
8. *The Cotton Club*	Orion	Francis Coppola
9. *Pinochio*	Buena Vista	Walt Disney
10. *El Cristal Encantado*	United States	J Henson & F

The Church has started to use video in educational and promotional work.

'... An interesting use of video is for social promotion and organisation. Maybe it is the most recent use, but also the most interesting and significant. This has been developed on the basis of pastoral work, for instance, that the Colombian Catholic Church does. Some of these groups have bought the video recorder, others have bought also the filming equipment and have used these resources in their work with marginal communities (many of which do not yet receive television transmissions), to promote development and organisation.'

Some groups working with grass-roots organisations, basically in the cities, have attempted to initiate the local populations involved into video production. Unfortunately, these efforts have not been successful, and they have had to turn to borrowing films and programmes from commercial firms or other national and international institutions.

According to information supplied by a researcher from Ceprodes, there is a certain amount of video infrastructure in education centres (universities, schools), in private enterprise and in some decentralised government institutions which is not being used to its full capacity.

Finally Cine Mujer, as well as other movie producers have started to use video as a tool in movie production.

The development of independent video in Colombia reflects the production boom in audio-visual material in all sectors ready to make use of affirmative and popular communication media.

TABLE 1

IMPORT TABLES OF VIDEOGRAPHIC EQUIPMENT
– PRODUCT: VIDEORECORDERS

Year	Movement Jan-Dec (US$)
1979	197,915
1980	4,176,033
1981	591,191
1982	950,000
1983	2,224,256
1984	1,386,390
1985*	1,824,469
Total	9,136680

Source: Incomex, accumulated year and country listings.

TABLE 2

IMPORT TABLES OF VIDEOGRAPHIC EQUIPMENT
– PRODUCT: MAGNETIC TAPES

Year	Movement Jan-Dec (US$)
1979	38,392
1980	442,408
1981	591,191
1982	950,000
1983	1,001,217
1984	275,510
1985*	95,614
Total	3,394,332

*June to August
Source: Incomex, accumulated year and country listings.

TABLE 3

COSTS PER UNIT (IN US$)

	Sale	Rental	No of films
Cinevideo	34	*	56
Magnum	33	1.6	22
Videotec	31	1.6	28
Video	31	1.6	12

* Does not rent on a per-unit basis.
Source: Interviews with Management.

Chapter 20

VENEZUELA

HARDWARE AND BLANK SOFTWARE

PRODUCTION

In Venezuela the 'manufacture' of video equipment and videocassettes is recent and of a limited scope. Sony of Venezuela C.A. assembles video recording (Betamax) domestic equipment. 3M Manufacturera de Venezuela and TUWEST C.A. (Tubos Westinghouse Stock Company) are implementing a project for local production of video tapes, which is organised in several stages. 3M S.A. has a technological agreement with TUWEST. The first stage is the winding of the tape on cassettes. In the second stage manufacturing of all the plastic components will start.

The biggest purchasers of unused tapes are the duplicators (30 in total). These companies account for 80 per cent of the local market.

According to estimates of duplicating firms, there are about 500–600 Video-stores (Video clubs, exchange, sale and rent stores). Of these 250 are located in Caracas. These companies define this market as an incipient one and in a process of adjustment, which means that some of these small establishments will disappear (due to management inefficiency) and new ones will appear.

We refer only to the half inch format, since the 3/4" and 1" formats are not produced domestically. These formats which are imported are used in the professional TV market and in the video production market.

Video producers prepare a certain amount of advertising, documentaries, commercial catalogues, correspondence material (of subsidiaries of the main offices, for example) and cinematography.

The Sales and Marketing Manager of 3M, felt that comparisons between the professional video market and the domestic one are not particularly useful because they are, according to his opinion, totally different.

The Beta format accounts for 80 per cent of the domestic market (1/2") and VHS accounts for the remaining 20 per cent.

DISTRIBUTION

In Venezuela there are no distributors of electronic products. The international manufacturers take care of local clients through their representatives in the country (which might be an assembly firm, an office or a big sales agency), or directly from the main offices. The same is true for video hardware and for software, of all types, models and formats.

In 1984, an approximate total of 2 million video cassettes (1/2" domestic) were imported. The main importing companies (foreign manufacturers), in order of their share of the market are: Sony, 3M Manufacturera de Venezuela and Racal. Kodak should be mentioned in fourth place. The other companies (National, Hitachi, Panasonic) import very small amounts. At a national level, these 'manufacturer importers' have about 24 retail stores of which 7 belong to 3M.

The main importers of professional-type video tapes are the following:

1"	Ampex Corp.
	3M Manufacturera de Venezuela
	Other Japanese manufacturers are Sony, Fuji, etc. Kodak is starting to penetrate in this area of business.
3/4"	Sony of Venezuela
	Ampex Corp.

Direct imports, by local clients, account for 80 per cent of total transactions of this type. The remaining 20 per cent are tapes purchased from the manufacturers' representatives located in the country. Tapes are imported in bulk directly from the factory by the main clients: TV channels, producers and editors. Ampex Corp and other companies have small stocks of professional-type video tapes for minor clients – small producers, for instance.

In 1956 Ampex Corp introduced 2" quadruplex type videorecording machines. For a very long time, they covered 100 per cent of the market. At present, there are only a couple of these machines operating. Nine years ago, they were displaced by the 1" recording machines, and three years ago they disappeared from the market.

The main 'importers-manufacturers' of video tape recording equipment are:

Ampex Corp which accounts for 90 per cent of the market in 1" Professional tapes.

Sony of Venezuela which takes 90 per cent of the market in 3/4" – U-Matic and BETA 1/2" – domestic tapes.

Others involved are Japanese companies such as JVC, Panasonic, etc.

HARDWARE

Studies, carried out by market research companies, estimate that about 600,000 domestic, 1/2" VCRs have been placed in the Venezuelan market. In 1985 approximately 20,000 units were placed in the market, but there has been practically no installation of new equipment which is one of the reasons why the market has not tended to grow.

There is a 1 per cent customs duty on imports of both professional and domestic VCRs and spare parts and since they come under 'regime 2' they are considered to be luxury items, for which there are no preferential dollar concessions. The government has thus directly and indirectly restricted imports in this sector, since they must be paid for in dollars.

Some electronic products also enter the country – in small lots – through wholesalers. In the case of domestic video machines, smuggling and the large number of imports by individuals must be taken into account. The number of imports by individuals increased steadily between 1975 and 1982.

Professional cameras used in the country are the Japanese Ikegami and the North American RCA, which together account for 80 per cent of the Venezuelan market. Some Hitachi cameras are also in use. In most instances they are bought directly by local clients from the international manufacturer.

Exports from the United States of America arrive by land, sea and air. This market is however mainly a professional one and is located in the capital city, Caracas. The local clients are the four television channels and 12 video tape producers and post-producers. These last firms use 1" recording machines and other sophisticated equipment (digital effect, electronic switchers, among others). They also use Telemovie apparatus with 35 and 16mm formats. The models used are RCA and Rancintel.

CONSUMPTION

A representative of Ampex Corp estimated that 99 per cent of the Venezuelan market operates on the basis of sales. Similarly, Video Express, estimated 99 per cent of the Venezuelan video market to be home-based and 1 per cent institutional. These figures are quite close to reality if we compare quantities of professional versus domestic video recording equipment distributed in the country, or the number of real and potential clients of both sectors. According to 3M Manufacturera de Venezuela, the present price of domestic equipment ($690) is beyond the purchasing power of the majority of the population.

VIDEOGRAMS

PRODUCTION

There are three television stations, eight main videotape production companies and nineteen video duplication firms in Venezuela.

The duplicating or copying firms reproduce, distribute, and market their products. Thus, in a list of the main national distributors we would have: Video Rodven, Video Hollywood-Video Games of Venezuela, Blancic Video, Video Express. There are no wholesalers in Venezuela, the only intermediary is the retailer.

According to the latest market study, these four companies share 98 per cent of the local market.

At present, there are 15 to 20 representatives of international producers in Venezuela and the different firms formally established in Venezuela sign contracts with those representatives and pay a royalty (copyright, production rights, etc) and are then legally authorised to launch the final product. According to the representative of Video, 60 new titles are issued (recorded video tapes) every month. That would mean an average of 12 titles for each of the duplicators:

> Video Rodven: 12
> Video Hollywood-Video Games of Venezuela: 12–14
> Blancic Video: 12
> Video Express: 8–12

The rest of the tapes are distributed by other companies.

An estimate of the level of business, in financial terms, may be obtained from import figures of pre-recorded software. These figures, for the last ten years, are given in Table 3.

CONSUMPTION

On the basis of interviews carried out with representatives of duplicating or copying companies and with those in charge of retail stores, we can conclude that the vast majority of tapes circulating in the domestic market, belong to the category 'Entertainment'. 'Right now, through the video, we are giving the consumer what he wants, [...] amusement and recreation ...' (Jose Bautista Suarez).

The duplicating companies, which are the main distributors of recorded tapes (films) in video form, do not normally reproduce or record material other than that designed purely for entertainment. According to the figures of the Foreign Trade Institute, in the last ten years (1975–1984) Venezuela has imported 15,357 kgs ($280,128) of language teaching tapes, which represents 6.4 per cent and 7.2 per cent respectively, of the total.

A representative from Hollywood Video estimated that the company distributes tapes in the following percentages:

%

1) Action films
2) Adventure films } 60
3) Children films
4) Terror and war films } 40

According to a spokesman from Video Express, entertainment films account for 99 per cent of the company's sales and this reflects the situation in the overall market.

Without doubt the other duplicating or copying companies follow sales patterns similar to those of the two companies mentioned.

Pre-recorded software is addressed mostly to adults and youngsters. Children's films are a small proportion of the total titles put on the market by companies. Hollywood Video sales are distributed in the following proportion: 75 per cent of recorded tapes are addressed to an adult audience and 25 per cent to an audience composed of young people and children.

The preceding estimates are strongly supported by the answers to interviews carried out in Video retail stores. In most of the video stores we visited (specifically in 5 of them) pornographic films are constantly being sold and rank – whether actually or potentially – very high among total tapes distributed.

CONCLUSION

USE OF VIDEO

In general, the video tape recorder is used in Venezuela to record TV programmes and to screen films. The introduction of this audio-visual technology into cultural, scientific and artistic endeavour is still marginal. The video recorder is not used massively for experimentation or communication. It does not have a collective or community use. Owners of video recorders rarely have a video camera and if they do it is used to make home movies.

For Jose Bautista Suarez the apparatus is at present used mainly to reproduce the tapes users buy, exchange or rent in video stores. Lately, this has been influenced by the fact that there is a scarcity of unused tapes (as a result of limited imports). 'If we had this type of material, TV programme recording would be encouraged'.

For Hector Azuz, the video recorder is being used to record from TV (40 per cent), to reproduce entertainment films (30 per cent) and the remaining 30 per cent is not being used. 'The demand for video tapes (films) does not correspond to the number of domestic appliances that exist which, according to the duplicators' estimates amount to 600,000 units'.

'Other use' of this technology, that is communication and dialogue among small groups, began in 1982 and 1983.

PARALLEL MARKET

The so-called video pirates offer the Venezuelan public a poor quality product. This is due to their *modus operandi*. Rather than duplicating simultaneously and massively from a matrix, where one piece of equipment sends the same signal to various recorders, they operate the second tape from the first, the third from the second, and from that one the fourth tape and so forth. This is known as the 'seven passings' in which the tape wears out and the clarity of both image and sound suffers.

In the past, 'video pirates' utilised unused tapes but now with the scarcity of material, in many cases they record on re-cycled tapes and thus put a very poor product on the market. They do not fix the price for their own merchandise, since they sell to the highest bidder. They distribute their tapes not only in video stores but also in apartments, houses and through peddlers. Their activity is an obstacle to improved distribution by legalised duplicating firms.

The proportion of piracy in the Venezuelan market has considerably diminished, for the following reasons:

-   Increased penetration and dissemination of the legal product means that the user tends to choose the better quality tapes. An additional advantage of the use of legal tapes is the right to claim for legal imperfections.
-   The legal duplicators refuse to sell original tapes to video pirates.
-   The co-operation of State bodies such as the armed Forces of Cooperation (AFC) and of the National Guard (NG).
-   The legal provisions now in force against 'video pirates'. The opinion of the Thirteenth Superior Court for Penal cases is that:

    '... it is an offence to reproduce, copy on duplicate without permission and with the purpose of obtaining profits, movie films on audio-visual tapes, normally called video-tapes or video-cassettes ...' (Silvia Martinez).

Duplicators believe that with an increasing number of new titles and new international producers, supported by various advertising resources (for instance TV commercials), video pirates may be virtually eliminated in two or three years' time.

Despite the fact that video pirates have not disappeared yet, the reduction of their profit margins is considered a success. A few years ago they covered practically 100 per cent of the local market.

'... a big organisation was operating in Venezuelan territory, dedicated to illegal and mass reproduction of those films, whose market covered all the area of the Caribbean and reached Brazil and Argentina ...' (Silvia Martinez).

It is estimated that today piracy accounts for between 15 per cent and 20 per cent of the domestic market.

TABLE 1

HARDWARE IMPORTS – VOLUME TOTAL AMOUNT IN THE LAST 10 YEARS (1975-1984)

Year	Value ($)
1975	878,875
1976	1,206,010
1977	2,279,220
1978	13,894,365
1979	15,968,981
1980	34,662,787
1981	48,548,327
1982	73,357,781
1983	14,595,680
1984	9,187,795
Total	214,579,821

Source: Foreign Trade Institute

TABLE 2

IMPORTS – BLANK TAPE VOLUME TOTAL IMPORTS IN THE LAST TEN YEARS (1975-1984)

Year	Value ($)
1975	495,118
1976	588,890
1977	814,102
1978	3,361,694
1979	6,565,636
1980	8,981,788
1981	11,038,589
1982	15,849,356
1983	5,157,313
1984	6,253,143
Total	59,105,143

Source: Foreign Trade Institute

TABLE 3

IMPORTS – VIDEOGRAMS TOTAL IMPORTS IN THE LAST TEN YEARS (1975–1984)

Year	Value ($)
1975	43,196
1976	54,740
1977	239,570
1978	339,359
1979	412,323
1980	93,543
1981	384,346
1982	695,971
1983	854,454
1984	135,792
Total	3,853,284

Source: Foreign Trade Institute

Chapter 21

CHILE

HARDWARE AND BLANK SOFTWARE

PRODUCTION

In Chile there is no video industry. No equipment or spare parts are manufactured, and all the equipment is of foreign origin, mainly Japan, North America and the Federal Republic of Germany. There is only one company that assembles manufactured television parts and some models of VHS video recorders – IRT, with premises on Vicuna Mackenna 333, Santiago. We are not aware of any future projects for manufacturing equipment or tapes.

DISTRIBUTION

Since there is no national production, distribution is based on import volumes. The negative attitude in providing information for the first part of this study becomes more acute in the second, due to the highly confidential nature of the data requested (as interested parties put it).

However, despite the lack of statistical information, working with import registries of the different companies we established a list of the official distributors of the main brand marks that confirms the supplies of existing equipment in the country.

IMPORTS

For Domestic Use. Privated individuals and companies may import equipment freely, with the sole condition of paying customs duties. Despite the fact that most imports are made through representatives, a large number are made by pirate companies, operating in Free Zone areas, mainly Panama. This situation, which was relatively important in the years 1980 to 1982, has lost much of its relevance because equipment 'illegally' imported – although sold at a lower price – does not have warranty or technical service.

Sixty thousand video-recorders entered the country legally through Customs. To this figure, must be added the number of machines illegally introduced into the country – for which no Customs duties are paid – which amount to 10,000, and finally equipment directly imported by institutions, individuals and organisations that have preferential duty treatment. This group would include churches, the Armed Forces and Embassies. Imports of equipment through Free Trade Zones (Africa, Iquique and Punta Arenas) are estimated to amount to 20,000 machines.

A researcher from ILET (Instituto Lationoamericano de Estudios Transnacionales) notes in an article entitled 'Communicacion Alternativa Video-Cassette: Perspectivas en America Latina' that there are about 100,000 machines installed in Chile or 45 for every 1,000 homes.

The distribution of equipment and tapes is made through the distributor's own points of sale and through electronic equipment stores located in the biggest cities and provinces. Unfortunately, the stores' listing is very partial. According to the sales manager of an electronic equipment store, the country's demand is well satisfied. Professional equipment and tapes are sold through the main office in Santiago. Sales for the provinces are made either through agents, or are directly imported by television stations or companies.

Sale and Rental

Production companies regularly rent their equipment. There are three officially recognised companies. Television stations are self-sufficient. With regard to domestic usage, the percentage of equipment rental is minimal and is much higher for pre-recorded tapes.

VHS/BETA Systems

At the beginning, the BETA system accounted for the majority of the market, but this situation has changed radically. Table 2 shows the growth of the JVC brand equipment. In 1985, Toshiba VHS equipment started to be available commercially in Chile, with a lower unitary value, but it is too soon to assess its market incidence.

CUSTOMS POLICIES

Customs duties are modified from time to time and the tariffs in force up to January 1986 were the following:

Value Added Tax, VAT: 20 per cent
General Tariffs on imports: 20 per cent
Additional tariff on video recorders: 50 per cent

CONSUMPTION

Domestic The consumption of domestic equipment covers two clearly distinct sectors. The first one is related to individuals with high and medium income levels who purchase equipment for entertainment purposes or as an alternative to films and television. The other group is institutional – schools, community groups – which consider video a support and motivation tool for teaching and dissemination activities.

An illustration of the behaviour of the market, is the tape consumption of different sectors, which indicates that the main purchasers of 1/2" inch tapes are videoclubs, with an average use of between 8 thousand and 12 thousand tapes a month. If we consider an annual turnover of roughly 300,000 tapes, we can infer that videoclubs consume between 35 per cent and 38 per cent of total tapes. Without considering the armed forces, town councils, intendancies and official government organisations (for which we do not have data), the other tape consumer sectors are probably alternative sectors and churches, followed by high and medium income schools. Individuals who have their own equipment probably only have a couple of tapes, which they erase when they want to record a new programme since they are not interested in having a video library.

At a professional level, the biggest tape consumers – in professional formats are, of course, television stations. In 1984, National Television of Chile consumed 6,260 tapes (1,460 of 1 inch and 4,800 of 3/4 inch), ie one third of total professional tapes imported during that year. Production companies consumed around 4,000 professional tapes (800 of 1 inch and 3,200 of 3/4 inch) and 5,000 of 1/2 inch.

VIDEOGRAMS

PRODUCTION

When video was introduced in 1976 it was an independent activity unrelated to television and in the following four years its development and production provided little interest.

In 1980, there was a big quantitative change. Advertising activity was booming, a factor which explains the creation of many production companies. Parallel to this, a favourable foreign exchange rate, derived from the prevailing economic policy, favoured the acquisition of high technology equipment.

Some enterprises which grew up during this period of expansion produce

documentaries both for social and educational use and at the request of institutions. Others are hired by official organisations to produce documentaries
for institutional use. Finally, there are producers who have production contracts with television stations. None of these enterprises produces for the
videoclub market.

There are a range of production organisations:

1. *Mixed Enterprises*, (movie and video), work almost exclusively in advertising and only occasionally produce a documentary either on their own or
   on request.
2. *Production Enterprises*, whose main activity is advertising, but produce
   documentaries upon request, either on their own or jointly with independent producers.
3. *Unofficial Productions*, making four documentaries a year.
4. *Official Production*, Ministries, Armed Forces etc.
5. *Institutional Production*, Universities, Museums and others.

Duplicationg Enterprises. In Chile there are no duplicating enterprises of the
types known in other countries, mainly due to the irregular situation within
which videoclubs operate. Videoclubs are perfectly legal in as much as they
pay municipal taxes. However, since they do not pay reproduction duties for
the rental or sale of pre-recorded tapes, their material is considered to be
'pirated'. A law was enacted in 1985 to protect copyright and to fight against
video and phonogram piracy.

Videoclubs that import their own tapes from the United States (in English)
or from Venezuela (with Spanish sub-titles) reproduce some copies and sell
them to other Videoclubs. Videoclubs make new copies on their own VHS or
BETA equipment. The number of copies made will depend on the demand
for the title.

Producers, who include duplicating among their services, do not consider
it very profitable. At the level of production in 3/4" and 1 inch formats, duplicating is a common activity. An exception is Promav, a company which does
duplicating to help finance its productions, since its budget supplied by the
Catholic University is very limited. Duplicating services are mostly for
individual or institutional use and are practically non-existent for the Videoclub
market.

DISTRIBUTION

Enterprises which distribute to Videoclubs. The material acquired for videoclubs
comes mainly from the United States, Panama and Venezuela.

Three individuals control the market and Law No 18,443, which came into
force in January 1987, will drastically change the present situation. The Law
provides for both fines and imprisonment for those who illegally reproduce

video tapes (and also phonograms). In the last few months, film and blank tape distributors have started up enterprises, with representation from international distributors.

There was no information available about the volume of business of individuals who supply videoclubs (they provide around 10 titles a week, roughly 500 a year) but it is known that small videoclubs have around 200 titles; medium size ones, between 500 and 800 and the big ones between 1,200 and 2,000.

Alternative Distributors. Alternative distributors operate on the basis of budgets provided by organisations involved in community development, popular education, trade unionism, human rights or popular culture. All these are non-profit organisations interested in disseminating videos that help or support their line of work. Users have access to these services either by signing formal agreements, free of charge, or paying a small fee. Services range from tape reproduction to loan of equipment.

CONSUMPTION

Number of Videos Entered through Customs. In 1984, information, provided by the Banco Central de Chile, indicates that 7,160 titles were imported through customs from 18 different countries, the largest number coming from the United States.

The major activity of producers is advertising. Their secondary activities include commissioned documentaries, institutional documentaries and, lastly, experimental films of which there is an average production of six to twenty titles a year.

An average of 400–500 documentaries (3/4" and 1") are produced each year. For commercials, the yearly average is 700 titles produced in Chile and 84 produced abroad and adapted in Chile. From 1980–84 it is estimated that 185 documentaries (3/4", 1/2" and 1") were produced independently, or at the request of institutions or alternative organisations. It is difficult to provide figures for productions made by television channels, but in general television stations distribute their programming as follows: 40 per cent–50 per cent, their own production; 5 per cent–10 per cent, production at specific request and 40 per cent–50 per cent purchases abroad, from world production centres or from big distributors. No statistics are kept on productions made by official production sources and no estimates can be made.

1. *Number of Videos Examined by the Movie Evaluation Board*

Year	Number of Videos
1983	4,745
1984	8,447
1985	6,116

Source: Movie Evaluation Board

The Board does not keep a registry of the titles according to categories or type. Nor does it differentiate between national and foreign production (although it can be estimated that the foreign production accounts for the highest proportion). The number of titles banned by censorship is irrelevant, since importers do not run the risk of importing titles which might be rejected by censorship.

Television Stations. Law No 17,377 which regulates Chilean television establishes that television channels should be primarily oriented to cultural and informational programming. The social market economy policy in force during the last decade establishes that television channels should be self-financing. The consequence of such a policy is a change in programming, which is basically oriented to entertainment, and a change in financing sources, which comes mainly from advertising.

The National Television Council, which is responsible for the application of Law 17,377, has had to order television channels to devote 2 hours a week to cultural programmes; to limit advertising time; to set a maximum of two hours a day for broadcasting foreign soap-operas (1 hour) and national soap-operas (1 hour).

It may be estimated that 10 per cent of Chilean National Television programming is direct broadcasting and the rest is pre-recorded. Pre-recorded production is composed of: 45 per cent production by the national channels; 5 per cent commissioned elsewhere or co-production, and 50 per cent of international origin, mainly North American. Total pre-recorded production can be divided in the following categories:

	%
Business/industry	–
Children/youngsters	7.5
Movies/entertainment, includes soap/operas & serials	63.3
Art	
General interest/educational }	9.8
Manual/instruction	–
Medicine/science	4.0
Sport	5.0
Popular culture/Music	5.6
Others (advertising, religious, miscellaneous)	5.8

It is interesting to note, from these figures, that 90 per cent of foreign pre-recorded tapes belong to the film and serials category.

The percentage figures are similar for the Television Corporation of the Catholic University of Chile, Channel 13. They do not however hold true for the Television Corporation of the University of Chile, Channel 11, which is a small station that tries to provide alternative programming to that broadcast by the big channels. The Television Corporation of the Catholic University of Valparaiso, which for budgetary reasons transmits only 4 hours a day, broadcasts material of which 60 to 70 per cent is cultural/educational.

Schools/Universities. Demand from schools and universities is in direct proportion to the number of their reproducing devices which is small. According to a spokesman from the Audio-Visual department of the Ministry of Education, the use of video is still in the early stages and its use is limited.

A study of the use of audio-visual media in private grammar schools and high schools, by Isabel Urzua and Tatiana Montes, reveals that video is preferred to other audio-visual techniques. Video ranks first with 31 per cent, followed by panoramic slides, 11 per cent; full-scale drawings, 20 per cent and others (films, illustrations and slides), 26 per cent. Audio-visual techniques are used in 88 per cent of the schools surveyed, because teachers consider them to be a useful aid in their teaching. The researchers selected a sample out of the 324 private schools in the metropolitan area of Santiago. The sample surveyed consisted of 32 schools, located in different neighbourhoods and communities. Free schools were not considered in the sample, only paying ones.

Training/Industries. Enterprises, industries, banks and laboratories are the best clients. They request documentaries for technical training of their employees. These enterprises also buy documentaries abroad, mainly in the United Kingdom and Spain.

Popular and Social Sectors. Demand from these sectors is mainly oriented to videos that reflect the historical, political and social situation of the country and of Latin America in general. Preference is also very high for musicals of committed singers/authors. The contents of independent production reveal the following categories for the 185 videos registered.

Number
86	Documentaries (Themes related to the socio-political, cultural and national situation)
68	Experimental (Video art and others)
15	Musicals (Includes video-clips)
15	Polemic (Social realism prevails)

This audience is increasing and has a selective and critical attitude to the material it requests or is offered.

Children's Videos. From the information gathered from videoclubs, children's material is composed of cartoons, children's television programmes, musicals and sports programmes. It accounts for 5 per cent–10 per cent of total demand. The percentage of children's programming shown on television channels whether produced by them or packed programming, amounts to 5 per cent to 10 per cent.

Pornographic Videos. The Prevention of Sexual Offences Brigade, is responsible for confiscating pornographic materials. According to the Chief Officer of the Brigade, the existing legislation is old-fashined and the sanctions are too mild; in addition it is very difficult to seize these materials. In 1984, approximately 200 videos were seized, but were quickly replaced. It is known that this type of material is exhibited in motels – of which there are about 100 in Santiago – and in private homes.

Few videoclubs have these titles and they would rather not take the risk. Users gain access to them through a password. There is speculation over the existence of national producers who prepare this type of material – it would seem that 99 per cent is of foreign origin.

Pornographic video is considered by the authorities, the specialised police force and the censorship bodies, as an irrelevant phenomenon.

It may be concluded that the consumption of pre-recorded video tapes centres around entertainment, television channels and videoclubs. The experience of ICTUS Producer and Distributor, reveals the importance of encouraging critical and discerning spectators through forms of alternative production, distribution and consumption. Finally, in schools and universities, teachers – more so than students – consider video as a support material in their teaching activities.

GENERAL CONSIDERATIONS AND PIRACY

Times and Modes of Usage. The information regarding specific time usage is very general. Talking with various users, we learned that they spend between 10 and 15 hours a week recording television programmes – mainly cultural and sports programmes which they then watch in the evenings or at weekends. These recordings are watched in family circles and are not meant for commercial use. The supplies of video devices is mainly composed of reproduction equipment, and those who have cameras (according to store salesmen and distributors) are very few and do not use them frequently (recording of special family events, and some professionals who record certain events for research purposes).

Pirate Tape Circulation in Videoclubs. The present legislation does not cover the payment of royalties for the rights of reproduction and screening of videograms and this has resulted in the proliferation of videoclubs and screenings by companies. Any individual or company, with adequate equipment, can duplicate from television, cinema films (this is not so common), or from video-cassette films. Not many people are involved in this activity, because of the high cost of good quality duplicating equipment. No more than four people supply videoclubs. In the provinces, the situation is quite different. The quality of the material is very poor (the same is true of many videoclubs in Santiago, especially those that duplicate from movies). In the provinces, the television programme market is much bigger, especially in those areas where only one channel can be seen. Entertainment programmes, musicals and scientific programmes are in the greatest demand.

The new legislation will change the present state of affairs. According to the opinion of some videoclub owners, the new norms and rules are a result of pressure exercised by transnational film corporations, who also want to have a share in the video business. According to these people, the payment of royalties will substantially increase the cost borne by users. The rental fee of a video-cassette, for three days, is now US$1.20. If royalties were paid, this amount would increase to 15 or 20 dollars.

The rental period of video-cassettes (three days), easily enables members to duplicate them. Videoclub owners ignore duplicating by users. Their main concern is piracy from other videoclubs, which is frequent especially with the most exclusive and box-office success titles.

Equipment Smuggling. According to the opinion of representatives from big brand names, the problem of smuggling is not as great as it was a few years ago. The high investment required to purchase a video-recorder, between 500 and 700 dollars, forces the purchaser to look for technical assistance and warranties, which he can only obtain from official representatives. It is true that a purchaser can buy a smuggled video recorder at half the market price; but the lack of technical assistance (service) is an important factor in a potential buyer's decision.

The effect of the new legislation on piracy and the way in which videoclubs will react – whether they will adapt to it or find the ways to elude it can only be analysed once the Law is brought into force.

TABLE 1

VIDEO IMPORTS - DOMESTIC*

	YEAR 1983 (in units)	YEAR 1984 (in units)	YEAR 1985 (in units) (until June)
AKAI	140	267	102
HITACHI	235	279	104
JVC	1,538	3,164	1,246
NATIONAL PANASONIC	1,523	2,414	388
TOSHIBA	386	789	71
PHILIPS	–	630	– (will resume imports in 1986)
SONY	1,030	1,45	229
SANYO	109	945	15
RCA	=	1,100	3
FISHER	–	350	73
KENWOOD	–	158	–
Other brands (NEC, SANSUI)	129	302	71

* We do not have exact figures for professional use but according to data provided by the sales manager of VIDEOCORP, the supplies of professional equipment is covered by SONY, (90 per cent-95 per cent) and the rest by JVC and National.

TABLE 2

	Year 1983	Year 1984	Year 1985 (until June)
VHS	3,436	8,536	1,950
BETA	1,626	3,425	313
VHS %	68	71	86
JVC/VHS %	45	37	64

Chapter 22

BELIZE

During the 1970s TV had little impact in Belize. In the north, residents of the then-prosperous sugar belt around Corozal could pick up Mexican TV signals, while in the far south some residents of Punta Gorda could receive Guatemalan TV. By 1980, television ownership was concentrated in Corozal and the low ownership for the Toledo District reflects the relative poverty of the area. Outside these two areas, there was no television broadcasting or reception in Belize; all other television sets were therefore used for video playback.

VCRs began to arrive in Belize in 1977 or 1978. One of the first customers for the large Quasar 1000 machine was Santine Castillo Ltd. Castillo bought a dozen machines in Miami, and quickly sold them.

Within a matter of months of the Quasar 1,000 machines became obsolete with the introduction of VHS and Betamax format machines, in particular the Quasar 500 VHS VCRs imported by Giovanni Smith. The market did not take off immediately; 'Nobody wanted to be the first,' recalled Smith in 1981, 'there was an attitude of wait and see'. (*Brukdown*, No 6, Dec 1981). Castillo began to sell the VHS models as well, and soon the VHS format dominated the market (Santiago Castillo).

As the sale of VCRs increased, so a tape rental business grew to match it. Tapes were flown from Miami to stock the libraries. 'A number of Belizeans in the US have set up shop to supply the market with the latest tapes. (Unfortunately, the commercials are usually left in),' commented *Brukdown* in 1979. One former video entrepreneur recalls a Miami apartment with 12 or 14 VCRs recording off air simultaneously.

The rental business was dominated by Castillo, with a library of 3,000 tapes, Smith (trading under the name of Nibble and Co) and Efrain Eguilar. Other smaller enterprises continually attempted to undercut the big three, sometimes by copying tapes rented from competitors – 'bootlegging the bootleggers' (1979

Brukdown). The price dropped from B$8 per rental to B$5 and B$3. Santiago Castillo estimates his business as being worth B$4,000 per month at its height.

The market situation changed radically in 1980 with the advent of Tropical Vision. The rental companies were well supplied from Miami, but the use of agents and carriage costs decreased profit margins, and although the timelag was acceptable for feature films and soap operas, it was unsatisfactory for popular sports events. Two businessmen, Emory King and Nestor Vasquez, saw 'a tremendous opportunity for someone to buy an earth station and make the tapes here,' (Emory King), utilising satellite signals to hook up to the American network. They bought a Harris 6 metre dish over land through Mexico, installed it at Tropical Park, 13 miles west of Belize City, and 'all we did was make taped – movies, specials and whatever we thought the public would want. We did a roaring trade. The first month we rented 1,000 pounds worth of tapes, and it went rapidly from one thousand to two to three to four to five over a period of several months. We were taking five or six thousand dollars a month in tape rentals, and then a 'fellow down the street' bought a dish and a transmitter and started transmitting television.' (Emory King).

The 'fellow down the street' was Arthur Hoare of CTV. In the Autumn of 1981 shortly after independence, CTV began to transmit a TV signal to some 24 subscribers who had paid upwards of B$3,500 for a 'decoding antenna'. Hoare maintained that he was 'amplifying' a signal, not transmitting it (1981 *Brukdown*). In December, David Jenkins, a local technician, discovered that by retuning the set the signal could be picked up for free, and despite attempts by CTV to change frequency, television reception became a possibility for the population at large for the price of conversion. Jenkins made a good living and the video market collapsed.

Castillo abandoned the rental business and now concentrates on importing televisions and blank videotapes in bulk as part of his other business interests. 'I'm still stuck with a few hundred pieces of tape, tape with material on it,' he says. Aguilar too abandoned video and emigrated. He left the remnants of his business in the hands of his brother Gilberto, a prominent cattle rancher, who says 'we were renting very little ... practically nothing. That's when I took over. It took me a few months to phase out gradually and that was it.' Smith transferred his interests to TV broadcasting in Orange Walk, and in the summer of 1985 was still trying to sell off his prerecorded tapes. Tropical Vision's business also dropped back to 1,000 per month within months, but King's reason for leaving the company and putting his capital into video production was different. Until 1983 any form of telecommunications transmission without a government licence was illegal, and no framework for issuing television broadcasting licences existed. Tropical attempted to obtain one without success, and in June 1982 'my partner insisted that we broadcast .... I sold my interest in the earth station and my partner started transmitting on a free channel and continued to make tapes and rent tapes which he does to this day. Presumably there's still a profit in it' (Emory King).

VIDEO DATA

OWNERSHIP

There are no official figures for video ownership in Belize, and unfortunately the Annual Trade Reports do not show video recorders as a separate category. Nonetheless a reasonable estimate is possible from available data.

OWNERSHIP OF TELEVISION, 1980

Belize

	Corozal	*City*	*Urban*	*Rural*	*National*
No of households	4,055	8,440	15,235	12,910	28,145
% owning TVs	35	6	12	7	10
No of TVs	1,419	533	1,828	904	2,815

(Households Expenditure Survey 1980)

If we assume that all television sets outside Corozal are for use with VCRs, and that video use in Corozal follows the urban average, this gives a figure of 487 VCRs, leaving 932 sets assumed to be solely for television reception. Deducting these from the national total gives an estimate for video ownership in 1980 of 1,883, rounded up to a figure of 2,000. Since the market for videos collapsed at the end of 1981, a final estimate for video ownership in 1985 is 2,500 units.

    Brukdown magazine estimated in December 1981 a total of 1,500–2,000. Santiago Castillo's estimate also confirms this figure. He believes that the 500 or so VCRs he sold between 1978 and 1982 represent 75 per cent of those commercially marketed, 'but then a lot of people brought them in themselves. I would say in Belize City itself you could find 700 video recorders, though I am not aware of how many people have got rid of theirs since the introduction of television'.

MANUFACTURE AND IMPORT OF VCRS AND BLANK VIDEOTAPE

No television receivers, video recorders or videotapes are manufactured in Belize. Imports are exclusively from the United States, although since the introduction of television broadcasting the market for video hardware and soft-ware has collapsed.

Brodie's, Belize City's largest department store, had 2 VCRs for sale in August 1985, one a National NV 1220 ($2,299) and a reconditioned Philco DTE ($995). The manager reported that both had been in stock since he took up his position in October 1984, and in that time he had not sold one.

Santiago Castillo says that he imports at most six VCRs a year, and those only to special order. He does not consider the risks of the re-export trade to Mexico to be justified by the return on the large investment required. Castillo imports videotape (JVC T 120 VHS) for wholesale distribution. His volume of sales is about 1,000 per year; his major customers are the TV stations. There is no VCR rental in Belize.

Video Usage

VHS is the only tape format now in use in Belize.

Since the introduction of television Belize has become singular if not unique in its use, for public broadcasting, of VCR technology, which was designed for domestic purposes, for public broadcasting.

TV stations which re-schedule do so by taping from satellite on VHS recorders and re-broadcasting from them. Advertising material distributed by foreign agencies on behalf of multinational companies is transferred from 3/4" tape to VHS for re-broadcast, and local production of advertisements and programmes is either on VHS direct, or, in the case of the larger-scale operations, shot in 3/4" and transferred to VHS for distribution.

Video recorders were then used principally for viewing programmes taken from American networks; 'location-shift' as well as time-shift. Since the advent of TV broadcasting, many video units are to be seen next to television sets, but are used little or not at all.

Santiago Castillo sums up the situation with regard to video use. 'In Belize nobody really uses the video for what is intended. The video recorder in Belize from the day it was introduced until today has always been used primarily as a playback unit. I once was researching with a company the possibility of making just a playback unit, that doesn't have a timer, doesn't have channels, doesn't have to record, none of this, just a simple playback unit at very inexpensive cost, the reason being that's all it's used for in Belize .... They don't feel the need to record TV programmes. Belize isn't a TV country as yet and the programmes shown on television suffice. I do not think the video market is going to expand. In the United States the video boom took a while to get started and here it will take 5 times longer. Maybe about the year 2,000 people will start using video recorders .... When they get more educated as to the use of the video recorder. In the meantime I think the only use for a video recorder in Belize will be, for example, illustrating lectures, one of the few applications I could see, and for religious purposes etc .... The home application has run down. For video to come back to Belize, the TV stations would have to close down or start showing such poor quality programmes that no-one would watch.'

In this regard, it will be interesting to observe if the closedown of the television station in Corozal, despite the ready alternative of Mexican television, leads to the resurgence of videotape rental of American programmes among the wealthier members of the community.

Video Production

The largest software production house is Great Belize Productions Ltd. The company has Panasonic 3/4" cameras and editing facilities. All its equipment, some $15,000 worth, was obtained from the United States through Santiago Castillo, who also supplies its tape stock. In the financial year 1983–84 GBP grossed approximately $120,000 (representing a loss of $20,000) and in 1984/85 lost $9,000 on a turnover of $140,000. 'I think that's remarkably good,' says owner Stewart Krohn.

GBP produces advertisements for the local market, public service announcements for governmental and private organisations, and short programmes commissioned locally (for example by political parties and the tourist association) and by American companies for re-editing in the United States and broadcast over American cable channels. The company is moving towards film assistance work (location shooting, local co-ordination, etc) such as its involvement with Peter Weir's *The Mosquito Coast* in October 1985.

Krohn estimates that advertising accounts for 50 per cent of the company's revenue and 75 per cent of its time. One of the services he provides is that of transferring foreign advertising tapes from 3/4" format to VHS for the TV companies. The advertising market is in decline due to economic recession and because demand is satisfied for the time being. It is also in the advertising sector that competition is the most severe. A number of smaller companies produce simple advertisements on a smaller budget, the simplest consisting of teletext messages overlaid on a coloured screen. 'Our reputation is one of doing good work but of being outrageously high-priced. We know our costs and even our 'outrageously high-priced work' is below our cost,' says Krohn.

One of GBP's competitors is Bel-Ad, which like Krohn and others such as Arts, Entertainments and Ads Unlimited, has tried to market video recordings of local events, such as sports events, beauty competitions and public occasions such as the visit of the Pope in 1983, for home viewing as well as television broadcast, but the attempts have not on the whole been commercially successful. In September 1985, a new company, Belize Audio Visual Tracks, again tried to exploit this market. Its first productions are a tape of the celebrations of the Battle of St George's Caye (10 September) and Independence Day (21 September) and a profile of the distinguished Belizean sculptor

George Gabb MBE. Whether this venture will be any more successful than its predecessors remains to be seen.

Krohn estimates GBP's output in 1984-5 as 50 advertisements, 12 public service announcements, one thirty-minute documentary and six twenty-minute documentaries. Since most video production is for TV re-broadcast, the problems of developing the industry are closely linked to the structure of that industry.

Stewart Krohn:'Because all of these stations get their programming free by satellite their only investment is the initial one in fixed assets. We have the proven capabilities to make quality productions of international standards. We cannot however finance serious local production which no-one will buy as long as they can get entertainment free. Television in Belize is pure entertainment. We think of it more broadly as a means of communication, as a means of education, but the country thinks of it solely as entertainment. We could spend $25,000 to produce a two part educational series on Maya archaeology, on history, the economy, or the social sciences, but who would finance it? The TV stations? Not only will they not pay for it, but if I want to air it on television, I must pay *them* for it.' He relates the story of how UNICEF had to pay some $1,800 to screen some short spots which had cost $2,000 to produce in pre-school education. 'They were broadcast, but not nearly as widely as they should have been. In the districts, where there's really no advertising market, a lot of the stations will broadcast free of charge, but in Belize City where the need of the coverage is greatest, they will not. If we were to try to produce on our own we would have to fund the production, and then pay for the airing. Everyone is aware that American television is blanketing the country, and undermining the culture, and the general feeling is that we need local productions, and local programmes. We are ready and able – and we're not the only ones – to make local productions but no-one is willing to take the steps needed to encourage such production .... At a conference set up by the Caribbean Institute of Mass Communication the Minister of Home Affairs said repeatedly 'We need local production'. What was done about it? Nothing.'

Krohn suggests three alternatives to encourage local video production. The first would be to establish a quota for local productions, and to refuse licences to operators who would not accept it. A second is to ban all except locally produced advertising. A third possibility would be to use licence revenue from set owners or station operators to subsidize local programmes. Krohn considers that all these measures would be resisted by the station operators as a threat to their income and that any governmental action which affected free public access to television would be a most unpopular. The option of a direct government subsidy for video production is not a practical reality for Belize's already hard-pressed public purse. 'So that's the situation from the production standpoint. We're fighting a losing battle.' One factor which might alter the situation in the medium term would be any measures taken by the American government or television and satellite companies to reduce the unrestricted access of the television stations to free programming from satellites.

Advertisers and some advertisements have come under attack in the press for racial stereotyping. The UDP controlled *The Beacon* in its Independence Day 1985 editorial demanded: 'Who the hell tells them that they can sell more merchandise by making caricatures of black Belizeans, as they once did in the States? Or that they will continue to be allowed to make public jokers of our people ...? Let us be very clear and concise. We Belizeans want to see no more ugly and degrading spectacles of ourselves on TV screens.' (*The Beacon* 21.9.85). Although the problem is not limited to Belizean productions, since many of the advertisements produced on behalf of multinational companies for use in the so-called Third World and screened in Belize contain similar stereotyping, such problems and the reaction to them limit the potential for development of the domestic video industry. The American network advertisements while by no means value-free are in general without the gross racist caricatures which *The Beacon* criticises.

Government Production

Two government departments have the resources to produce video.

The oldest established is the Video Production Unit of the Government Information Service (GIS). Unesco supplied the unit's equipment, which consists of 2 Sony cameras (one portable), with a 3/4" playback unit. The unit has no editing facilities, which severely limits its development potential.

Its projects so far fall into four areas. *Belize Today* is a weekly local news bulletin, of exceptionally good quality for a programme edited in-camera, broadcast, presumably, from a variety of tapes, and using non-professionals front of camera. (The newsreader is a secretary in one of the ministries). When the research for this study was being carried out in August 1985 the programme had been temporarily suspended due to equipment failure.

Face the Nation, a panel discussion on current affairs, simultaneously videotaped and broadcast on radio, broke new ground in the media presentation of politics in Belize. The programme was extremely controversial when first broadcast in early 1985 and the GIS felt that it tended to become one-sided as time went on. In addition the logistical difficulties of producing the programme in Belize City were felt to be too costly in resources for the Belmopan-based Unit. The GIS therefore decided to discontinue the series.

The Prime Minister holds regular press conferences every 4 to 6 weeks. These are taped by the GIS for TV transmission, and also by Great Belize Productions Ltd (GBP) for archive purposes on behalf of the People's United Party (PUP). These broadcasts were also revolutionary in terms of public debate, the PUP government having had a reputation for extreme secrecy. The Unit is not satisfied with the presentation of the conferences and believes that quality would be substantially improved by the acquisition of a switching unit. The cost, some US$4,400, is however, prohibitive.

The unit is also called upon to shoot promotional material for other government agencies and the GIS finds this a strain on its limited resources.

The GIS Unit acquired its tape stock from a number of different sources. At first, its tapes were acquired via GBP, subsequently via a purchasing agent in Miami, and currently through the offices of the Belize Permanent Representative to the United Nations in New York. None of these arrangements have proved entirely satisfactory.

The Video Production Unit of the Ministry of Education Curriculum Development Unit received its equipment from the Japanese Government in February 1985. The Unit has 2 cameras (JVX GX-5700; Sony DXC 1820K), 1 1/2" VCR (JVC BR-6200U), 2 3/4" VCR (JVC CR-6650U, Sony VO 4800 portable), 2 1/2" editing recorders (JVC BR-8600), 2 3/4" editing recorders (JVC CR 8250U), I JVC RM 86U editing control unit and a VICTOR VS-1500 titler with camera. In addition the unit received monitors and 100 blank tapes.

At present, the unit has no air-conditioned storage facilities but hopes to use VCRs for teacher education in regional centres, and also, if sufficient equipment can be obtained from international aid sources, to have tapes re-broadcast by the TV stations for simultaneous viewing in schools. A number of problems in addition to that of resources need to be overcome before the project can be implemented. One of these is a problem of government licensing; another is estimation of the optimum time of broadcast and the attendant alterations to the school timetables. Possibly most difficult would be the question of financing the broadcasts if the co-operation of the TV stations is not forthcoming.

The Unit's priorities in the use of video are:

1. Teacher Education
2. Primary Maths and Science
3. Secondary Science

The Unit Staff also anticipate claims being made on their resources by other government agencies.

The unit sees a number of difficulties in establishing its operations. One problem is that of sources of educational videotapes for the video library it would like to establish for teachers.

It also shares two difficulties with the GIS unit. The first is that video equipment was provided without any increase in funding, with the result that any activities in the new medium mean a reduction of resources for other projects. A second problem is that of servicing. Manufacturers supply servicing literature to authorised service centres only. There are no such centres in Belize, although a number of technicians in both the public and private sector have the expertise to carry out the work. The problem is exacerbated by the fact that although there is little equipment in the country, it is made by a variety of manufacturers.

One of the GIS cameras developed a serious fault; the cost price of the item was US$5,500. The repair bill, including carriage charges to the United States, was US$4,500. In addition to the expense, work was interrupted for a considerable period.

Community Use

Although use of video by and for the community remains an area of enormous untapped potential, initiatives have been taken in a number of areas.

Cynthia Higninio Ellis has probably been using video in the community for as long as anyone in Belize. She has been using video in women's groups since at least 1981, especially in rural areas. In this area the National 'Breast is Best' League has financed a series of public announcements for TV broadcast.

A number of individuals have begun to use video in furtherance of their professional work. Santiago Castillo described attending a lecture on the dangers of drug abuse given by one of Belize's two psychiatrists, and illustrated with video. When Asst Superintendent Willoughby of the Belize City Police was in charge of police training he borrowed a video camera and made his own training films. The head of the Tourist Association, Mrs Jean Shaw, has a number of videos for the promotion of tourism.

Religious groups have not been slow to exploit the potential of the new medium. Belize is a highly religious society, 91.6 per cent of the population professing Christianity, predominantly Roman Catholic (61.7 per cent) and Anglican (11.8 per cent) (Abstract of Statistics 1985). Belize is heavily penetrated by missionaries for new Christian sects, especially among its Maya and Kakchi communities. The Caribbean Council of Churches has identified this as a major social problem (quoted *The Reporter* 27.10.85). Television has brought media evangelists to the attention of the Belizean viewer, and an American-based evangelical movement sponsors regular 'one minute sermons'. The Catholic Apostolate presents a 30 minute programme on Sundays and the Baptist Library provides videotapes on religious themes.

Finally, as in the rest of the world, those whose origins lie in the Indian sub-continent have access to videos of Bombay musicals.

CRIME

According to Asst Superintendent Willoughby of the Belize City Police, law enforcement agencies do not see any basis in Belizean law for taking action over 'video crime'. Certainly no such action has ever been taken. Copyright legislation would only be enforceable in respect of individual items copyrighted in Belize in his opinion.

With respect to pornography, he feels that existing laws relating to obscenity are sufficient to deal with any new developments due to video.

A Censorship Board with very strict guidelines regulates films and film posters under the Cinematograph Ordinance, but this specifically excludes 'an exhibition given in private premises to which the public are not admitted whether on payment or otherwise' (Section 16).

Video material is covered by the wide-ranging Undesirable Publications Ordinance 1953. Section 2 defines 'publication' as including 'all written or printed matter and anything, whether of a nature similar to written or printed matter or not, containing any visible representation, or by its form, shape or in any manner capable of suggesting words or ideas, and every copy and reproduction of such a publication.'

The Minister has absolute discretion to prohibit the import, publishing, sale, offer for sale, distribution, possession and reproduction of any material he considers 'contrary to the public interest' on pain of a $1,000 fine and/or 1 year's imprisonment for a first offence (Section 4). Under Section 6, packages may be inspected by the Postmaster General, customs officers, the police or by any other official designated by the minister.

In addition the Post Office Regulations (1966) prohibit the conveyance by post of 'any indecent or obscene print, painting, photograph, cinematograph film, lithograph, engraving, book, card or written communication, or any indecent or obscene article whether similar to the above or not' (Part 1 Section 9).

No evidence was found to support rumours of hard-core pornographic videos being shown at one location in Belize City, nor could anyone be found who claimed to have actually seen transmisisons from the Playboy Channel apparently broadcast late at night by some TV stations in the districts. Asst Superintendent Willoughby said that video pornography was 'not a problem'. Nonetheless imported pornography is frequently cited in press editorials and letters as a reason for perceived increases in the rate of violent crime (eg *Amandala* 3.5.85). In this context it may be that what is meant are satellite broadcasts of film material more explicit than is permitted by the Censorship Board.

In 1982 it seemed to the casual observer that the novelty of television had attracted many young people off the streets, so that is seemed safer to walk at night; in 1985 the owner of one of the San Ignacio stations, told an American interviewer that television had helped to divert young people from vice (quoted *The Voice* 25.8.85).

VIDEO RENTAL

Tropical Vision seems to be the only company still renting videotapes, although owner Nestor Vasques claims that 'there are others who do not admit to being in the business'. Like his former competitors, Vasquez says 'we got stuck with these things'. He maintains an interest in tapes primarily because of their use in advertising.

Tropical Vision's library is small, certainly not more than 500 tapes. 'Movies are number one; network movies are most popular' because the cinemas in Belize City are still well patronised. Tropical's stock list confirms this; it contains not more than a dozen sports tapes and a handful of children's and music programmes. Vasques says that although music tapes would undoubtedly be popular in theory, in practice the youth market does not have the income for tape rental. Several interviewees claimed that the mainstay of Tropical's rental business was popular soap operas such as *Dynasty* and *Dallas*. Tropical now broadcasts *Dallas* and began to show *Dynasty* on 5 November 1985.

Vasquez says his rental business, $5,000 per month at its peak (Emory King), declined by 50 per cent in 1982, and was down to 10 per cent of its peak figure by 1983. As an indicator of the decline in video use, he says that the maintenance business fell off in proportion. At present, he says 'the video business is very poor .... More TV and cable licences will put an end to video'.

CONCLUSION

There can of course be no conclusion to this book in the real sense of the word, since the speed at which the world video markets continue to develop and change would invalidate within a very short space of time any conclusive arguments derived from the studies presented here. It is therefore more appropriate to offer a number of observations about recent developments which have emerged as central to the debate in all the studies. These elements may be grouped into five distinct but interrelated areas: (1) continued growth and expansion; (2) technological developments; (3) developments in the relationship between video, TV and the cinema; (4) recent changes in the Third World video experience; and (5) recommendations for further research.

1. According to *Screen Digest* — the monthly publication which is the most reliable source of figures for the audio-visual media — the global figure for total video units had reached 168.96 million by the end of 1987. This figure is expected to reach 200 million by the end of 1988. The publication indicates clearly that these must be seen as 'best guess' estimates, given the difficulty of collating available data, but the editors are careful to cross-check their sources. The *Digest* now refers to the average VCR population of the world (in terms of TV homes) reaching 50 per cent whilst reporting that JVC now envisage a penetration level of some 70-80 per cent in the not too distant future. The only question mark here concerns whether or not the conventional VHS system will maintain its current market position.

In December 1987, *Screen Digest* indicated that (a) 17 countries have a higher than 50 per cent penetration figure of video in TV households, and (b) a further 10 have a higher than 40 per cent penetration. These are listed as:
(a) Australia, Bahrain, Hong Kong, Iceland, Ireland, Kuwait, Lebanon, Malaysia, Netherlands Antilles, New Zealand, Nigeria, Panama, Qatar, Singapore, United Arab Emirates, United Kingdom and the United States of America.
(b) Bermuda, Canada, Cyprus, German Federal Republic, India, Ireland, Luxembourg, Netherlands, Philippines and Saudi Arabia.

In order to put these figures in perspective, it should be noted that such countries as Netherlands Antilles, Nigeria, Panama and India have a relatively low number of TV sets in private homes in relation to the size of the population. The high figures therefore reflect the fact that middle class homes are increasingly likely to have a video as well as a television set.

It is also reported that there are now six countries which sell more than 1 million video sets a year and the 1987 growth percentages are given as follows:

Western Europe	25.2	Eastern Europe	44.7
The Far East	20.9	North Africa	58.0
Australasia	23.2	Rest of Africa	54.6
Asia	42.0	South America	39.9
North America	33.5	Central America	53.7
The Middle East	20.1		

It will be noted that *Screen Digest*'s grouping and nomenclature of the countries of the world is slightly different from ours but the figures give an interesting account of current growth rates. As mentioned earlier, it is perhaps to be expected that the highest percentage growth rates are to be found in Eastern Europe, Africa and Central America, because these are the regions which have the lowest current market penetration. Thus, while the percentages are high, the number of units remains low. Nevertheless, *Screen Digest* indicates that there are significant changes in attitude to video in Eastern Europe. This is particularly true in the Soviet Union where Philips have made a production agreement with the government, and in Hungary and Czechoslovakia.

2. Recent developments in the field of video technology have also been striking. To begin on the negative side, the Philips V 2000 system has ceased production and the Sony Betamax format may not be continued for long, particularly now that Sony have decided to begin marketing VHS units under their own brand name (the first time in the company's history that such a move has been made). The relatively new 8 mm format is also beginning to weaken in marketing terms. Kodak, for example, have ceased production.

On the positive side, CD Video which will be available in late 1988 was demonstrated by Philips in March 1987. It is designed to provide a video adjunct to CD audio players; and in April 1987, Super VHS was announced by JVC. This system provides much better image and sound definition and is already marketed in the United States where it is a considerable improvement on the 525 line NTSC system. This new system plays tapes recorded on the old format machines, although the reverse is not possible. It remains to be seen whether it will be attractive in countries which have either a PAL or SECAM 625 system which already provide a better quality of image than the American counterpart.

However, the major developments in non-professional video hardware are to be found in the gradual introduction of new editing and dubbing equipment. A new generation of VHS editing suites using digital and computer technology will eventually replace 'crash' editing and allow ½″ cassettes to be edited with the same degree of sophistication as is possible with ¾″ U Matic and 1″ reel to reel machines. In fact, it is being suggested that digitalized VHS will give greater multi-image editing fidelity than is currently possible on standard 1″ editing suites. Furthermore, this new digitalized equipment will eradicate the quality loss that occurs every time a dubbed tape is dubbed. Some of the implications and possibilities of these developments will be discussed below.

Over the same period, there have been further related developments such as the continuing evolution of the European C MAC and D2 MAC generating the EU MAC system; Sony's further promotion of its HDTV system; the nearing of a launch date for DBS, to list the more obvious areas of technological innovation. Their implications will be briefly indicated below.

3. It was clear when domestic video first appeared that it would create and occupy an intriguing space between cinema and television. In addition to the broadcasting facilities it provides, video not only offers a technology that enables movies to be viewed in the home but may also be used to replace public screenings where no film projection equipment is available. It was this possibility that led many film professionals to fear that the power of video would lead to the demise of the cinema. However, as a number of the studies show, in many countries in the world, video does not so much replace cinema but rather operates as an adjunct to it — many people who are keen cinema-goers also use video for film screening purposes. Their commitment is to audio-visual culture in general and those countries where cinema-going was in greatest decline and where video has made a big impact have begun to see a slight resurgence in cinema audience figures.

Whilst video now seems unlikely to usurp the role of *cinema*, it does appear that, despite the resistance of most film-makers and technicians, it will eventually usurp the primacy, or even the very existence, of *film* and its attendant technologies. There is clearly a considerable difference between private or family domestic viewing on the one hand, and the public shared experiences of a large screen on the other; therefore it seems highly likely that these two viewing spaces will continue to exist side by side in one form or another.

However, the development of wide, large and flat screen, high definition television systems *and* of satellite distribution networks (and in particular DBS) will undoubtedly mean that the cinema of the future will operate with video projection systems and not film projectors. There have already been demonstrations of very high quality video projection systems which fill a screen large enough for a small cinema and some are already in commercial operation. What is required now is for DBS satellites to provide the distribution system by beaming down to a small reception dish on the roof of the cinema which will obviate the need for the costly and slow business of transporting heavy film cans around the world.

4. It is in the developing countries that recent developments in video and its future potential appear the most exciting. Over the last few years, as may be seen from the studies, video has come to offer a technology that is not tied to the conventional and highly expensive ones of broadcast television, nor to its modes of production and distribution systems. In short, video has done nothing less than create a new audio-visual space.

Within the Latin American sub-continent in countries such as Chile, Brazil and Nicaragua, one can already see the use of what the West would consider to be non-broadcast video technology to produce and distribute television programmes which are 'alternative' to those that predominate within most countries and around the world. Similar experiments are taking place in many other countries. It is interesting to note examples of not only minority but even majority groups using low priced video technology to further their cause and to generate different and alternative types of news broadcasts in particular, and television programming in general. In other words, the notion that technological criteria should provide a baseline for determining whether or not a programme can be transmitted, as is the case in the countries with long-established and wealthy broadcasting institutions, is being called into question. The development of these new technologies encourages a focusing on the *content* of a programme rather than on its electronic quality.

Some of the studies refer to the international video software flows that are being developed particularly by minority communities living outside their country of origin. The flow of Indian films to the United Kingdom and Canada, and the international flow of tapes to Yugoslav communities outside their country are examples here. Recent use was made of such a channel when a tape commissioned by the Indian Government concerning events at the golden temple at Amritsar was circulated in the United States, Canada and Western Europe.

Changes which lie ahead — and in the fairly near future — may be far-reaching indeed. The increasing technological sophistication of VHS hardware, particularly in the field of editing and dubbing suites, provides low cost systems of television production. These systems may not meet the electronic specifications of the major broadcasting organizations, but they can be used to produce technically high quality programmes indistinguishable by the general public from broadcast television. Whether such productions are officially sanctioned by a government — in the case of countries that cannot afford to undertake full-scale conventional television production — or are undertaken by semi-official or clandestine organizations, makes little technical difference. What is significant is that it is now possible, with this new technology, to produce low cost TV for a multiplicity of large or small audiences around the world. Images, music, sounds and voices which hitherto would not have appeared on a television set, can now be seen and heard.

5. Because video is such a new phenomenon, and has expanded at a rate that far exceeds even the industry's expectations and forecasts, relatively little non-commercial research has been conducted in this area. One of the reasons may have been a lack of data and this book was designed in part to fill that gap. It is nevertheless clear that, in addition to the monitoring process, there is a great deal of research which needs to be undertaken if we are to remain abreast of developments in the fastest growing area of the audio-visual world.

In conclusion, it may therefore be useful to describe some areas for possible future research.

It is of course clear that statistical or numerical data will have to be refined and updated constantly. Research into video hardware should focus not on video recorders but rather on cameras and editing, and dubbing suites. This will involve documenting not only the world-wide flow of equipment but also, and more importantly, reporting on the way in which and for what purposes such equipment is used.

Further research into the world-wide flow of pre-recorded video software is required. This will involve an analysis of both the flow of videograms (commercially produced films and television programmes) circulating internationally for commercial profit *and* the flow of tapes made by a wide range of 'alternative' groups — community, political, educational, religious, trade union, women's, ethnic minority, minority rights groups, etc. In this latter area of research, it would be necessary to investigate not only who was responsible for producing such work, but also who the target groups were, how programmes were circulated and how they were received. Having obtained equipment, the creation of 'alternative' consistently efficient systems of distribution is the most complex — and continues to be the seemingly most insoluble — problem that all film and video makers face.

Government policy-making in this area also lends itself to research. Again the focus should be wide enough to cover both problems such as censorship and positive policy-making in support of 'alternative' video and television production. Such policies might encourage the provision of 'alternative' audio-visual messages within the country, but are more likely to be concerned with the provision of programming which is an alternative to that provided by the international television companies.

Audience research should also be given priority and one of the areas which is among the more manageable, would be an investigation of the potential role of video in multi-language societies. Undoubtedly, with the spread of satellite transmitted television programmes, the power and influence of the world's dominant languages and cultures is going to increase. It would therefore be worthwhile to look at the ways in which alternative video distribution systems might contribute to the continuation and preservation of the multiplicity of the world's languages, cultures and communities.

These are some of the questions that need to be addressed. The problems attendant upon this type of research on a world scale are so daunting that at times it appears impossible. The complexity of social, cultural, political, religious differences are such as to make comparisons meaningless and the cost prohibitive. Nevertheless, with the financial support of international agencies, it might be possible to begin to design certain research models and to undertake some intitial, and much needed, fieldwork.

Manuel Alvarado
9 June 1988